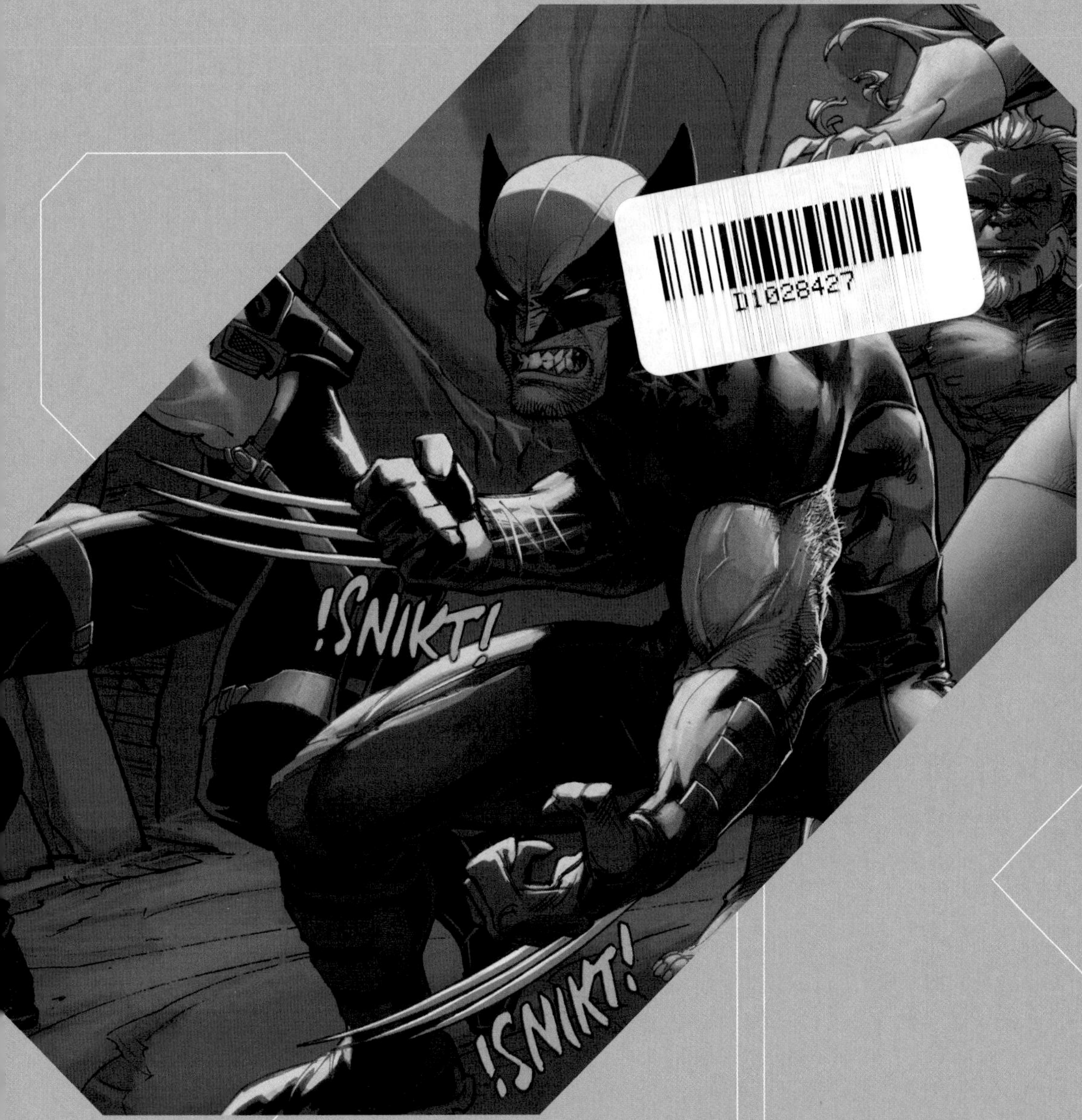
!SNIKT!
!SNIKT!

[kra_]
[koa_]

[dawn_of_x]

DAWN OF X VOL. 7. Contains material originally published in magazine form as MARAUDERS (2019) #7, EXCALIBUR (2019) #7-#8, NEW MUTANTS (2019) #7, X-MEN (2019) #7 and WOLVERINE (2020) #1. First printing 2020. ISBN 978-1-302-92760-8. Published by MARVEL WORLDWIDE, INC., a subsidiary of MARVEL ENTERTAINMENT, LLC. OFFICE OF PUBLICATION: 1290 Avenue of the Americas, New York, NY 10104. © 2020 MARVEL No similarity between any of the names, characters, persons, and/or institutions in this magazine with those of any living or dead person or institution is intended, and any such similarity which may exist is purely coincidental. **Printed in the U.S.A.** KEVIN FEIGE, Chief Creative Officer; DAN BUCKLEY, President, Marvel Entertainment; JOHN NEE, Publisher; JOE QUESADA, EVP & Creative Director; TOM BREVOORT, SVP of Publishing; DAVID BOGART, Associate Publisher & SVP of Talent Affairs; Publishing & Partnership; DAVID GABRIEL, VP of Print & Digital Publishing; JEFF YOUNGQUIST, VP of Production & Special Projects; DAN CARR, Executive Director of Publishing Technology; ALEX MORALES, Director of Publishing Operations; DAN EDINGTON, Managing Editor; SUSAN CRESPI, Production Manager; STAN LEE, Chairman Emeritus. For information regarding advertising in Marvel Comics or on Marvel.com, please contact Vit DeBellis, Custom Solutions & Integrated Advertising Manager, at vdebellis@marvel.com. For Marvel subscription inquiries, please call 888-511-5480. **Manufactured between 6/26/2020 and 7/28/2020 by LSC COMMUNICATIONS INC., KENDALLVILLE, IN, USA.**

10 9 8 7 6 5 4 3 2 1

DAWN OF X

Volume
07

X-Men created by Stan Lee & Jack Kirby

Writers:	**Jonathan Hickman, Benjamin Percy, Gerry Duggan & Tini Howard**
Pencilers:	**Rod Reis, Adam Kubert, Stefano Caselli, Wilton Santos, Marcus To & Leinil Francis Yu**
Inkers:	**Rod Reis, Adam Kubert, Stefano Caselli, Oren Junior, Sean Parsons, Marcus To, Roberto Poggi, Victor Nava & Leinil Francis Yu**
Color Artists:	**Rod Reis, Frank Martin, Edgar Delgado, Erick Arciniega & Sunny Gho**
Letterers:	**VC's Cory Petit & Joe Caramagna**

Cover Art:	**Rod Reis; Adam Kubert & Frank Martin; Russell Dauterman & Matthew Wilson; Mahmud Asrar & Matthew Wilson; and Leinil Francis Yu & Sunny Gho**

Head of X:	**Jonathan Hickman**
Design:	**Tom Muller**
Assistant Editors:	**Annalise Bissa & Chris Robinson**
Editor:	**Jordan D. White**

Collection Cover Art:	**Adam Kubert & Frank Martin**

Collection Editor:	**Jennifer Grünwald**
Assistant Managing Editor:	**Maia Loy**
Assistant Managing Editor:	**Lisa Montalbano**
Editor, Special Projects:	**Mark D. Beazley**
VP Production & Special Projects:	**Jeff Youngquist**
SVP Print, Sales & Marketing:	**David Gabriel**
Editor in Chief:	**C.B. Cebulski**

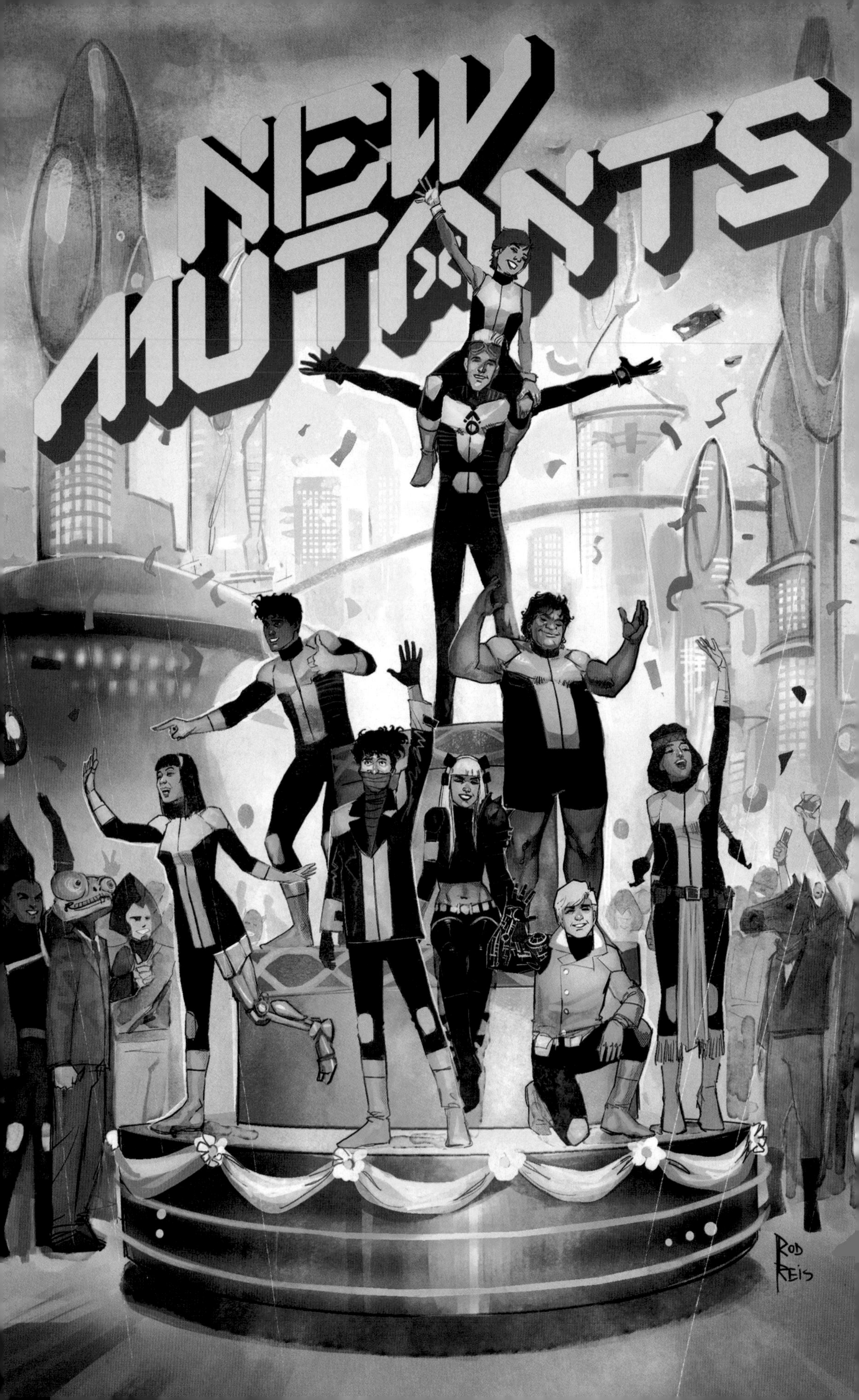
NEW MUTANTS
ROD REIS

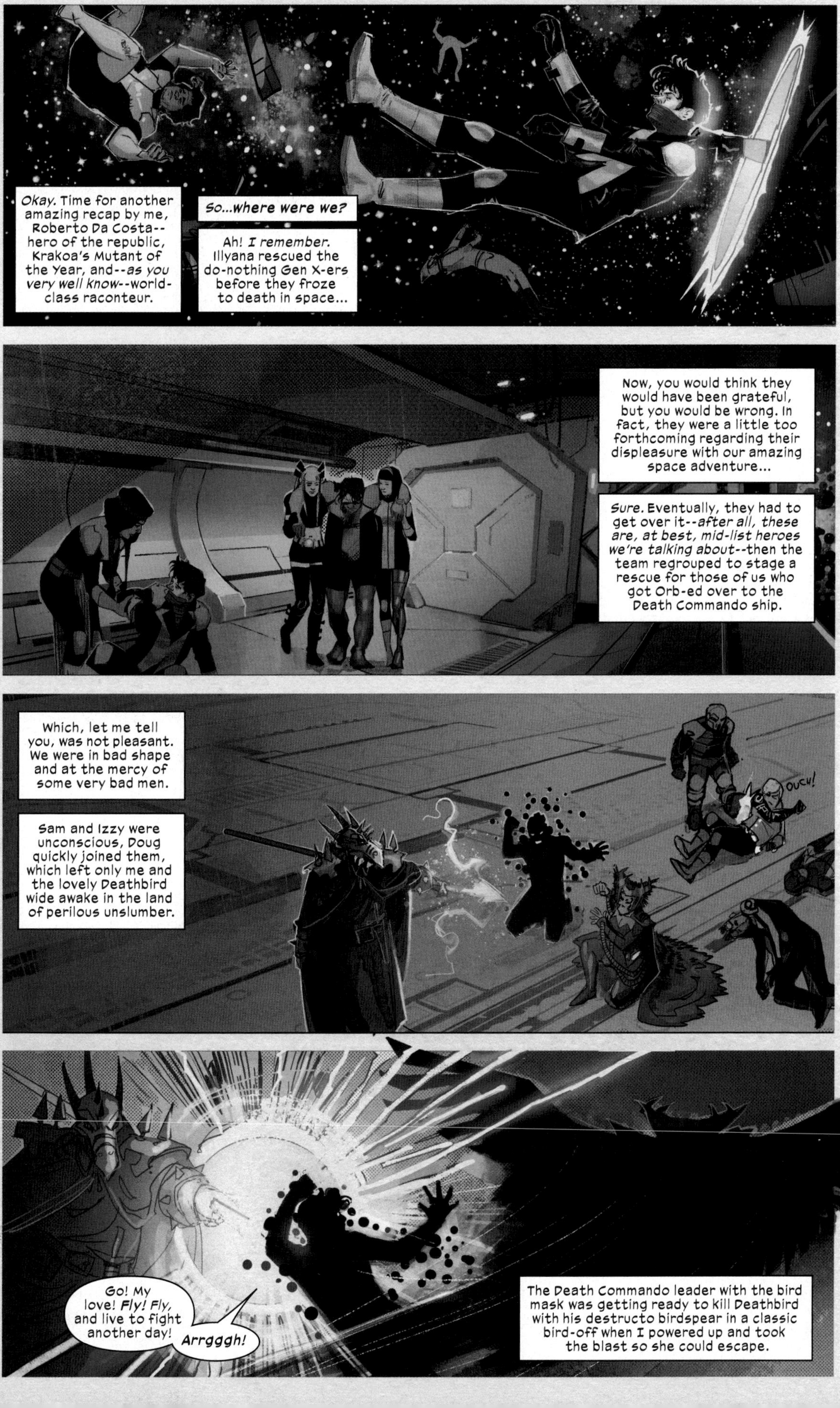
Okay. Time for another amazing recap by me, Roberto Da Costa--hero of the republic, Krakoa's Mutant of the Year, and--as you very well know--world-class raconteur.
So...where were we?
Ah! I remember. Illyana rescued the do-nothing Gen X-ers before they froze to death in space...
Now, you would think they would have been grateful, but you would be wrong. In fact, they were a little too forthcoming regarding their displeasure with our amazing space adventure...
Sure. Eventually, they had to get over it--after all, these are, at best, mid-list heroes we're talking about--then the team regrouped to stage a rescue for those of us who got Orb-ed over to the Death Commando ship.
Which, let me tell you, was not pleasant. We were in bad shape and at the mercy of some very bad men.
Sam and Izzy were unconscious, Doug quickly joined them, which left only me and the lovely Deathbird wide awake in the land of perilous unslumber.
OUCH!
Go! My love! Fly! Fly, and live to fight another day!
Arrgggh!
The Death Commando leader with the bird mask was getting ready to kill Deathbird with his destructo birdspear in a classic bird-off when I powered up and took the blast so she could escape.

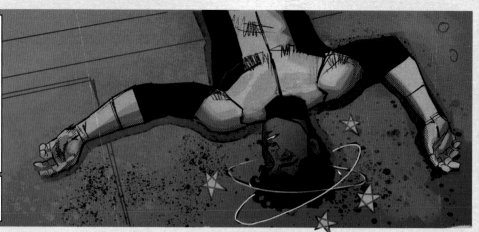

And, look, I know what you're thinking. Was this a calculated move on my part to establish myself narratively as a hero in Deathbird's mind, or am I just heroic in general and incapable of not doing hero-like things?

Yes. Yes, to both. Yes, *forever.* Deal with it.

Later, we were being tortured...

(Mostly Doug, because he cries the most and the loudest, and torturers are generally emotionally fragile babies who need validation that their work "matters.")

AAAAAAAAAAAAAAA

ZZZZZ

Butterscotch puddin'! The password is butterscotch puddin'!

It doesn't have a g! *NO G!*

But then Deathbird busted in and *saved us.*

She took the bird head of the bird guy who said he was going to take hers.

Which, I gotta say, was both a little gross and a bit of a turn-on.

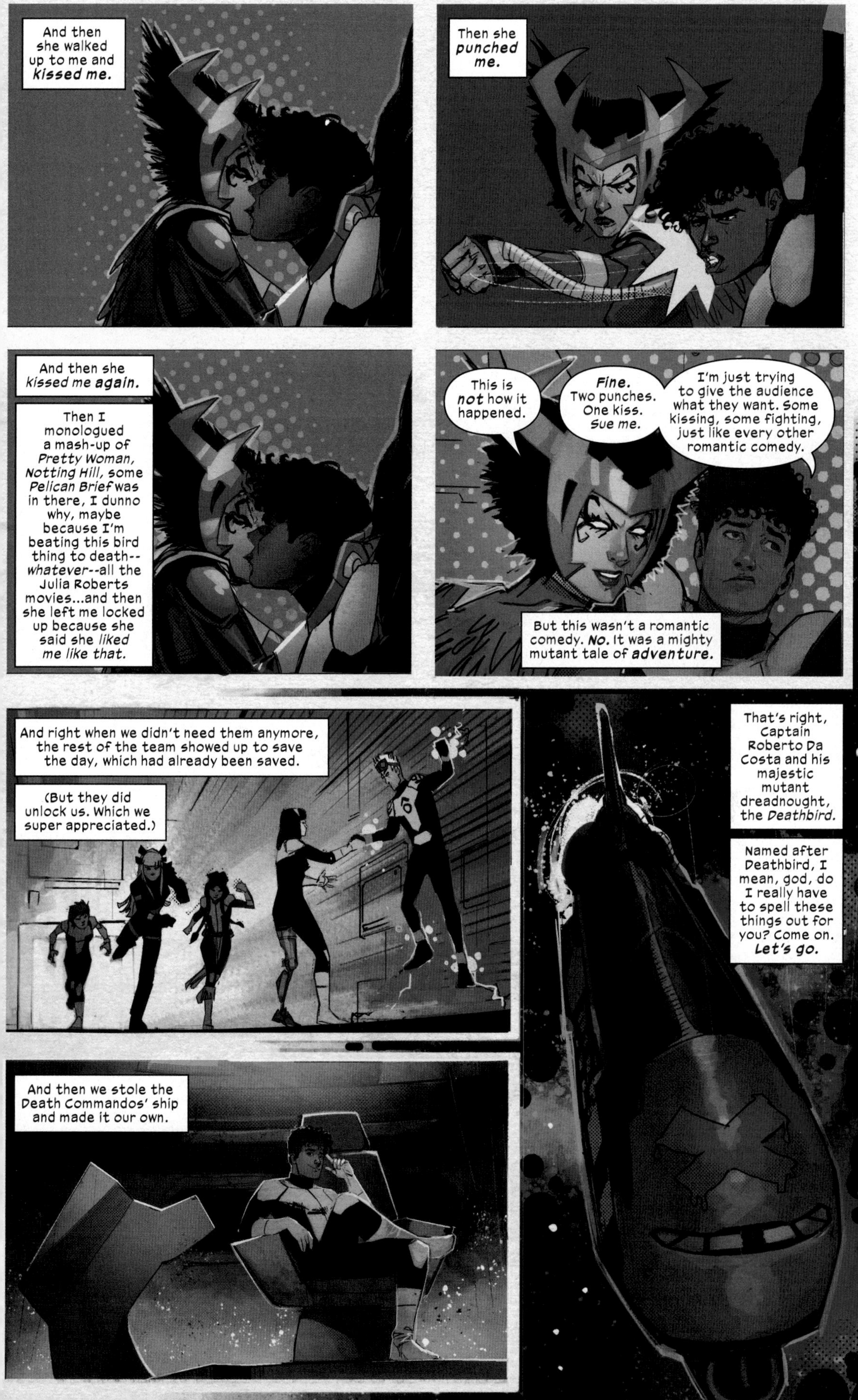
And then she walked up to me and *kissed me.*
Then she *punched me.*
And then she *kissed me again.*
Then I monologued a mash-up of *Pretty Woman, Notting Hill,* some *Pelican Brief* was in there, I dunno why, maybe because I'm beating this bird thing to death--*whatever*--all the Julia Roberts movies...and then she left me locked up because she said she *liked* me like that.
This is *not* how it happened.
Fine. Two punches. One kiss. *Sue me.*
I'm just trying to give the audience what they want. Some kissing, some fighting, just like every other romantic comedy.
But this wasn't a romantic comedy. *No.* It was a mighty mutant tale of *adventure.*
And right when we didn't need them anymore, the rest of the team showed up to save the day, which had already been saved.
(But they did unlock us. Which we super appreciated.)
And then we stole the Death Commandos' ship and made it our own.
That's right, Captain Roberto Da Costa and his majestic mutant dreadnought, the *Deathbird.*
Named after Deathbird, I mean, god, do I really have to spell these things out for you? Come on. *Let's go.*

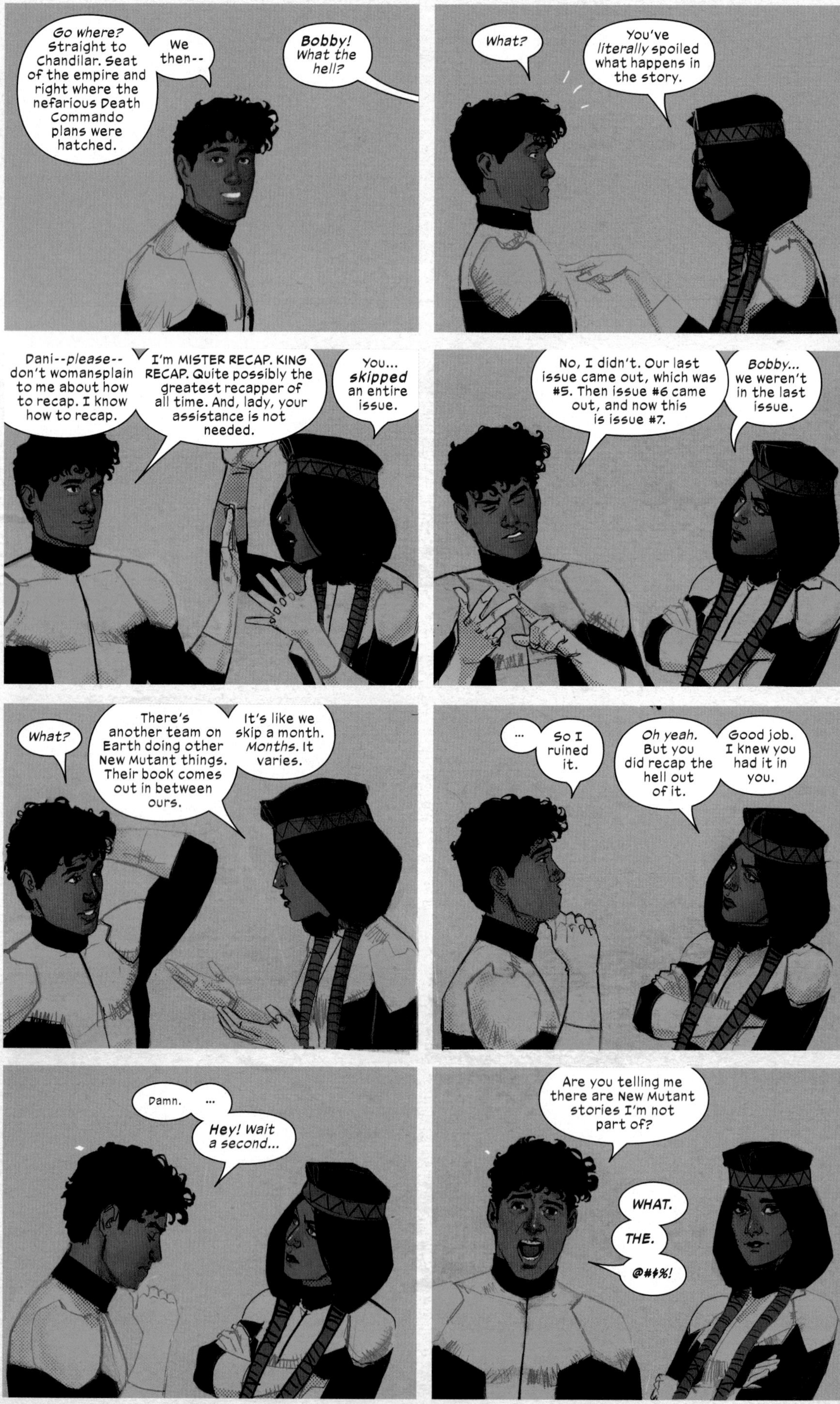
Go where? Straight to Chandilar. Seat of the empire and right where the nefarious Death Commando plans were hatched.
We then--
Bobby! What the hell?
What?
You've literally spoiled what happens in the story.
Dani--please--don't womansplain to me about how to recap. I know how to recap.
I'm MISTER RECAP. KING RECAP. Quite possibly the greatest recapper of all time. And, lady, your assistance is not needed.
You... skipped an entire issue.
No, I didn't. Our last issue came out, which was #5. Then issue #6 came out, and now this is issue #7.
Bobby... we weren't in the last issue.
What?
There's another team on Earth doing other New Mutant things. Their book comes out in between ours.
It's like we skip a month. Months. It varies.
...
So I ruined it.
Oh yeah. But you did recap the hell out of it.
Good job. I knew you had it in you.
Damn.
...
Hey! Wait a second...
Are you telling me there are New Mutant stories I'm not part of?
WHAT.
THE.
@#¢%!

[kra_[0.7]
[koa_[0.7]

[kra_[0.X]
[koa_[0.X]

WHAT THE @#$%, INDEED?

Sorry, Bobby.

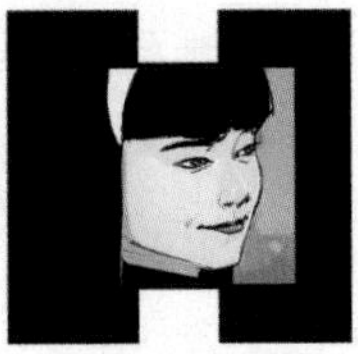
Karma

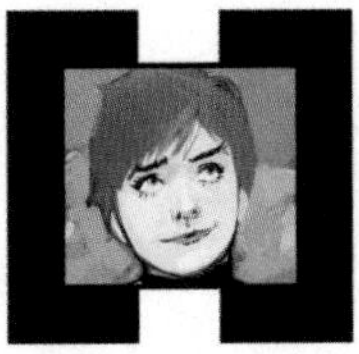
Wolfsbane

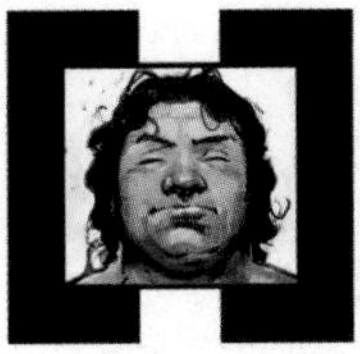
Mondo

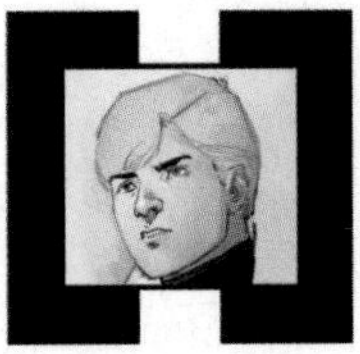
Cypher

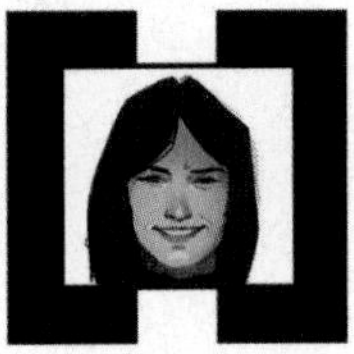
Mirage

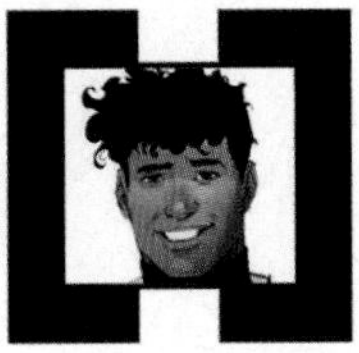
Sunspot

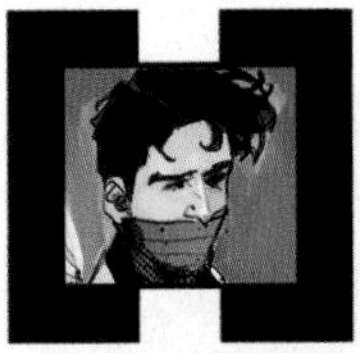
Chamber

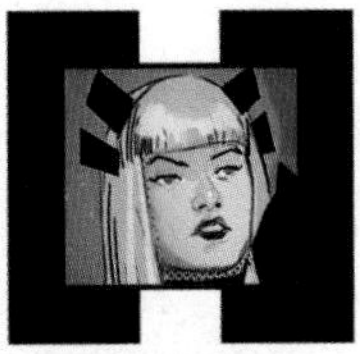
Magik

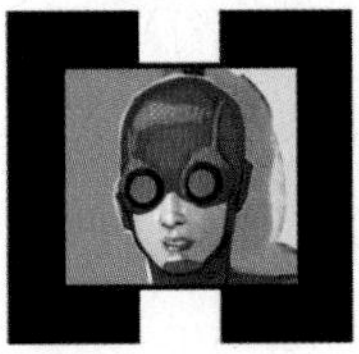
Smasher

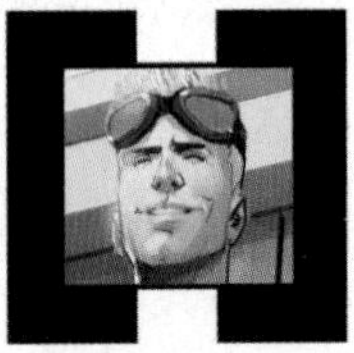
Cannonball

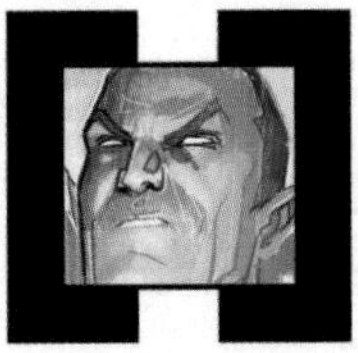
Gladiator

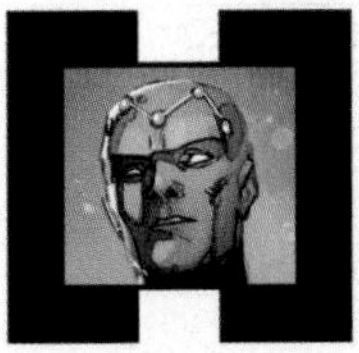
Mentor

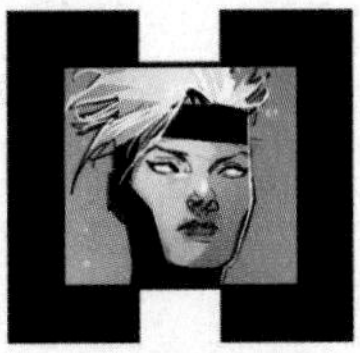
Oracle

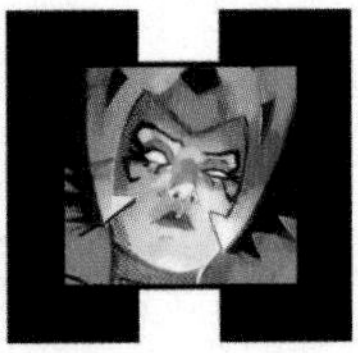
Deathbird

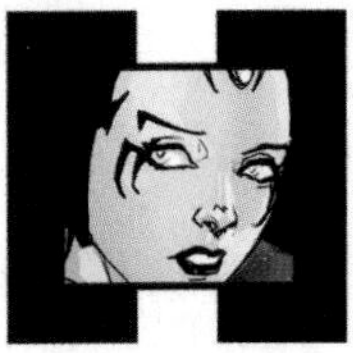
Xandra

[kra_[0.7]...]
[koa_[0.7]...]

[and..beyond.]

[00_lets_go__X]
[00_to_space_X]

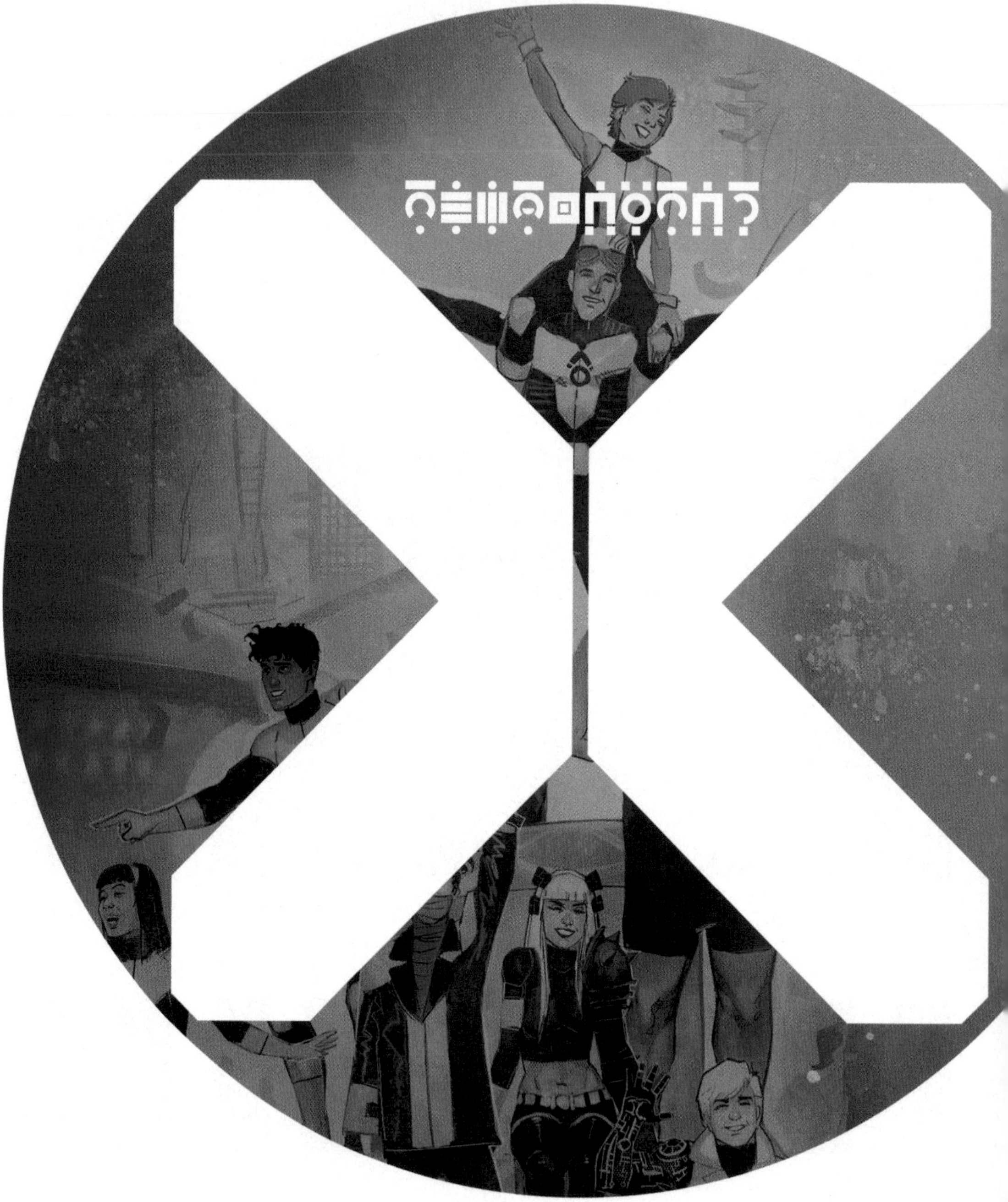

JONATHAN HICKMAN.............................[WRITER]
ROD REIS.....................................[ARTIST]
VC's TRAVIS LANHAM.........................[LETTERER]
TOM MULLER...................................[DESIGN]

ROD REIS................................[COVER ARTIST]

NICK RUSSELL.............................[PRODUCTION]

JONATHAN HICKMAN..........................[HEAD OF X]
ANNALISE BISSA....................[ASSISTANT EDITOR]
JORDAN D. WHITE..............................[EDITOR]
C.B. CEBULSKI.......................[EDITOR IN CHIEF]

[07] NEW MUTANTS

[ISSUE SEVEN]..................SPOILERS

[00_lets_go__X]
[00_to_space_X]

[00_00.....0]
[00_00.....7]

[00_good____]
[00_times___]

[00_in_____]

[00_space___]

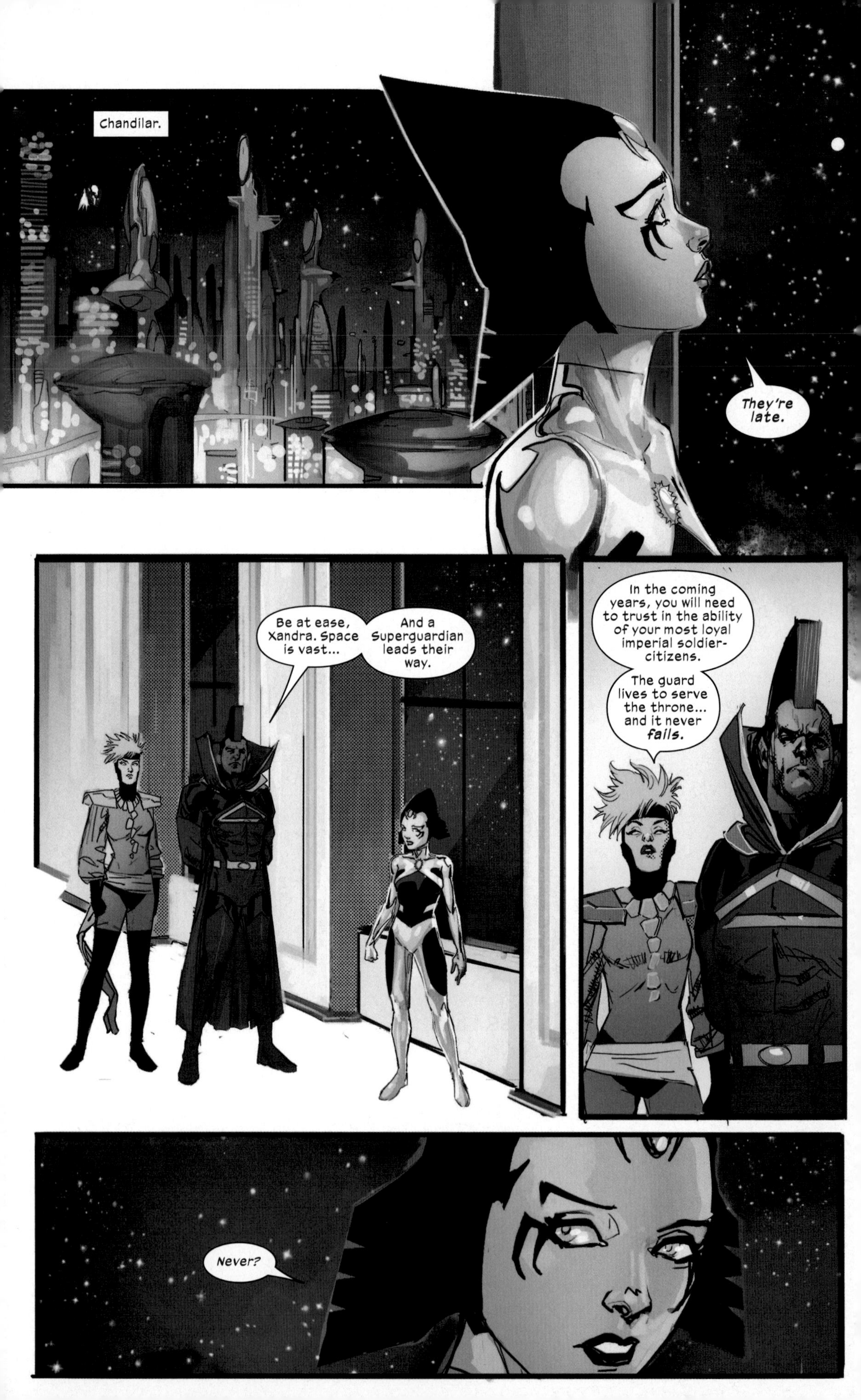
Chandilar.
They're late.
Be at ease, Xandra. Space is vast...
And a Superguardian leads their way.
In the coming years, you will need to trust in the ability of your most loyal imperial soldier-citizens.
The guard lives to serve the throne... and it never *fails.*
Never?

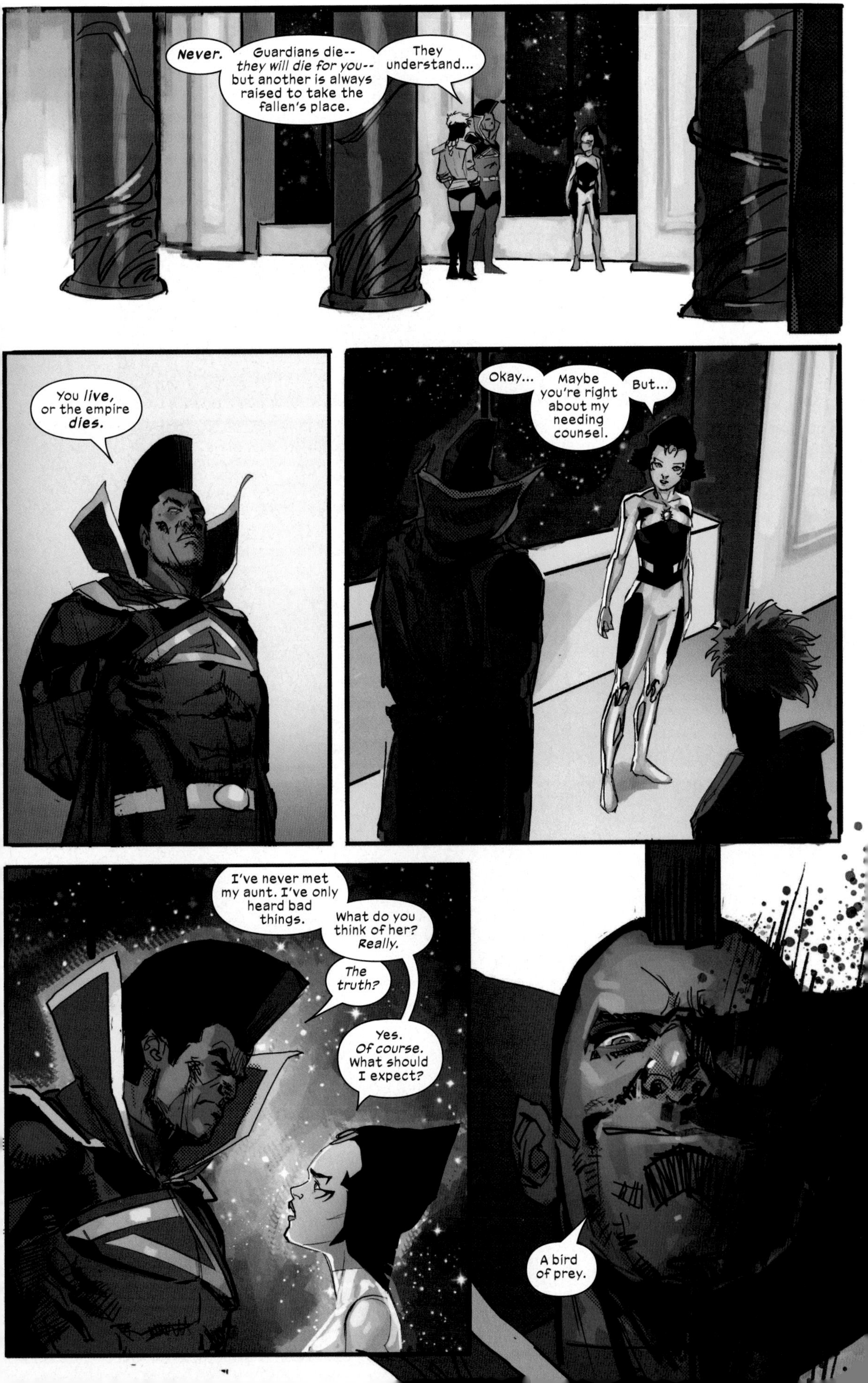
Never.
Guardians die-- they will die for you-- but another is always raised to take the fallen's place.
They understand...
You live, or the empire dies.
Okay...
Maybe you're right about my needing counsel.
But...
I've never met my aunt. I've only heard bad things.
What do you think of her? Really.
The truth?
Yes. Of course. What should I expect?
A bird of prey.

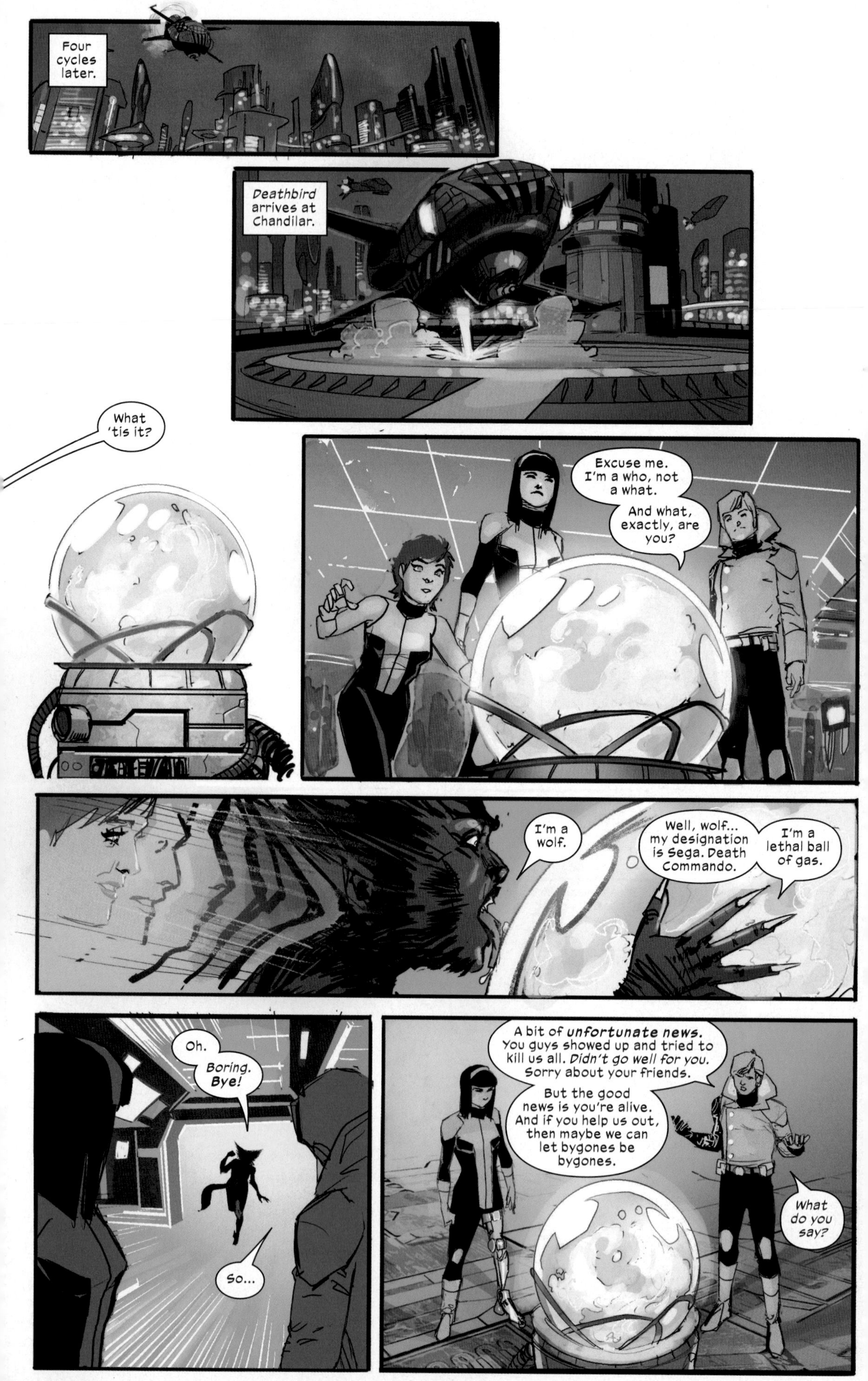

Four cycles later.
Deathbird arrives at Chandilar.
What 'tis it?
Excuse me. I'm a who, not a what.
And what, exactly, are you?
I'm a wolf.
Well, wolf... my designation is Sega. Death Commando.
I'm a lethal ball of gas.
Oh.
Boring. Bye!
So...
A bit of unfortunate news. You guys showed up and tried to kill us all. Didn't go well for you. Sorry about your friends.
But the good news is you're alive. And if you help us out, then maybe we can let bygones be bygones.
What do you say?

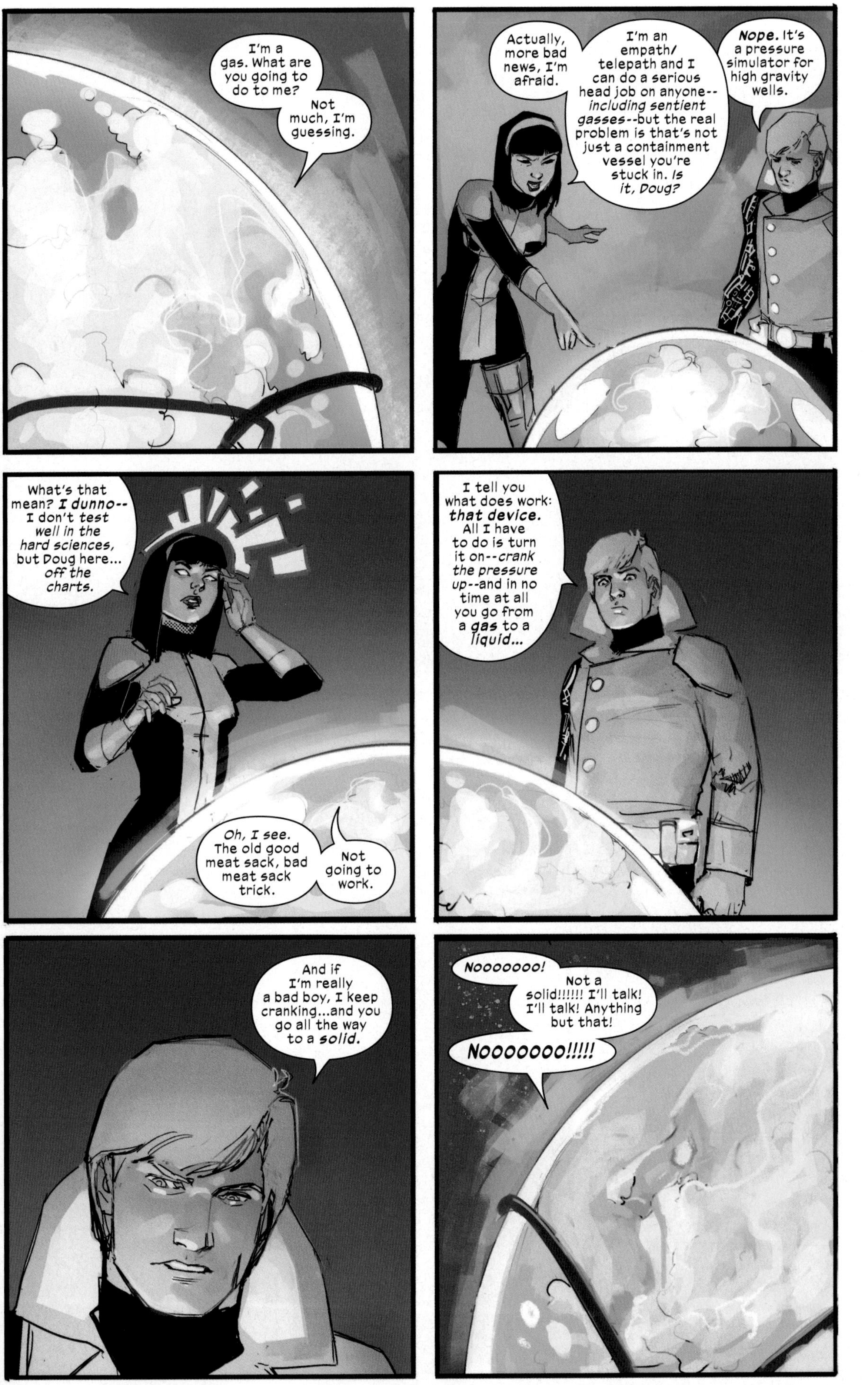
I'm a gas. What are you going to do to me?
Not much, I'm guessing.
Actually, more bad news, I'm afraid.
I'm an empath/ telepath and I can do a serious head job on anyone-- including sentient gasses--but the real problem is that's not just a containment vessel you're stuck in. Is it, Doug?
Nope. It's a pressure simulator for high gravity wells.
What's that mean? I dunno-- I don't test well in the hard sciences, but Doug here... off the charts.
Oh, I see. The old good meat sack, bad meat sack trick.
Not going to work.
I tell you what does work: that device. All I have to do is turn it on--crank the pressure up--and in no time at all you go from a gas to a liquid...
And if I'm really a bad boy, I keep cranking...and you go all the way to a solid.
Noooooo!
Not a solid!!!!!! I'll talk! I'll talk! Anything but that!
NOOOOOO!!!!!

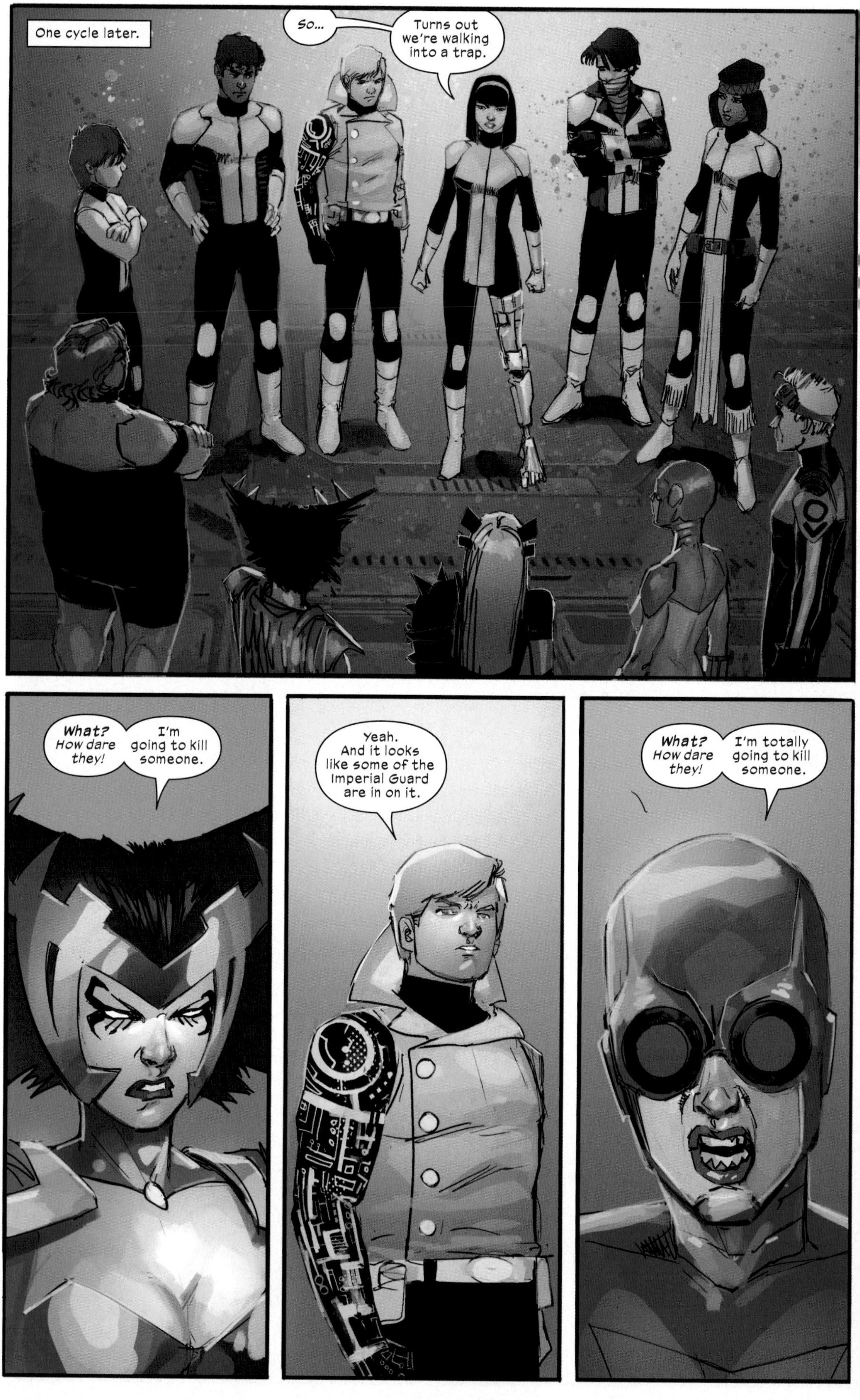
One cycle later.
So...
Turns out we're walking into a trap.
What? How dare they!
I'm going to kill someone.
Yeah. And it looks like some of the Imperial Guard are in on it.
What? How dare they!
I'm totally going to kill someone.

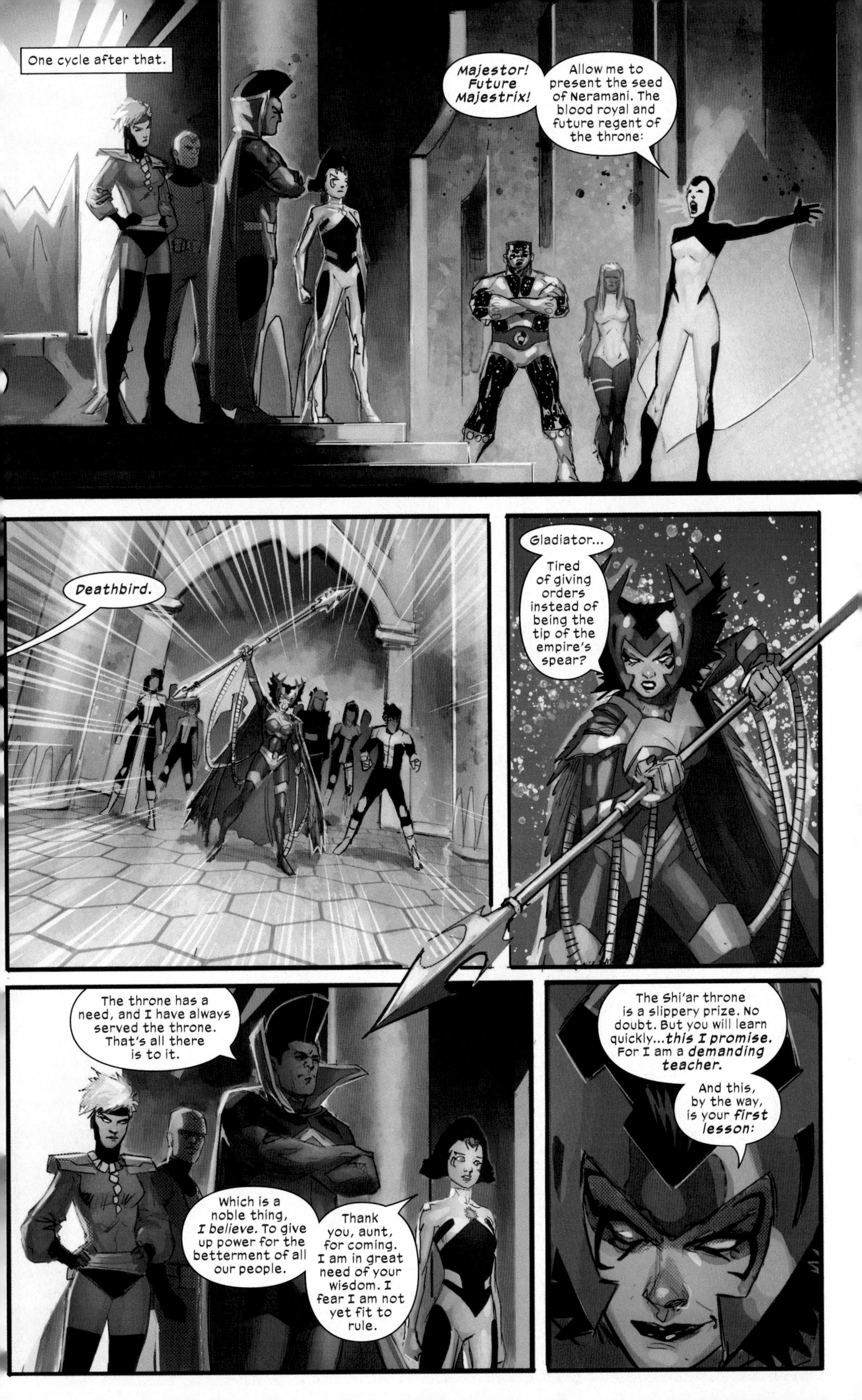

One cycle after that.
Majestor! Future Majestrix!
Allow me to present the seed of Neramani. The blood royal and future regent of the throne:
Deathbird.
Gladiator...
Tired of giving orders instead of being the tip of the empire's spear?
The throne has a need, and I have always served the throne. That's all there is to it.
Which is a noble thing, *I believe.* To give up power for the betterment of all our people.
Thank you, aunt, for coming. I am in great need of your wisdom. I fear I am not yet fit to rule.
The Shi'ar throne is a slippery prize. No doubt. But you will learn quickly...*this I promise.* For I am a *demanding teacher.*
And this, by the way, is your *first lesson:*

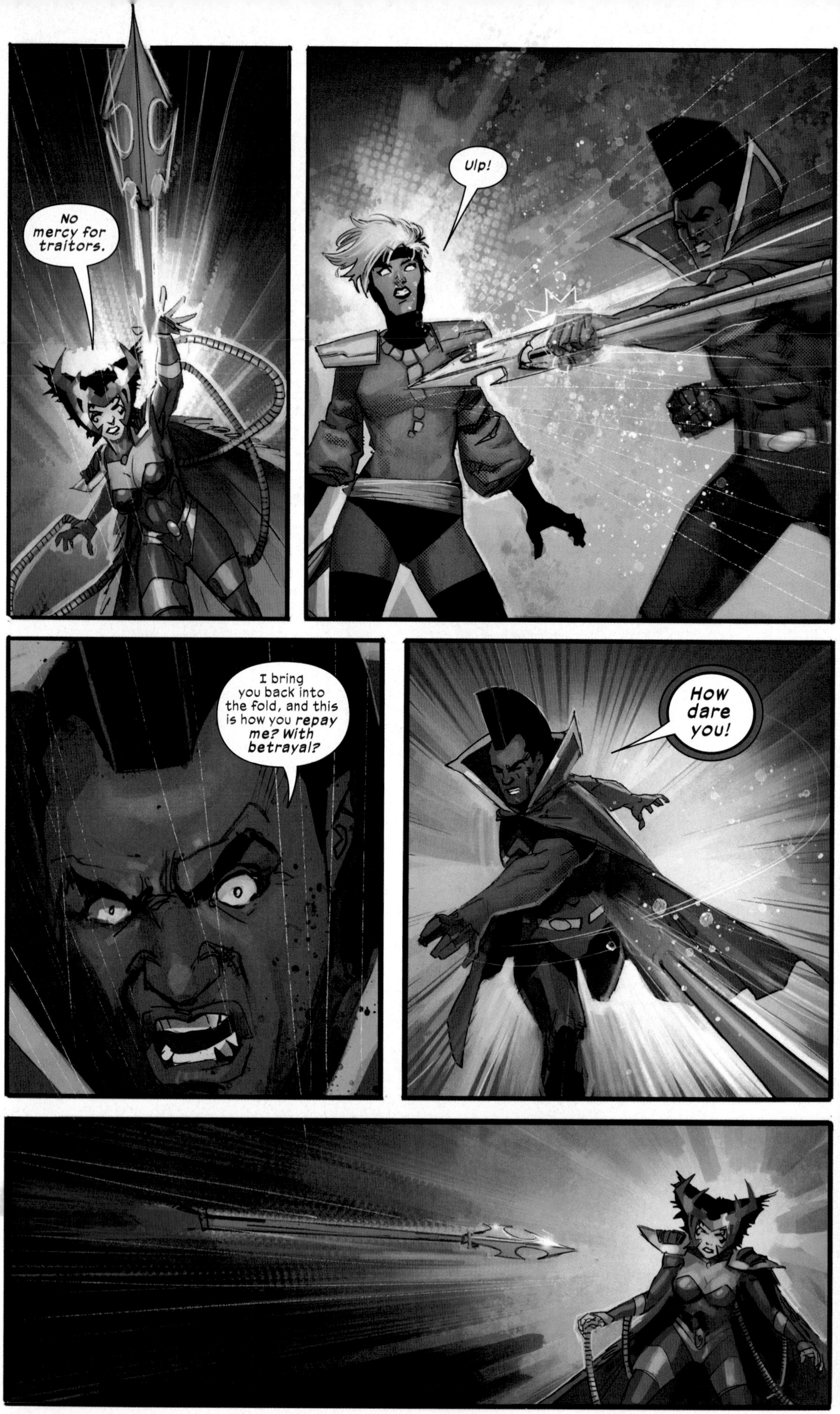
No mercy for traitors.
Ulp!
I bring you back into the fold, and this is how you *repay me?* *With betrayal?*
How dare you!

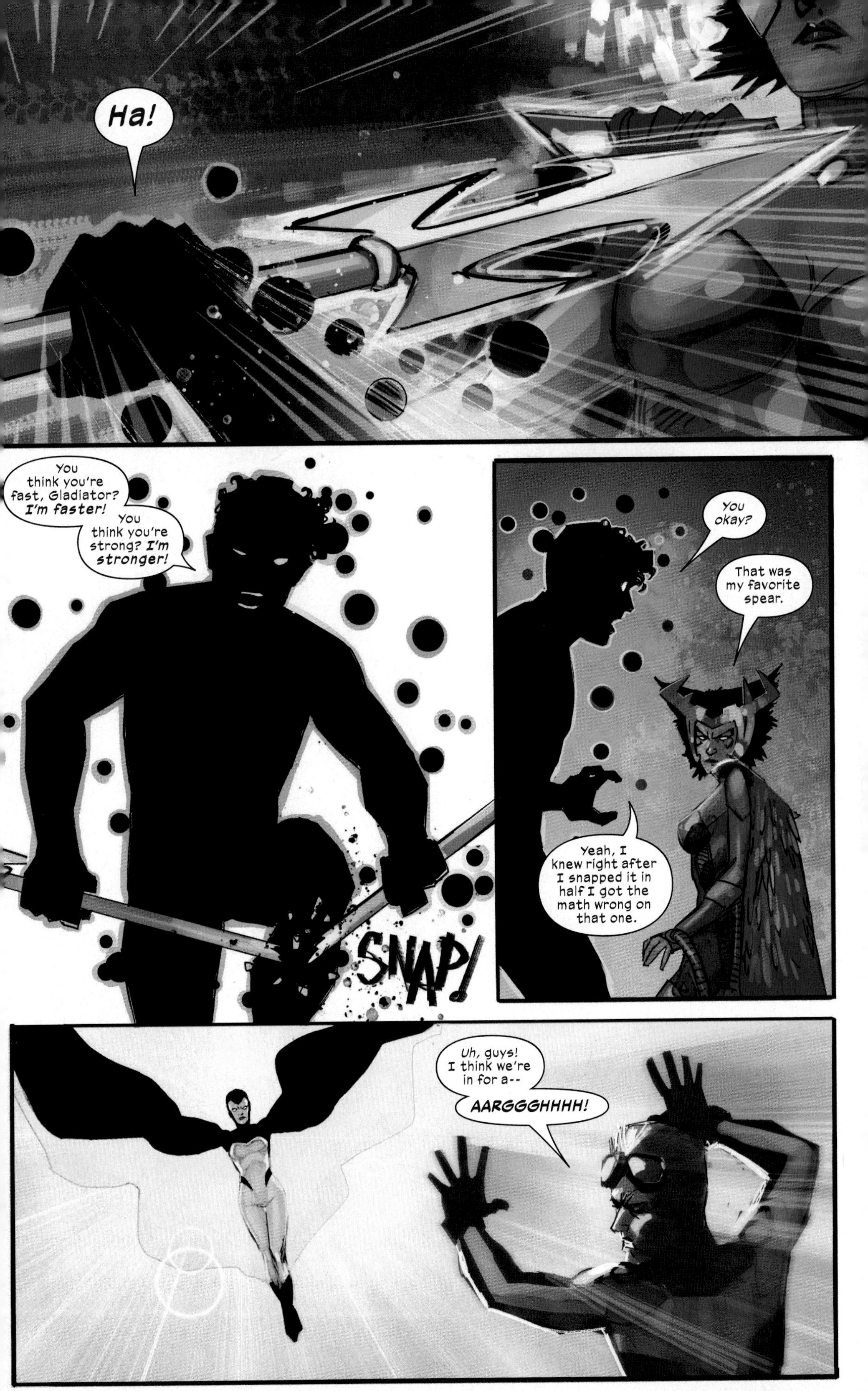
Ha!
You think you're fast, Gladiator? I'm faster!
You think you're strong? I'm stronger!
SNAP!
You okay?
That was my favorite spear.
Yeah, I knew right after I snapped it in half I got the math wrong on that one.
Uh, guys! I think we're in for a--
AARGGGHHHH!

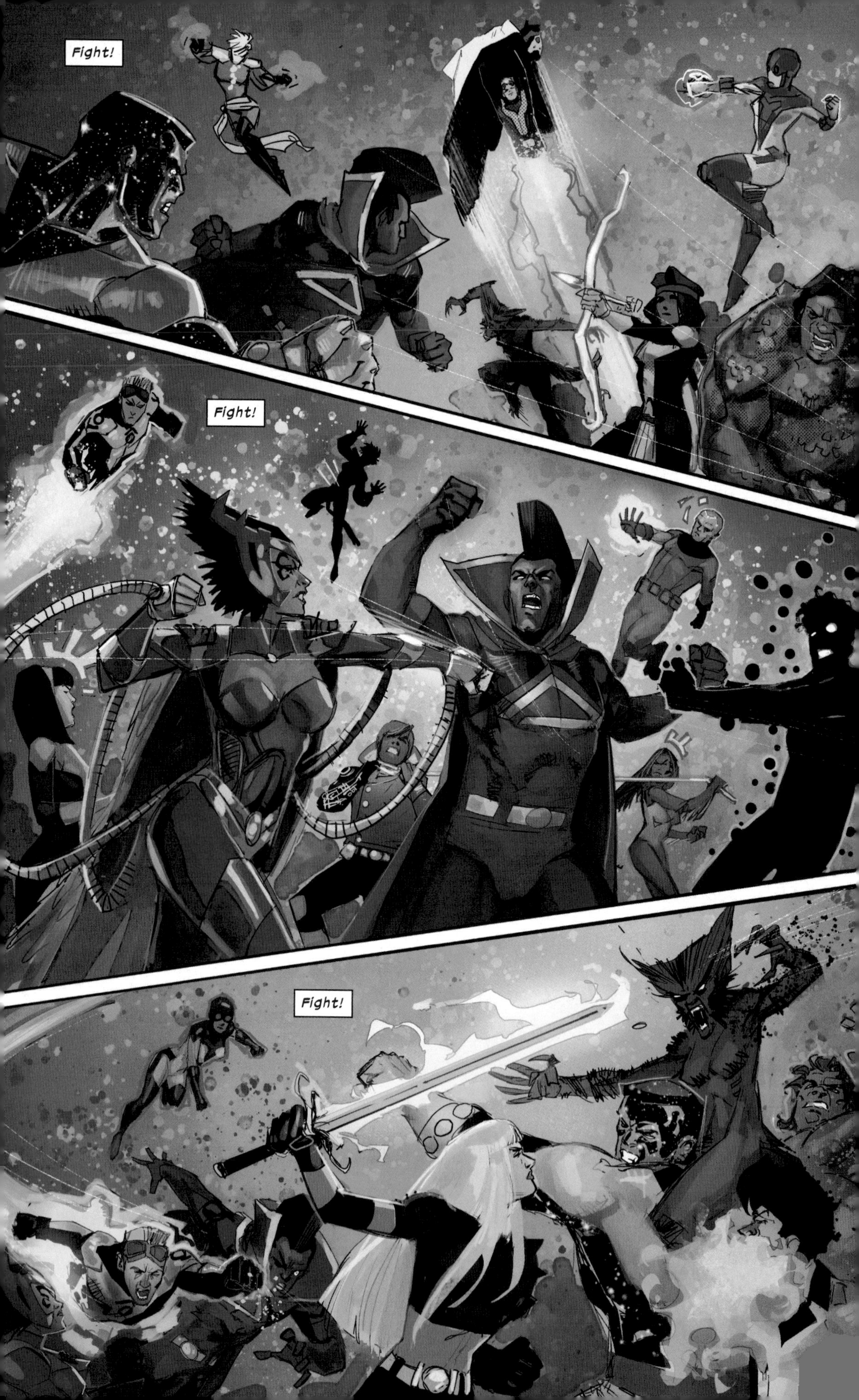
Fight!
Fight!
Fight!

FIGHT!

Normally, this fight would have gone on for seventeen glorious pages. Women and men would have triumphed, male and female aliens would have fallen. Maybe vice versa. Maybe not. But now there's only one way to tell...and all you need is a pair of dice.

LET'S GET IT ON!

ROUND ONE:
Roll one die each to choose a combatant from a side - [one mutant, one guardsman].

MUTANTS			GUARDIANS	
1.MIRAGE	[1d6]	...........................1.	MANTA	[1d6]
2.SMASHER	[1d6]	..............................2.	EARTHQUAKE	[1d6]
3.MONDO	[1d6]	...........................3.	QUASAR	[1d6]
4.CHAMBER	[1d6]	...........................4.	STARBOLT	[1d6]
5.WOLFSBANE	[1d6]	.............................5.	FLASHFIRE	[1d6]
6.KARMA	[1d6]	...........................6.	HUSSAR	[1d6]

Then roll for damage for each character [1d6 or 2d6]. Whoever rolls the highest number wins, and the lower number is eliminated. [If both numbers are the same, BOTH characters are eliminated.] Play until one team is eliminated.

ROUND TWO:
The eliminated team is then allowed to introduce their final three players. [On the initial roll, 1/4 = character 1, 2/5 = character 2, 3/6 = character 3.] Play until one team is, again, eliminated. If the winning team lost the first round, then the losing team can use their final three players. Then, again, play until one team is eliminated.

MUTANTS			GUARDIANS	
1.CANNONBALL	[2d6]	..............................1.	MENTOR	[2d6]
2.SUNSPOT	[2d6]	..............................2.	ORACLE	[2d6]
3.MAGIK	[2d6]	..............................3.	GLADIATOR	[2d6]

VICTORY:
After one team is eliminated, the winning team does not get to claim victory until they scream DEATHBIRD at the top of their lungs. Seriously, you can't win without doing this. It's in the official rules. You're reading them.

DEATHBIRD!

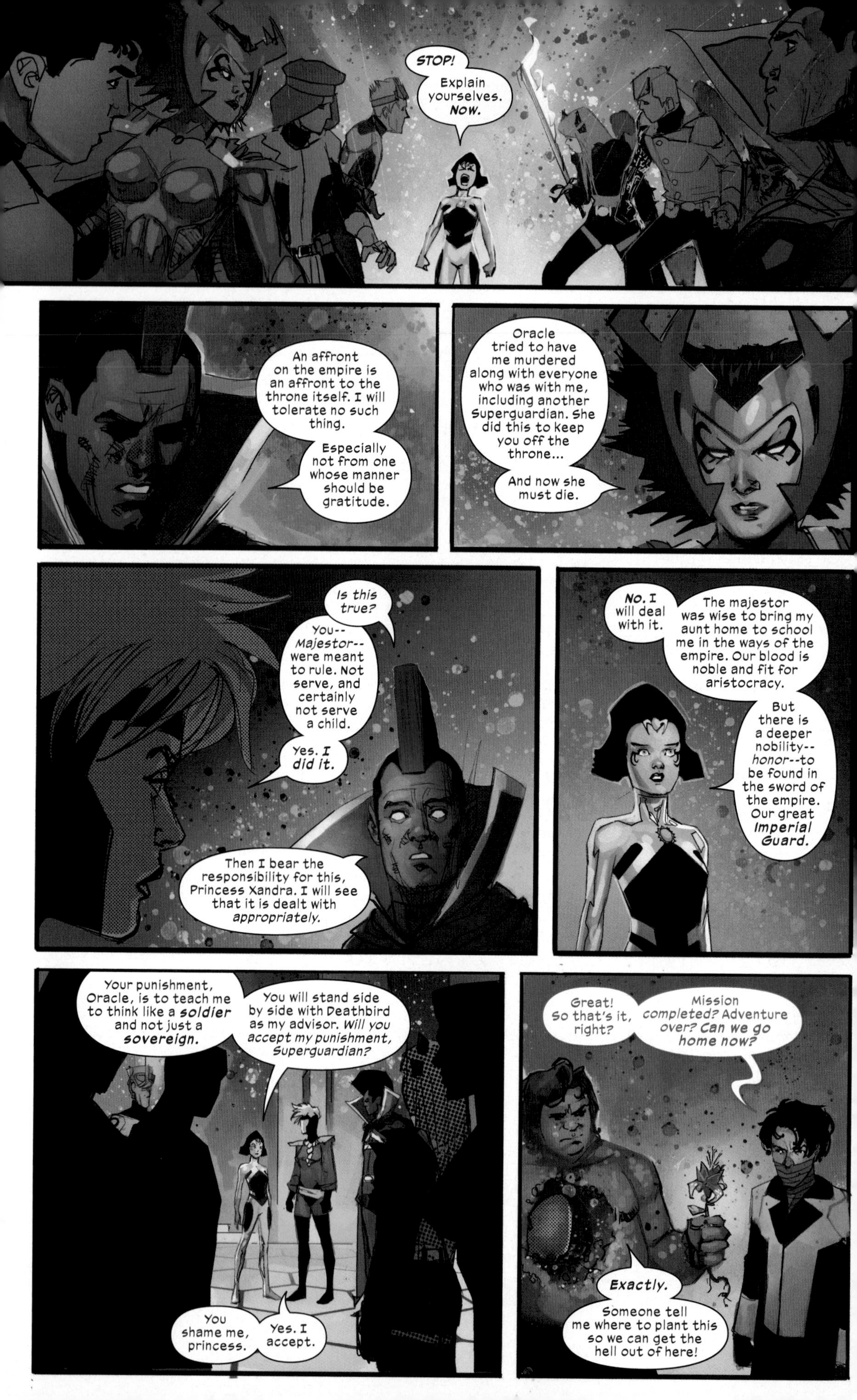
STOP!
Explain yourselves. NOW.
An affront on the empire is an affront to the throne itself. I will tolerate no such thing.
Especially not from one whose manner should be gratitude.
Oracle tried to have me murdered along with everyone who was with me, including another Superguardian. She did this to keep you off the throne...
And now she must die.
Is this true?
You-- Majestor-- were meant to rule. Not serve, and certainly not serve a child.
Yes. I did it.
Then I bear the responsibility for this, Princess Xandra. I will see that it is dealt with appropriately.
No. I will deal with it.
The majestor was wise to bring my aunt home to school me in the ways of the empire. Our blood is noble and fit for aristocracy.
But there is a deeper nobility-- honor--to be found in the sword of the empire. Our great Imperial Guard.
Your punishment, Oracle, is to teach me to think like a soldier and not just a sovereign.
You will stand side by side with Deathbird as my advisor. Will you accept my punishment, Superguardian?
You shame me, princess.
Yes. I accept.
Great! So that's it, right?
Mission completed? Adventure over? Can we go home now?
Exactly.
Someone tell me where to plant this so we can get the hell out of here!

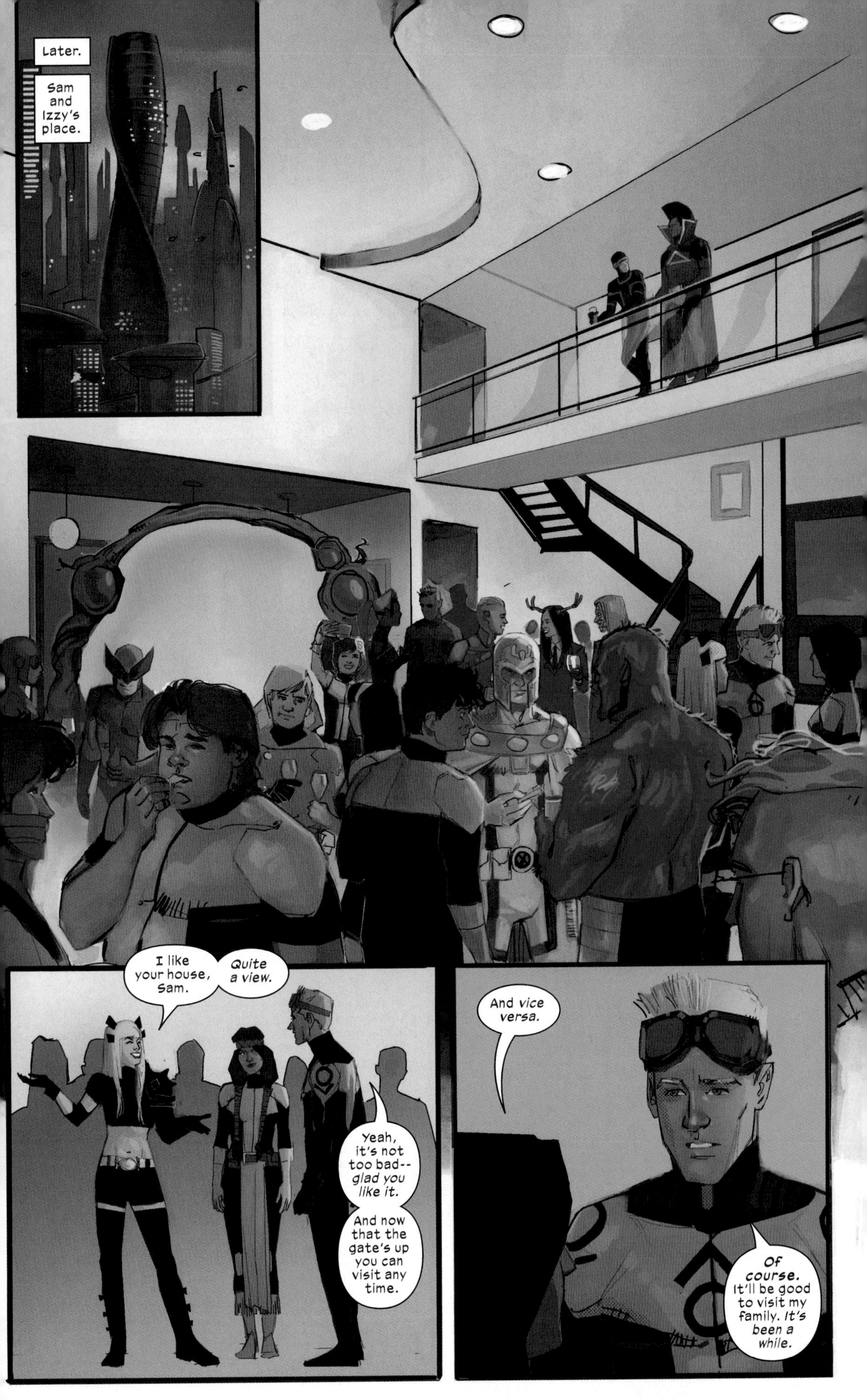

Later.
Sam and Izzy's place.
I like your house, Sam.
Quite a view.
Yeah, it's not too bad-- glad you like it.
And now that the gate's up you can visit any time.
And vice versa.
Of course. It'll be good to visit my family. It's been a while.

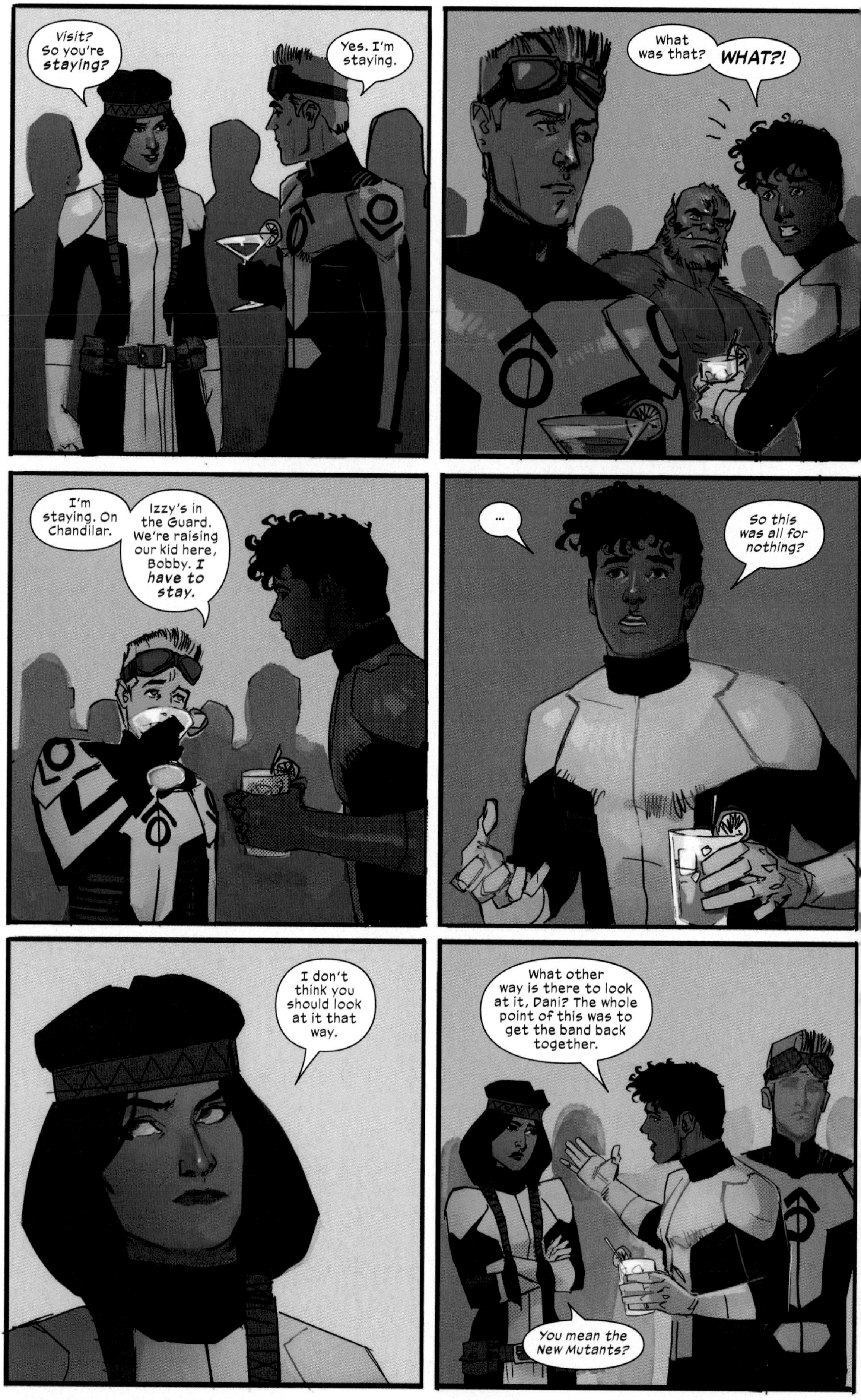

Visit? So you're *staying?*
Yes. I'm staying.
What was that?
WHAT?!
I'm staying. On Chandilar.
Izzy's in the Guard. We're raising our kid here, Bobby. ***I have to stay.***
...
So this was all for nothing?
I don't think you should look at it that way.
What other way is there to look at it, Dani? The whole point of this was to get the band back together.
You mean the New Mutants?

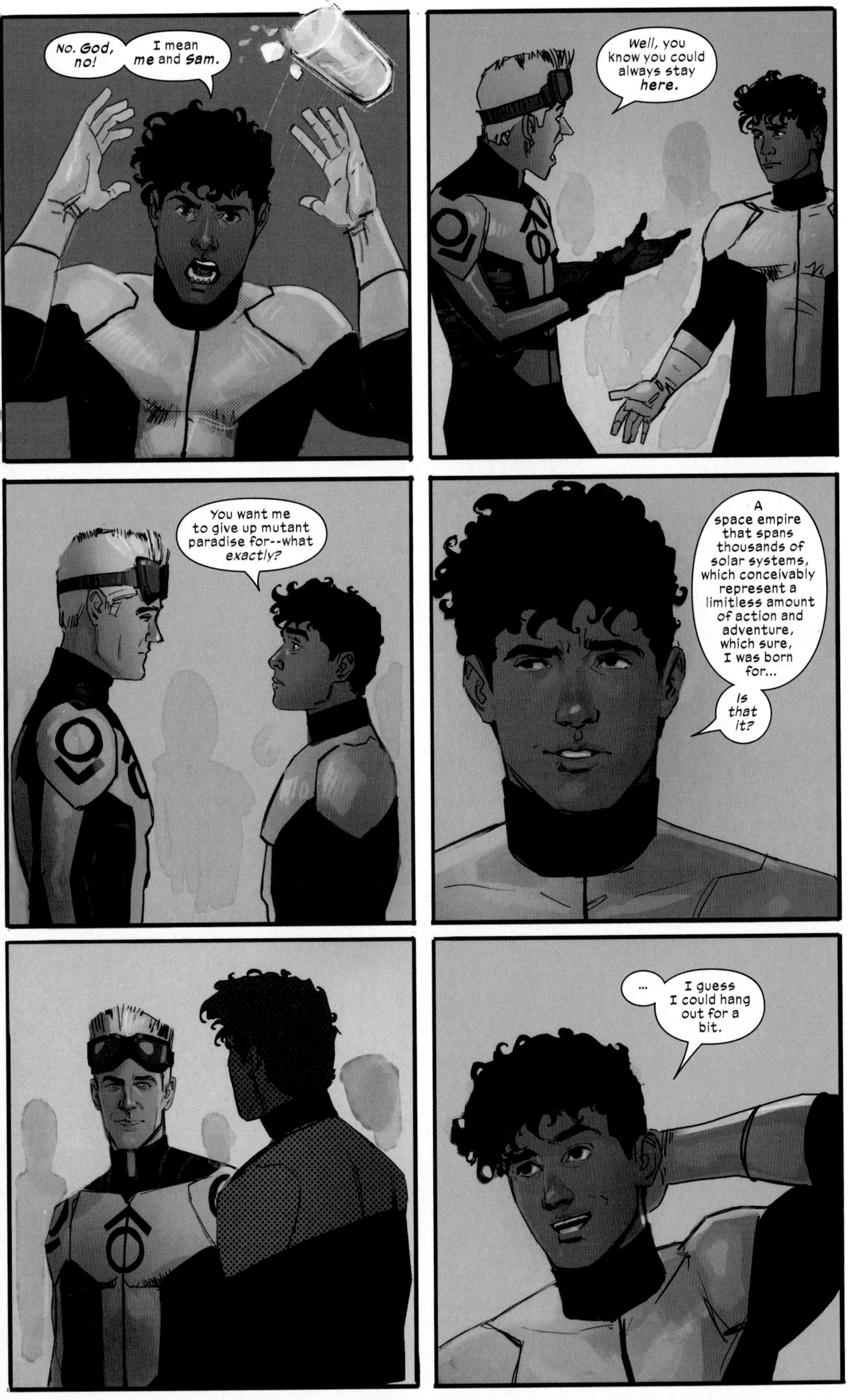
No. God, no!
I mean me and Sam.
Well, you know you could always stay here.
You want me to give up mutant paradise for--what exactly?
A space empire that spans thousands of solar systems, which conceivably represent a limitless amount of action and adventure, which sure, I was born for...
Is that it?
...
I guess I could hang out for a bit.

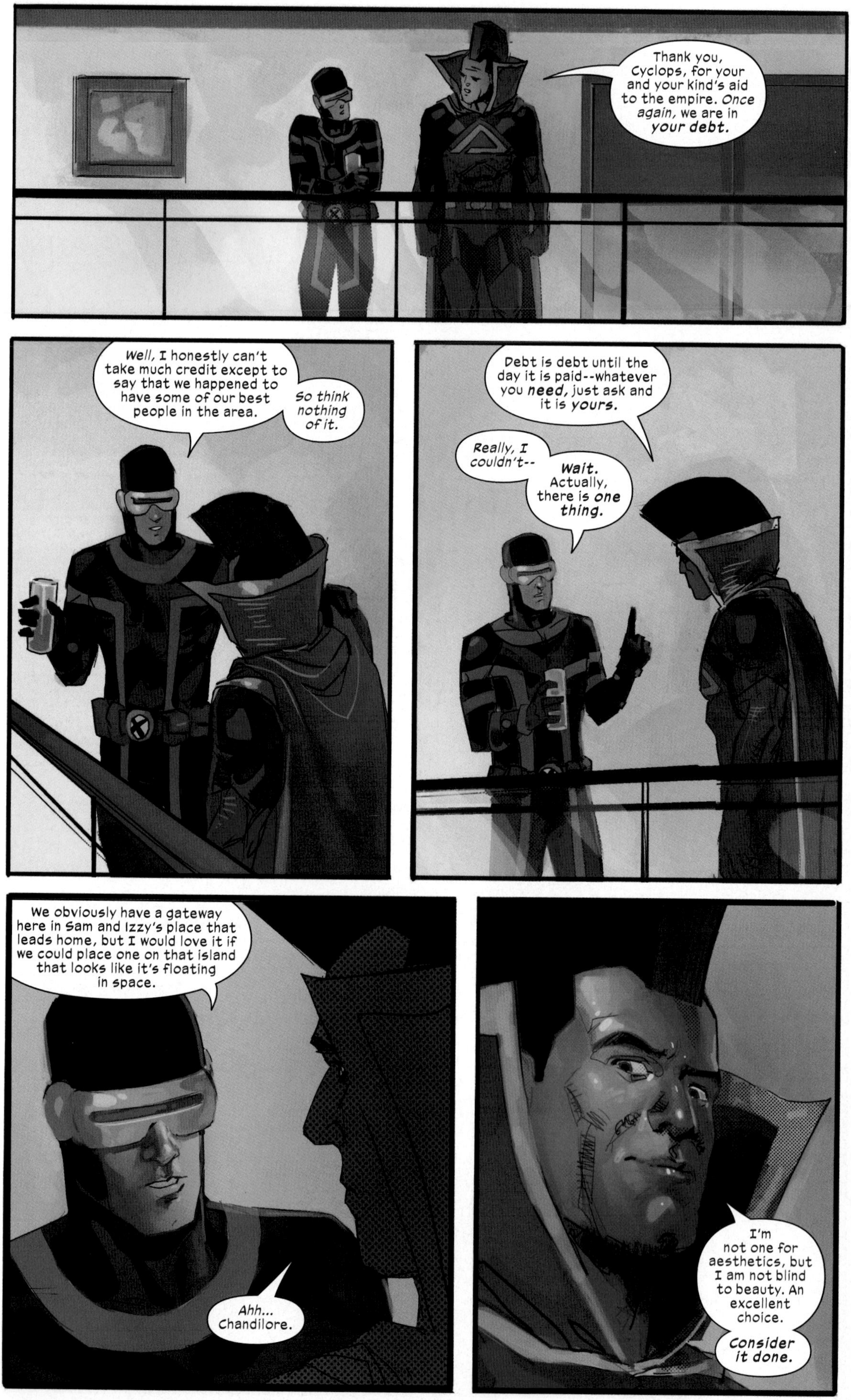
Thank you, Cyclops, for your and your kind's aid to the empire. *Once again,* we are in ***your debt.***
Well, I honestly can't take much credit except to say that we happened to have some of our best people in the area.
So think nothing of it.
Debt is debt until the day it is paid--whatever you ***need,*** just ask and it is ***yours.***
Really, I couldn't--
Wait. Actually, there is ***one thing.***
We obviously have a gateway here in Sam and Izzy's place that leads home, but I would love it if we could place one on that island that looks like it's floating in space.
Ahh... Chandilore.
I'm not one for aesthetics, but I am not blind to beauty. An excellent choice.
Consider it done.

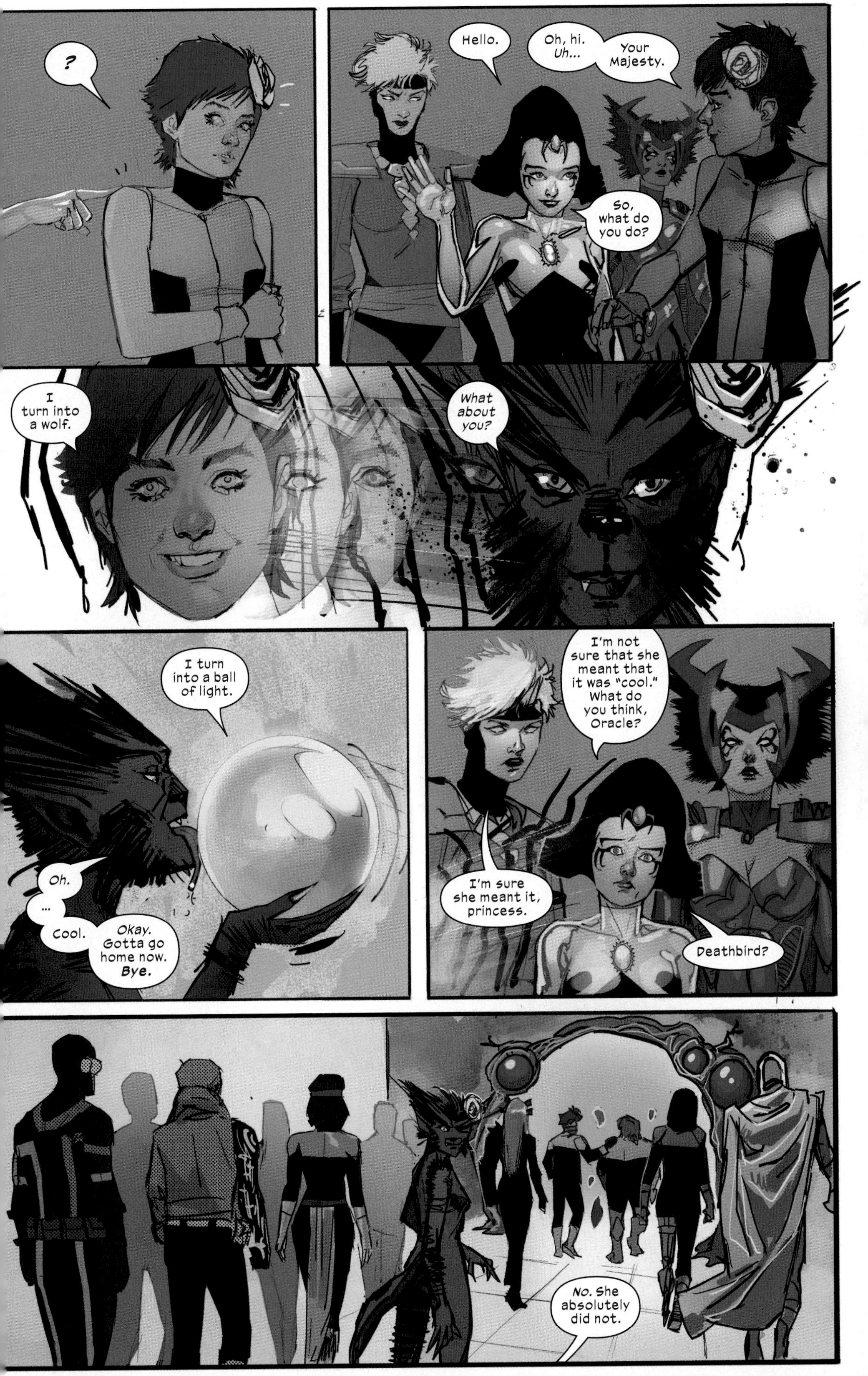
?
Hello.
Oh, hi. Uh...
Your Majesty.
So, what do you do?
I turn into a wolf.
What about you?
I turn into a ball of light.
Oh.
...
Cool.
Okay. Gotta go home now. Bye.
I'm not sure that she meant that it was "cool." What do you think, Oracle?
I'm sure she meant it, princess.
Deathbird?
No. She absolutely did not.

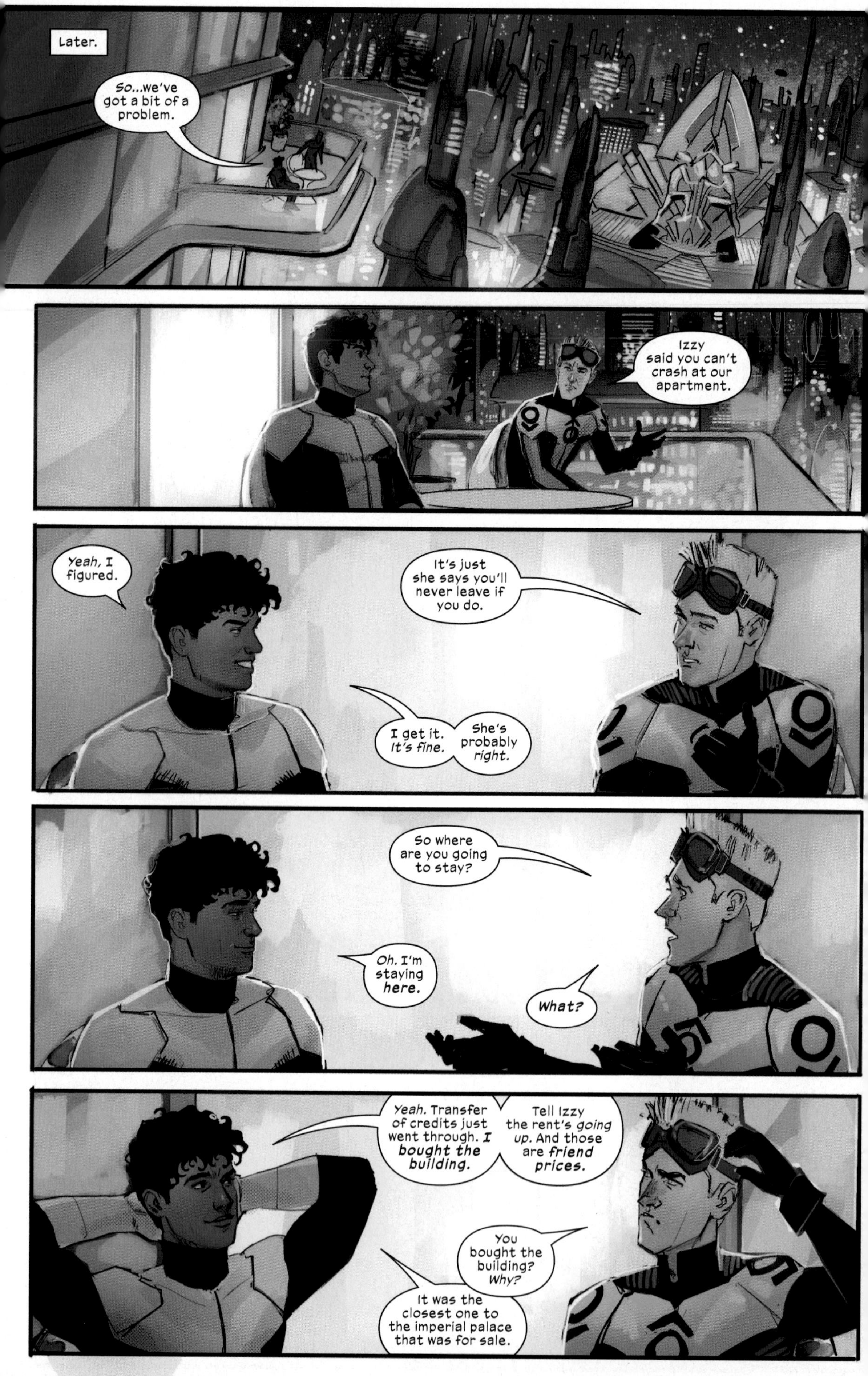
Later.
So...we've got a bit of a problem.
Izzy said you can't crash at our apartment.
Yeah, I figured.
It's just she says you'll never leave if you do.
I get it. It's fine.
She's probably right.
So where are you going to stay?
Oh. I'm staying here.
What?
Yeah. Transfer of credits just went through. I bought the building.
Tell Izzy the rent's going up. And those are friend prices.
You bought the building? Why?
It was the closest one to the imperial palace that was for sale.

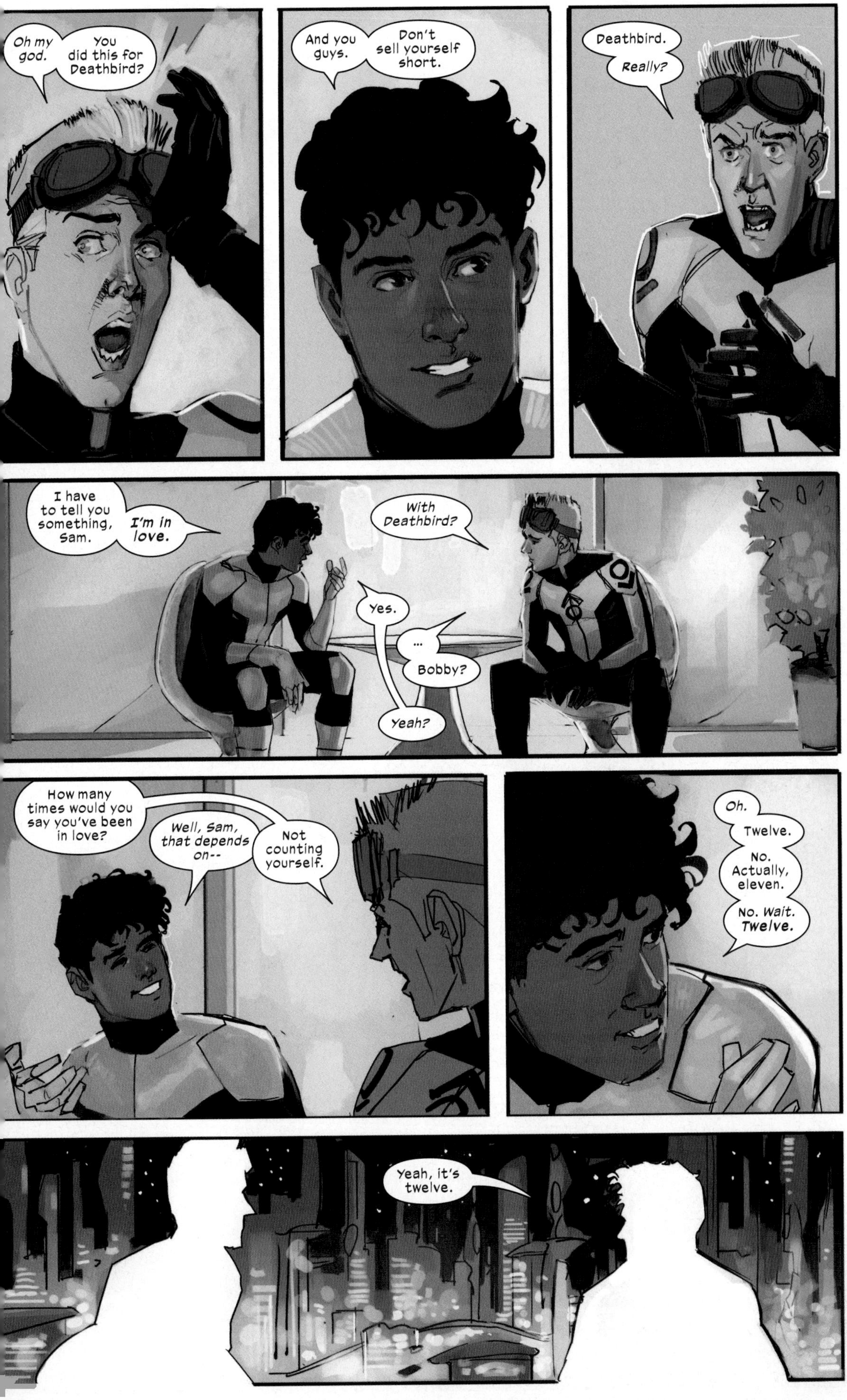
Oh my god.
You did this for Deathbird?
And you guys.
Don't sell yourself short.
Deathbird.
Really?
I have to tell you something, Sam.
I'm in love.
With Deathbird?
Yes.
...
Bobby?
Yeah?
How many times would you say you've been in love?
Well, Sam, that depends on--
Not counting yourself.
Oh.
Twelve.
No. Actually, eleven.
No. Wait. Twelve.
Yeah, it's twelve.

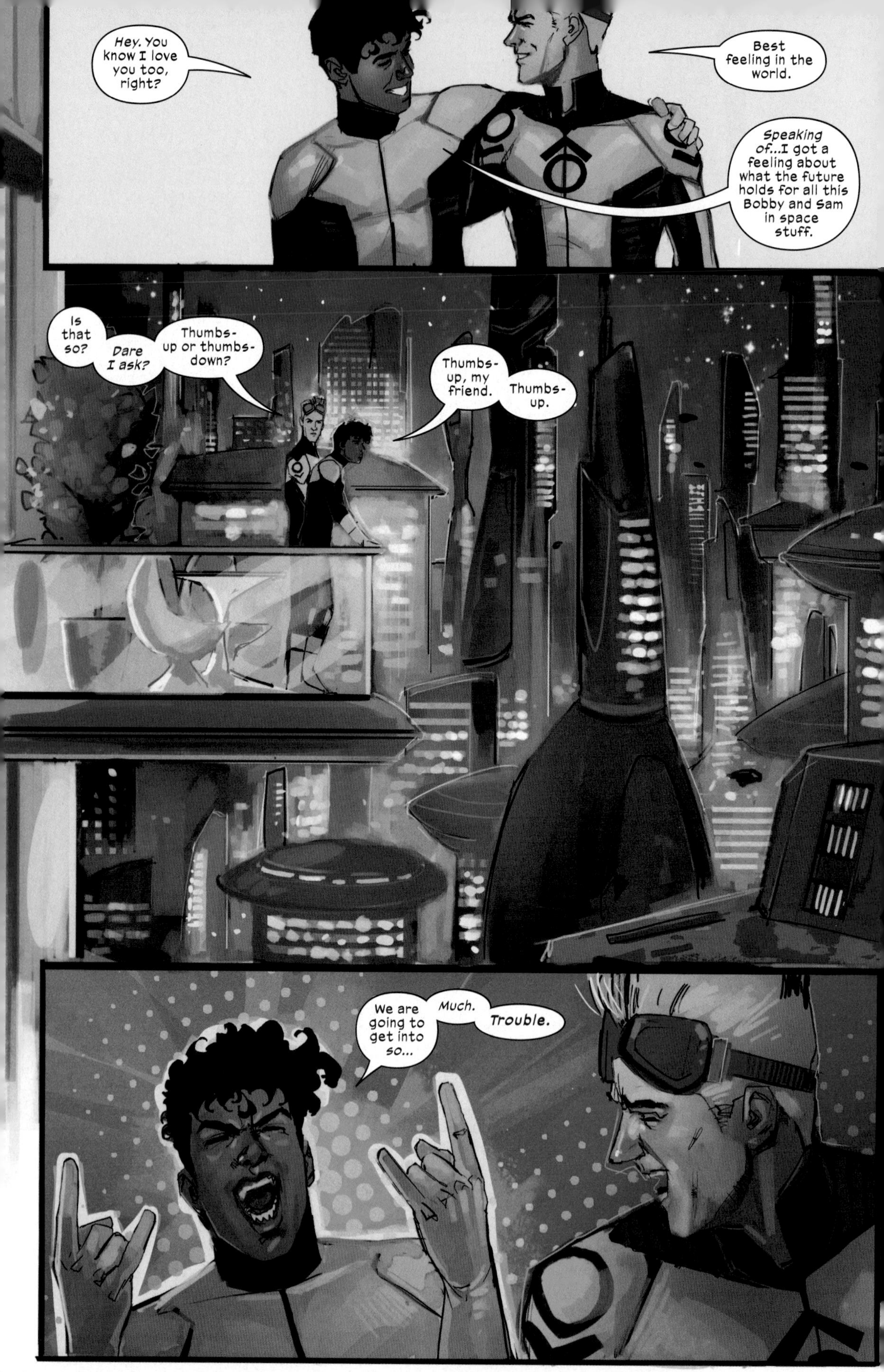

Hey. You know I love you too, right?
Best feeling in the world.
Speaking of...I got a feeling about what the future holds for all this Bobby and Sam in space stuff.
Is that so?
Dare I ask?
Thumbs-up or thumbs-down?
Thumbs-up, my friend.
Thumbs-up.
We are going to get into so...
Much.
Trouble.

[dawn_of_x]

[kra_]
[koa_]

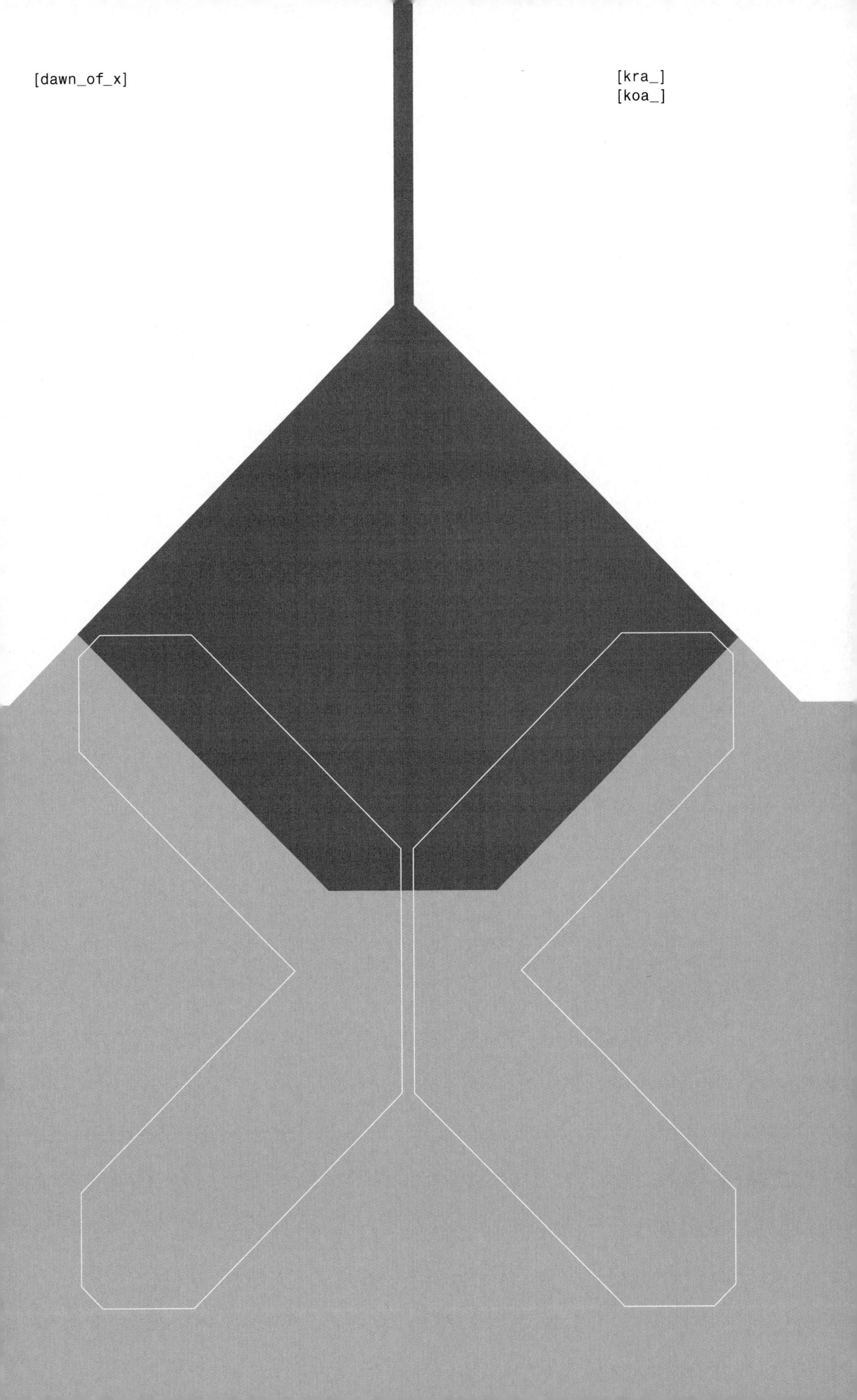

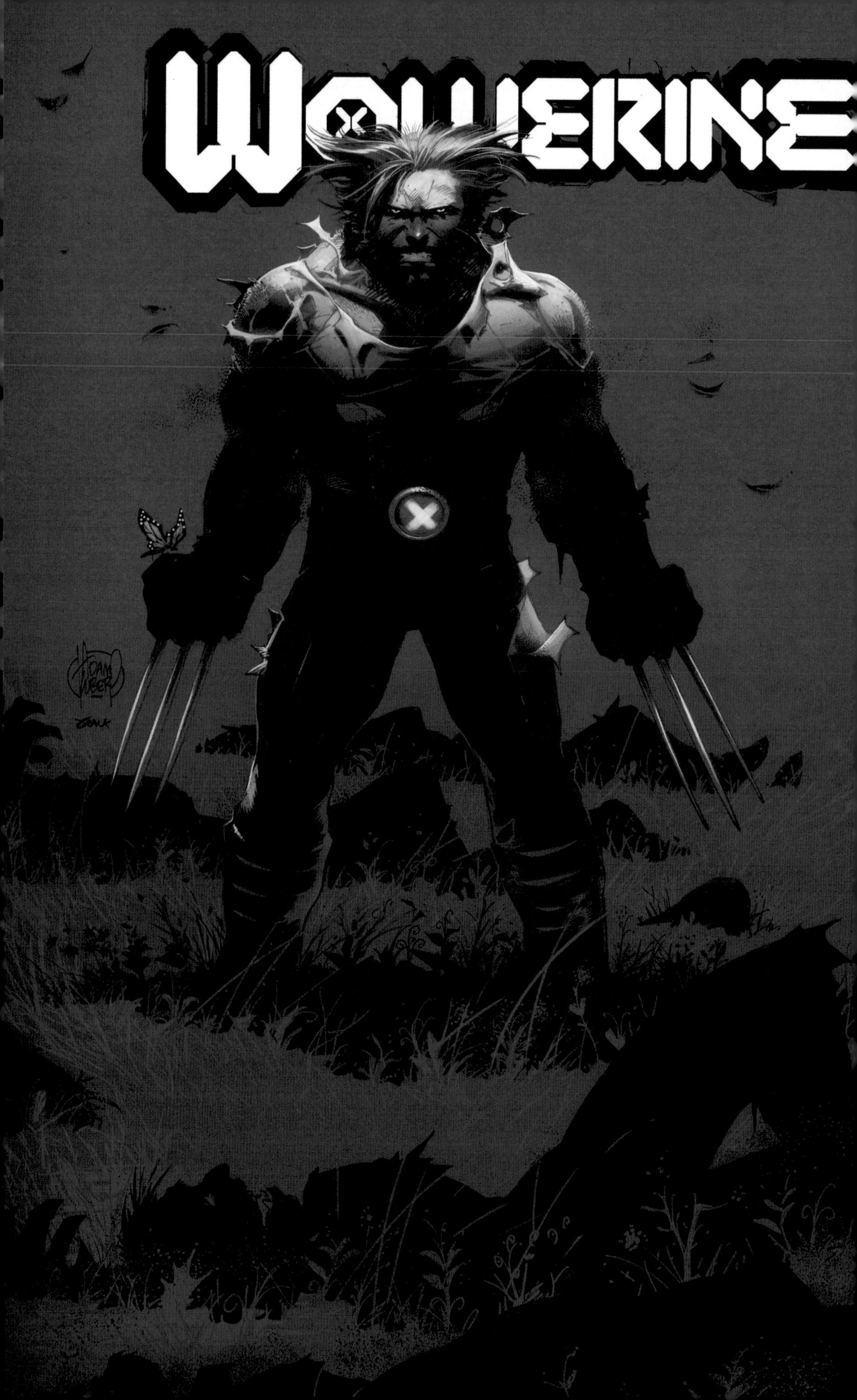
WOLVERINE

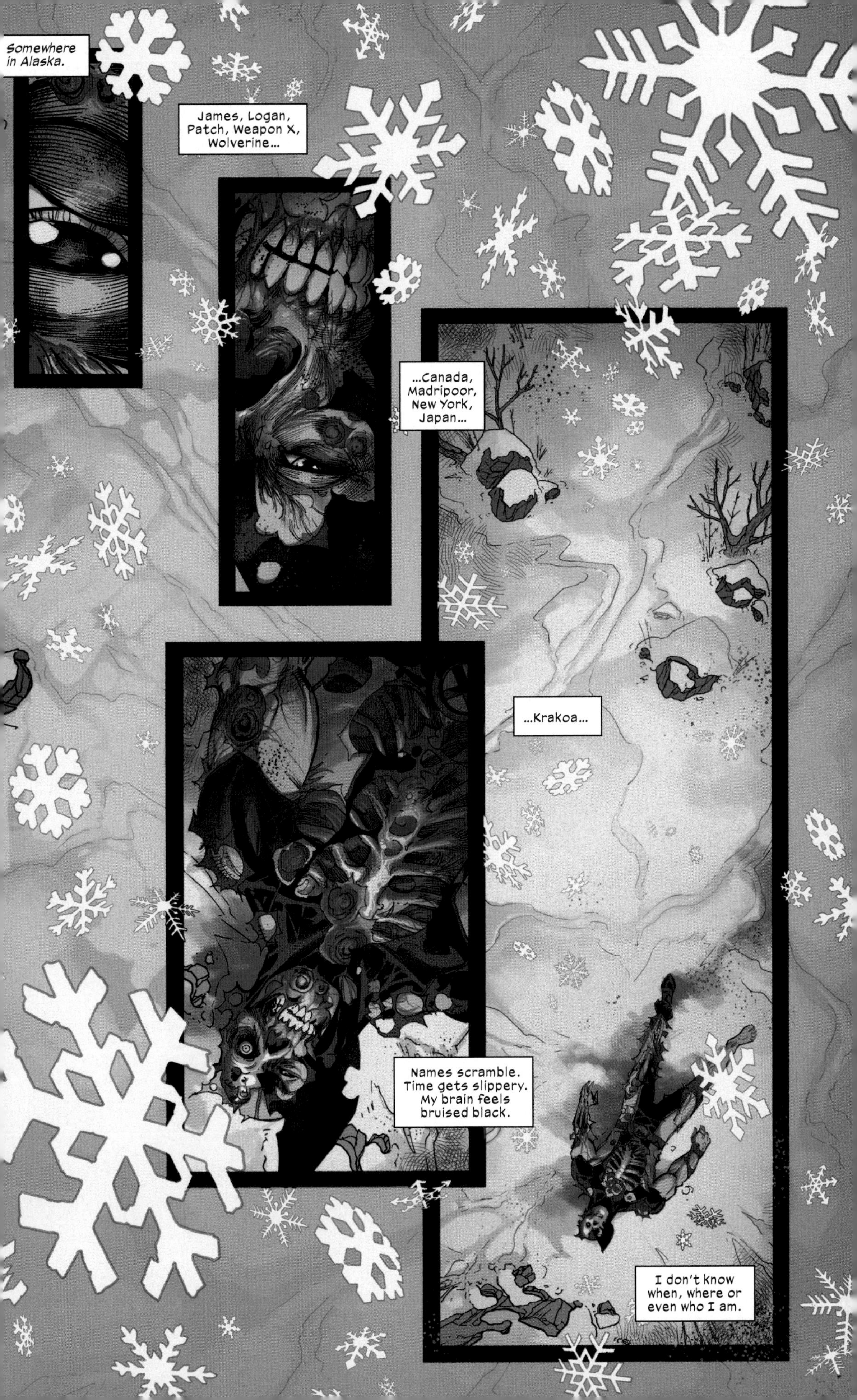
Somewhere in Alaska.
James, Logan, Patch, Weapon X, Wolverine...
...Canada, Madripoor, New York, Japan...
...Krakoa...
Names scramble. Time gets slippery. My brain feels bruised black.
I don't know when, where or even who I am.

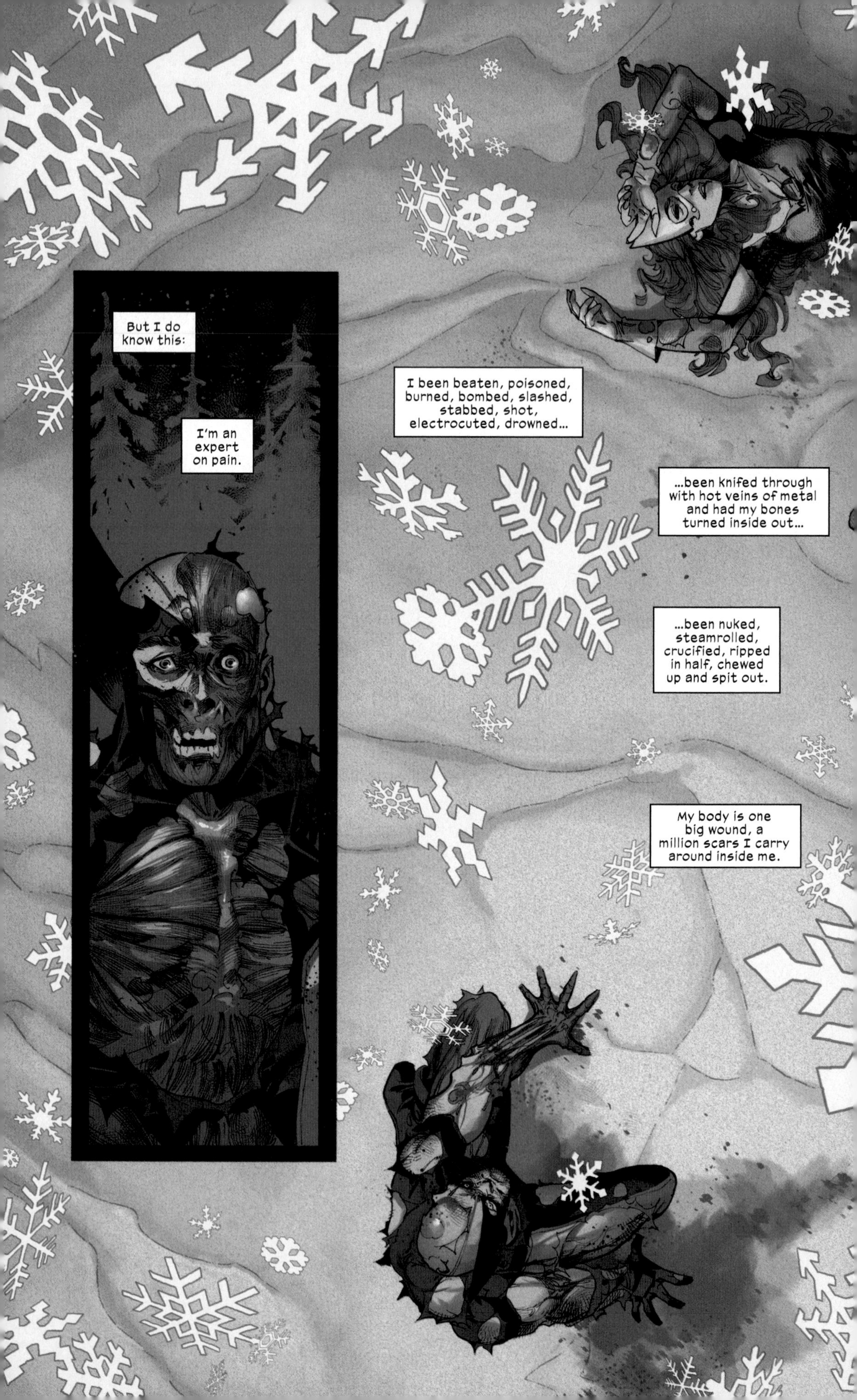
But I do know this:
I'm an expert on pain.
I been beaten, poisoned, burned, bombed, slashed, stabbed, shot, electrocuted, drowned...
...been knifed through with hot veins of metal and had my bones turned inside out...
...been nuked, steamrolled, crucified, ripped in half, chewed up and spit out.
My body is one big wound, a million scars I carry around inside me.

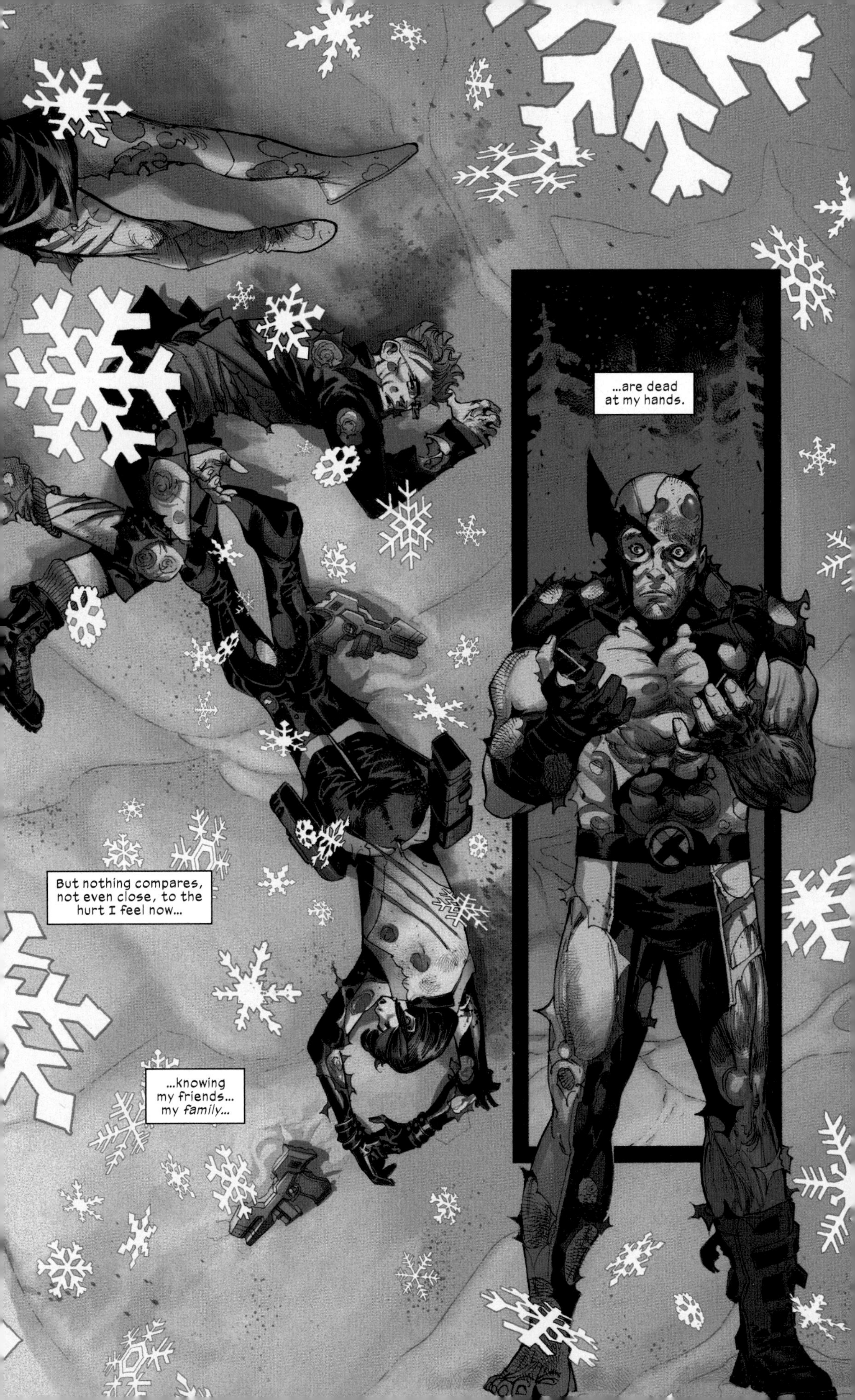
But nothing compares, not even close, to the hurt I feel now...
...knowing my friends... my *family*...
...are dead at my hands.

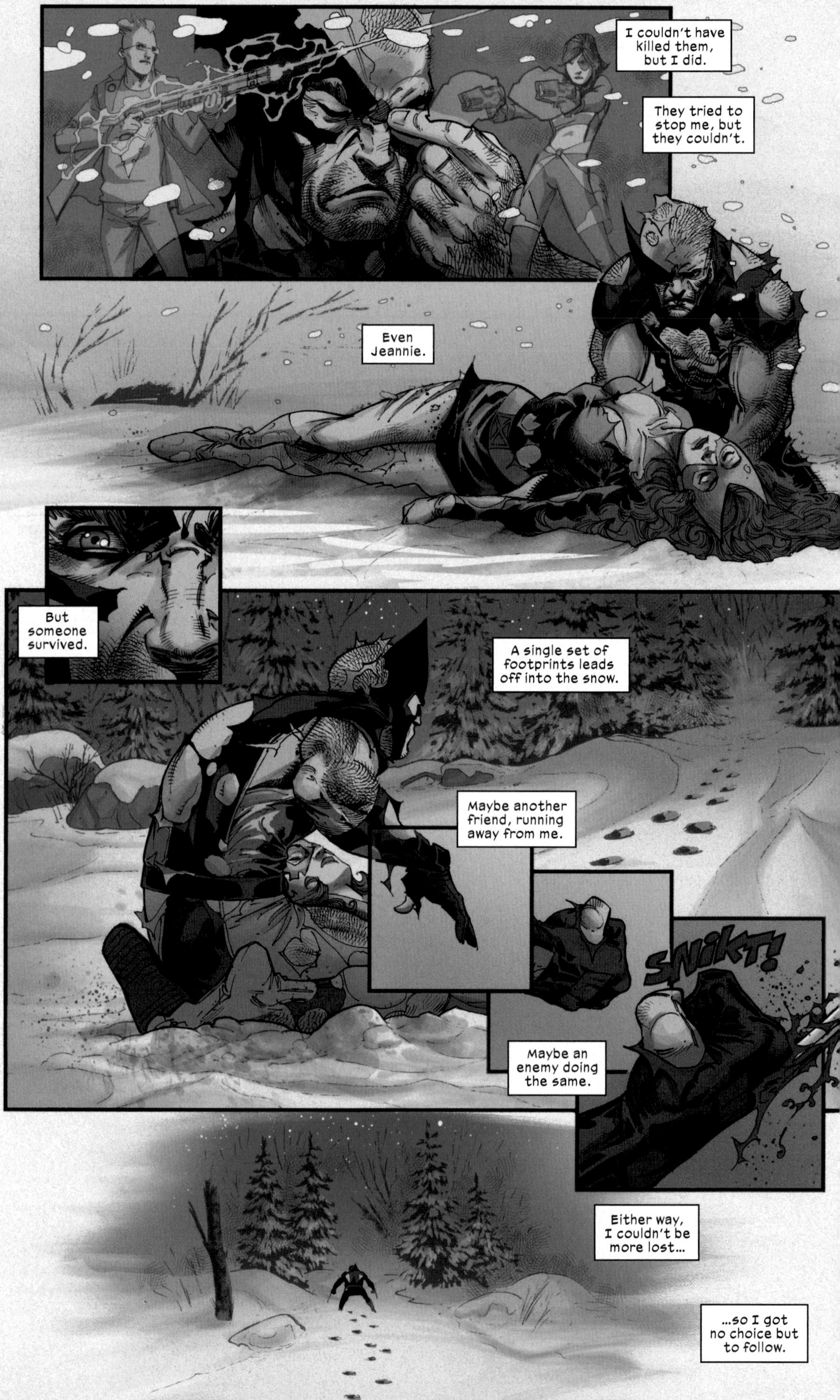
I couldn't have killed them, but I did.
They tried to stop me, but they couldn't.
Even Jeannie.
But someone survived.
A single set of footprints leads off into the snow.
Maybe another friend, running away from me.
Maybe an enemy doing the same.
SNIKT!
Either way, I couldn't be more lost...
...so I got no choice but to follow.

[kra_[0.1]
[koa_[0.1]

[kra_[0.X]
[koa_[0.X]

IF YOU REALLY WANT TO TANGLE WITH SOMEONE

Mutants around the world are flocking to the island-nation of Krakoa for safety, security and to be part of the first mutant society -- *even* Wolverine.

Yet, in spite of the wealth and opportunity ahead, Wolverine remains poised for the worst...

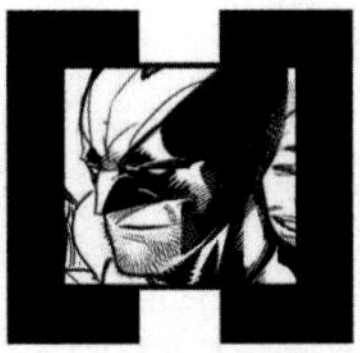
Wolverine

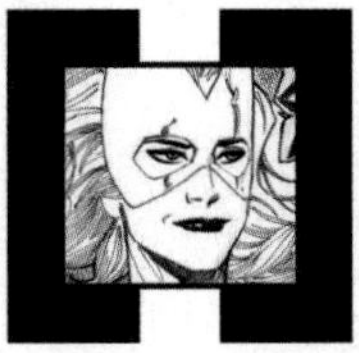
Marvel Girl

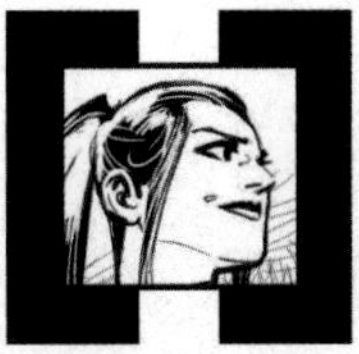
Kate Pryde

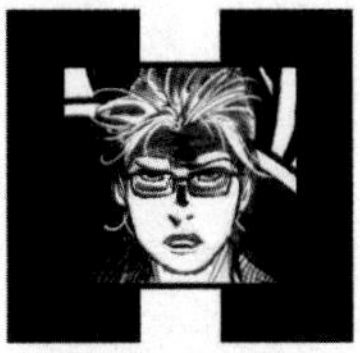
Sage

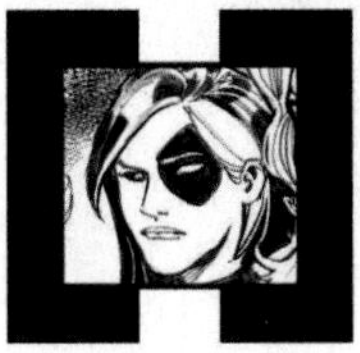
Domino

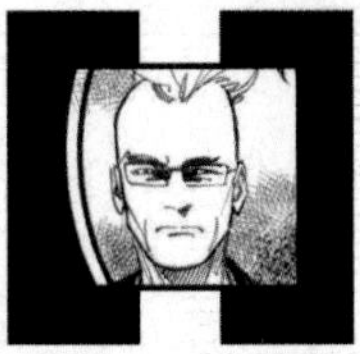
Kid Omega

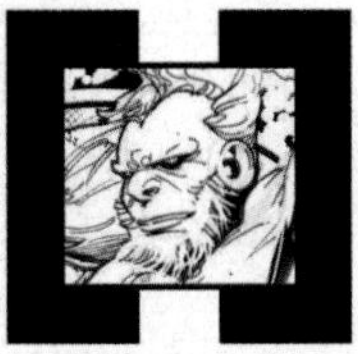
Gateway

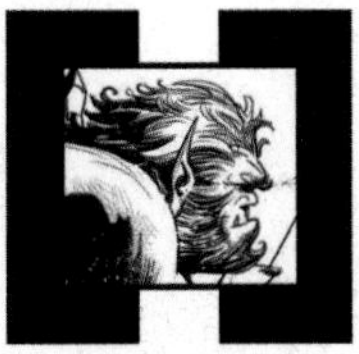
Beast

[00_best_]
[00_there]

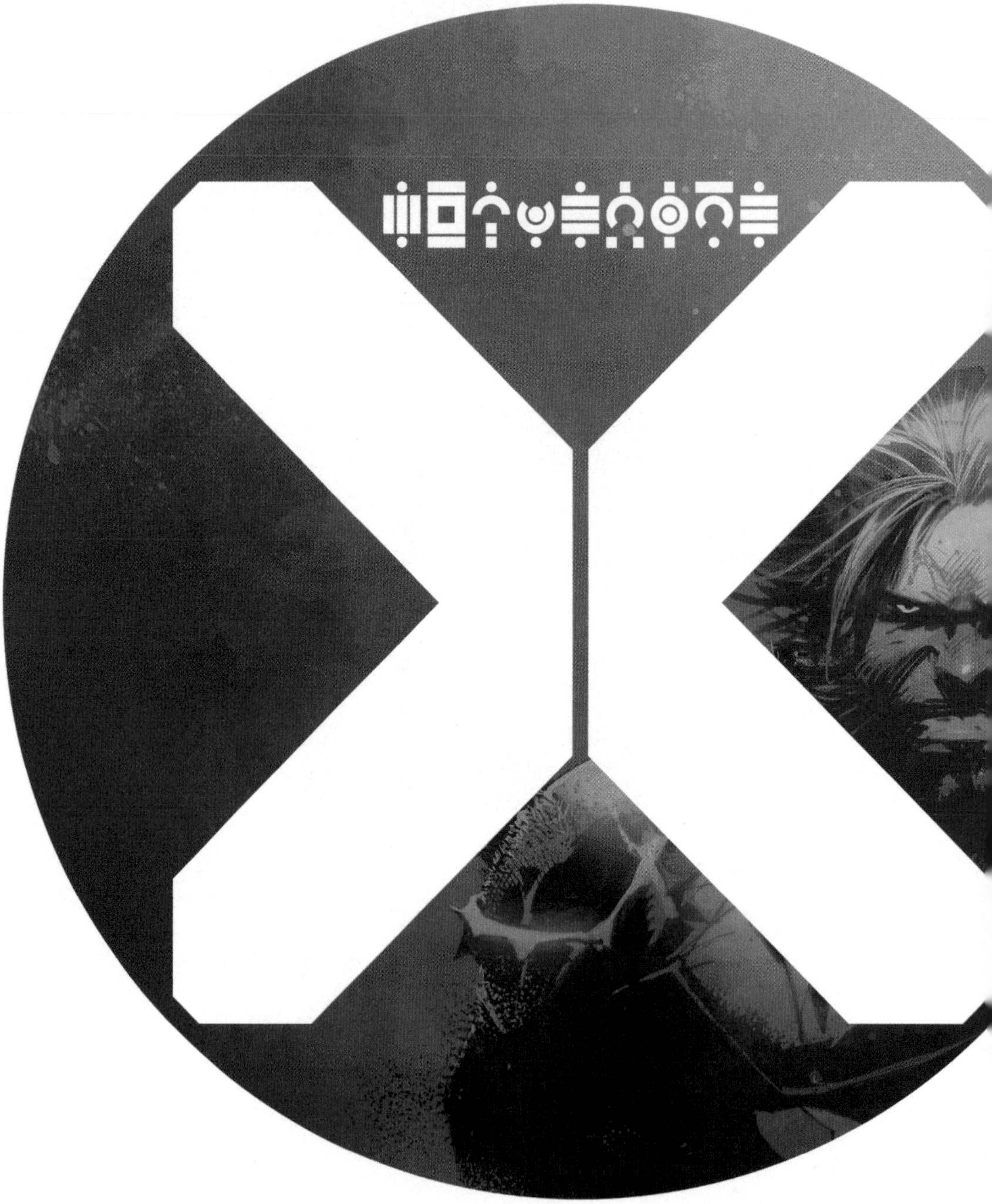

BENJAMIN PERCY................................[WRITER]
ADAM KUBERT...................................[ARTIST]
FRANK MARTIN.............................[COLOR ARTIST]
VC's CORY PETIT..............................[LETTERER]
TOM MULLER....................................[DESIGN]

ADAM KUBERT & FRANK MARTIN..............[COVER ARTISTS]

ALEX ROSS / CHIP KIDD / JEEHYUNG LEE / JIM LEE &
JASON KEITH / RAHZZAH / R.B. SILVA & MARTE GRACIA /
SKOTTIE YOUNG /
GABRIELE DELL'OTTO..............[VARIANT COVER ARTISTS]

NICK RUSSELL...............................[PRODUCTION]

JONATHAN HICKMAN...........................[HEAD OF X]
CHRIS ROBINSON.......................[ASSISTANT EDITOR]
JORDAN D. WHITE...............................[EDITOR]
C.B. CEBULSKI.........................[EDITOR IN CHIEF]

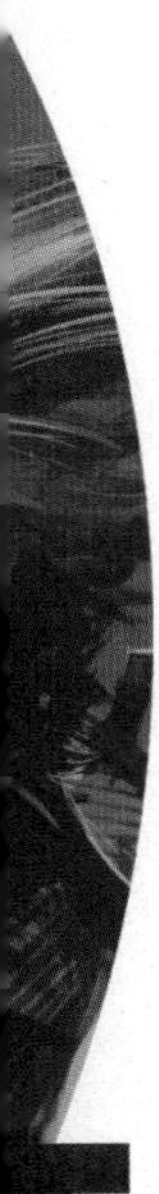

[01] WOLVERINE

[ISSUE ONE]............THE FLOWER CARTEL

[dawn_of_x]

[kra_]
[koa_]

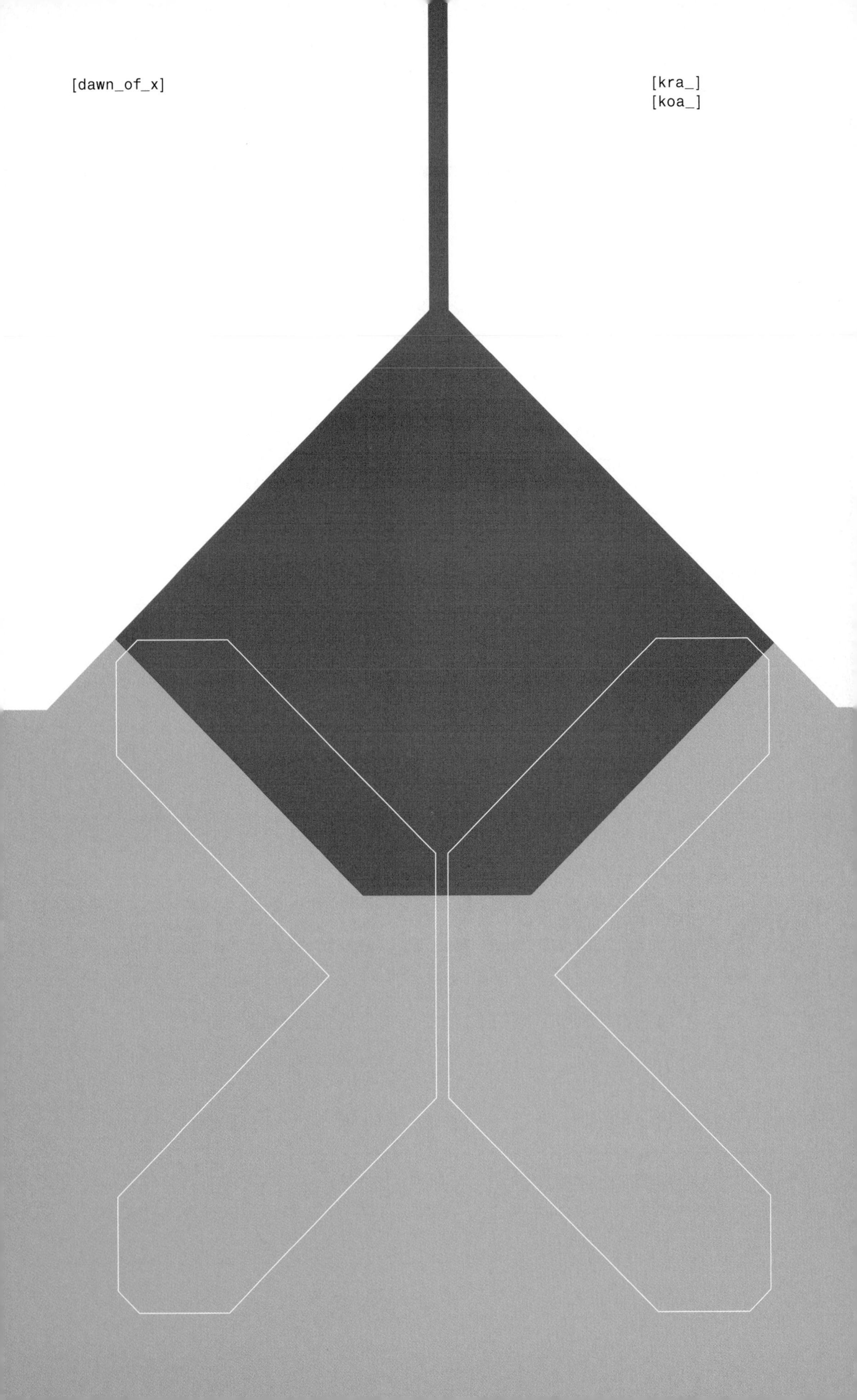

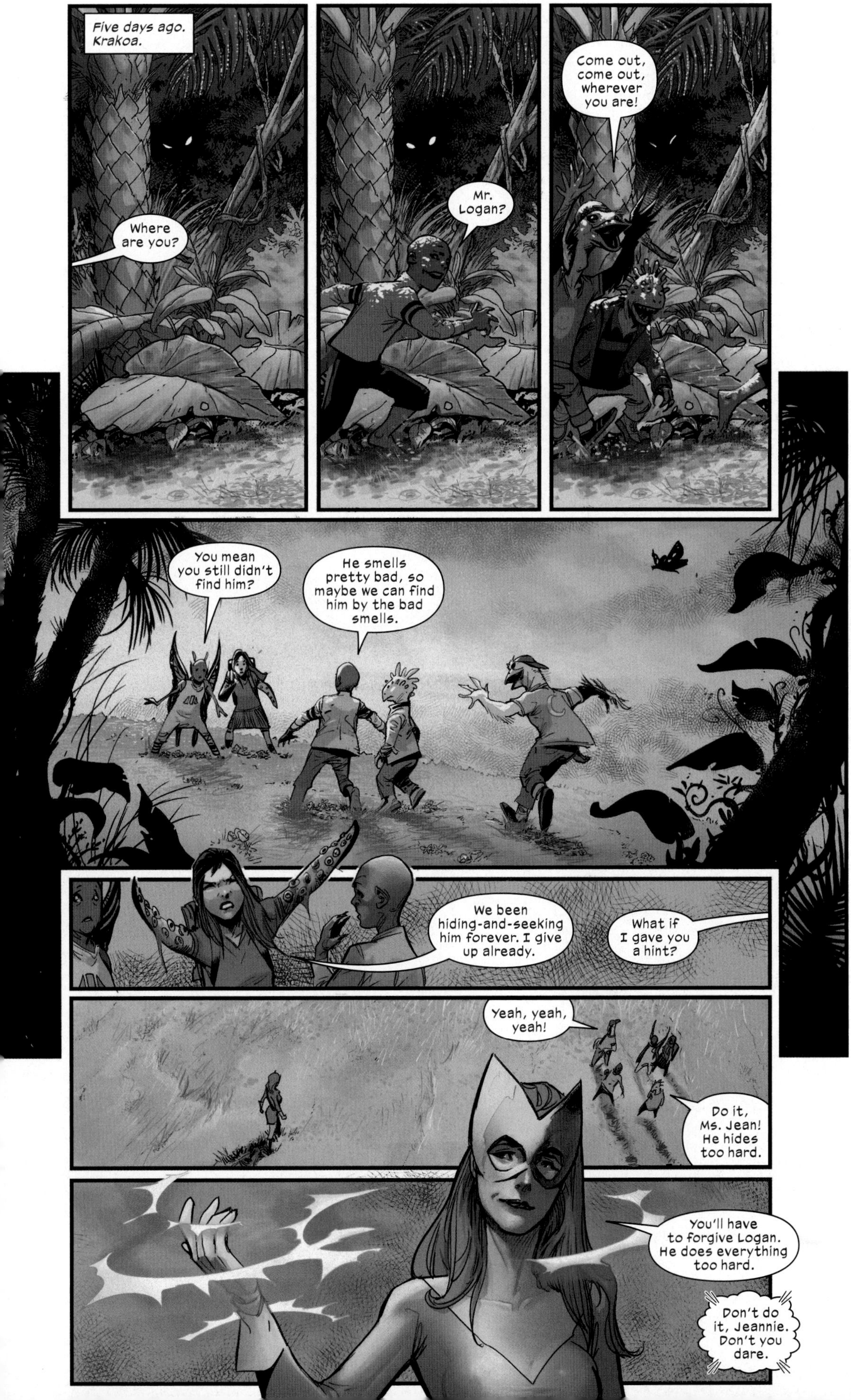

Five days ago. Krakoa.
Where are you?
Mr. Logan?
Come out, come out, wherever you are!
You mean you still didn't find him?
He smells pretty bad, so maybe we can find him by the bad smells.
We been hiding-and-seeking him forever. I give up already.
What if I gave you a hint?
Yeah, yeah, yeah!
Do it, Ms. Jean! He hides too hard.
You'll have to forgive Logan. He does everything too hard.
Don't do it, Jeannie. Don't you dare.

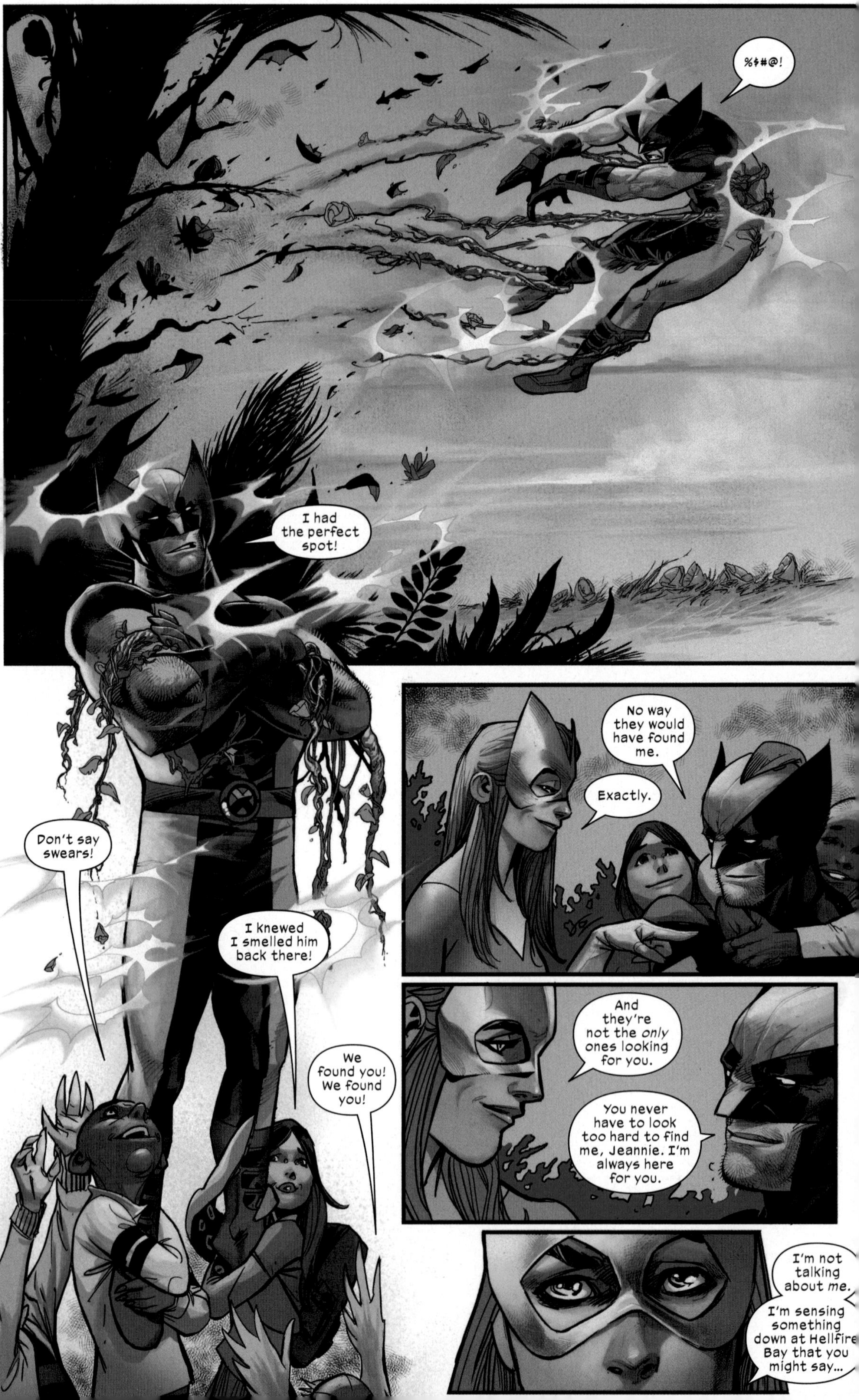
%$#@!
I had the perfect spot!
Don't say swears!
I knewed I smelled him back there!
We found you! We found you!
No way they would have found me.
Exactly.
And they're not the *only* ones looking for you.
You never have to look too hard to find me, Jeannie. I'm always here for you.
I'm not talking about *me*.
I'm sensing something down at Hellfire Bay that you might say...

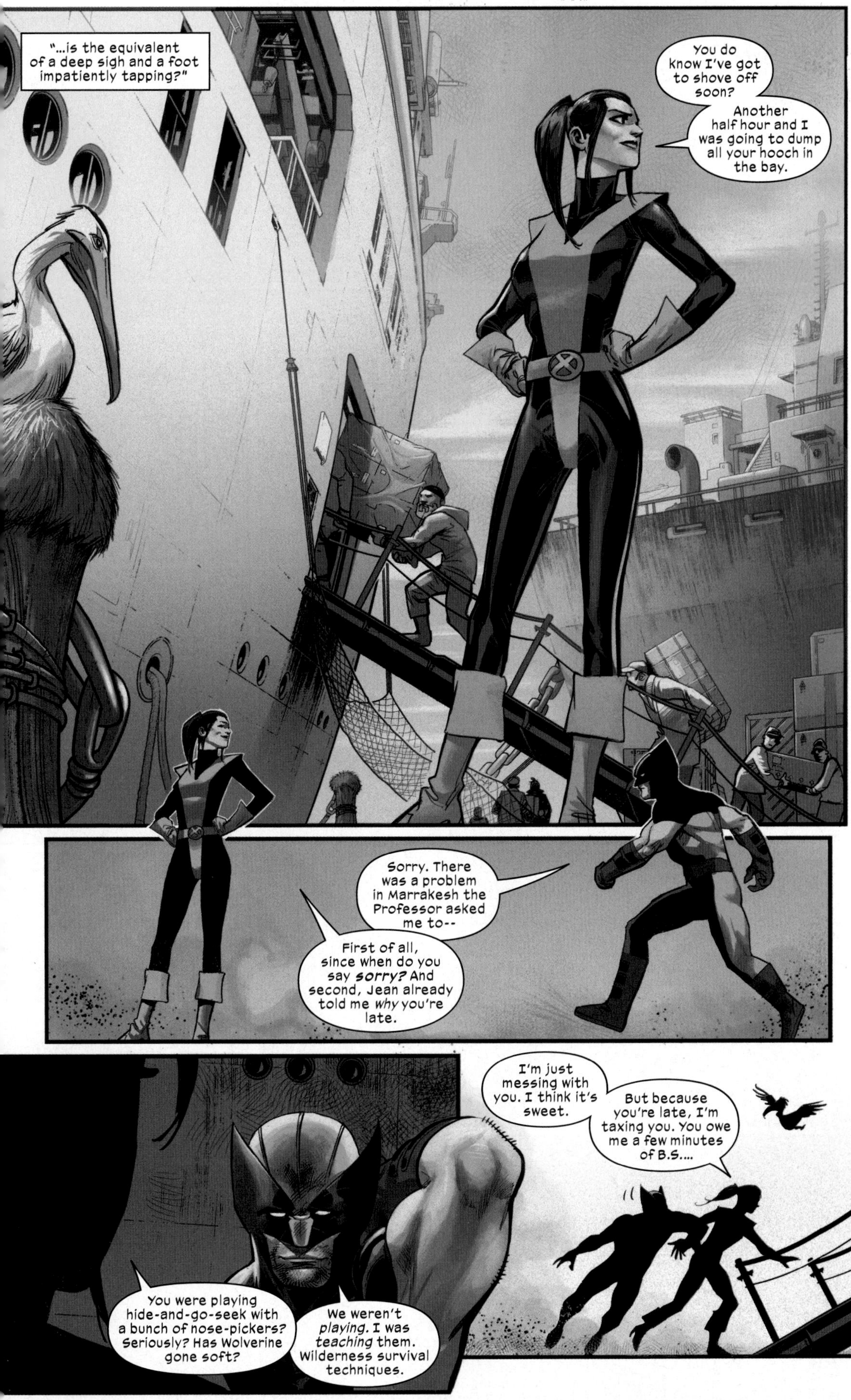
"...is the equivalent of a deep sigh and a foot impatiently tapping?"
You do know I've got to shove off soon?
Another half hour and I was going to dump all your hooch in the bay.
Sorry. There was a problem in Marrakesh the Professor asked me to--
First of all, since when do you say *sorry?* And second, Jean already told me *why* you're late.
You were playing hide-and-go-seek with a bunch of nose-pickers? Seriously? Has Wolverine gone soft?
We weren't *playing*. I was *teaching* them. Wilderness survival techniques.
I'm just messing with you. I think it's sweet.
But because you're late, I'm taxing you. You owe me a few minutes of B.S....

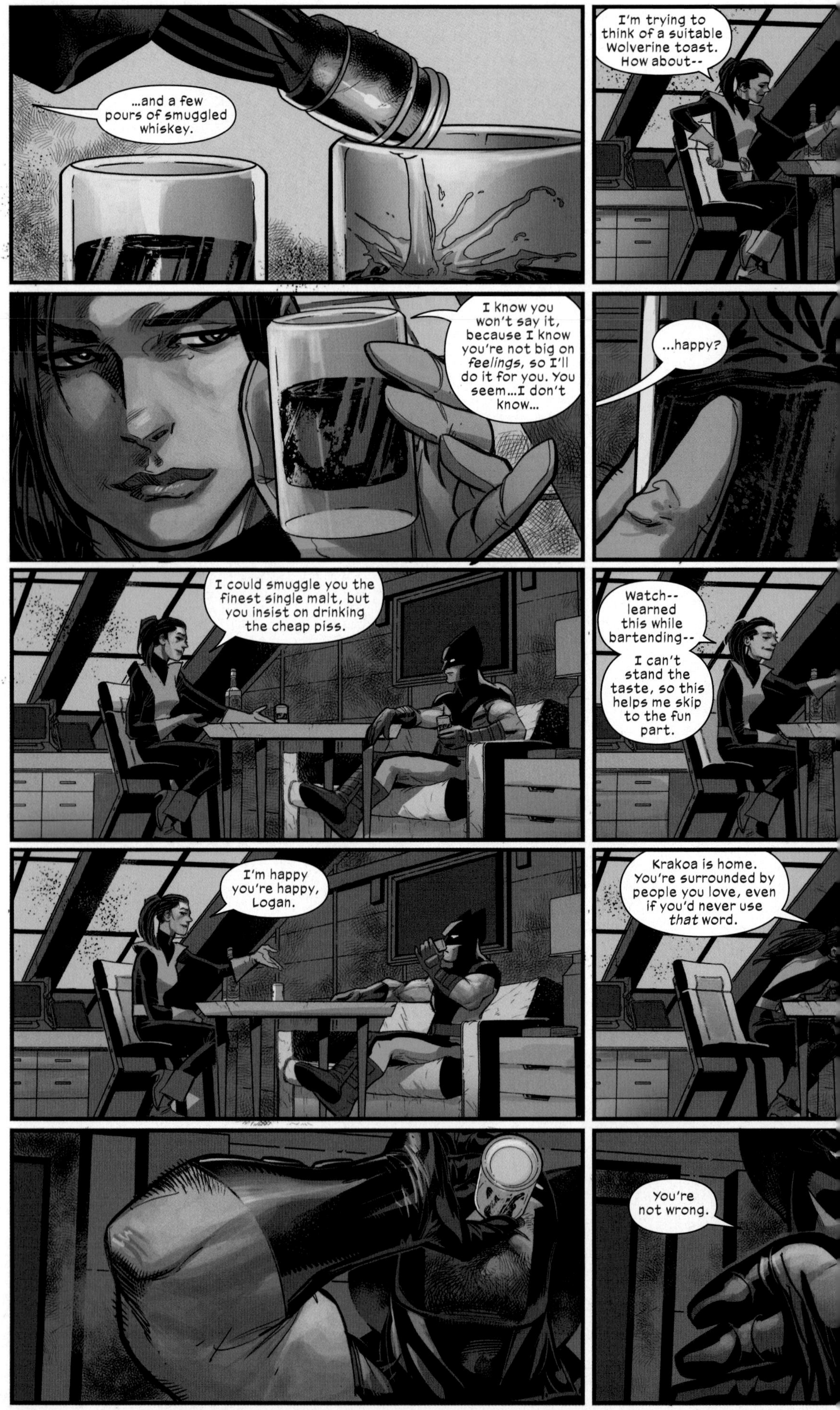
...and a few pours of smuggled whiskey.
I'm trying to think of a suitable Wolverine toast. How about--
I know you won't say it, because I know you're not big on *feelings*, so I'll do it for you. You seem...I don't know...
...happy?
I could smuggle you the finest single malt, but you insist on drinking the cheap piss.
Watch-- learned this while bartending--
I can't stand the taste, so this helps me skip to the fun part.
I'm happy you're happy, Logan.
Krakoa is home. You're surrounded by people you love, even if you'd never use *that* word.
You're not wrong.

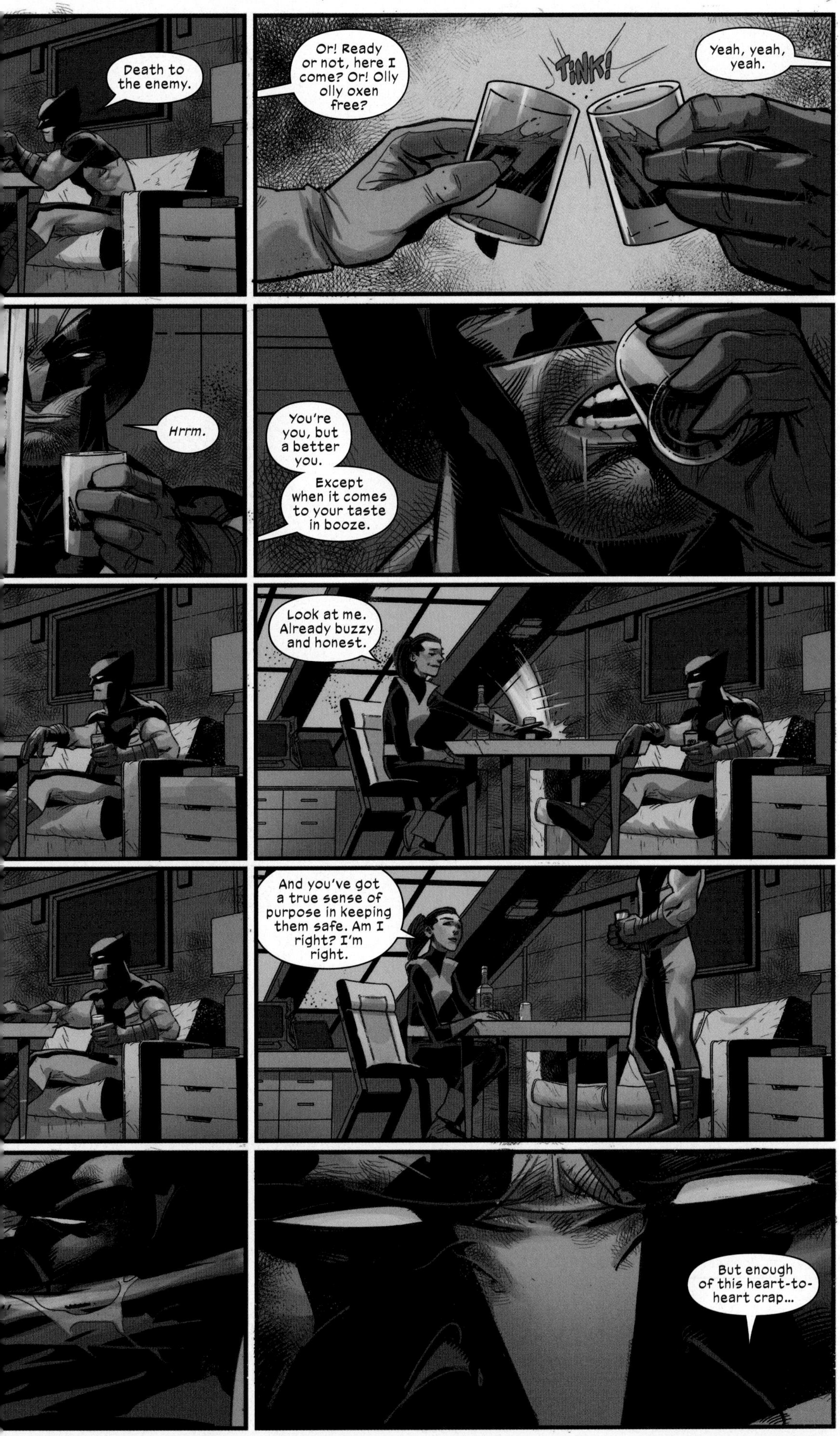
Death to the enemy.
Or! Ready or not, here I come? Or! Olly olly oxen free?
TINK!
Yeah, yeah, yeah.
Hrrm.
You're you, but a better you.
Except when it comes to your taste in booze.
Look at me. Already buzzy and honest.
And you've got a true sense of purpose in keeping them safe. Am I right? I'm right.
But enough of this heart-to-heart crap...

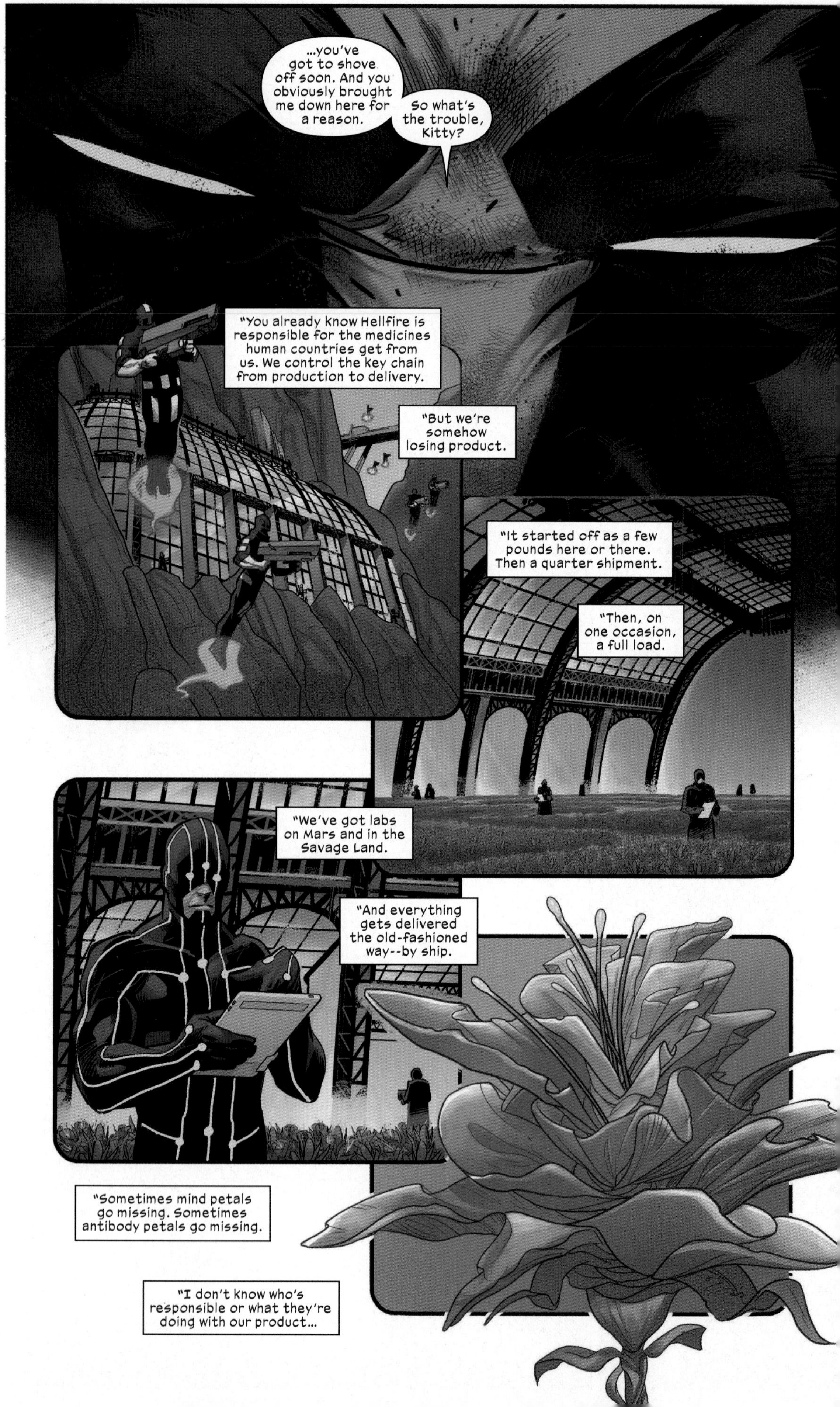
...you've got to shove off soon. And you obviously brought me down here for a reason.
So what's the trouble, Kitty?
"You already know Hellfire is responsible for the medicines human countries get from us. We control the key chain from production to delivery.
"But we're somehow losing product.
"It started off as a few pounds here or there. Then a quarter shipment.
"Then, on one occasion, a full load.
"We've got labs on Mars and in the Savage Land.
"And everything gets delivered the old-fashioned way--by ship.
"Sometimes mind petals go missing. Sometimes antibody petals go missing.
"I don't know who's responsible or what they're doing with our product...

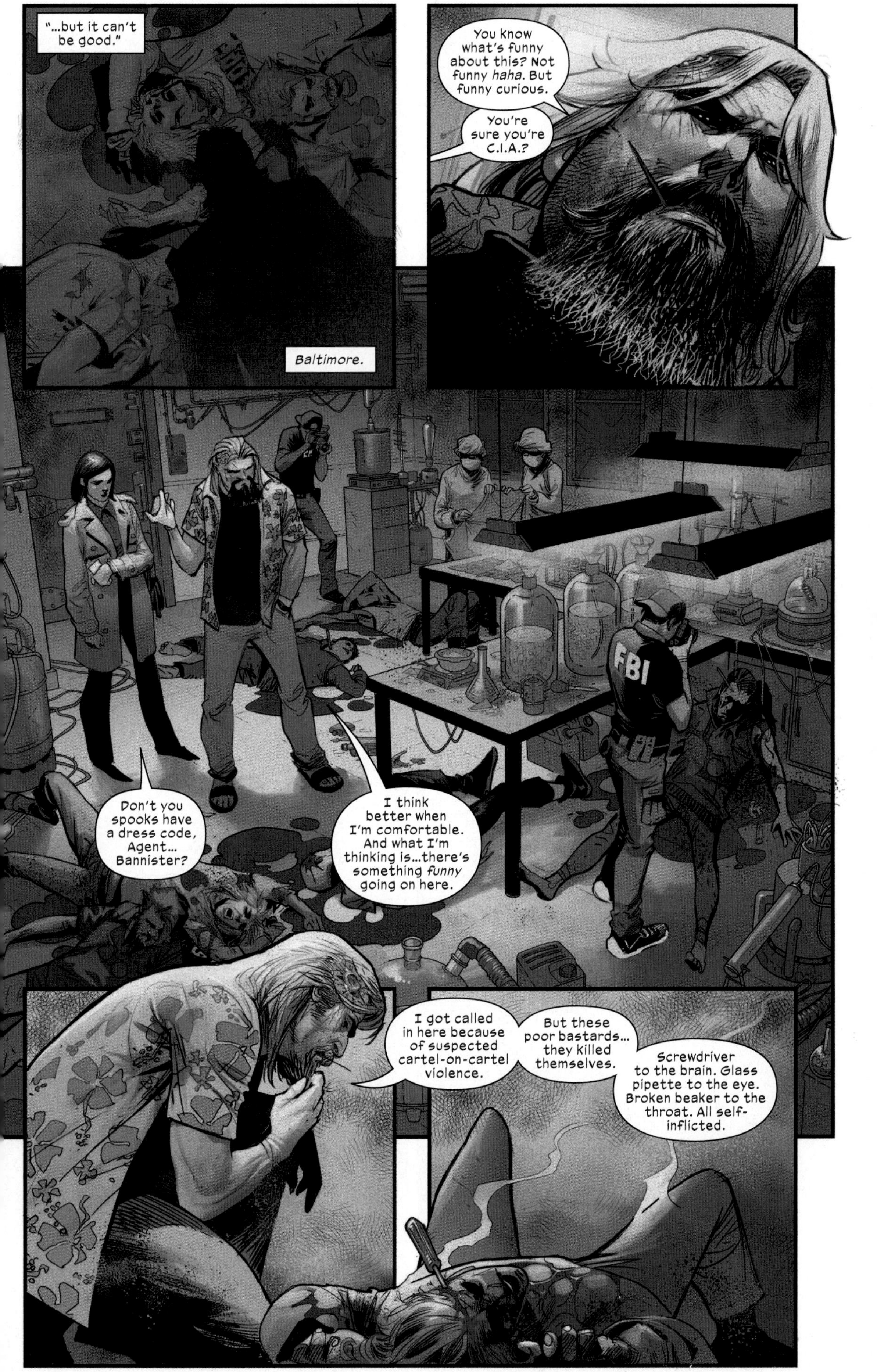
"...but it can't be good."
Baltimore.
You know what's funny about this? Not funny *haha*. But funny curious.
You're sure you're C.I.A.?
Don't you spooks have a dress code, Agent... Bannister?
I think better when I'm comfortable. And what I'm thinking is...there's something *funny* going on here.
FBI
I got called in here because of suspected cartel-on-cartel violence.
But these poor bastards... they killed themselves.
Screwdriver to the brain. Glass pipette to the eye. Broken beaker to the throat. All self-inflicted.

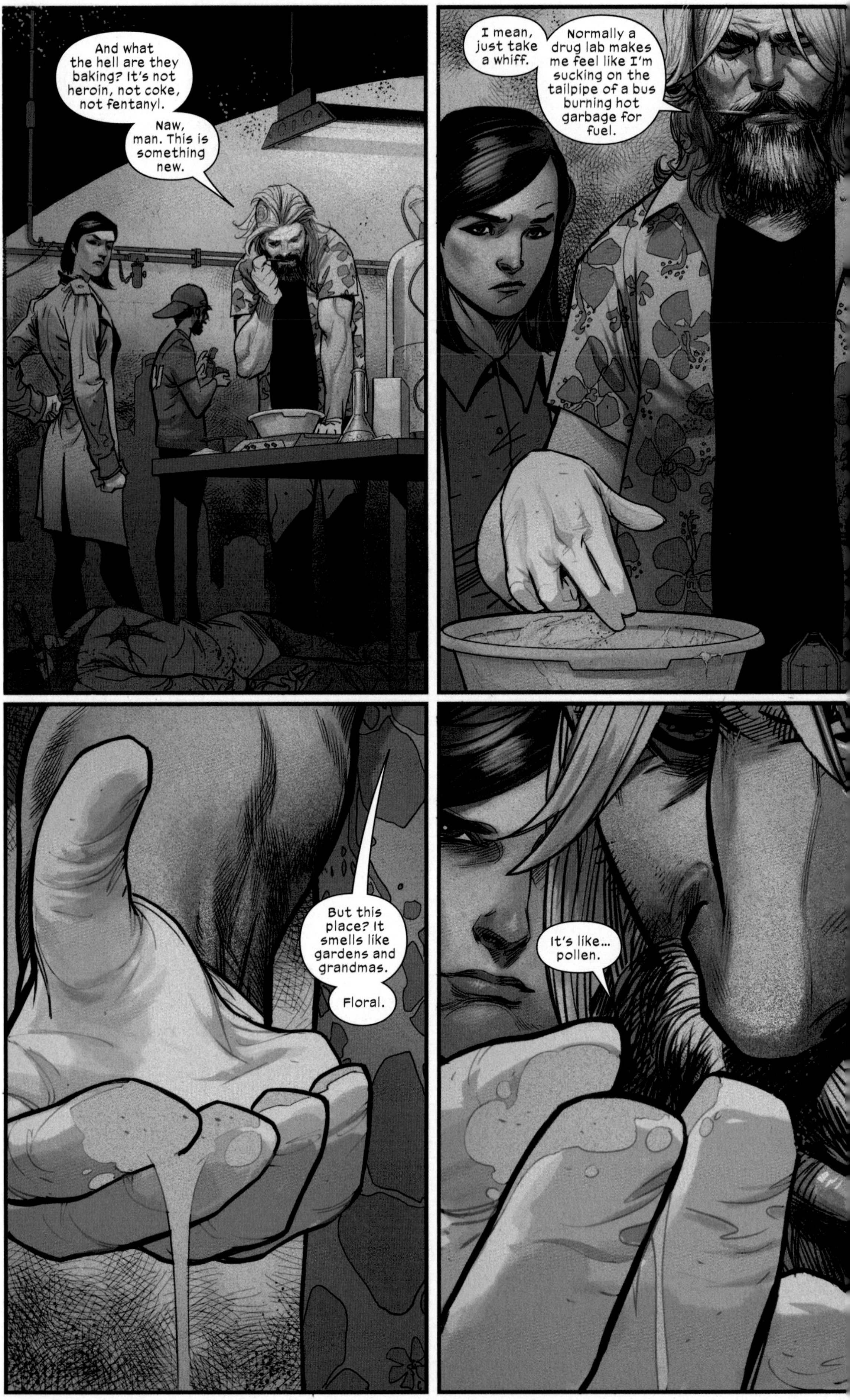
And what the hell are they baking? It's not heroin, not coke, not fentanyl.
Naw, man. This is something new.
I mean, just take a whiff.
Normally a drug lab makes me feel like I'm sucking on the tailpipe of a bus burning hot garbage for fuel.
But this place? It smells like gardens and grandmas.
Floral.
It's like... pollen.

POLLEN

Pollen has become an epidemic-level street drug in a short space of time. There are many versions available worldwide, but the only consistent source and product comes from the so-called Flower Cartel, which is believed to be involved in a violent campaign to wipe out any competition and interference.

Jeff Bannister is a senior narcotics agent notable for his decorated history in the Sinaloa and Chihuahua states of Mexico as well as his undercover work in Colombia and Venezuela. He is divorced, but after his daughter was diagnosed with leukemia two years ago, he requested and was granted a stateside transfer.

Ever since he began investigating pollen, he has been reporting to multiple superiors, one of whom he suspects heads a shadow group within the agency devoted to mutant surveillance.

When he proposed to arrange a covert operation—with a team posing as members of the narcotics trade eager to do business with the Flower Cartel—he did not run into the usual tangle of red tape and debriefings but instead received an immediate green light and seemingly unlimited resources.

Bannister's orders are unclear. On the one hand, his superiors seem to wholeheartedly endorse his proposal to crack down on the Flower Cartel.

On the other hand, he has taken several calls from the FBI, FBN, DEA, FDA and even the State Department. They all cite dissatisfaction with the manufacture, regulation and distribution of Krakoan pharmaceuticals. They have (so far unproven) suspicions that a mounting black market may tie back to the Hellfire Trading Company.

They have asked him to consider -- if the situation permits, of course -- keeping channels open.

Because collaborating with the drug traffickers will allow for a campaign of espionage, subversion, sabotage and -- possibly -- profit.

The Flower Cartel has since proposed a meeting.

The location: deep country Alaska.

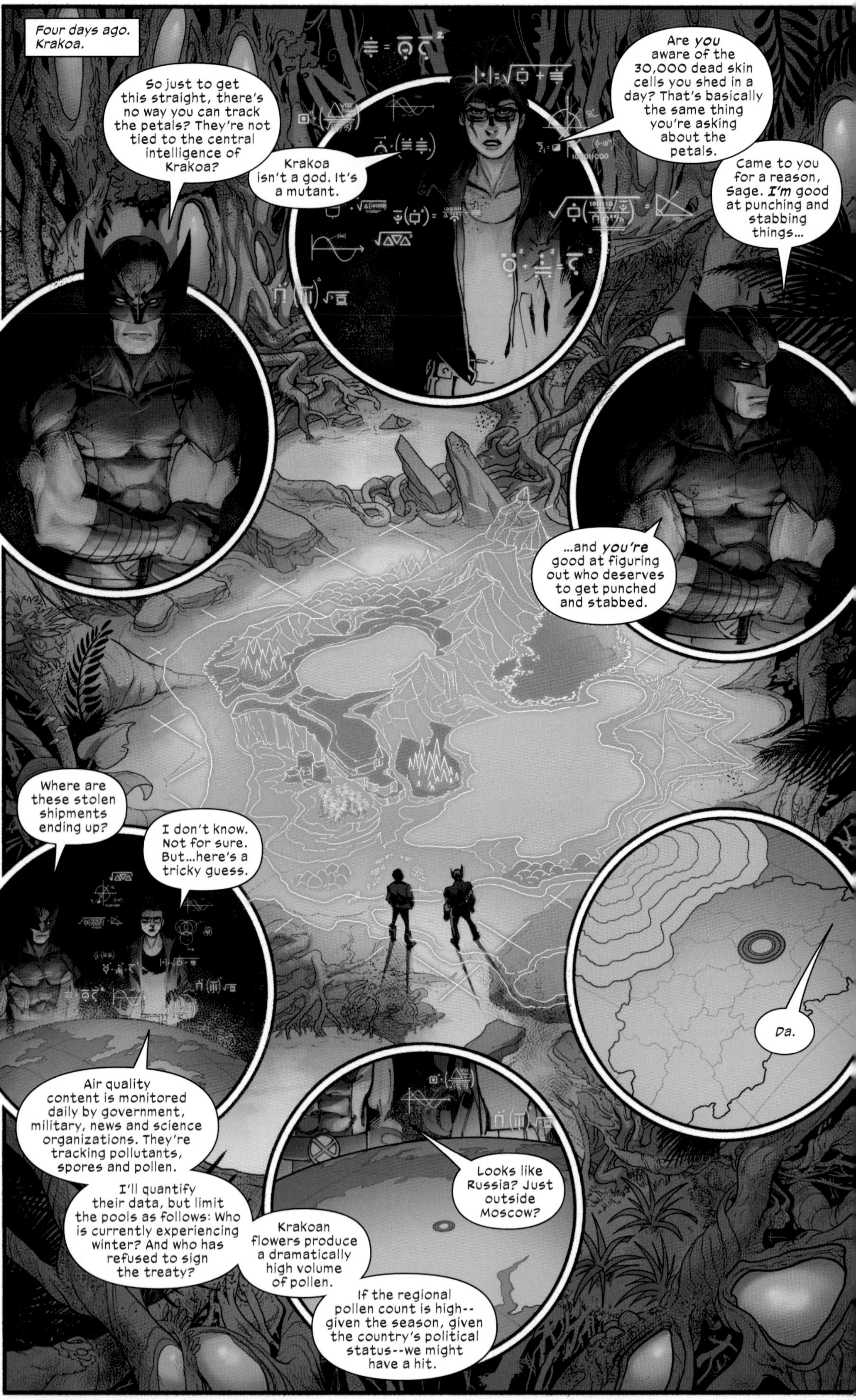

Four days ago. Krakoa.
So just to get this straight, there's no way you can track the petals? They're not tied to the central intelligence of Krakoa?
Krakoa isn't a god. It's a mutant.
Are *you* aware of the 30,000 dead skin cells you shed in a day? That's basically the same thing you're asking about the petals.
Came to you for a reason, Sage. ***I'm*** good at punching and stabbing things...
...and *you're* good at figuring out who deserves to get punched and stabbed.
Where are these stolen shipments ending up?
I don't know. Not for sure. But...here's a tricky guess.
Air quality content is monitored daily by government, military, news and science organizations. They're tracking pollutants, spores and pollen.
I'll quantify their data, but limit the pools as follows: Who is currently experiencing winter? And who has refused to sign the treaty?
Krakoan flowers produce a dramatically high volume of pollen.
If the regional pollen count is high--given the season, given the country's political status--we might have a hit.
Looks like Russia? Just outside Moscow?
Da.

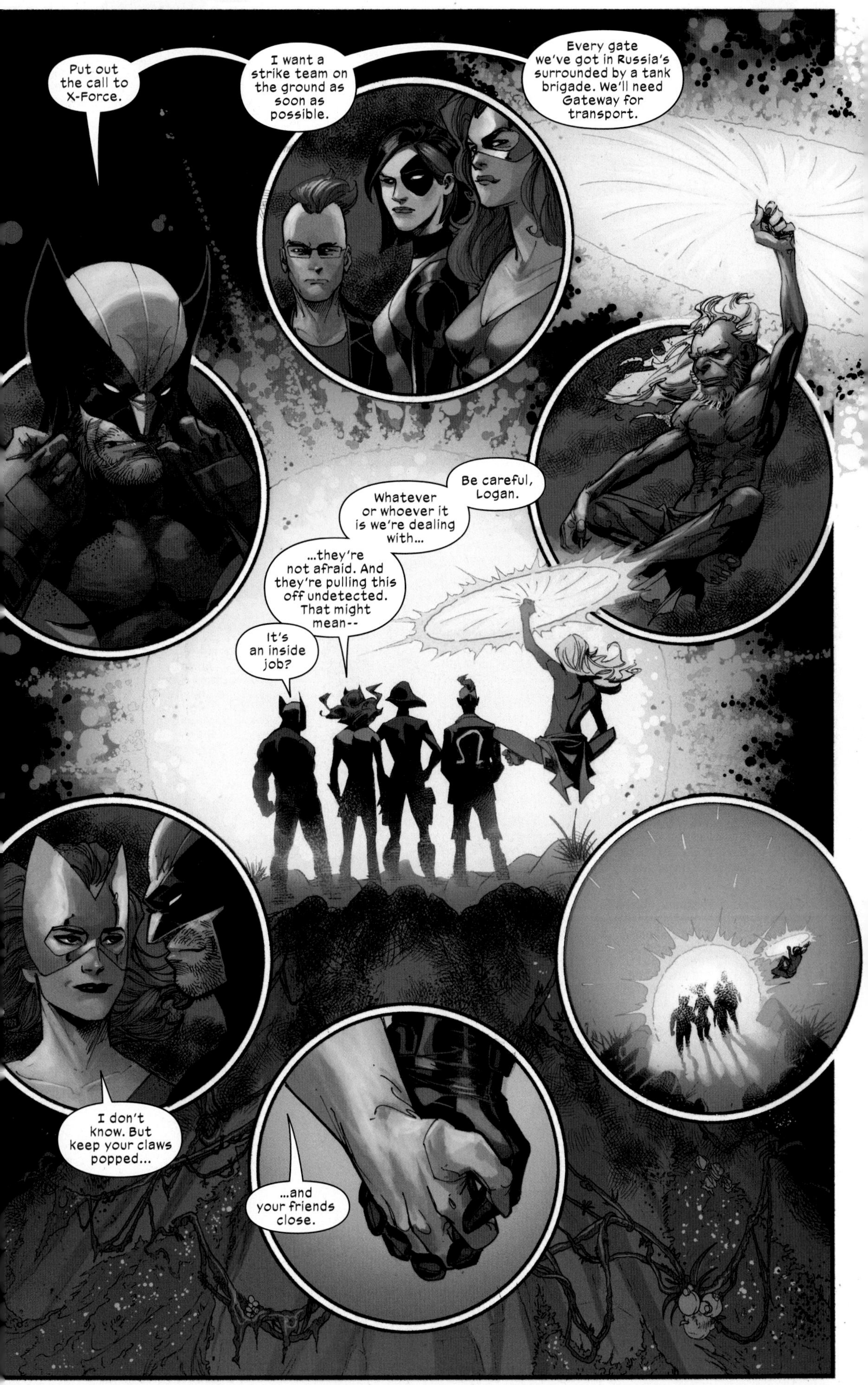
Put out the call to X-Force.
I want a strike team on the ground as soon as possible.
Every gate we've got in Russia's surrounded by a tank brigade. We'll need Gateway for transport.
Whatever or whoever it is we're dealing with...
Be careful, Logan.
...they're not afraid. And they're pulling this off undetected. That might mean--
It's an inside job?
I don't know. But keep your claws popped...
...and your friends close.

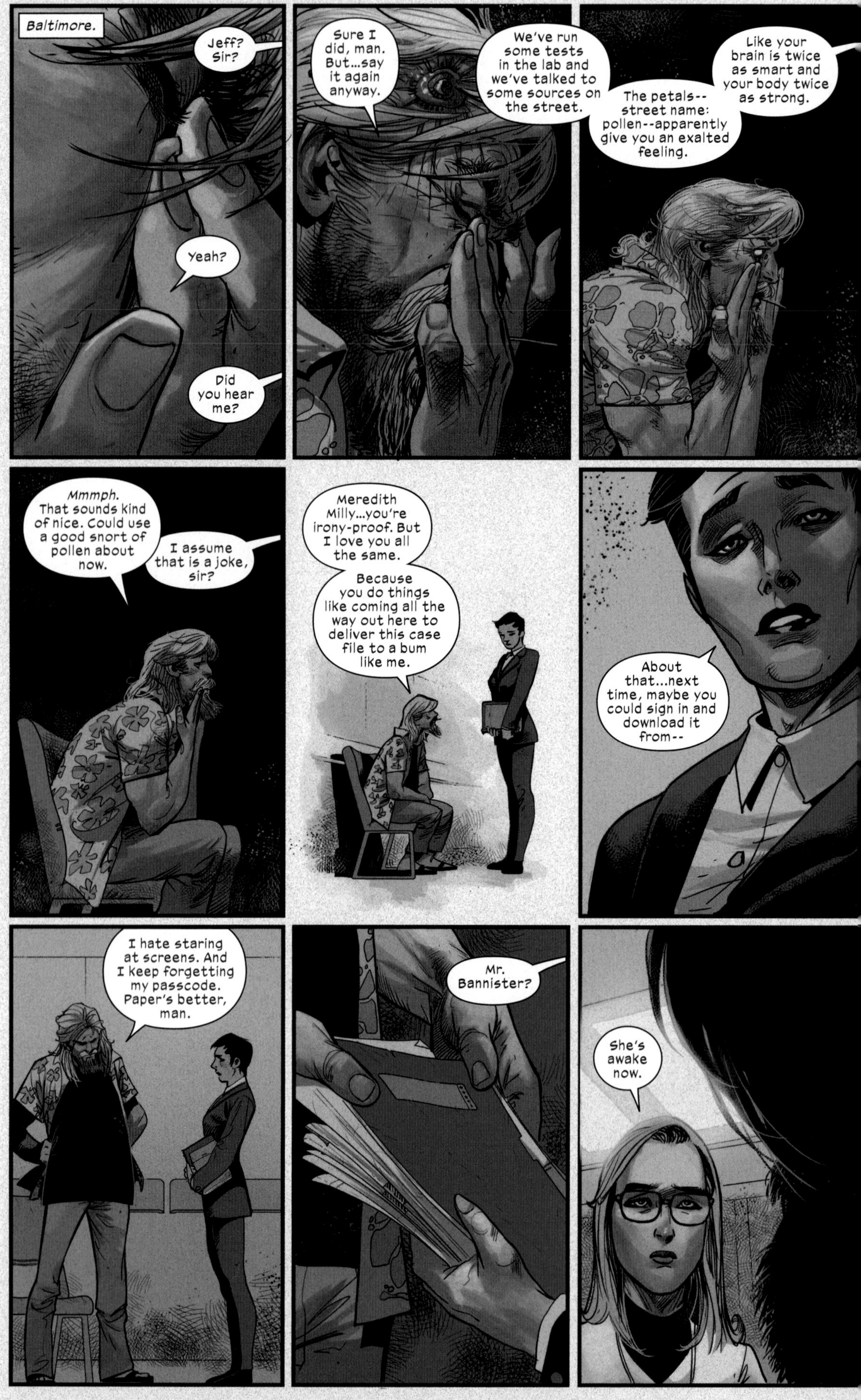

Baltimore.
Jeff? Sir?
Yeah?
Did you hear me?
Sure I did, man. But...say it again anyway.
We've run some tests in the lab and we've talked to some sources on the street.
The petals--street name: pollen--apparently give you an exalted feeling.
Like your brain is twice as smart and your body twice as strong.
Mmmph. That sounds kind of nice. Could use a good snort of pollen about now.
I assume that is a joke, sir?
Meredith Milly...you're irony-proof. But I love you all the same.
Because you do things like coming all the way out here to deliver this case file to a bum like me.
About that...next time, maybe you could sign in and download it from--
I hate staring at screens. And I keep forgetting my passcode. Paper's better, man.
Mr. Bannister?
She's awake now.

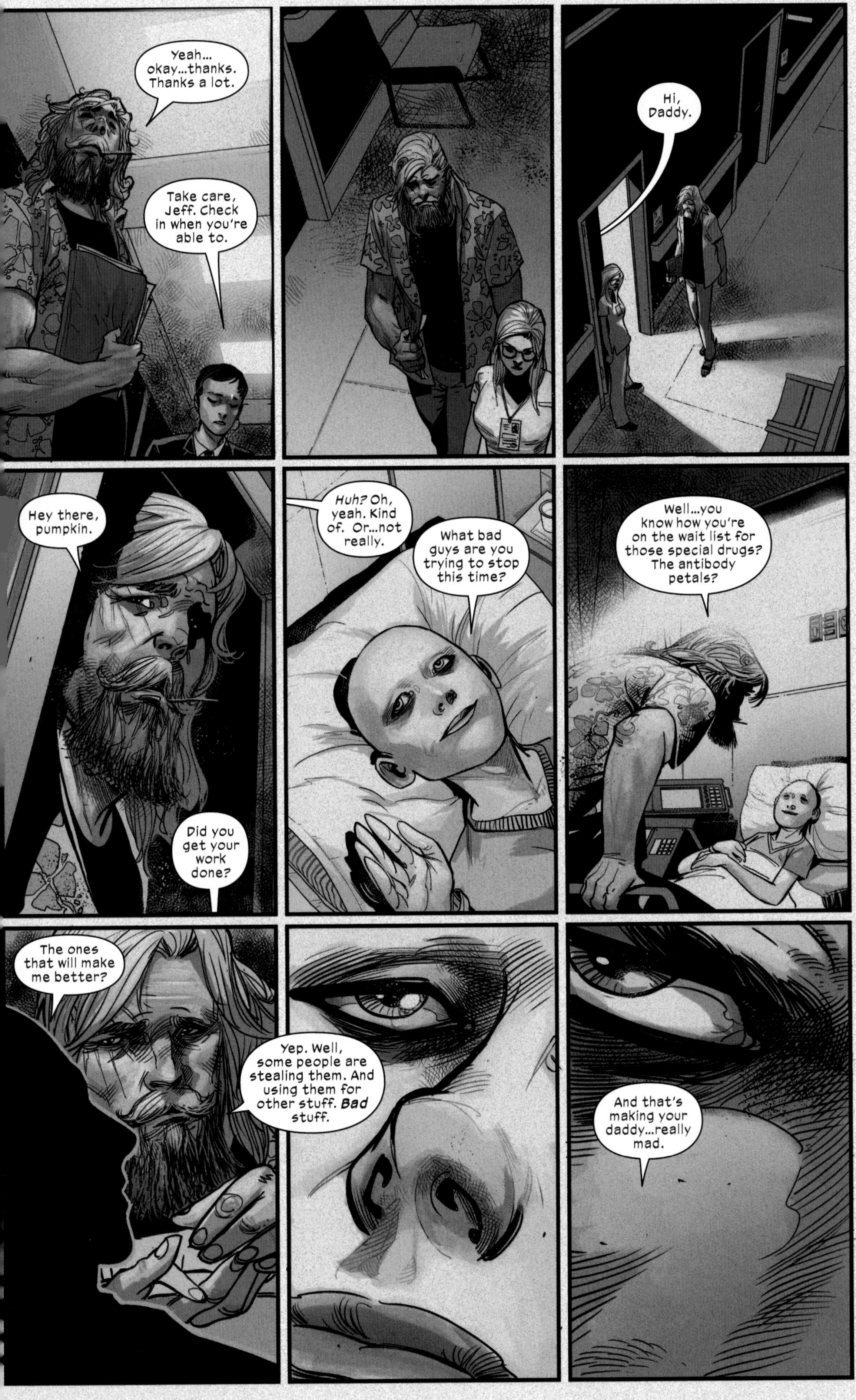
Yeah... okay...thanks. Thanks a lot.
Take care, Jeff. Check in when you're able to.
Hi, Daddy.
Hey there, pumpkin.
Did you get your work done?
Huh? Oh, yeah. Kind of. Or...not really.
What bad guys are you trying to stop this time?
Well...you know how you're on the wait list for those special drugs? The antibody petals?
The ones that will make me better?
Yep. Well, some people are stealing them. And using them for other stuff. ***Bad*** stuff.
And that's making your daddy...really mad.

THE ORDER OF X

There have always been those humans who recognized mutants as higher beings, touched by divinity. But since the declaration of sovereignty, their numbers have grown dramatically, as if the new dawn broke with an ethereal light.

At this time, the Order of X has no definitive leader or practice or text or belief system. No roof over its church, so to speak.

But there are commonalities evolving among the various branches and thousands of parishioners worldwide.

They regularly gather around Krakoan gates, prostrating their bodies, praying and pleading. Should a mutant appear, some parishioners will collapse in seizure and speak in tongues. Others will rush the mutant, their hands hungry for a touch, as if some essence might carry over to them.

There have been reports of men and women disrobing and offering themselves naked to the mutants. Their bodies are altars upon which they might produce the ultimate form of worship: a child that carries the X-Gene.

Some branches wear an X around their necks like a crucifix or Star of David, but scarification and branding seems to be the standard for adornment. Xs are sometimes carved over the eyes or across the chest or the face, but the mouth is the most frequent site for etching.

Though their overall theology appears to be based on devotion and humility, there are extremists who appear to believe that the sacrifice and consumption of *Homo superior* is the path to a higher plane.

—

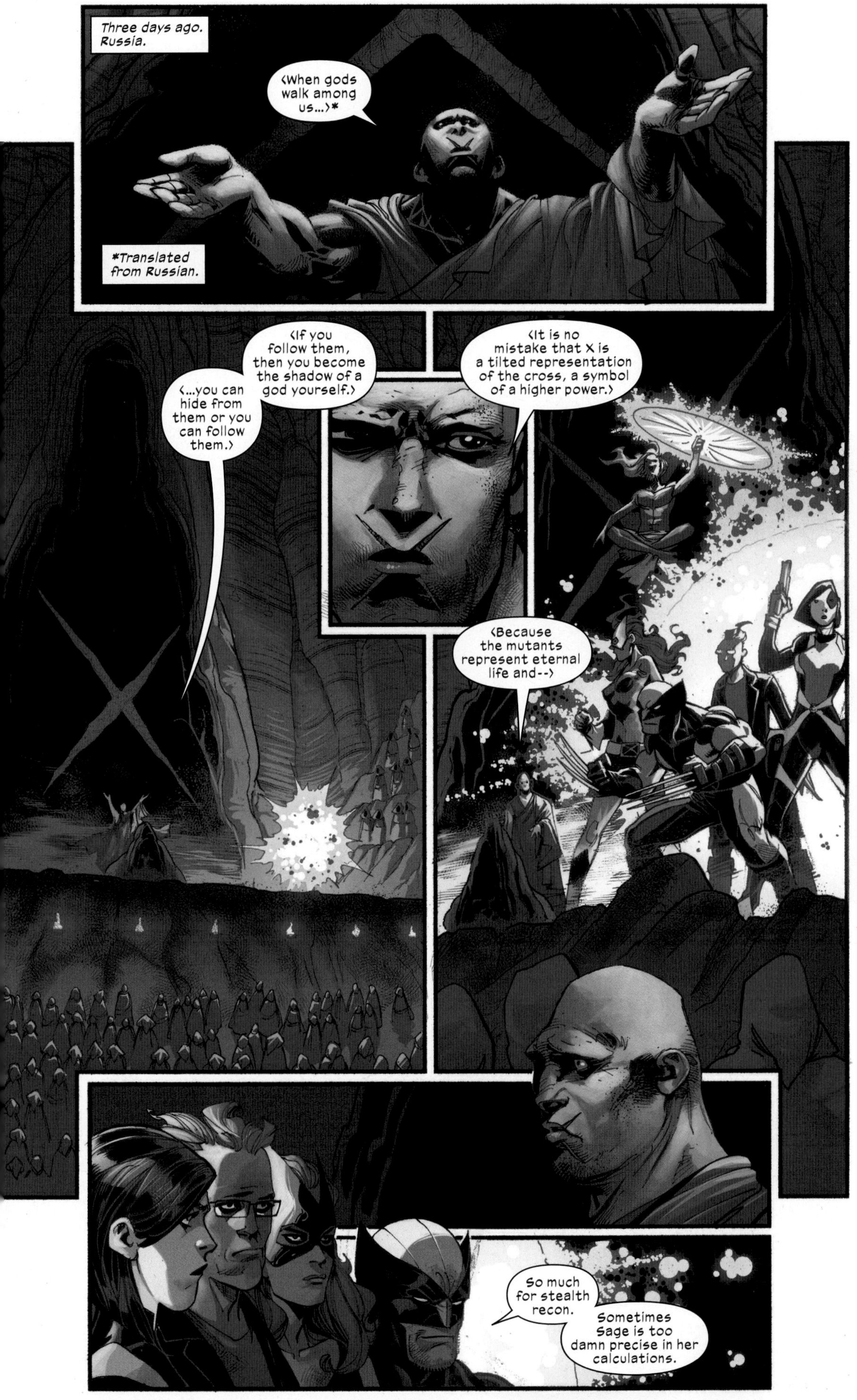

Three days ago. Russia.
‹When gods walk among us...›*
*Translated from Russian.
‹...you can hide from them or you can follow them.›
‹If you follow them, then you become the shadow of a god yourself.›
‹It is no mistake that X is a tilted representation of the cross, a symbol of a higher power.›
‹Because the mutants represent eternal life and--›
So much for stealth recon.
Sometimes Sage is too damn precise in her calculations.

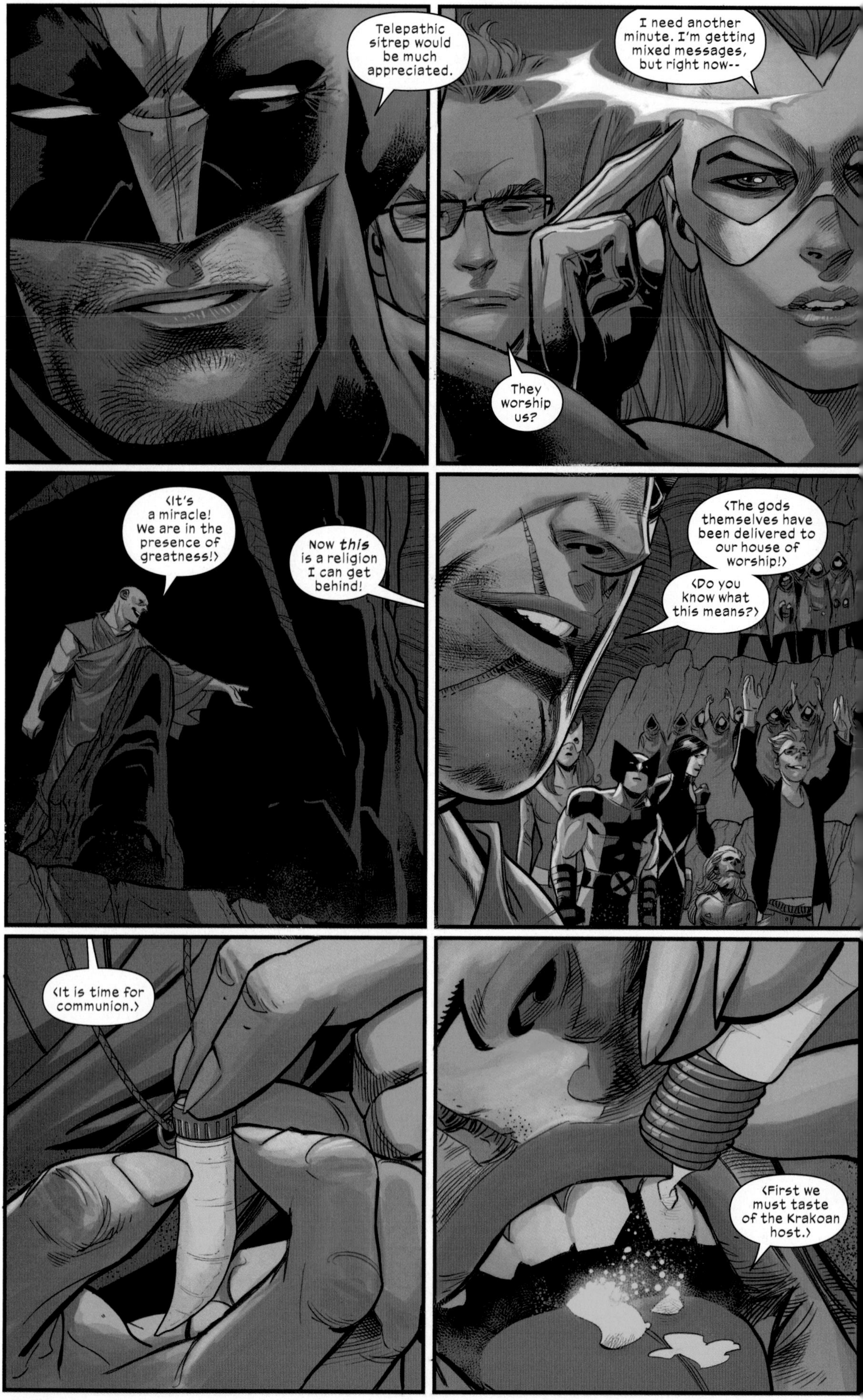
Telepathic sitrep would be much appreciated.
I need another minute. I'm getting mixed messages, but right now--
They worship us?
<It's a miracle! We are in the presence of greatness!>
Now *this* is a religion I can get behind!
<The gods themselves have been delivered to our house of worship!>
<Do you know what this means?>
<It is time for communion.>
<First we must taste of the Krakoan host.>

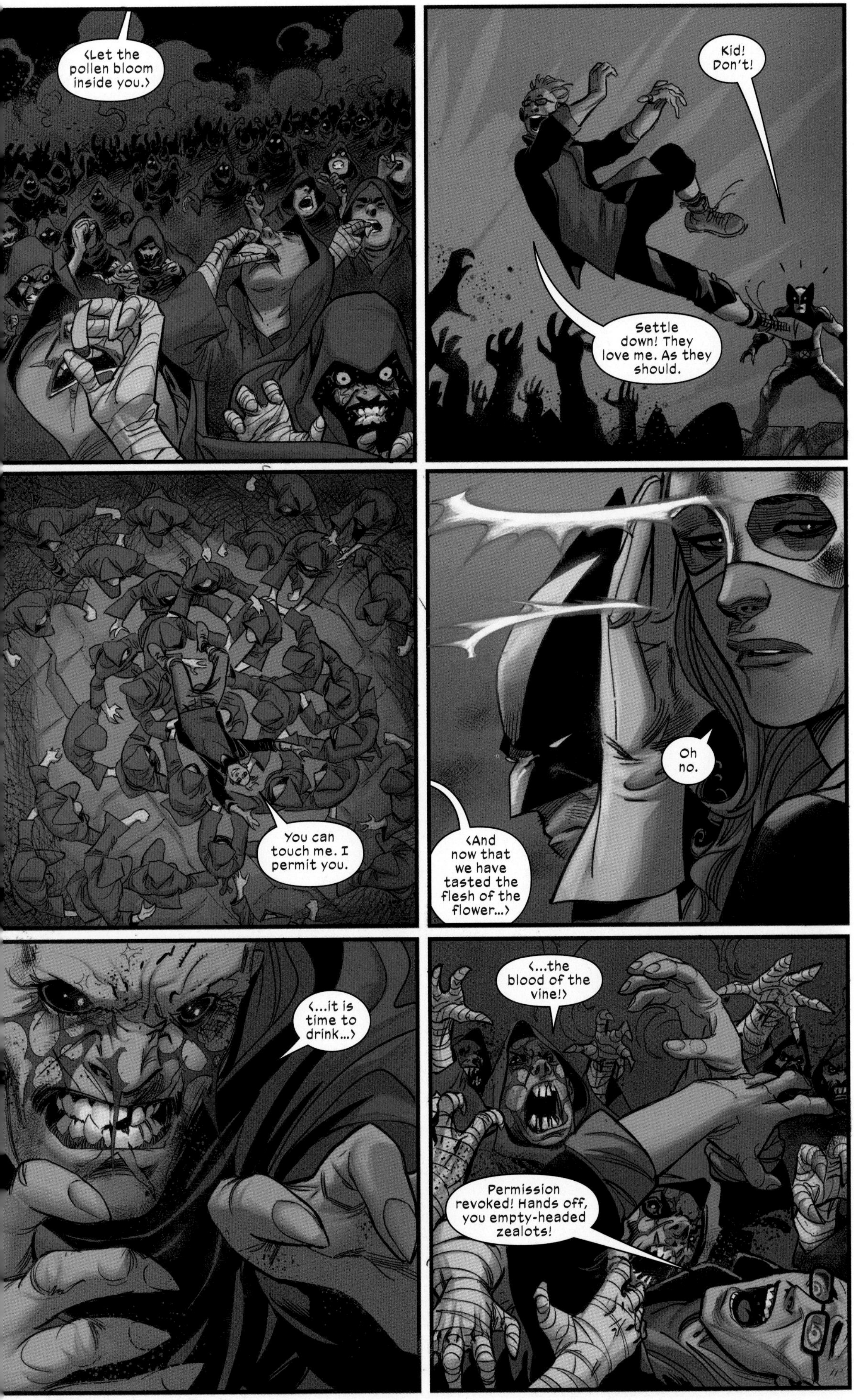

‹Let the pollen bloom inside you.›
Kid! Don't!
Settle down! They love me. As they should.
You can touch me. I permit you.
Oh no.
‹And now that we have tasted the flesh of the flower...›
‹...it is time to drink...›
‹...the blood of the vine!›
Permission revoked! Hands off, you empty-headed zealots!

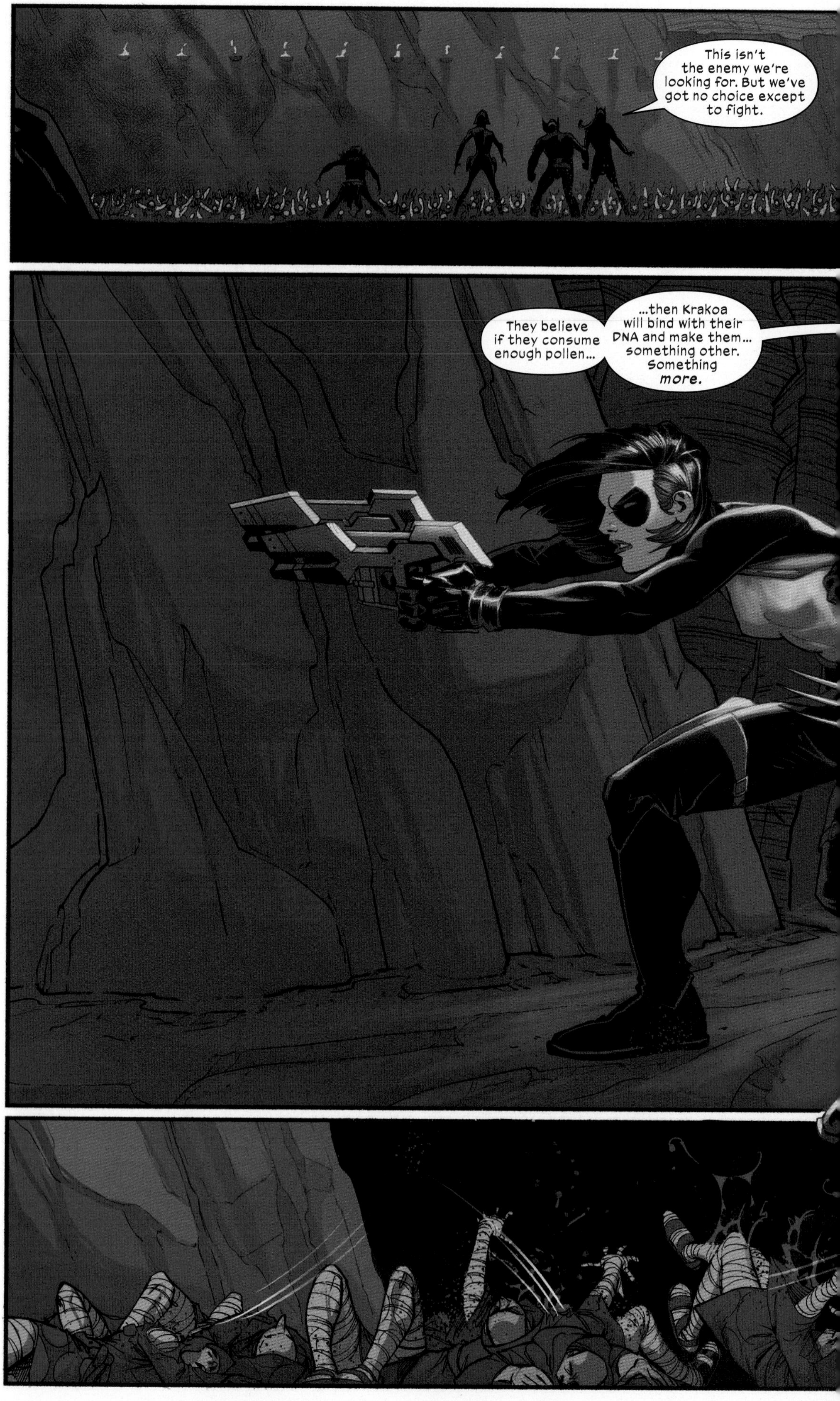
This isn't the enemy we're looking for. But we've got no choice except to fight.
They believe if they consume enough pollen...
...then Krakoa will bind with their DNA and make them... something other. Something *more.*

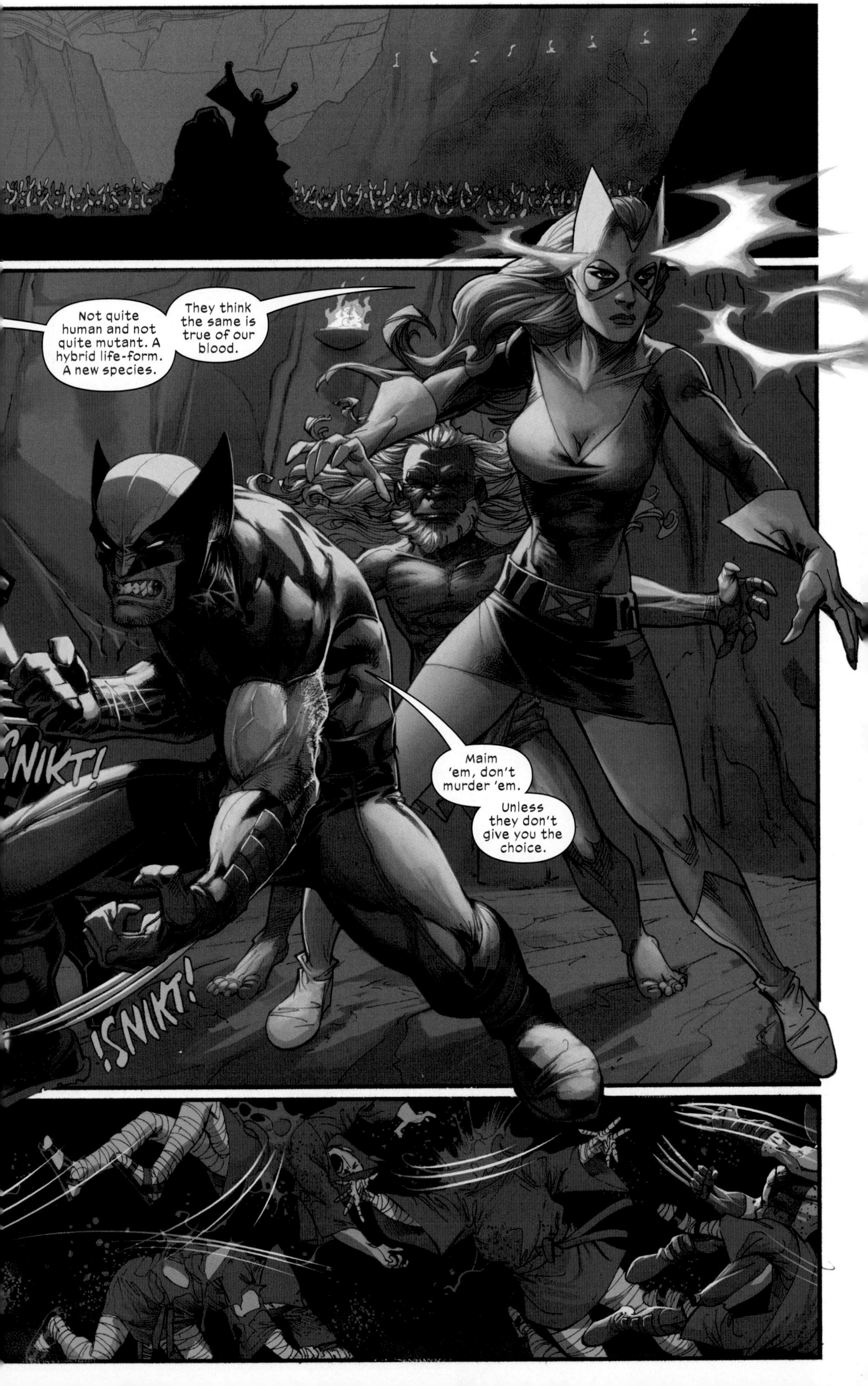
Not quite human and not quite mutant. A hybrid life-form. A new species.
They think the same is true of our blood.
SNIKT!
SNIKT!
Maim 'em, don't murder 'em.
Unless they don't give you the choice.

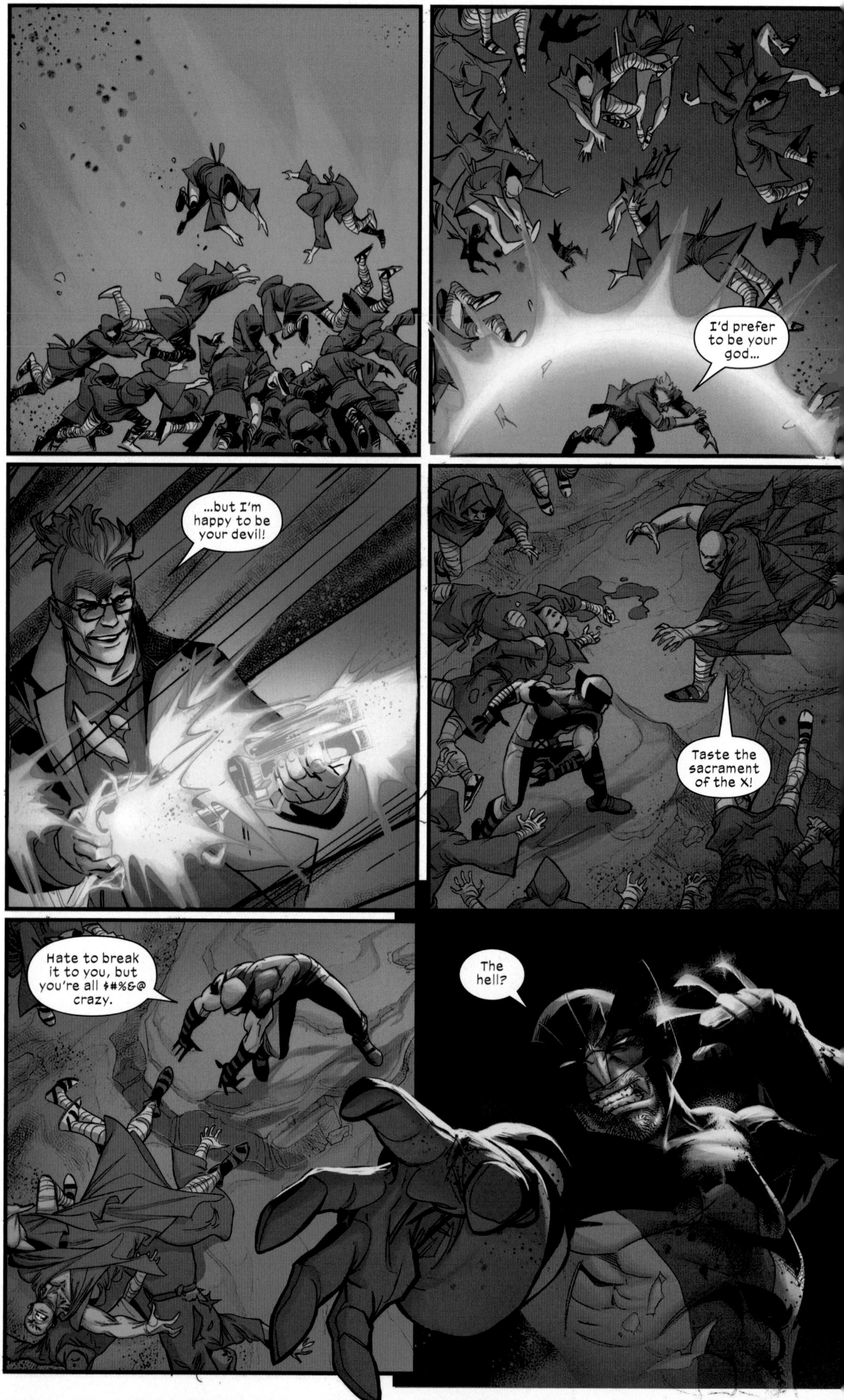
I'd prefer to be your god...
...but I'm happy to be your devil!
Taste the sacrament of the X!
Hate to break it to you, but you're all $#%&@ crazy.
The hell?

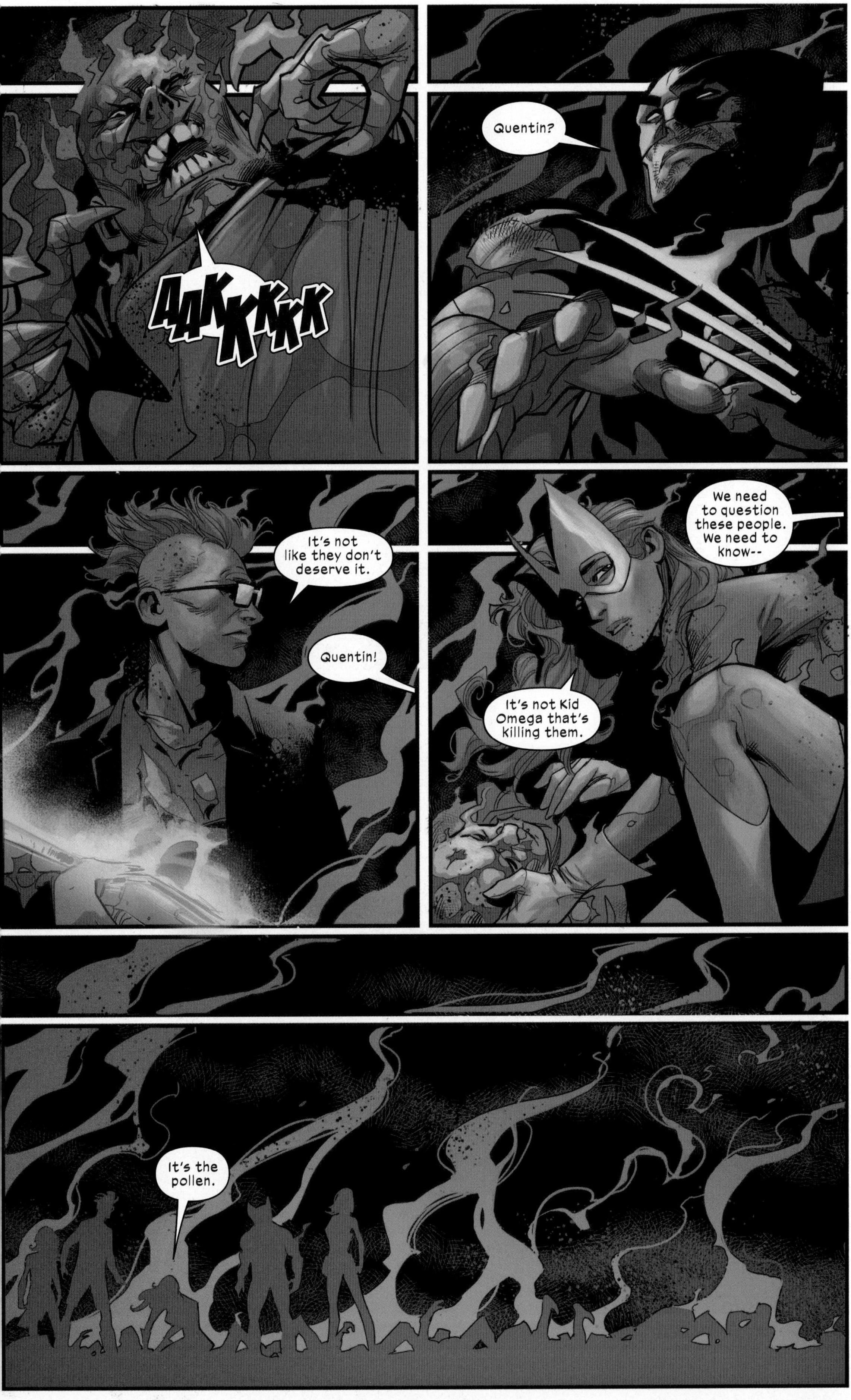
AAKKKKKK
Quentin?
It's not like they don't deserve it.
Quentin!
We need to question these people. We need to know--
It's not Kid Omega that's killing them.
It's the pollen.

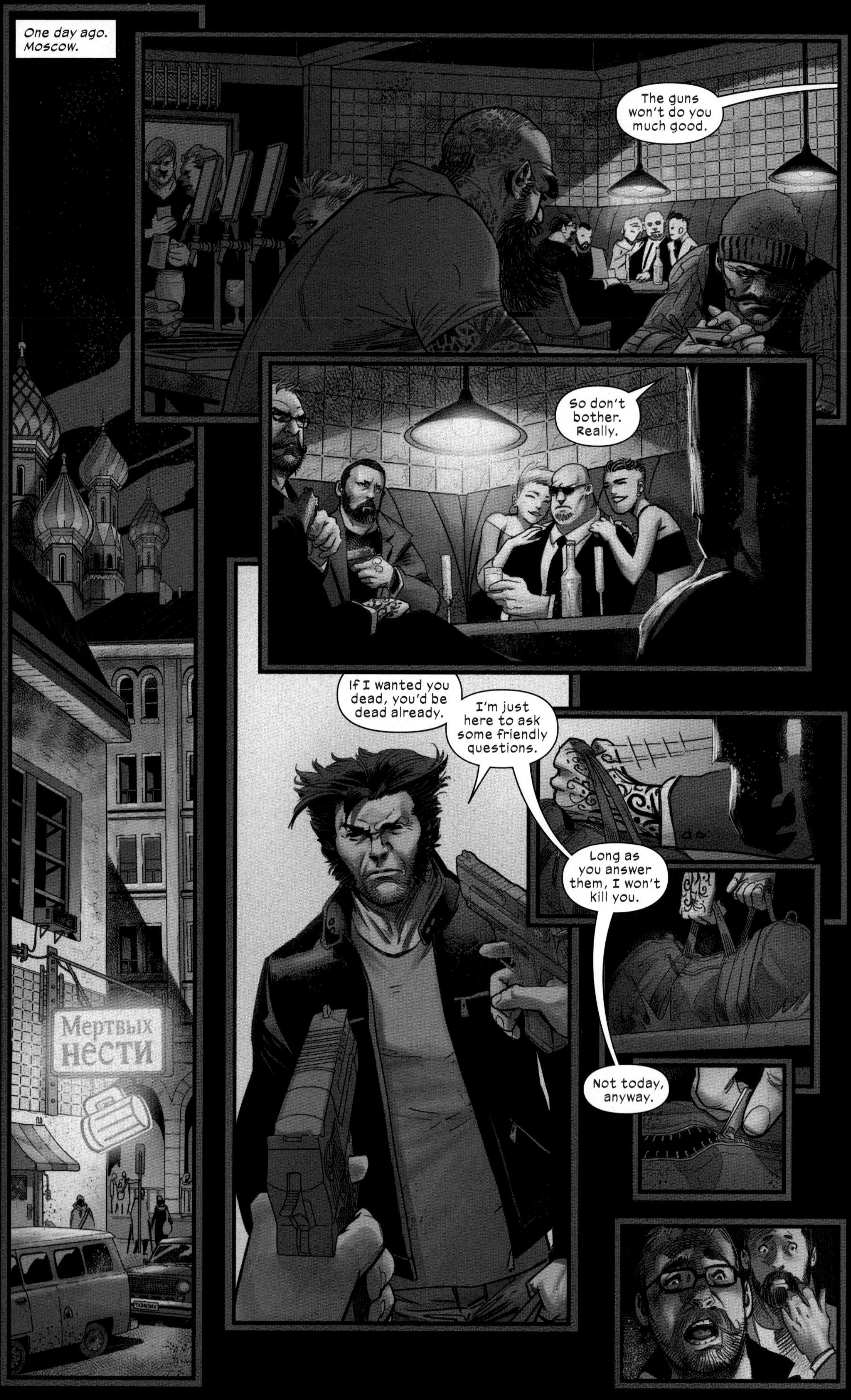
One day ago. Moscow.
The guns won't do you much good.
So don't bother. Really.
Мертвых нести
If I wanted you dead, you'd be dead already.
I'm just here to ask some friendly questions.
Long as you answer them, I won't kill you.
Not today, anyway.

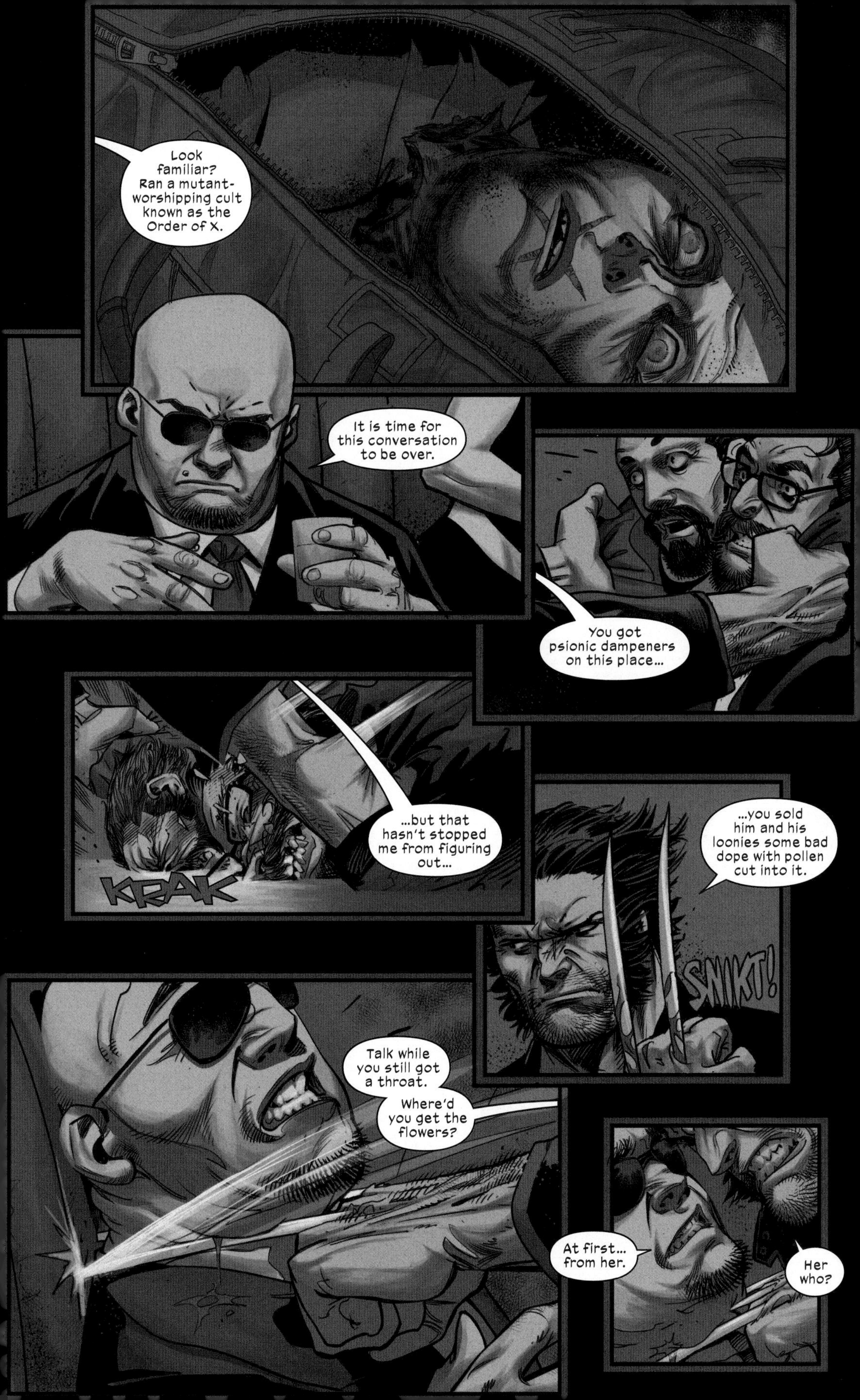
Look familiar? Ran a mutant-worshipping cult known as the Order of X.
It is time for this conversation to be over.
You got psionic dampeners on this place...
...but that hasn't stopped me from figuring out...
KRAK
...you sold him and his loonies some bad dope with pollen cut into it.
SNIKT!
Talk while you still got a throat.
Where'd you get the flowers?
At first... from her.
Her who?

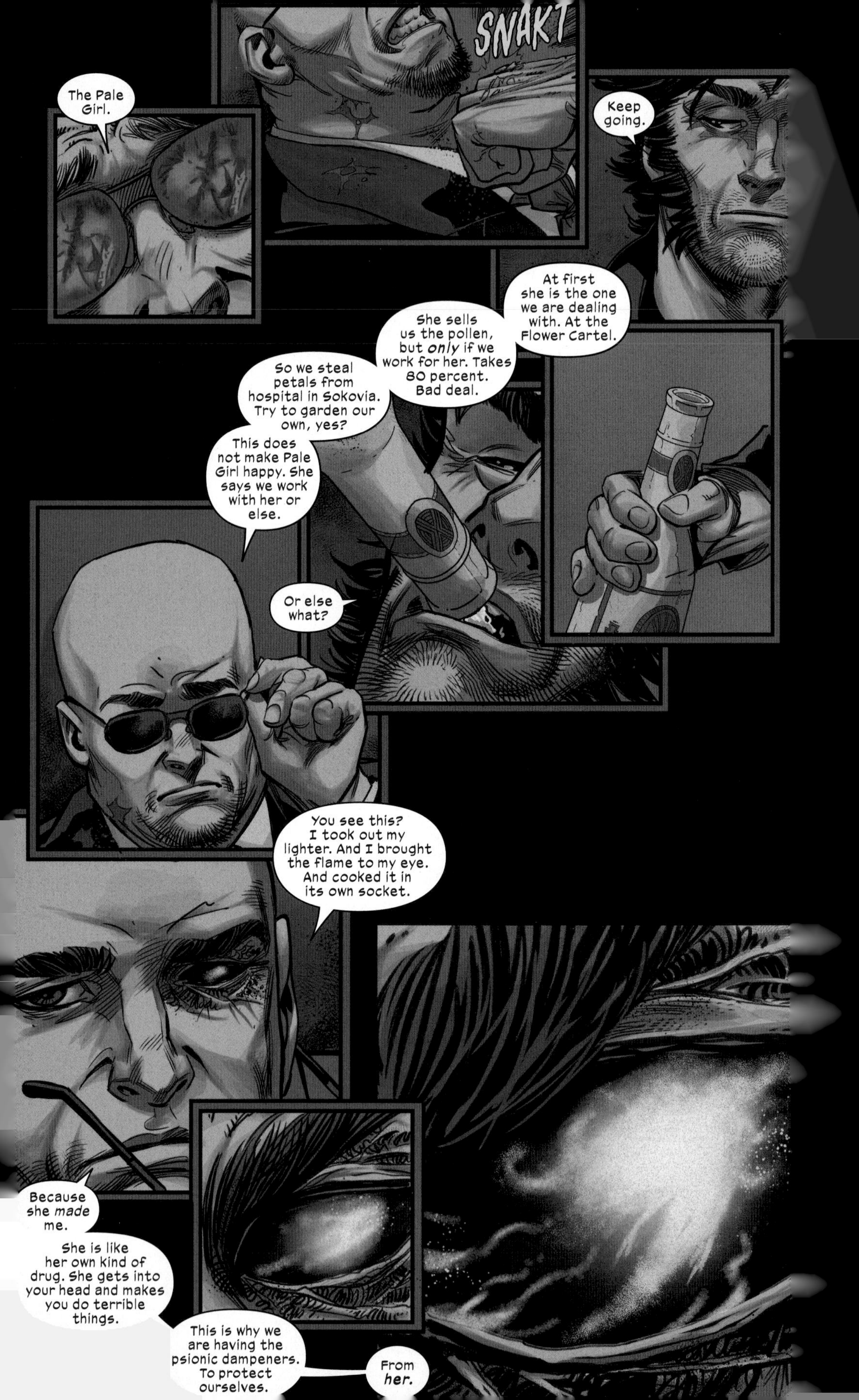
SNAKT
The Pale Girl.
Keep going.
At first she is the one we are dealing with. At the Flower Cartel.
She sells us the pollen, but *only* if we work for her. Takes 80 percent. Bad deal.
So we steal petals from hospital in Sokovia. Try to garden our own, yes?
This does not make Pale Girl happy. She says we work with her or else.
Or else what?
You see this? I took out my lighter. And I brought the flame to my eye. And cooked it in its own socket.
Because she *made* me.
She is like her own kind of drug. She gets into your head and makes you do terrible things.
This is why we are having the psionic dampeners. To protect ourselves.
From *her*.

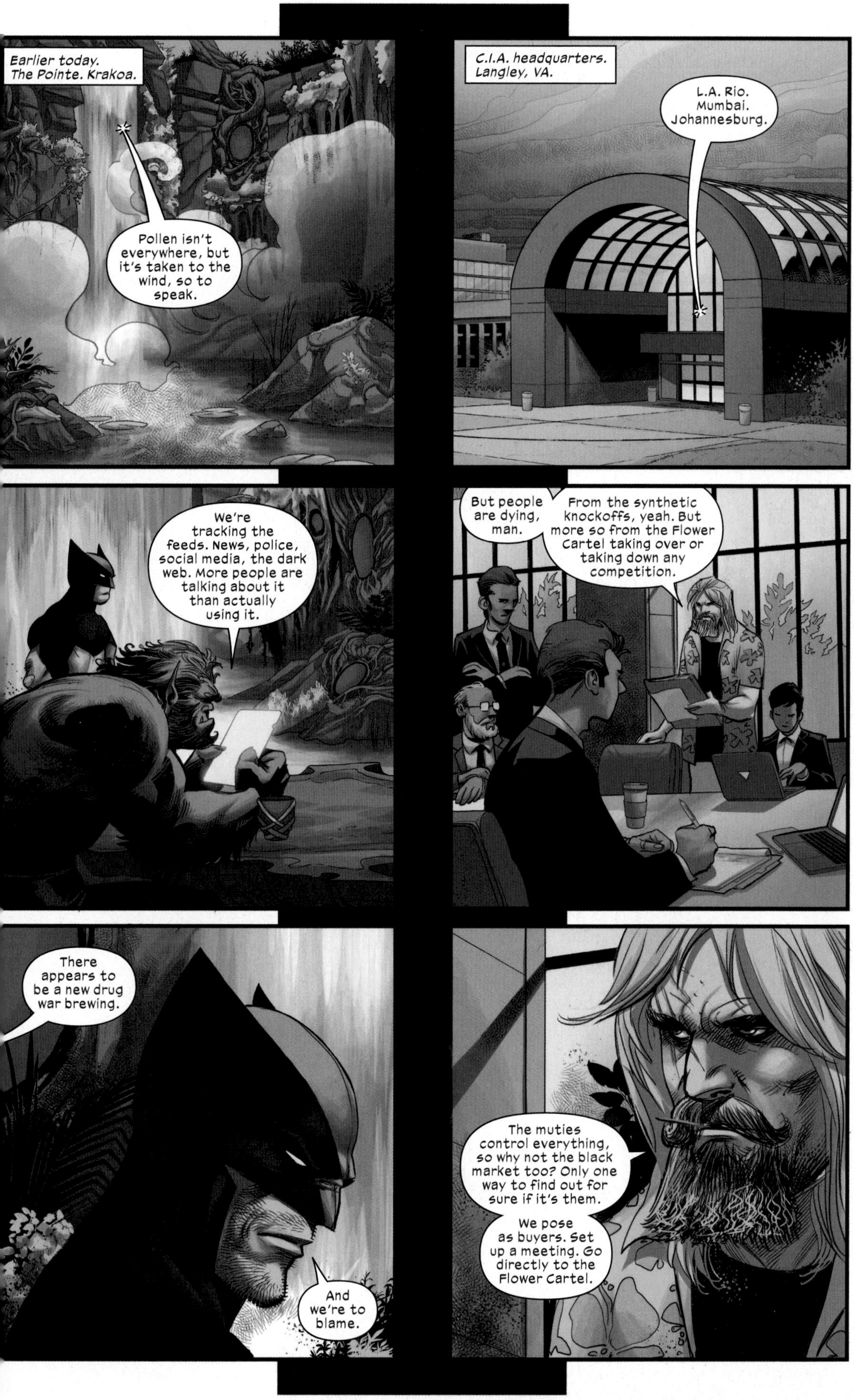
Earlier today. The Pointe. Krakoa.
Pollen isn't everywhere, but it's taken to the wind, so to speak.
C.I.A. headquarters. Langley, VA.
L.A. Rio. Mumbai. Johannesburg.
We're tracking the feeds. News, police, social media, the dark web. More people are talking about it than actually using it.
But people are dying, man.
From the synthetic knockoffs, yeah. But more so from the Flower Cartel taking over or taking down any competition.
There appears to be a new drug war brewing.
And we're to blame.
The muties control everything, so why not the black market too? Only one way to find out for sure if it's them.
We pose as buyers. Set up a meeting. Go directly to the Flower Cartel.

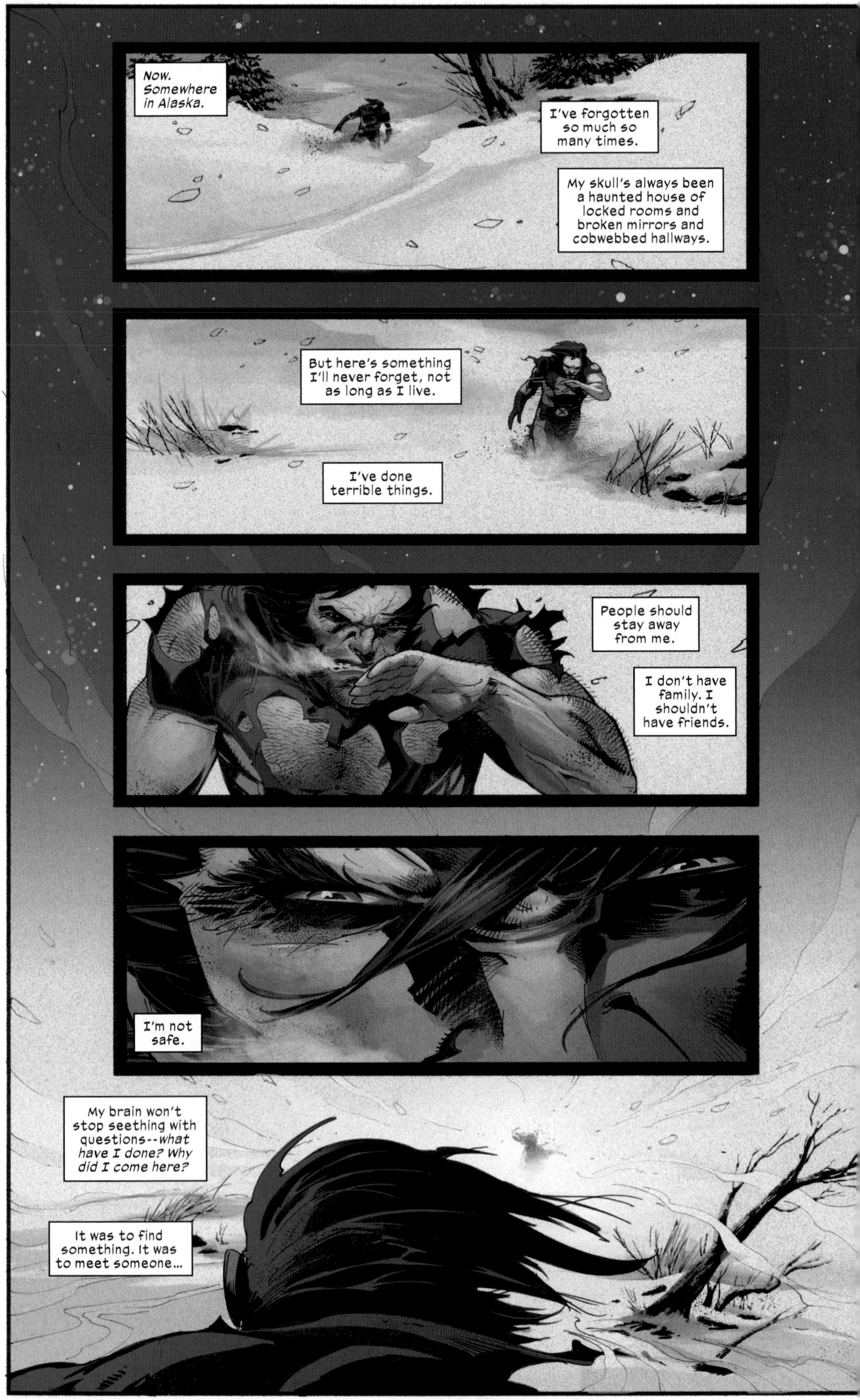
Now. Somewhere in Alaska.
I've forgotten so much so many times.
My skull's always been a haunted house of locked rooms and broken mirrors and cobwebbed hallways.
But here's something I'll never forget, not as long as I live.
I've done terrible things.
People should stay away from me.
I don't have family. I shouldn't have friends.
I'm not safe.
My brain won't stop seething with questions--*what have I done? Why did I come here?*
It was to find something. It was to meet someone...

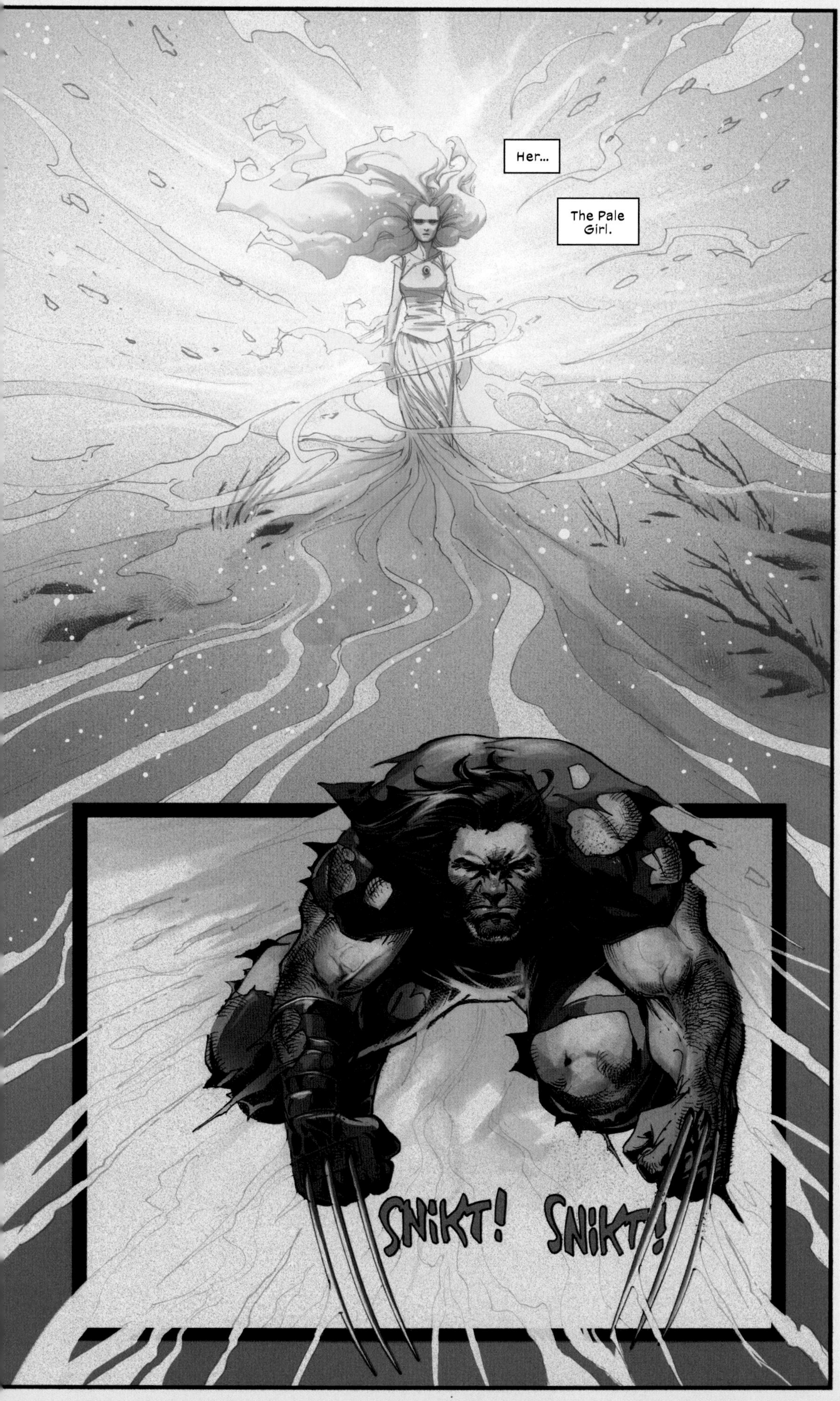
Her...
The Pale Girl.
SNIKT! SNIKT!

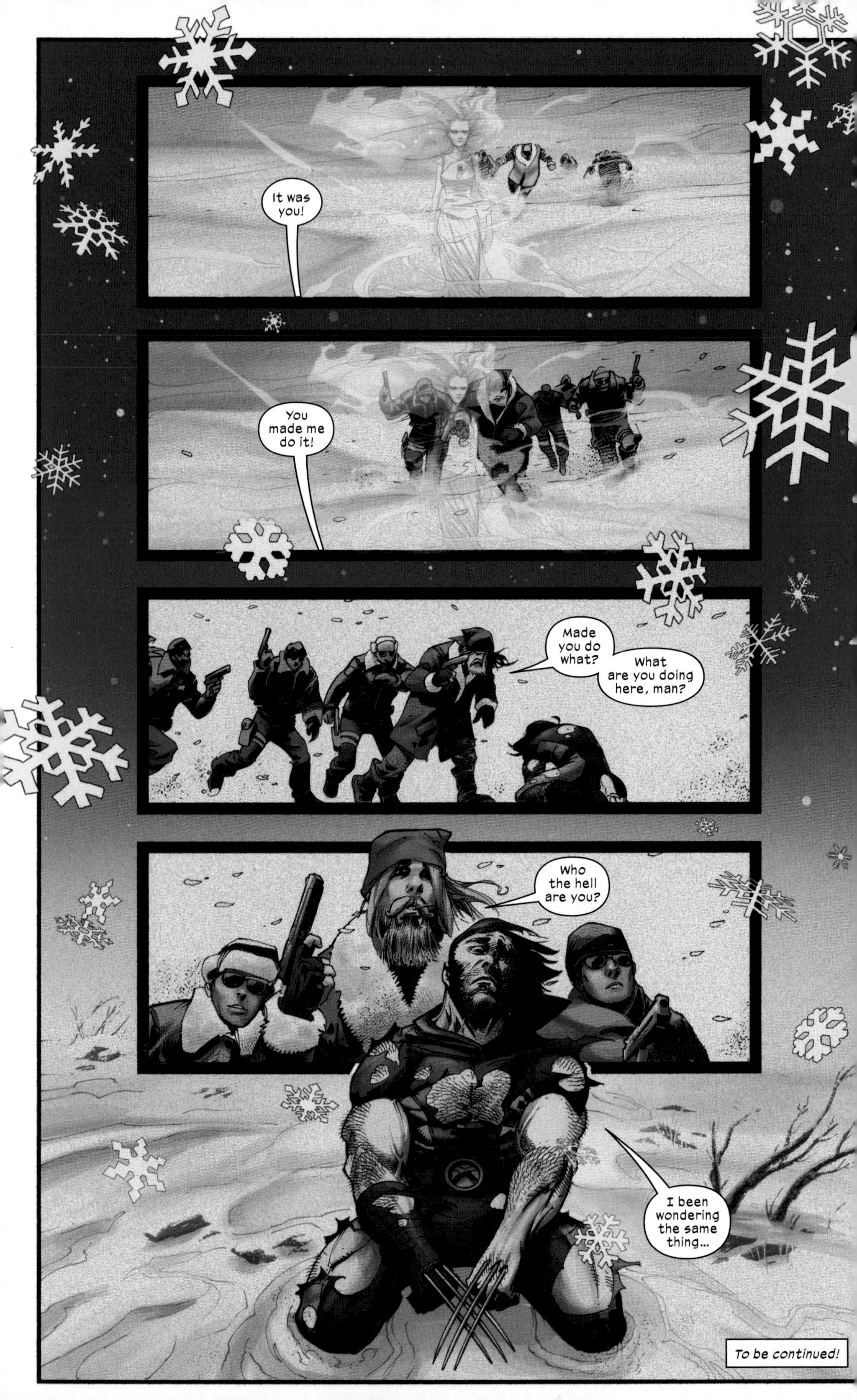
It was you!
You made me do it!
Made you do what?
What are you doing here, man?
Who the hell are you?
I been wondering the same thing...
To be continued!

[dawn_of_x]

[kra_]
[koa_]

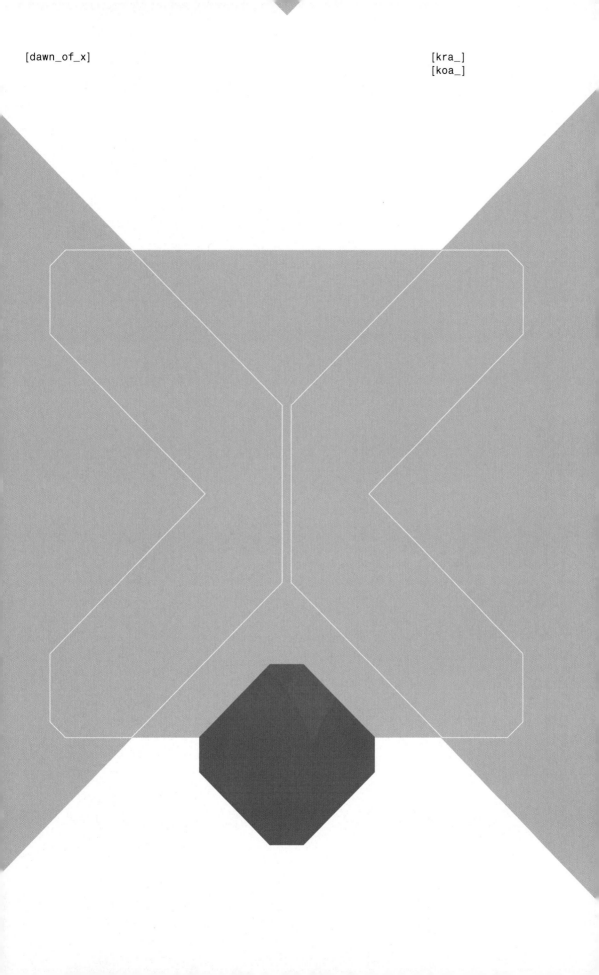

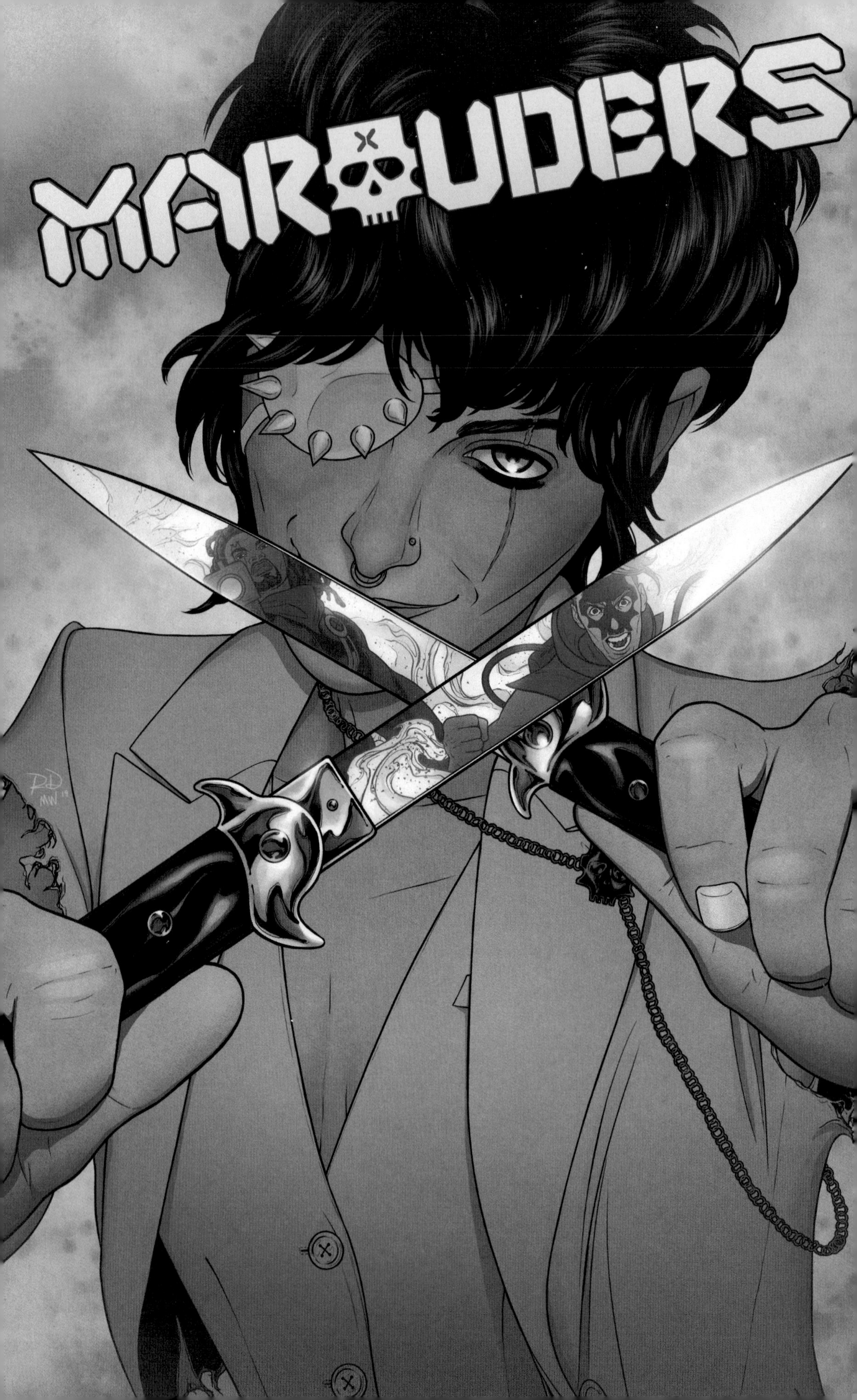
MARAUDERS

[kra_[0.7]
[koa_[0.7]

[kra_[0.X]
[koa_[0.X]

A CUT ABOVE

Homines Verendi, a new organization with wealth and political connections, means to undermine mutantkind's new society -- and will go to great lengths to do so!

In response, Emma Frost and the Hellfire Trading Company will need new allies by their side to face enemies from without *and within...*

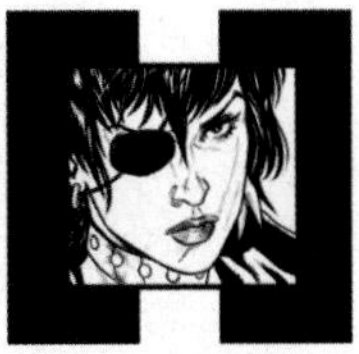

Callisto

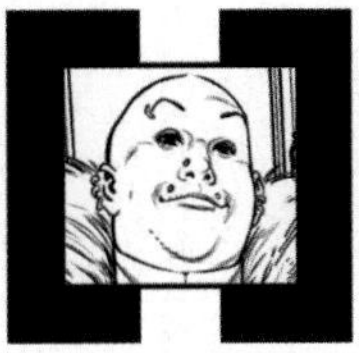

Jumbo Carnation

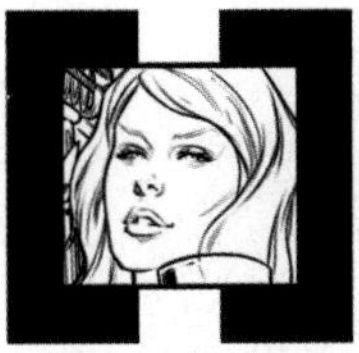

Emma Frost

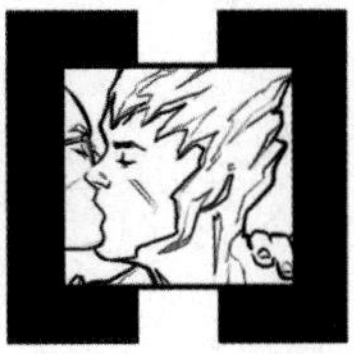

Iceman

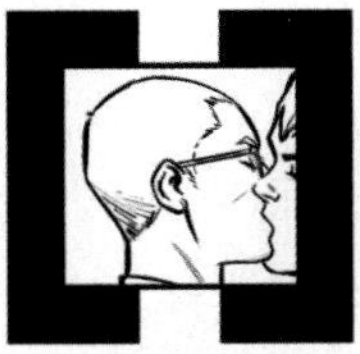

Christian Frost

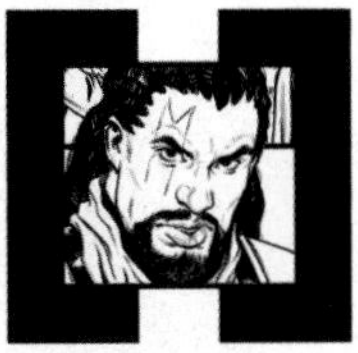

Bishop

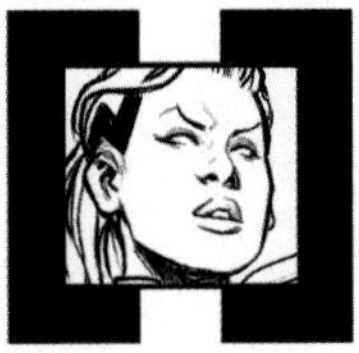

Storm

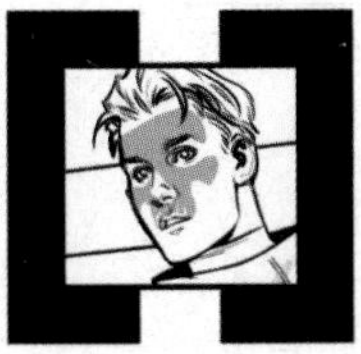

Pyro

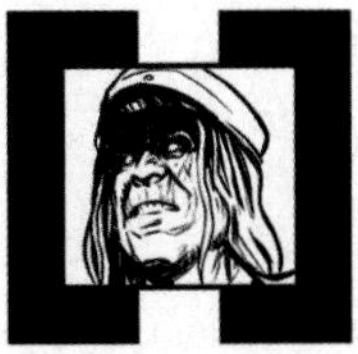

Masque

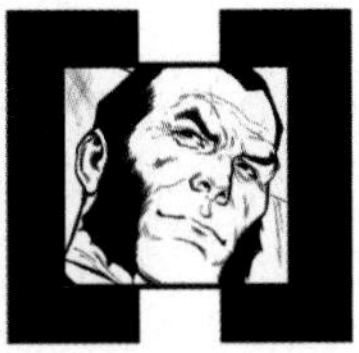

Sebastian Shaw

[00_mutant_piracy]
[00_sea_shores_X_]

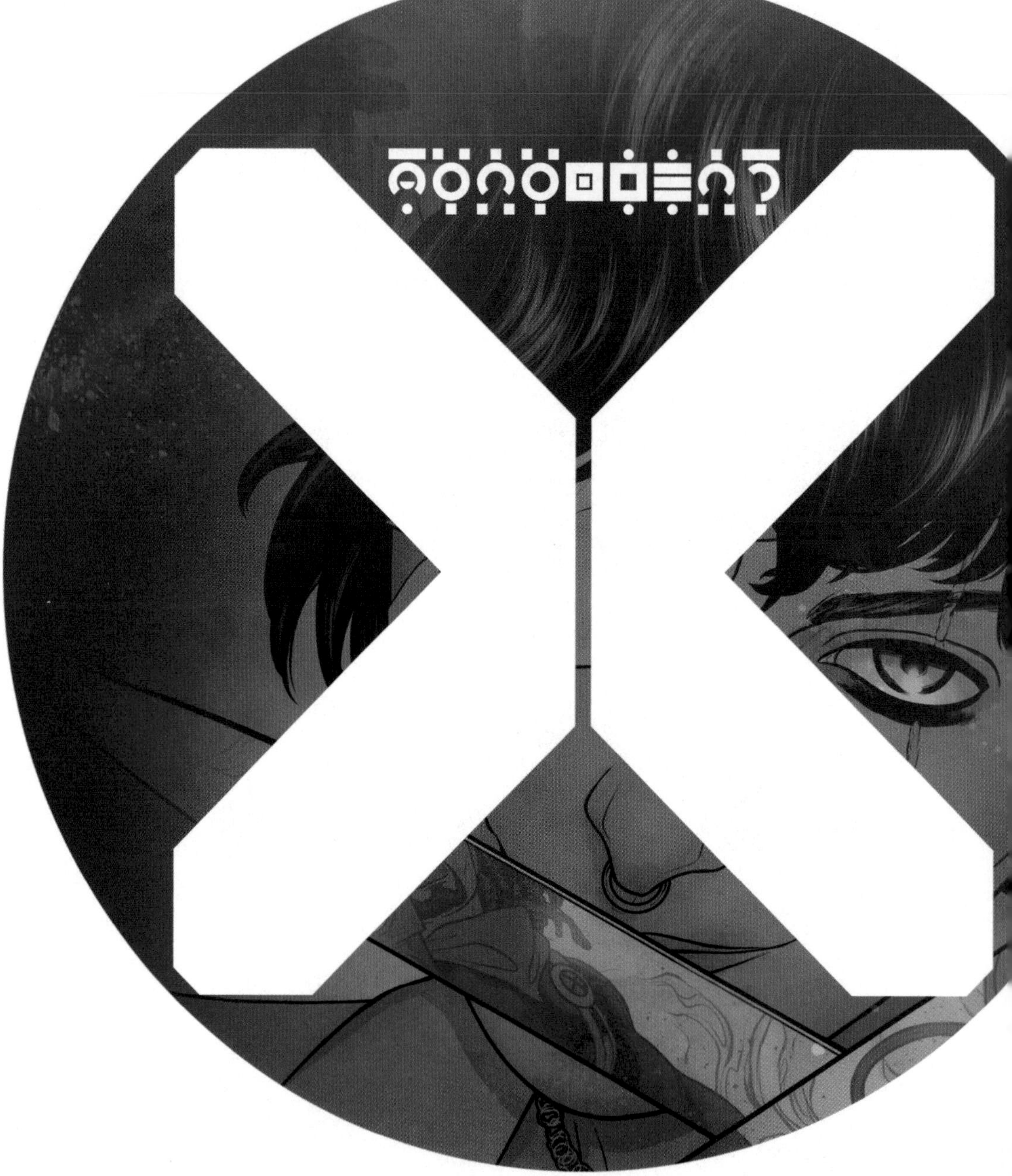

[00_mutant_piracy]
[00_sea_shores_X_]

GERRY DUGGAN..................................[WRITER]
STEFANO CASELLI...............................[ARTIST]
EDGAR DELGADO...........................[COLOR ARTIST]
VC's CORY PETIT...........................[LETTERER]
TOM MULLER....................................[DESIGN]

RUSSELL DAUTERMAN & MATTHEW WILSON......[COVER ARTISTS]

NICK RUSSELL..............................[PRODUCTION]

JONATHAN HICKMAN...........................[HEAD OF X]
CHRIS ROBINSON......................[ASSISTANT EDITOR]
JORDAN D. WHITE...............................[EDITOR]
C.B. CEBULSKI........................[EDITOR IN CHIEF]

[07] MARAUDERS

[ISSUE SEVEN]......FROM EMMA, WITH LOVE

[00_mutant_piracy]
[00_sea_shores_X_]

[00_00...0]
[00_00...7]

[00_boat__]
[00______]

[00______]

[00_____X]

TEXT MESSAGE-- UNKNOWN SENDER

Katherine Pryde, we met briefly once in Washington, DC. You likely won't remember me, and I'm afraid I can't tell you my name, but I hope you'll believe what I am about to write, because it's true. Kade Kilgore and Manuel Enduque have made two drug purchases through shell companies in Madripoor. One of those drugs was Krakoan medicines. The other was poison. It doesn't take a genius to guess what those little turds are planning. I give you this info in the hope that your people can avert a tragedy that will hurt some already hurting human souls. I don't have the jurisdiction, and Madripoor authorities seem to have been paid off by something new called Verendi. I'll send a second message after this one with the coordinates of the warehouse where I believe the drugs were shipped to. If you are the woman I think you are, you will try your damnedest to keep sick people from dying for something as stupid as hurting your new nation's economy. Good luck. Don't bother replying to either message. This burner phone is going into the Potomac after I hit Send.

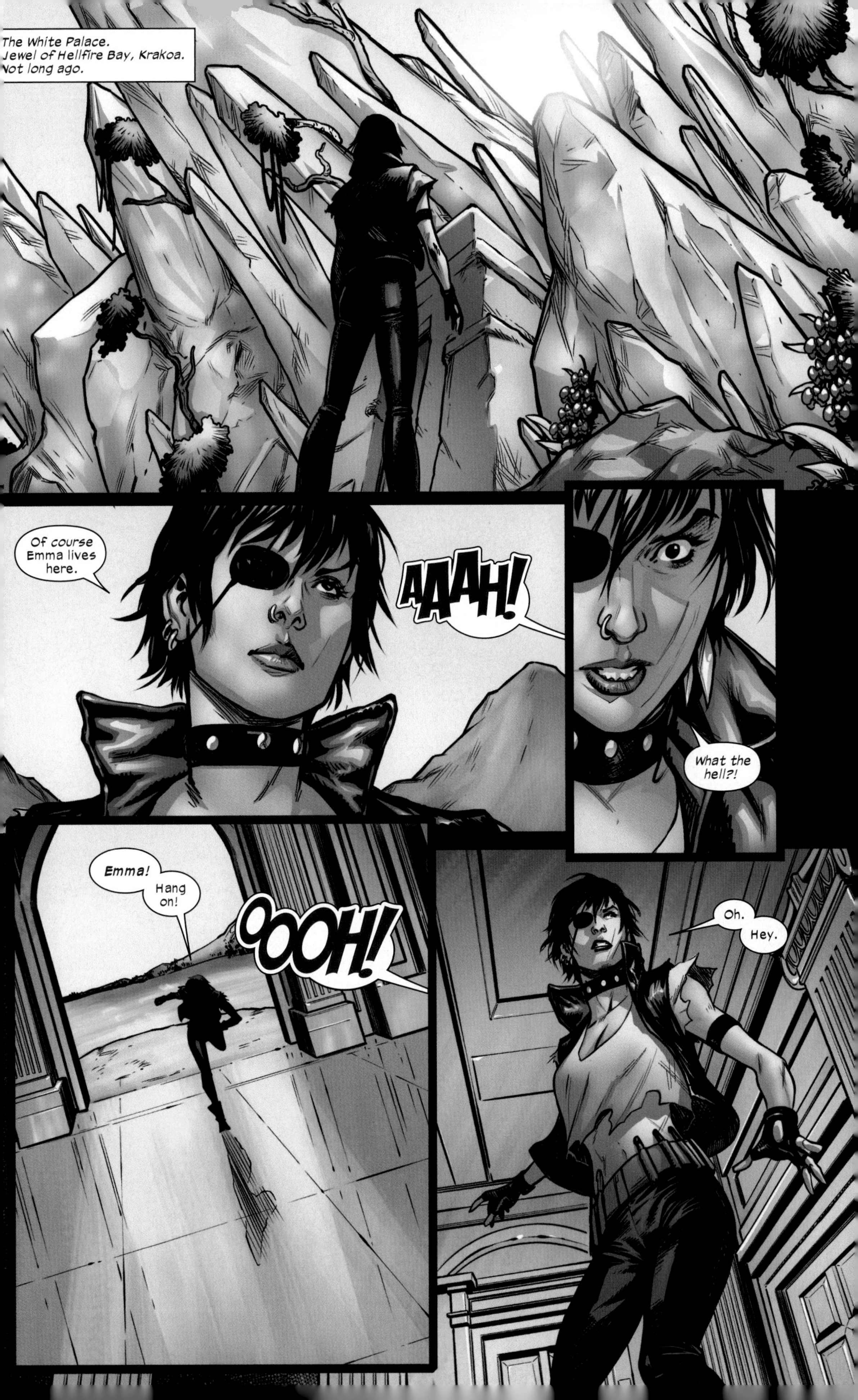
The White Palace.
Jewel of Hellfire Bay, Krakoa.
Not long ago.
Of course Emma lives here.
AAAH!
What the hell?!
Emma! Hang on!
OOOH!
Oh. Hey.

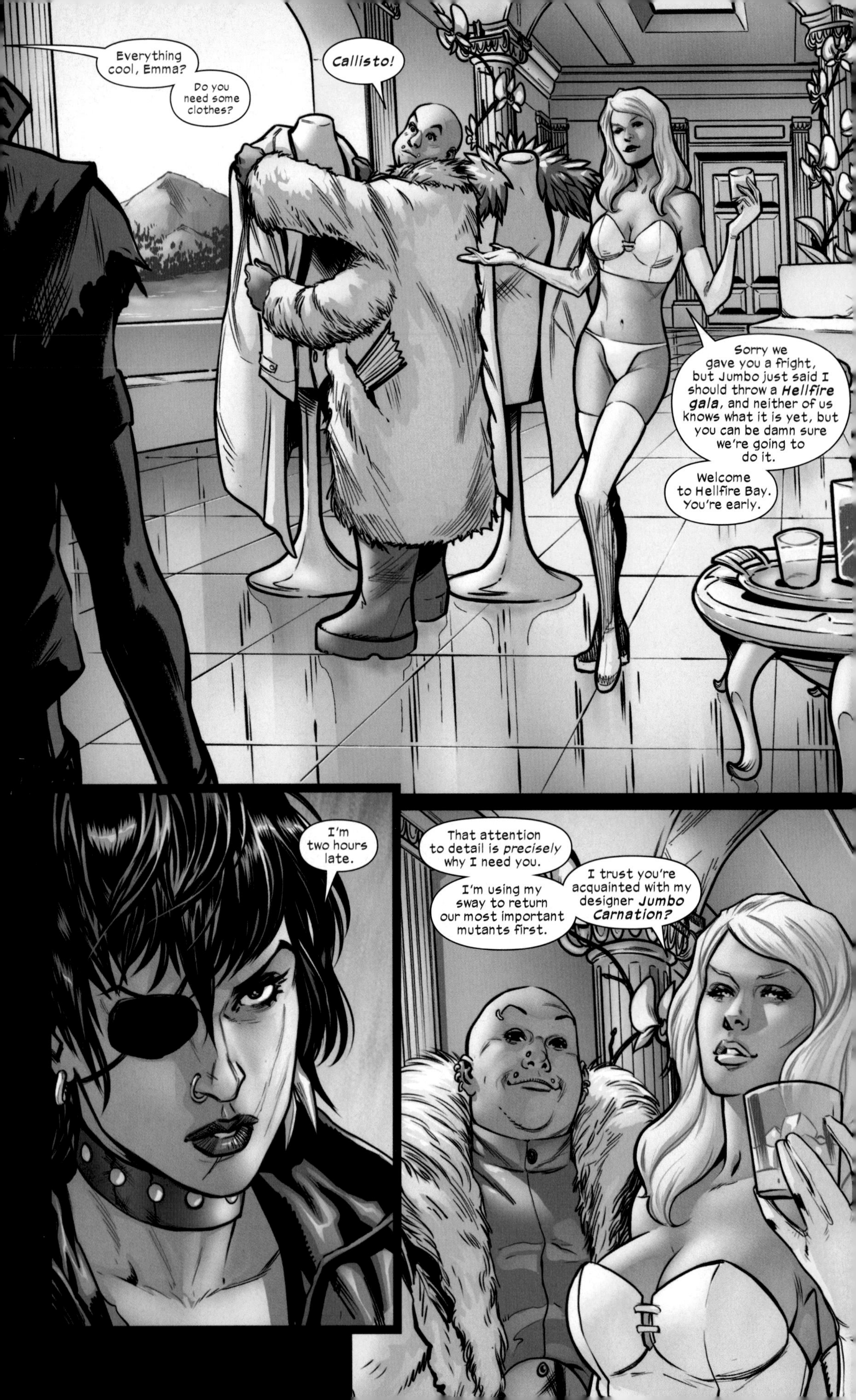

Everything cool, Emma?
Do you need some clothes?
Callisto!
Sorry we gave you a fright, but Jumbo just said I should throw a Hellfire gala, and neither of us knows what it is yet, but you can be damn sure we're going to do it.
Welcome to Hellfire Bay. You're early.
I'm two hours late.
That attention to detail is precisely why I need you.
I'm using my sway to return our most important mutants first.
I trust you're acquainted with my designer Jumbo Carnation?

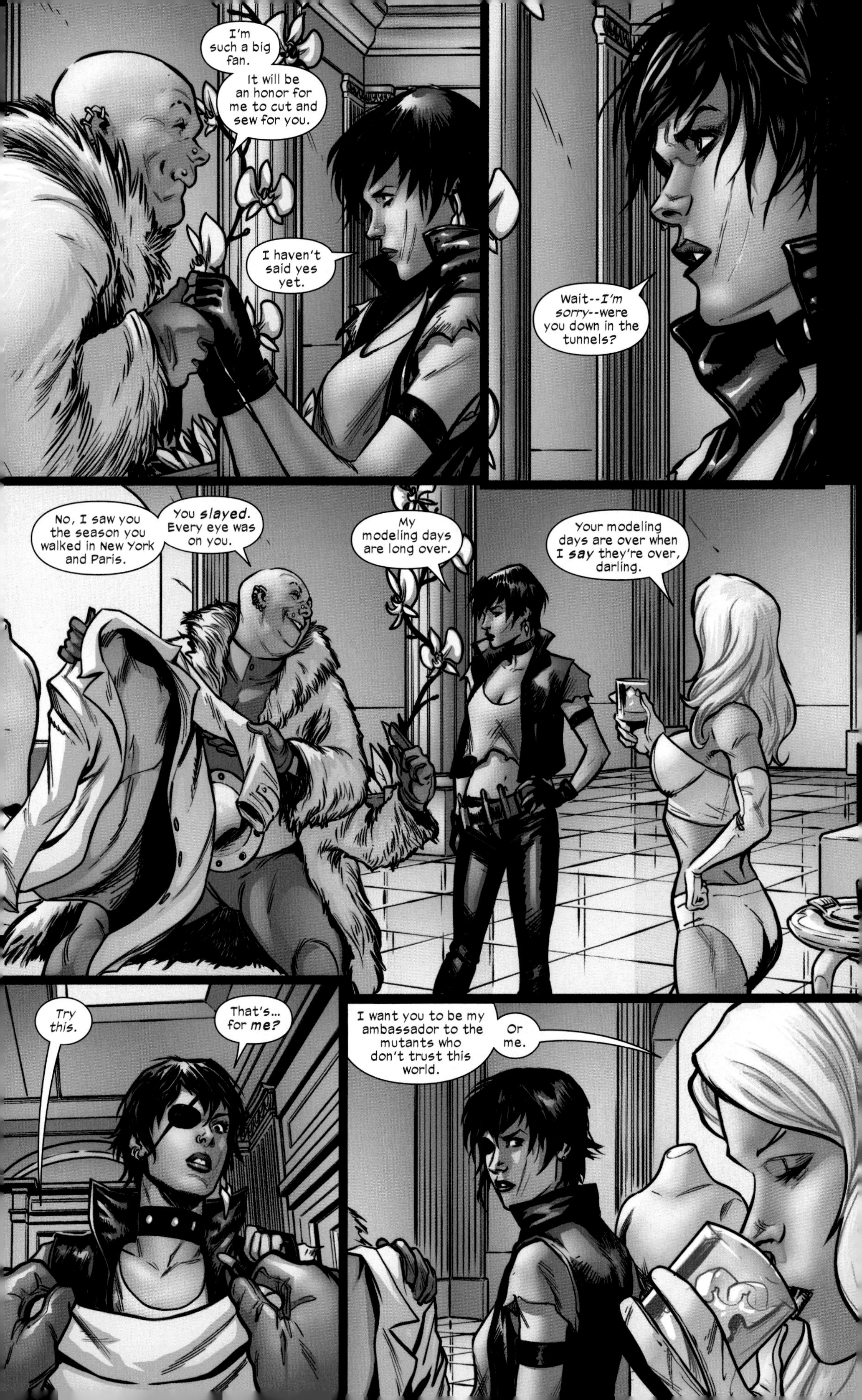

I'm such a big fan.
It will be an honor for me to cut and sew for you.
I haven't said yes yet.
Wait--*I'm sorry*--were you down in the tunnels?
No, I saw you the season you walked in New York and Paris.
You *slayed*. Every eye was on you.
My modeling days are long over.
Your modeling days are over when I *say* they're over, darling.
Try this.
That's... for *me?*
I want you to be my ambassador to the mutants who don't trust this world.
Or me.

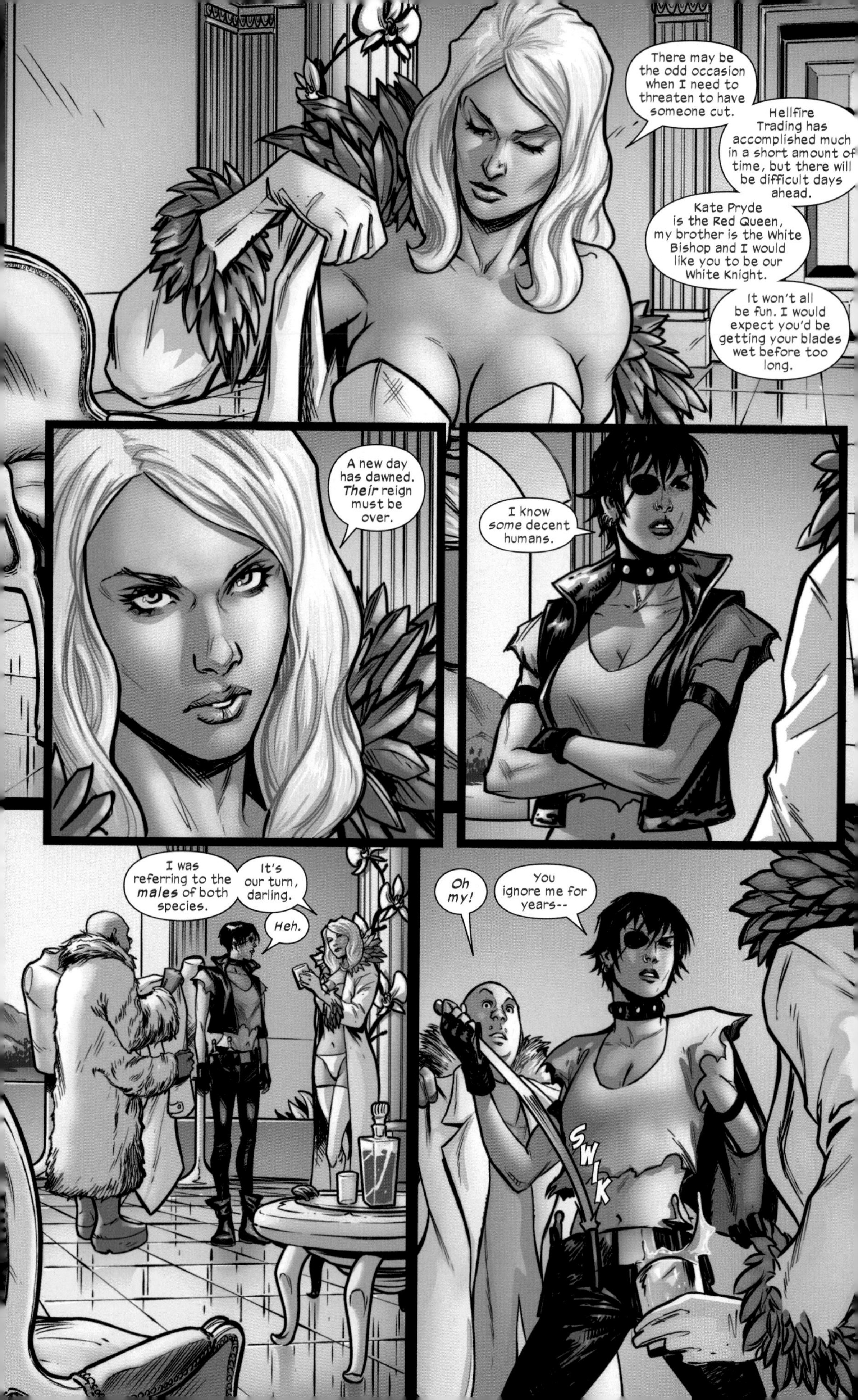
There may be the odd occasion when I need to threaten to have someone cut.
Hellfire Trading has accomplished much in a short amount of time, but there will be difficult days ahead.
Kate Pryde is the Red Queen, my brother is the White Bishop and I would like you to be our White Knight.
It won't all be fun. I would expect you'd be getting your blades wet before too long.
A new day has dawned. *Their* reign must be over.
I know *some* decent humans.
I was referring to the *males* of both species.
It's our turn, darling.
Heh.
Oh my!
You ignore me for years--
SWIK

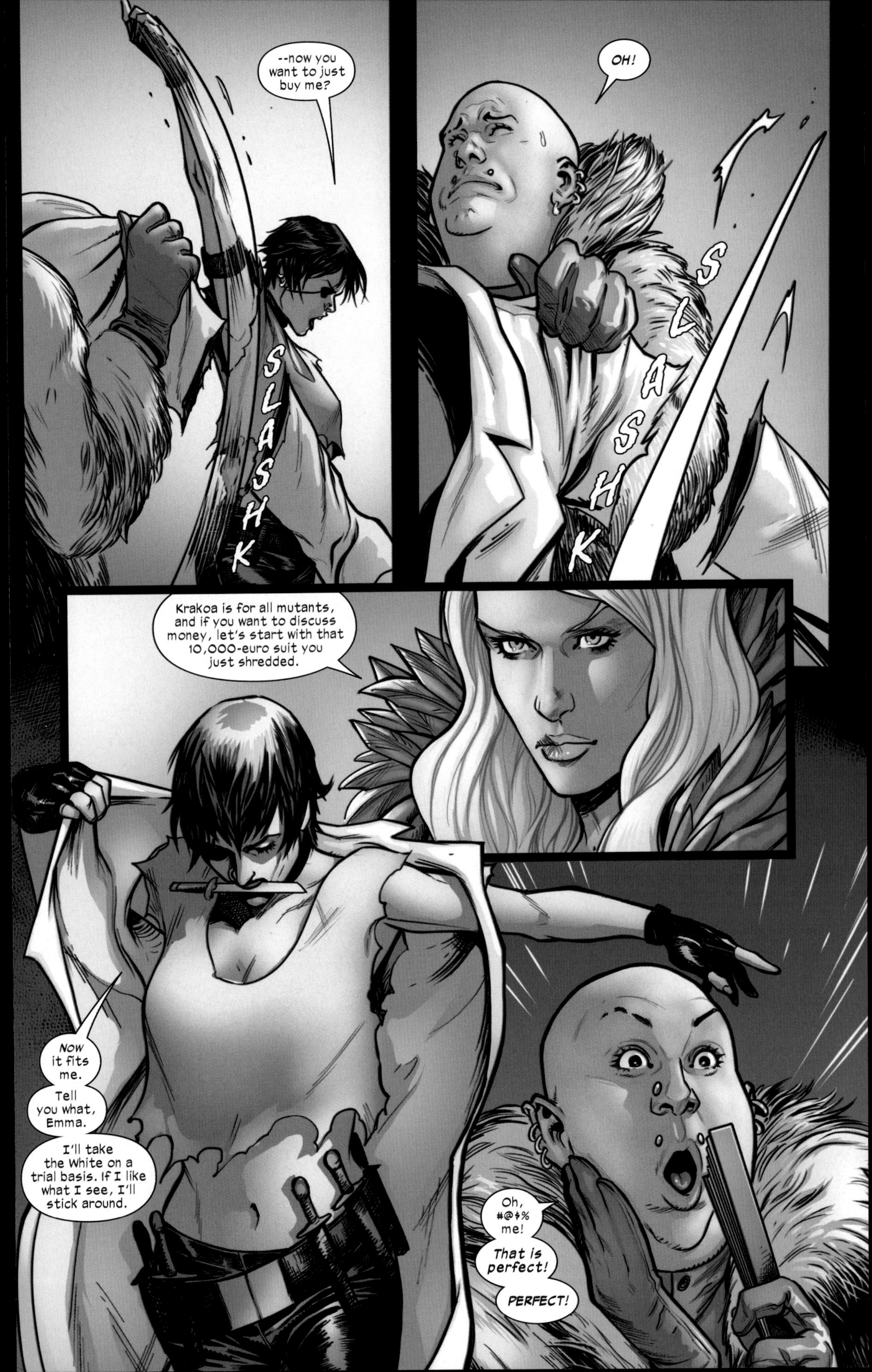
--now you want to just buy me?
SLASHK
OH!
SLASHK
Krakoa is for all mutants, and if you want to discuss money, let's start with that 10,000-euro suit you just shredded.
NOW it fits me.
Tell you what, Emma.
I'll take the White on a trial basis. If I like what I see, I'll stick around.
Oh, #@$% me!
That is perfect!
PERFECT!

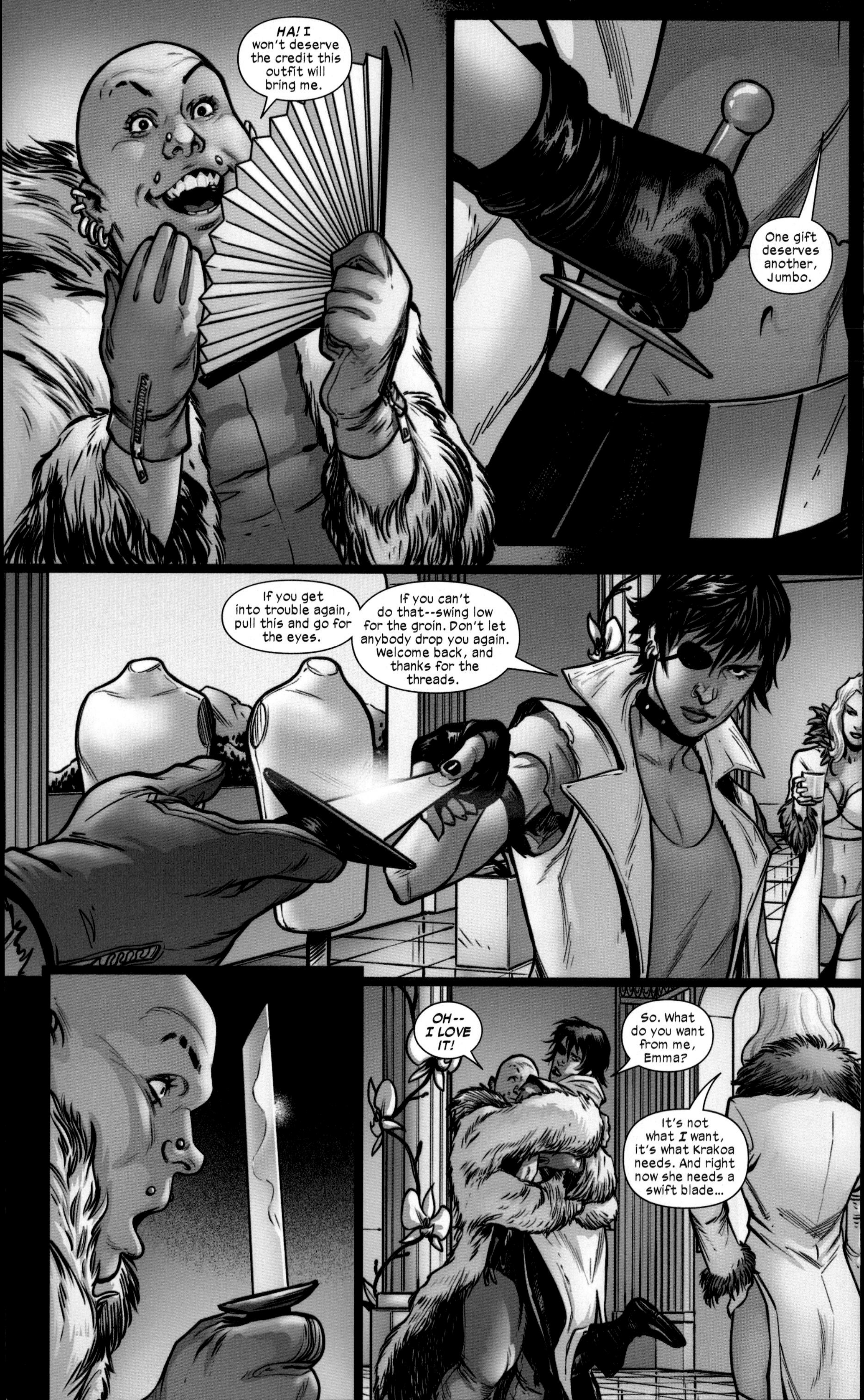
HA! I won't deserve the credit this outfit will bring me.
One gift deserves another, Jumbo.
If you get into trouble again, pull this and go for the eyes.
If you can't do that--swing low for the groin. Don't let anybody drop you again. Welcome back, and thanks for the threads.
OH-- I LOVE IT!
So. What do you want from me, Emma?
It's not what I want, it's what Krakoa needs. And right now she needs a swift blade...

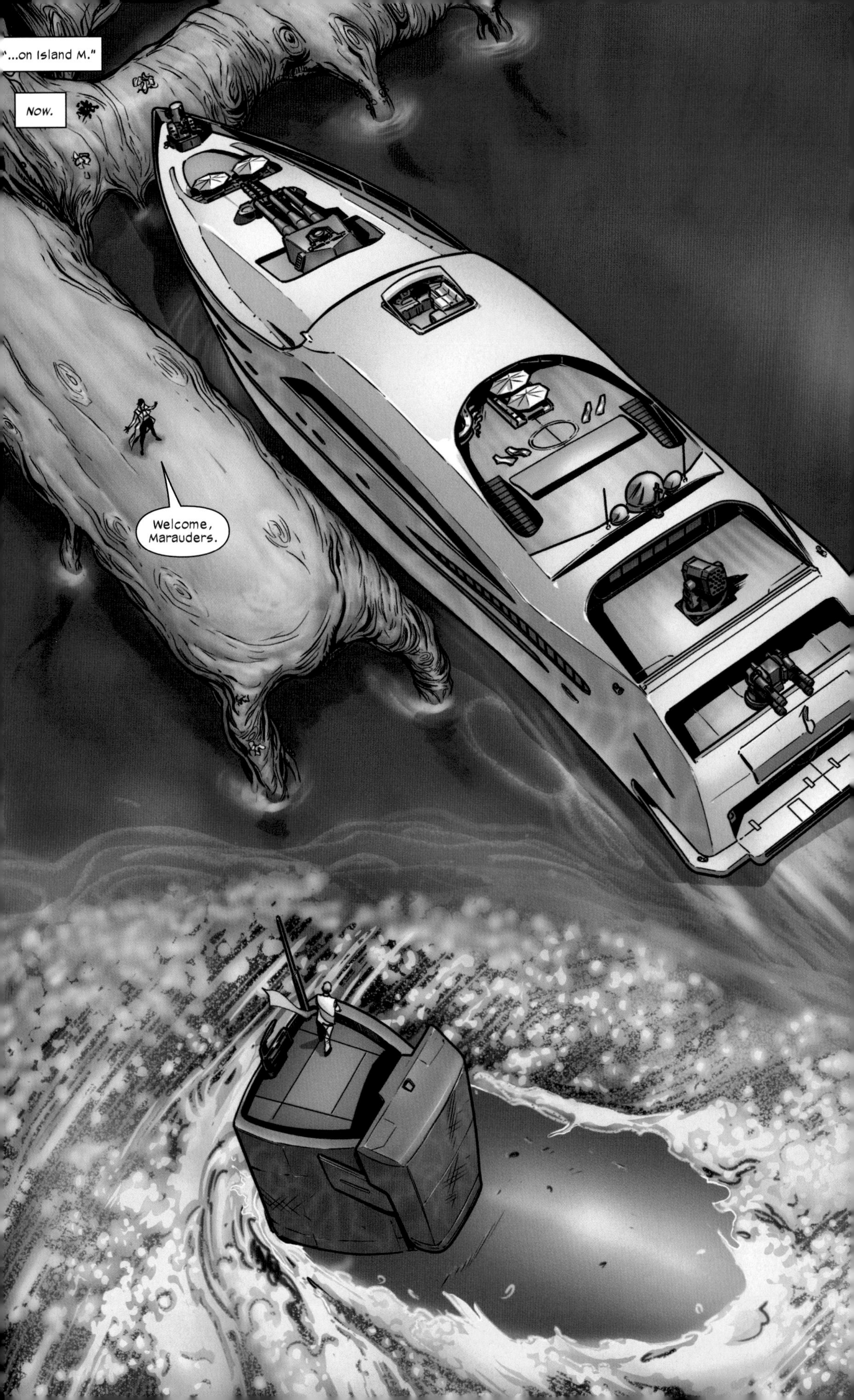
"...on Island M."
Now.
Welcome, Marauders.

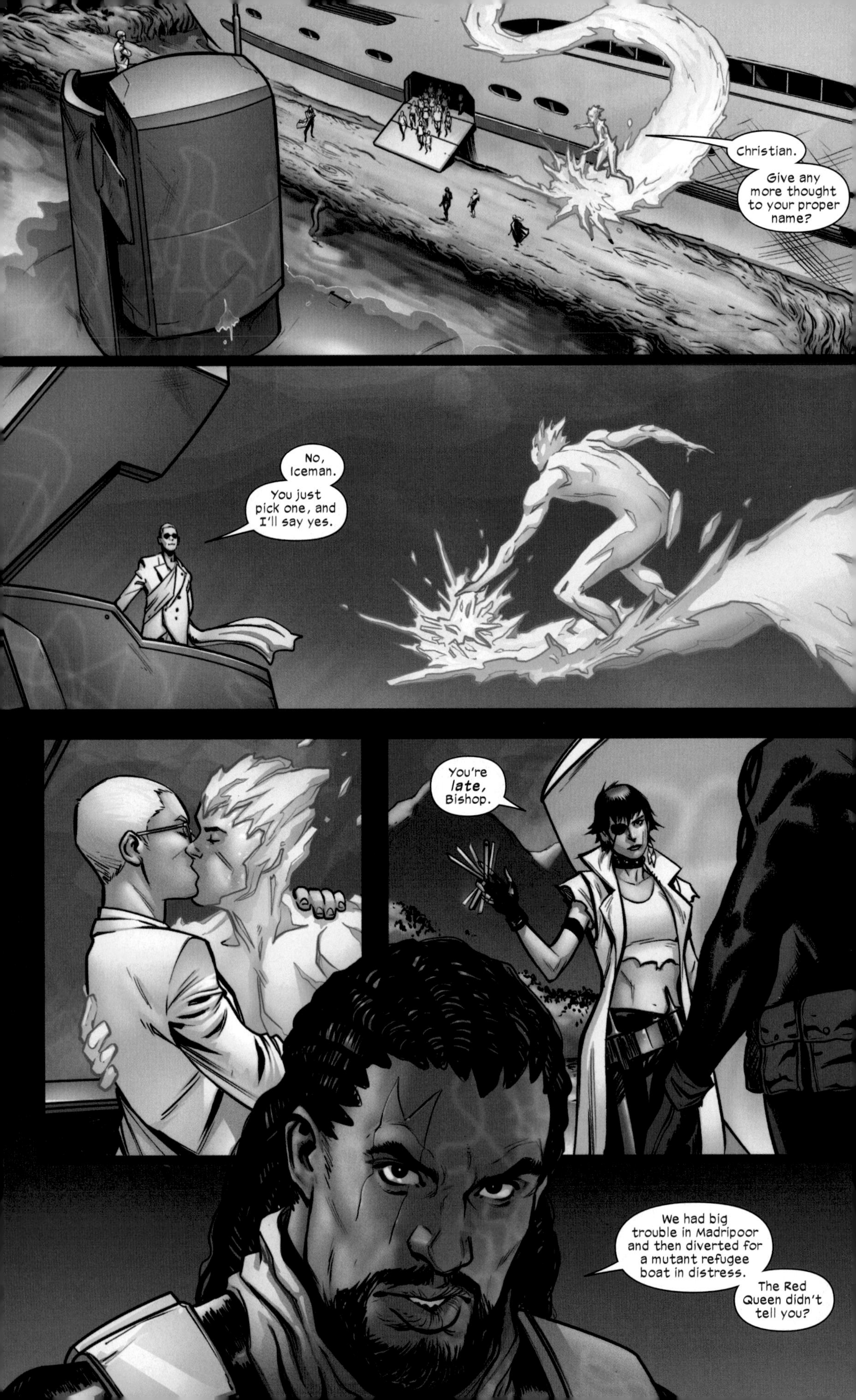
Christian.
Give any more thought to your proper name?
No, Iceman.
You just pick one, and I'll say yes.
You're *late,* Bishop.
We had big trouble in Madripoor and then diverted for a mutant refugee boat in distress.
The Red Queen didn't tell you?

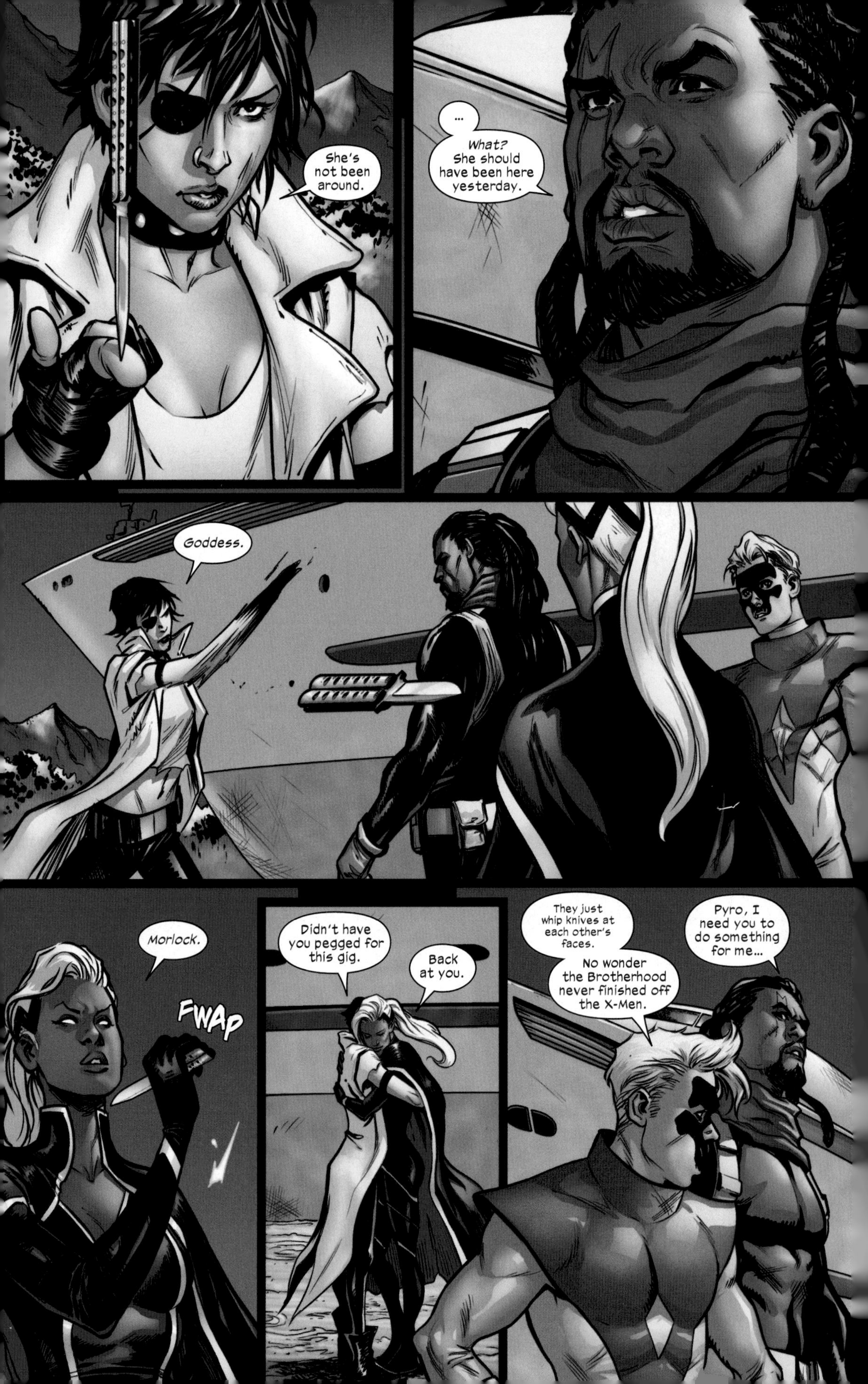
She's not been around.
...
What? She should have been here yesterday.
Goddess.
Morlock.
FWAP
Didn't have you pegged for this gig.
Back at you.
They just whip knives at each other's faces.
No wonder the Brotherhood never finished off the X-Men.
Pyro, I need you to do something for me...

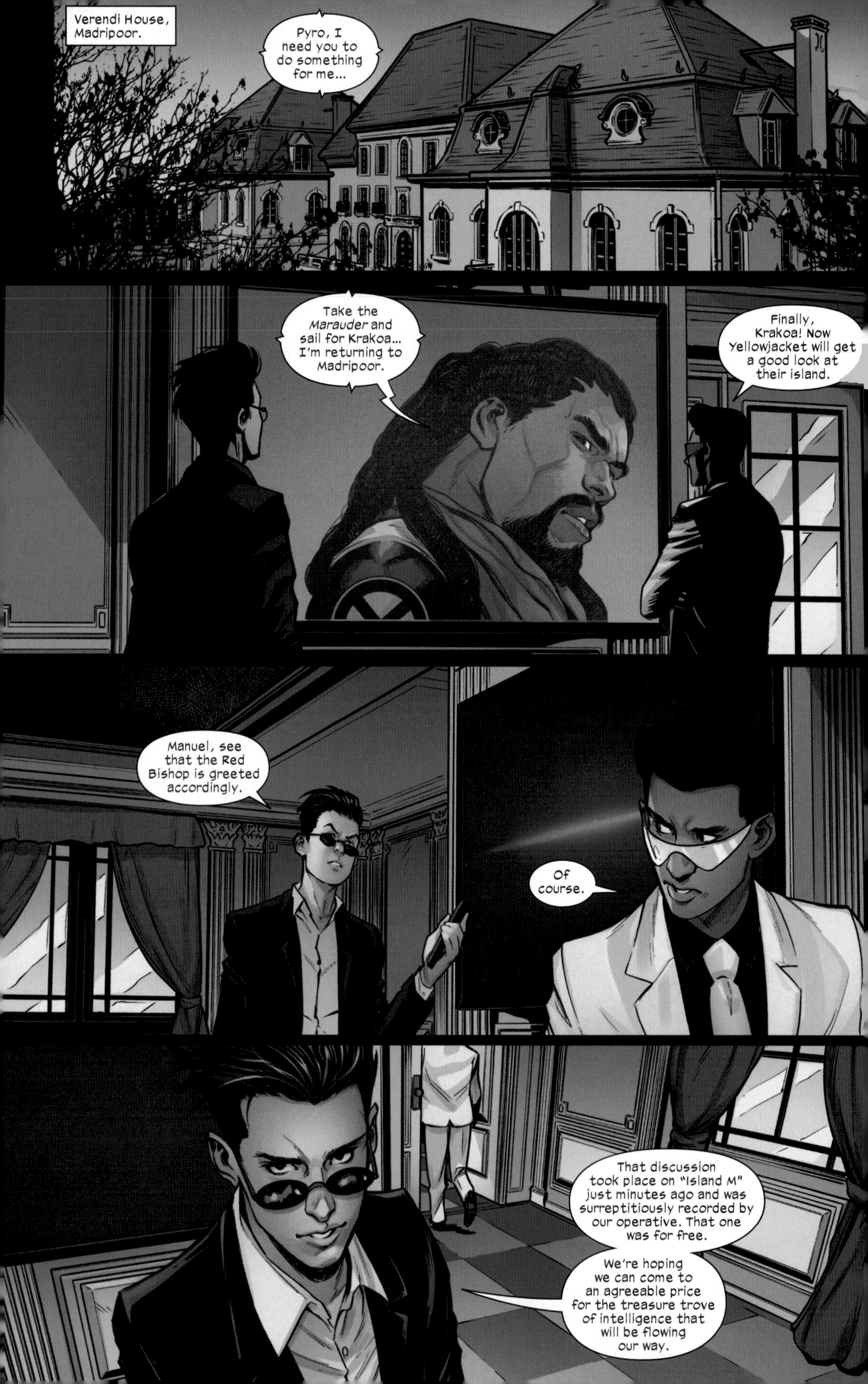

Verendi House, Madripoor.
Pyro, I need you to do something for me...
Take the *Marauder* and sail for Krakoa... I'm returning to Madripoor.
Finally, Krakoa! Now Yellowjacket will get a good look at their island.
Manuel, see that the Red Bishop is greeted accordingly.
Of course.
That discussion took place on "Island M" just minutes ago and was surreptitiously recorded by our operative. That one was for free.
We're hoping we can come to an agreeable price for the treasure trove of intelligence that will be flowing our way.

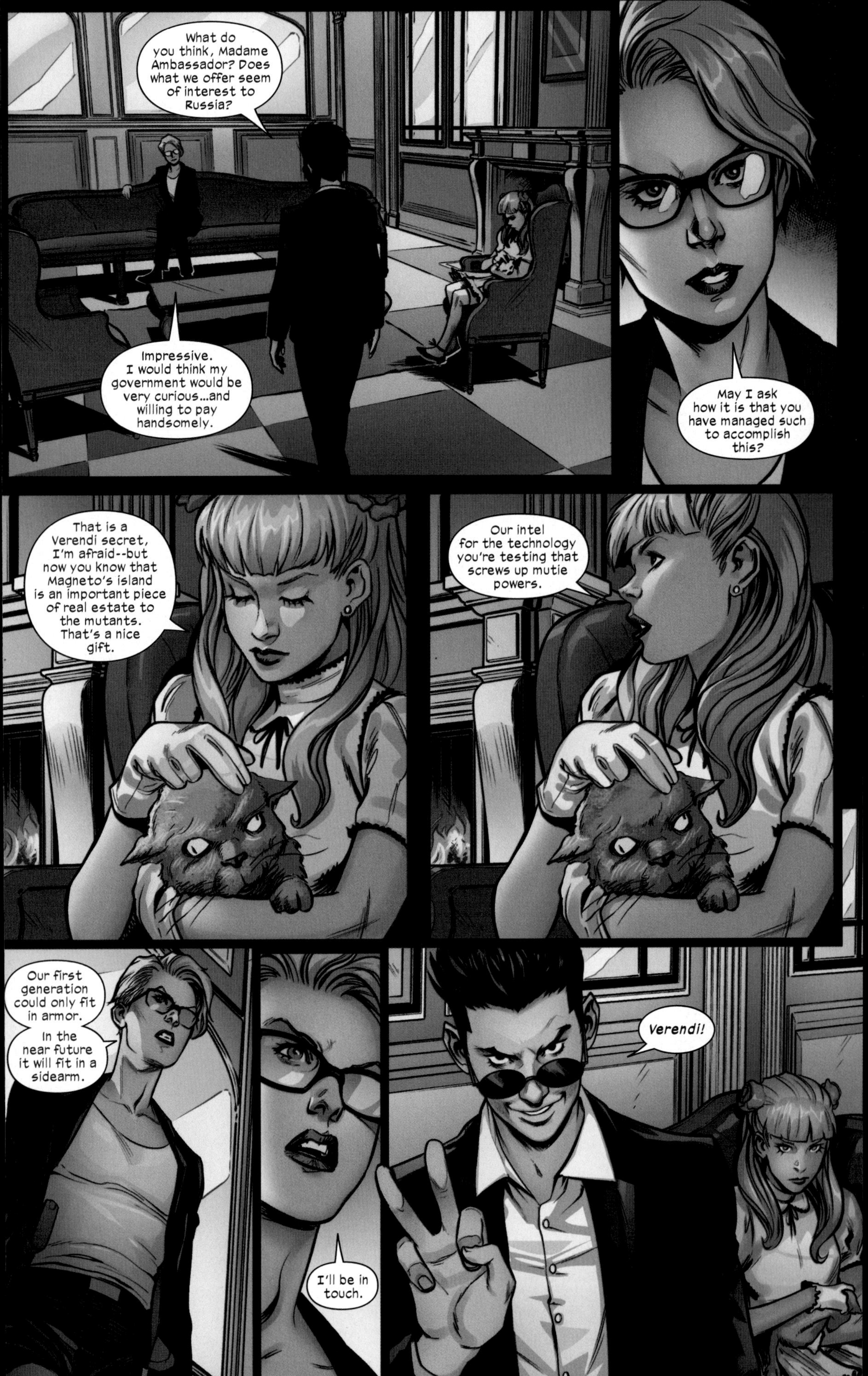
What do you think, Madame Ambassador? Does what we offer seem of interest to Russia?
Impressive. I would think my government would be very curious...and willing to pay handsomely.
May I ask how it is that you have managed such to accomplish this?
That is a Verendi secret, I'm afraid--but now you know that Magneto's island is an important piece of real estate to the mutants. That's a nice gift.
Our intel for the technology you're testing that screws up mutie powers.
Our first generation could only fit in armor.
In the near future it will fit in a sidearm.
I'll be in touch.
Verendi!

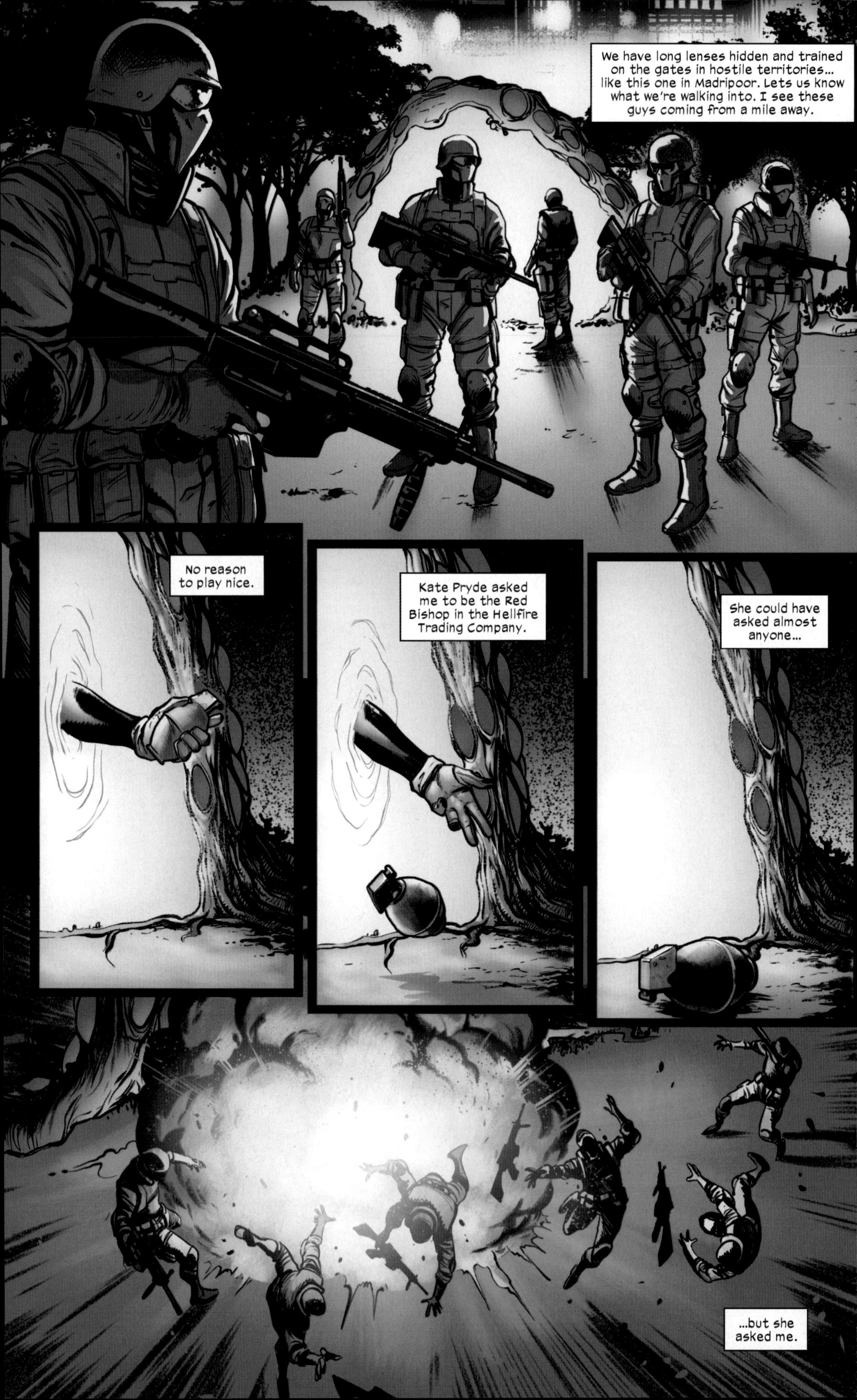
We have long lenses hidden and trained on the gates in hostile territories... like this one in Madripoor. Lets us know what we're walking into. I see these guys coming from a mile away.
No reason to play nice.
Kate Pryde asked me to be the Red Bishop in the Hellfire Trading Company.
She could have asked almost anyone...
...but she asked me.

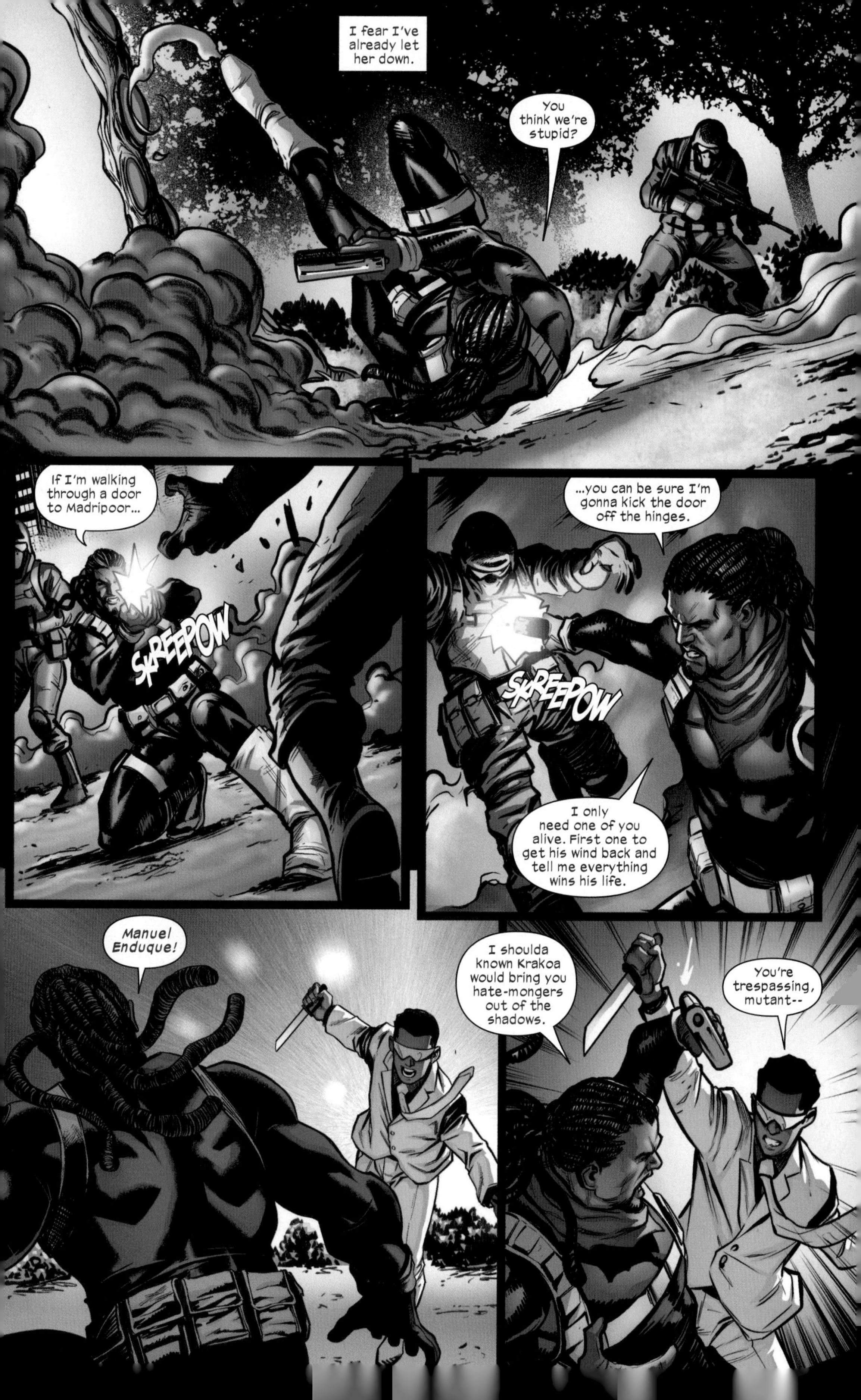
I fear I've already let her down.
You think we're stupid?
If I'm walking through a door to Madripoor...
SKREEPOW
...you can be sure I'm gonna kick the door off the hinges.
SKREEPOW
I only need one of you alive. First one to get his wind back and tell me everything wins his life.
Manuel Enduque!
I shoulda known Krakoa would bring you hate-mongers out of the shadows.
You're trespassing, mutant--

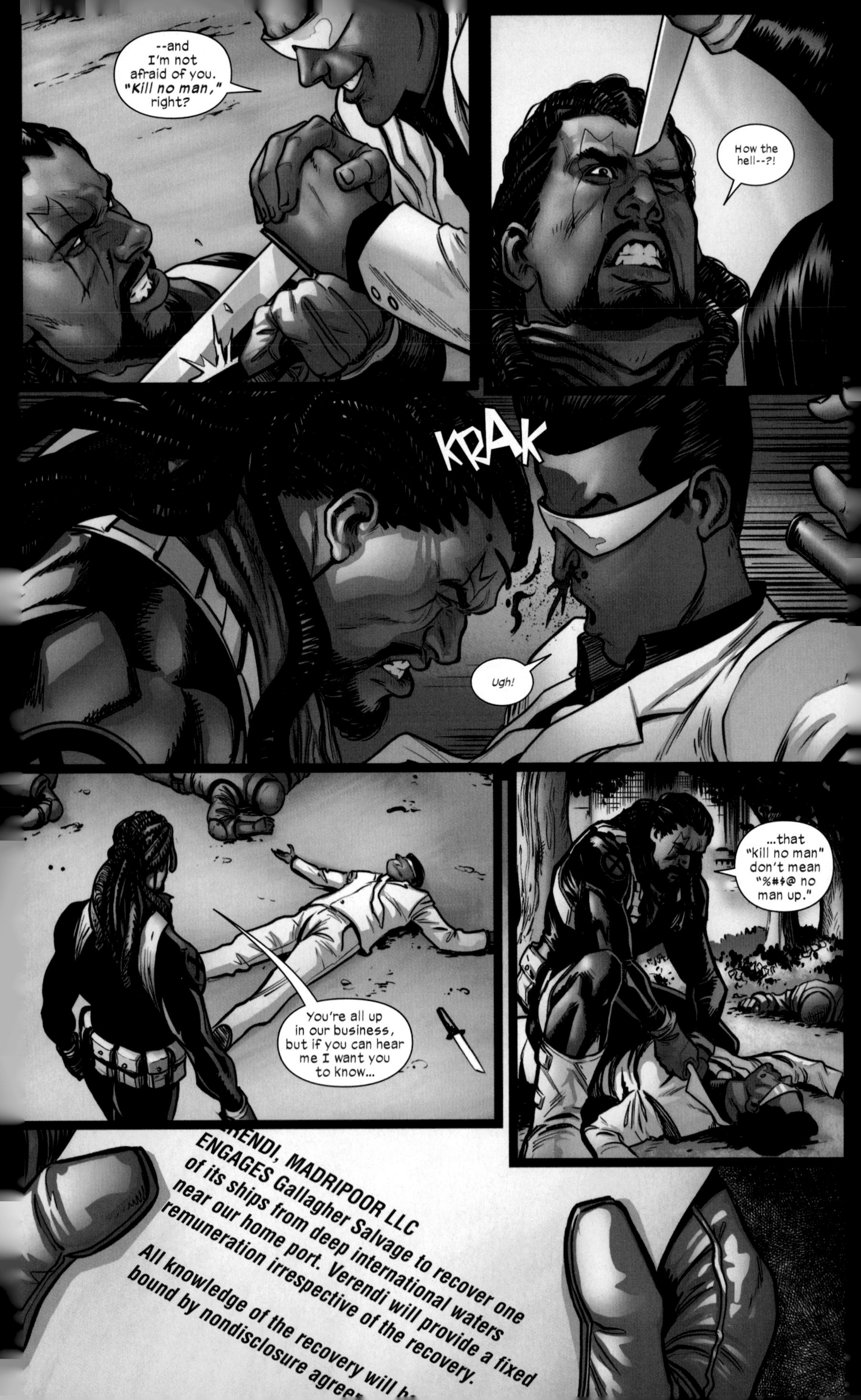
--and I'm not afraid of you. "Kill no man," right?
How the hell--?!
KRAK
Ugh!
You're all up in our business, but if you can hear me I want you to know...
...that "kill no man" don't mean "%#$@ no man up."
RENDI, MADRIPOOR LLC
ENGAGES Gallagher Salvage to recover one of its ships from deep international waters near our home port. Verendi will provide a fixed remuneration irrespective of the recovery.
All knowledge of the recovery will
bound by nondisclosure

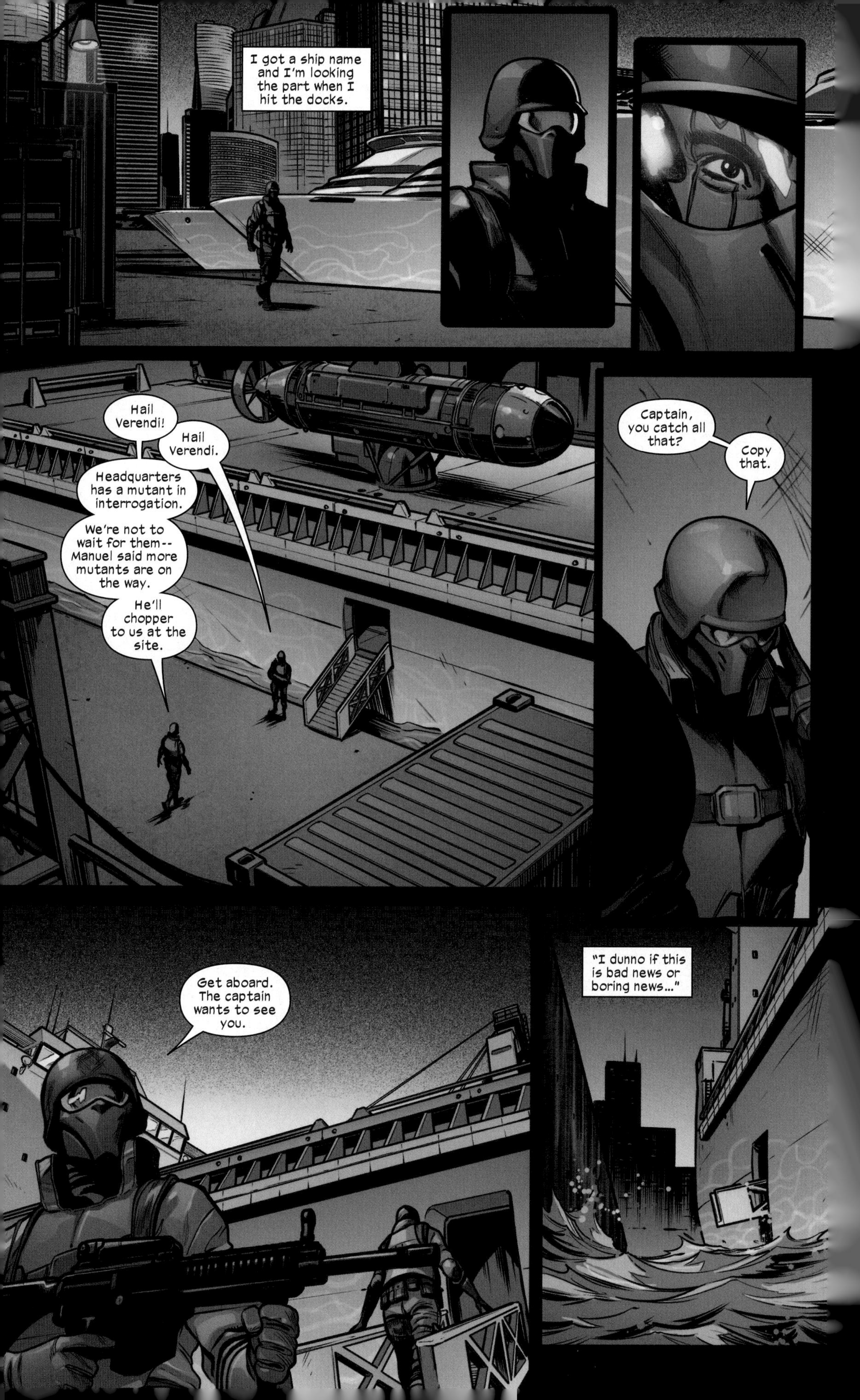
I got a ship name and I'm looking the part when I hit the docks.
Hail Verendi!
Hail Verendi.
Headquarters has a mutant in interrogation.
We're not to wait for them--Manuel said more mutants are on the way.
He'll chopper to us at the site.
Captain, you catch all that?
Copy that.
Get aboard. The captain wants to see you.
"I dunno if this is bad news or boring news..."

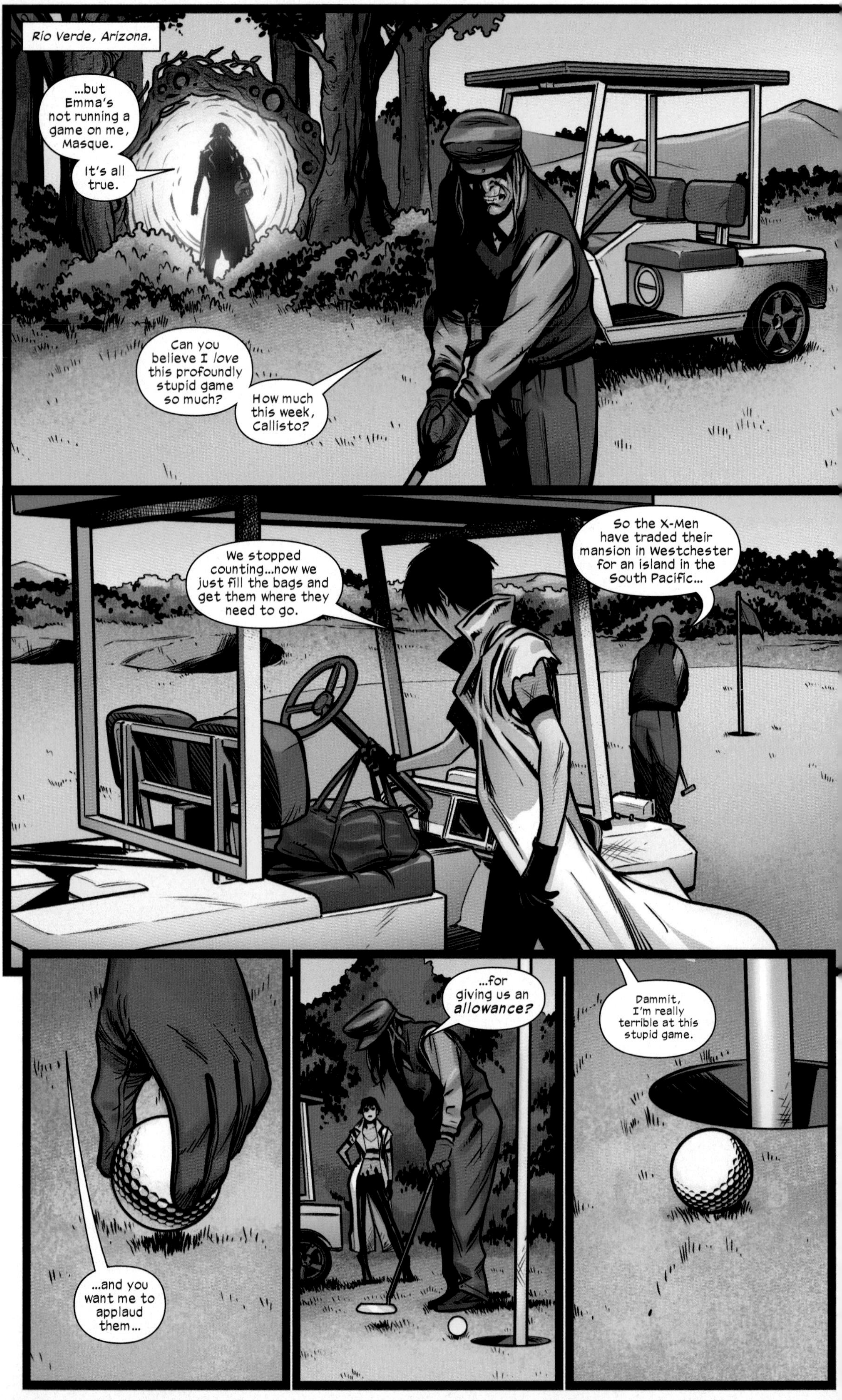
Rio Verde, Arizona.
...but Emma's not running a game on me, Masque.
It's all true.
Can you believe I *love* this profoundly stupid game so much?
How much this week, Callisto?
We stopped counting...now we just fill the bags and get them where they need to go.
So the X-Men have traded their mansion in Westchester for an island in the South Pacific...
...and you want me to applaud them...
...for giving us an *allowance?*
Dammit, I'm really terrible at this stupid game.

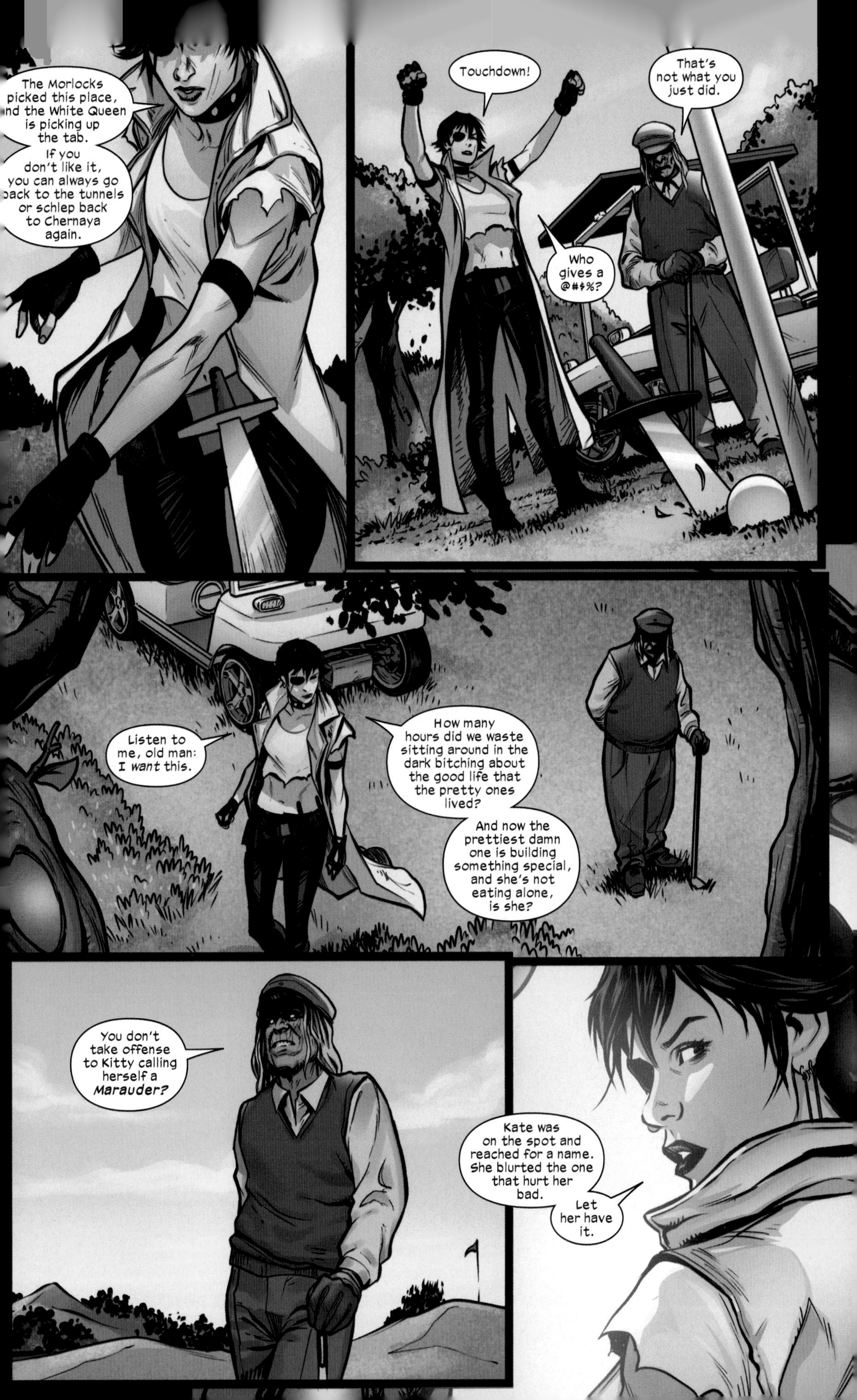
The Morlocks picked this place, and the White Queen is picking up the tab.
If you don't like it, you can always go back to the tunnels or schlep back to Chernaya again.
Touchdown!
That's not what you just did.
Who gives a @#$%?
Listen to me, old man: I *want* this.
How many hours did we waste sitting around in the dark bitching about the good life that the pretty ones lived?
And now the prettiest damn one is building something special, and she's not eating alone, is she?
You don't take offense to Kitty calling herself a *Marauder?*
Kate was on the spot and reached for a name. She blurted the one that hurt her bad.
Let her have it.

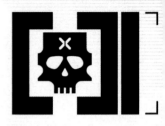

TOP SECRET EYES-ONLY ACCESS

FROM: THE X-DESK
TO: ▮▮▮▮▮▮▮▮
SUBJECT: RE: Krakoa

—

Working from home, pending review of my status. As requested, my mother gave blood once to the boys at USAMRIID, but that's over. She's not a test subject. I understand the importance of studying the patients on the Krakoan drugs, but I don't know how much time she's had put back on the clock and I can't spend it back in doctors' offices.

When the Krakoan drugs were unveiled a few weeks ago, I reached out to an old friend in the DEA and arranged to have marked currency sent to the Hellfire Trading Company for one of our aboveboard purchases from a YES country.

Those bills have begun circulating in and around Rio Verde, Arizona. I haven't had a chance to roll out that way yet, but a quick internet search turned up the following threads. They make for a fun read. It's looking like Krakoa is a capitalistic country with some very strong socialist programs and possibly a retiree community? There's nothing out in Rio Verde except planned communities and golf courses. Odd, right?

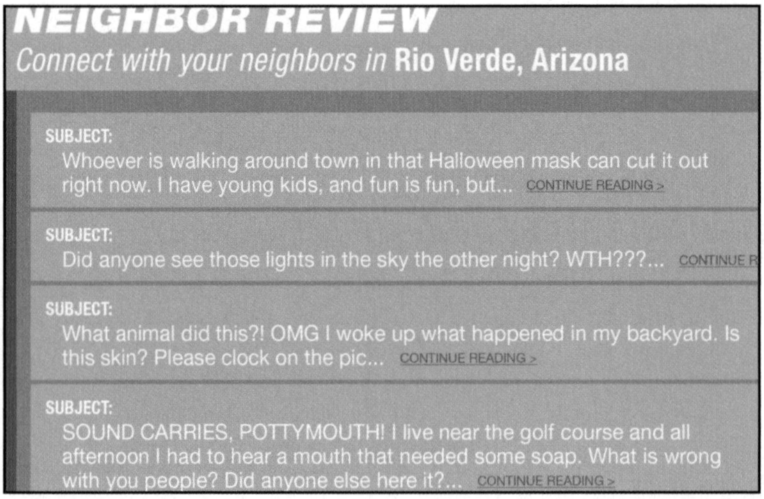

NEIGHBOR REVIEW
Connect with your neighbors in **Rio Verde, Arizona**

SUBJECT:
Whoever is walking around town in that Halloween mask can cut it out right now. I have young kids, and fun is fun, but... CONTINUE READING >

SUBJECT:
Did anyone see those lights in the sky the other night? WTH???... CONTINUE P

SUBJECT:
What animal did this?! OMG I woke up what happened in my backyard. Is this skin? Please clock on the pic... CONTINUE READING >

SUBJECT:
SOUND CARRIES, POTTYMOUTH! I live near the golf course and all afternoon I had to hear a mouth that needed some soap. What is wrong with you people? Did anyone else here it?... CONTINUE READING >

—

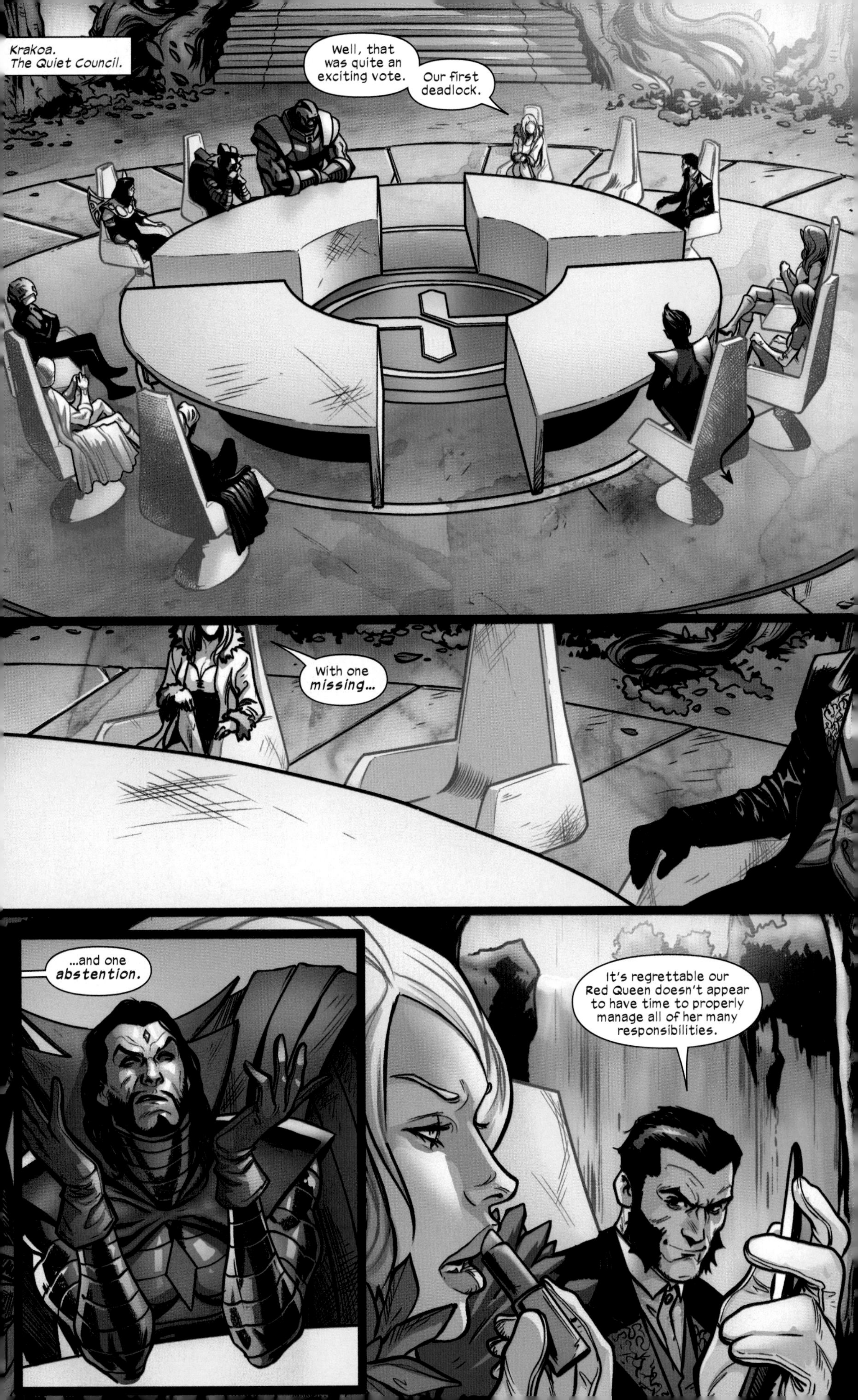
Krakoa.
The Quiet Council.
Well, that was quite an exciting vote.
Our first deadlock.
With one missing...
...and one abstention.
It's regrettable our Red Queen doesn't appear to have time to properly manage all of her many responsibilities.

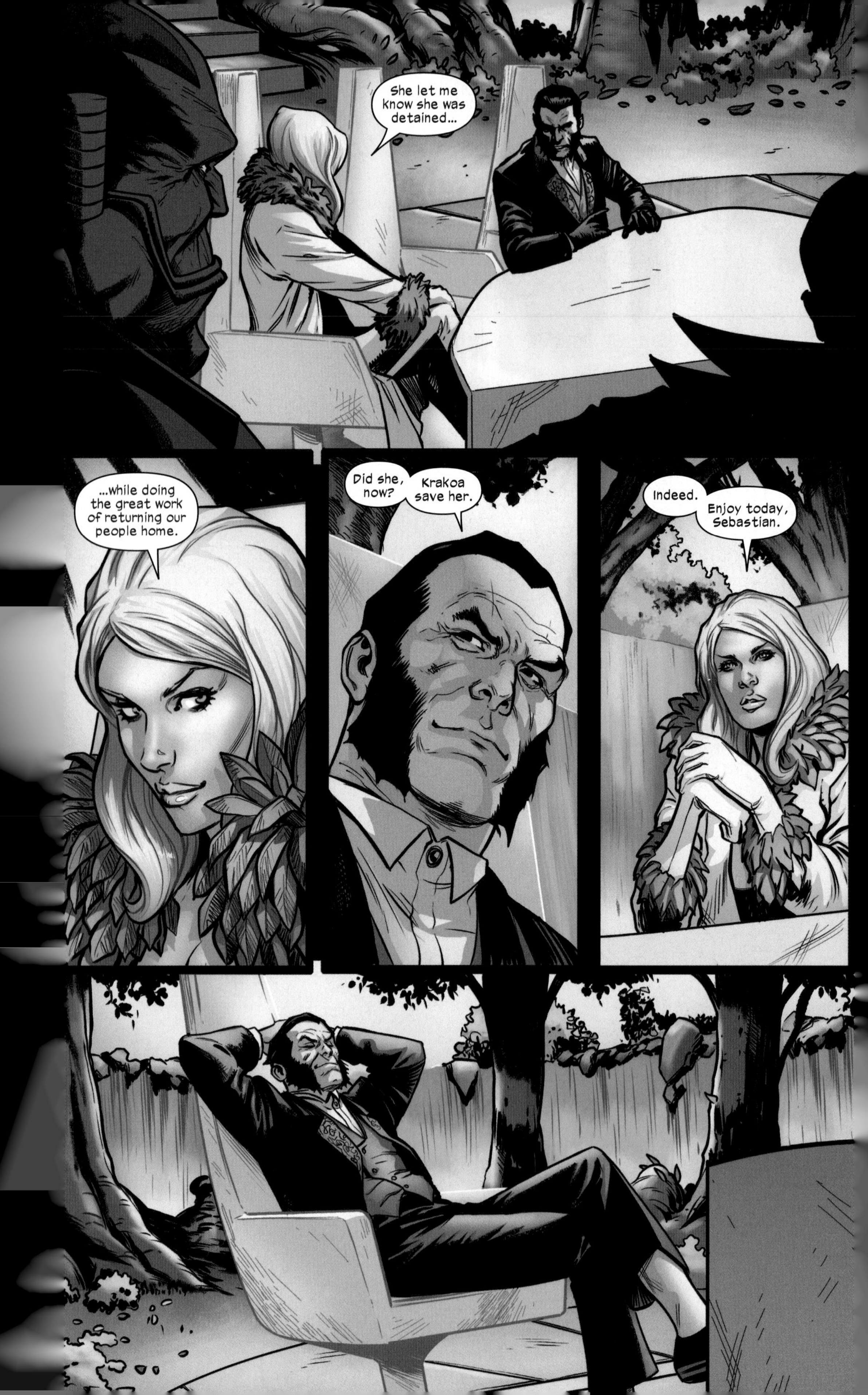
She let me know she was detained...
...while doing the great work of returning our people home.
Did she, now?
Krakoa save her.
Indeed.
Enjoy today, Sebastian.

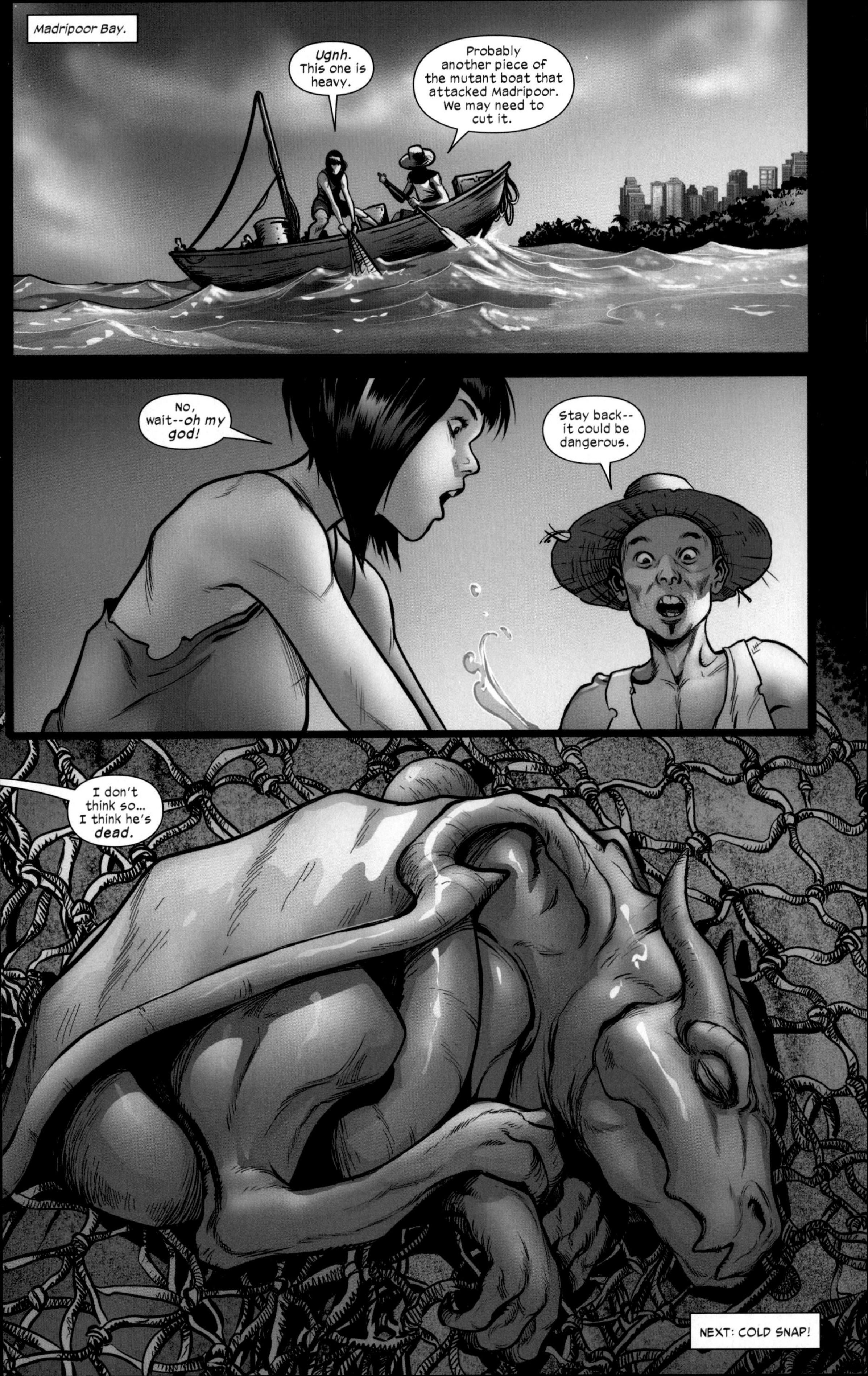
Madripoor Bay.
Ugnh. This one is heavy.
Probably another piece of the mutant boat that attacked Madripoor. We may need to cut it.
No, wait--*oh my god!*
Stay back--it could be dangerous.
I don't think so... I think he's *dead.*
NEXT: COLD SNAP!

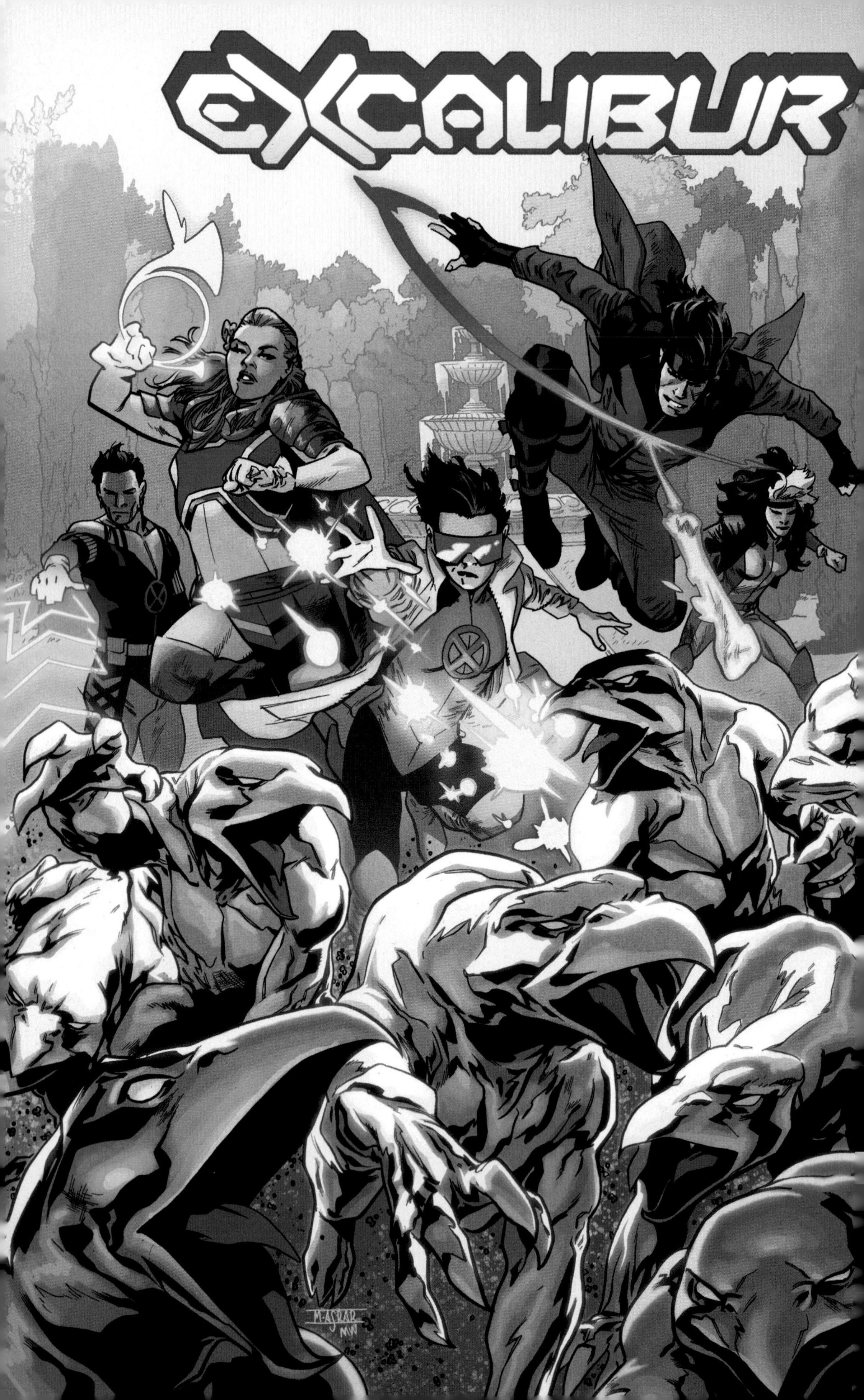
EXCALIBUR
M·ASRAR
MW

[ava_[0.7]
[lon_[0.7]

[ava_[0.X]
[lon_[0.X]

THE HUNT IS ON

EXCALIBUR reigns! With evil sorceress Morgan Le Fay defeated and Brian Braddock freed from her clutches, Apocalypse has maneuvered his pick for king onto the throne: Jamie Braddock! Jamie may be a mad choice...but Apocalypse always has his reasons.

And despite no longer being possessed, Brian's time under Morgan Le Fay's sway changed him -- into a man who unwillingly wields the Sword of Might...

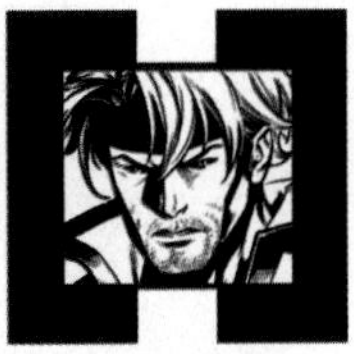

Gambit

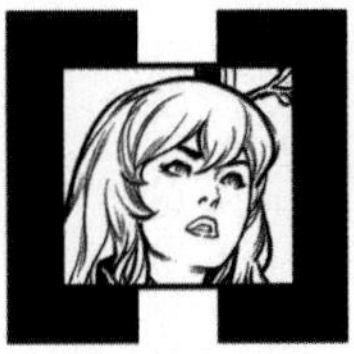

Rogue

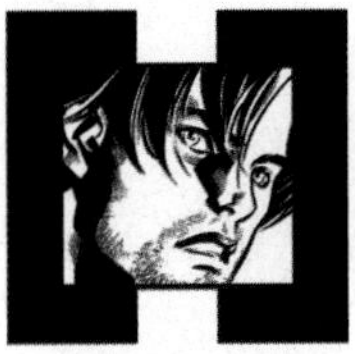

Rictor

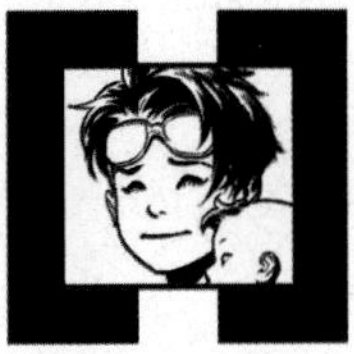

Jubilee

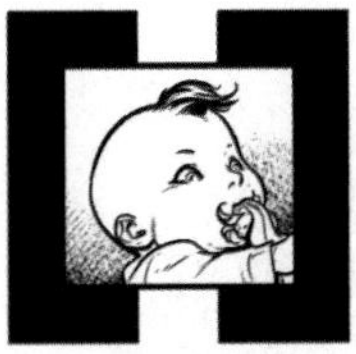

Shogo

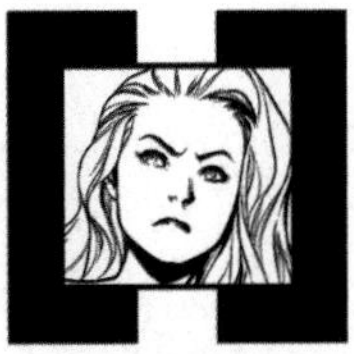

Captain Britain

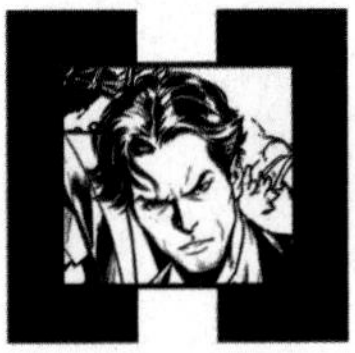

Pete Wisdom

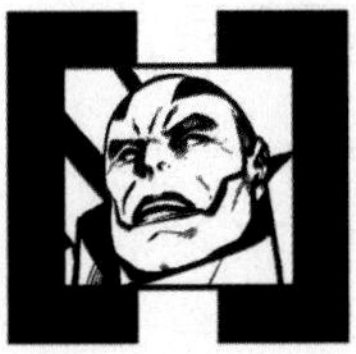

Apocalypse

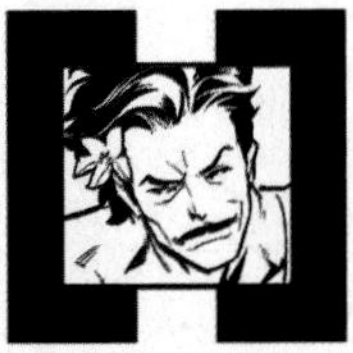

Jamie Braddock

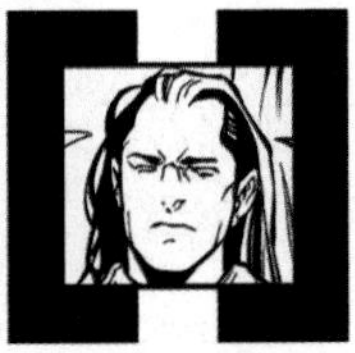

Exodus

[ava_[0.7]...]
[lon_[0.7]...]

[Tally....HO.]

[00_so_below_X]
[00_as_above_X]

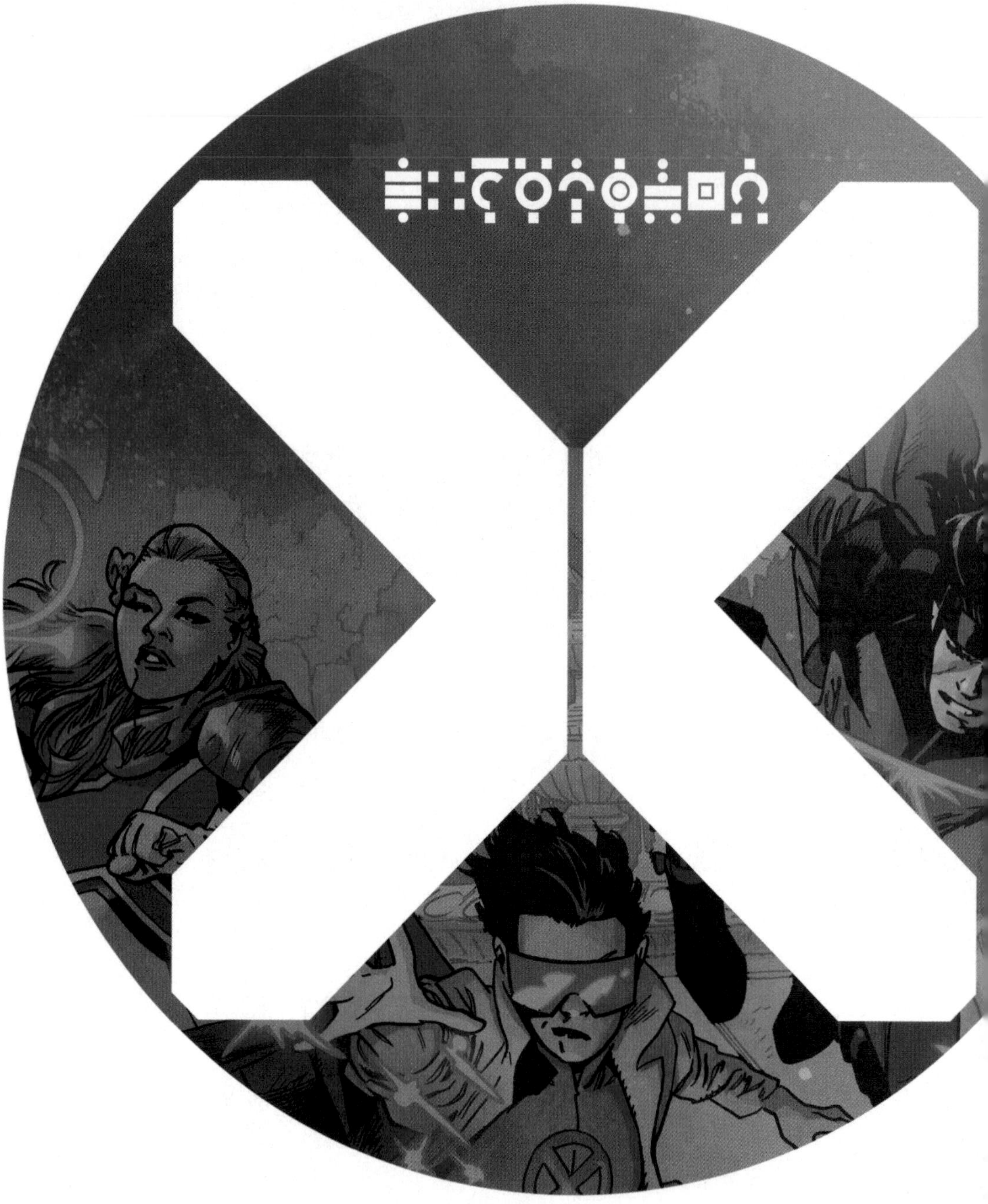

[00_so_below_X]
[00_as_above_X]

TINI HOWARD....................................[WRITER]
WILTON SANTOS..................................[PENCILER]
OREN JUNIOR....................................[INKER]
ERICK ARCINIEGA.........................[COLOR ARTIST]
VC's CORY PETIT.............................[LETTERER]
TOM MULLER.....................................[DESIGN]

MAHMUD ASRAR & MATTHEW WILSON...........[COVER ARTISTS]

BEN OLIVER.......................[VARIANT COVER ARTIST]

NICK RUSSELL...............................[PRODUCTION]

JONATHAN HICKMAN............................[HEAD OF X]
ANNALISE BISSA.......................[ASSISTANT EDITOR]
JORDAN D. WHITE................................[EDITOR]
C.B. CEBULSKI.........................[EDITOR IN CHIEF]

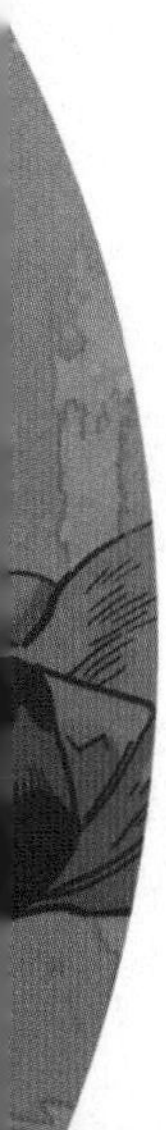

[07] EXCALIBUR

[ISSUE SEVEN]................VERSE VII:
......THE UNSPEAKABLE AND THE UNEATABLE

[00_so_below_X]
[00_as_above_X]

[00_00.....0]
[00_00.....7]

[00__fine___]
[00_day_____]

[00_for_a___]

[00___hunt__]

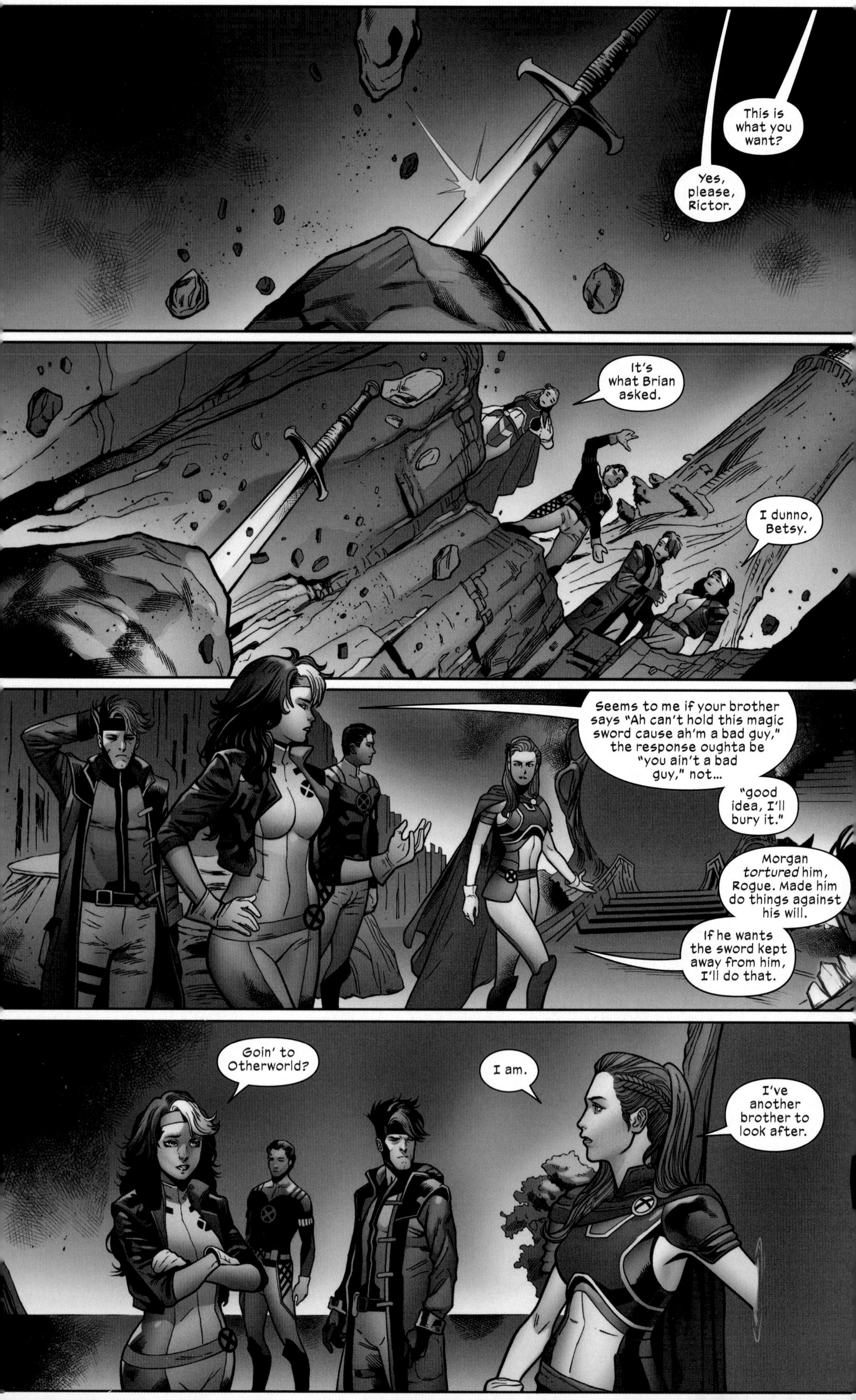
This is what you want?
Yes, please, Rictor.
It's what Brian asked.
I dunno, Betsy.
Seems to me if your brother says "Ah can't hold this magic sword cause ah'm a bad guy," the response oughta be "you ain't a bad guy," not...
"good idea, I'll bury it."
Morgan *tortured* him, Rogue. Made him do things against his will.
If he wants the sword kept away from him, I'll do that.
Goin' to Otherworld?
I am.
I've another brother to look after.

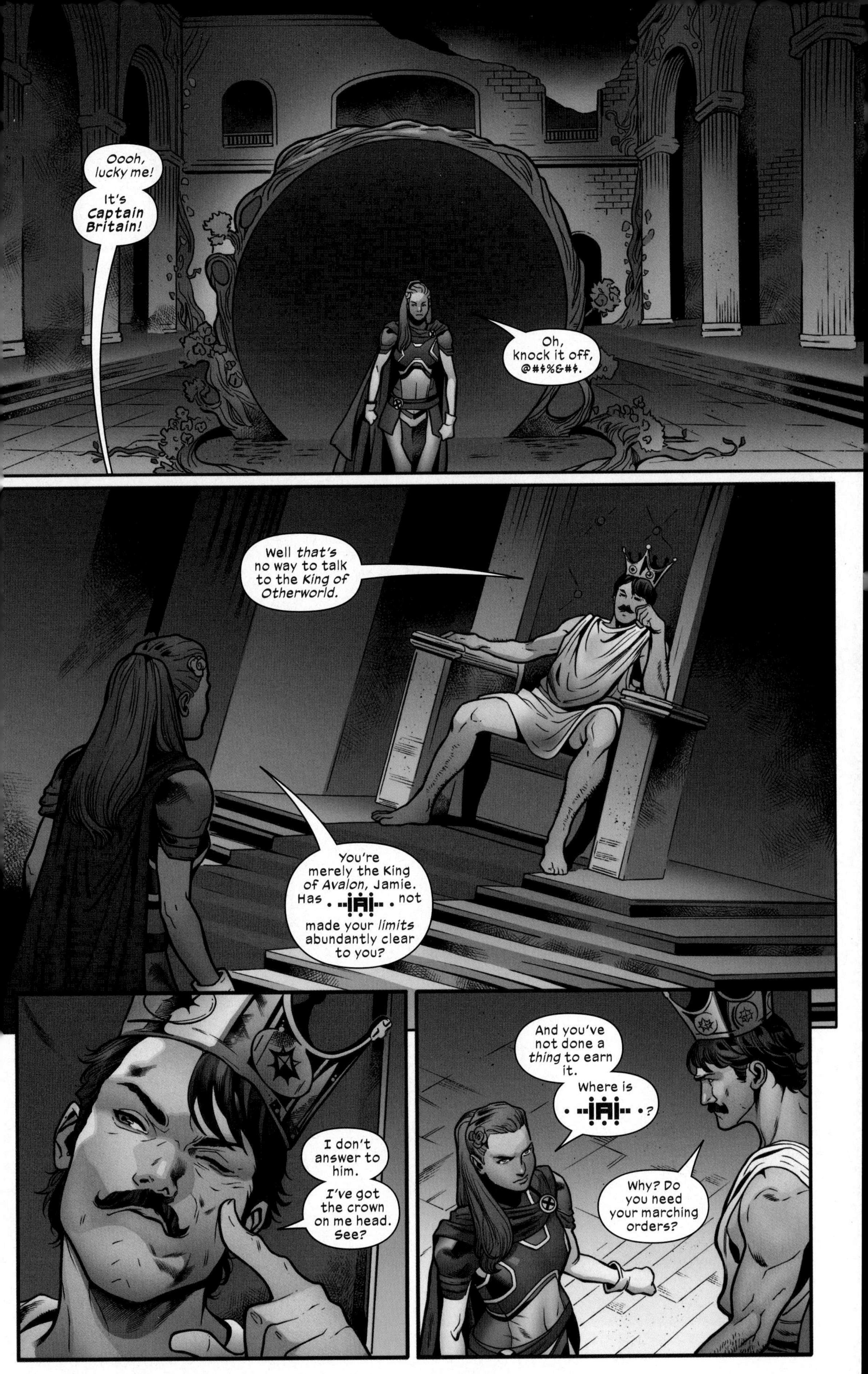
Oooh, lucky me!
It's Captain Britain!
Oh, knock it off, @#$%&#$.
Well that's no way to talk to the King of Otherworld.
You're merely the King of Avalon, Jamie. Has •-[glyph]-• not made your limits abundantly clear to you?
I don't answer to him.
I've got the crown on me head. See?
And you've not done a thing to earn it.
Where is •-[glyph]-•?
Why? Do you need your marching orders?

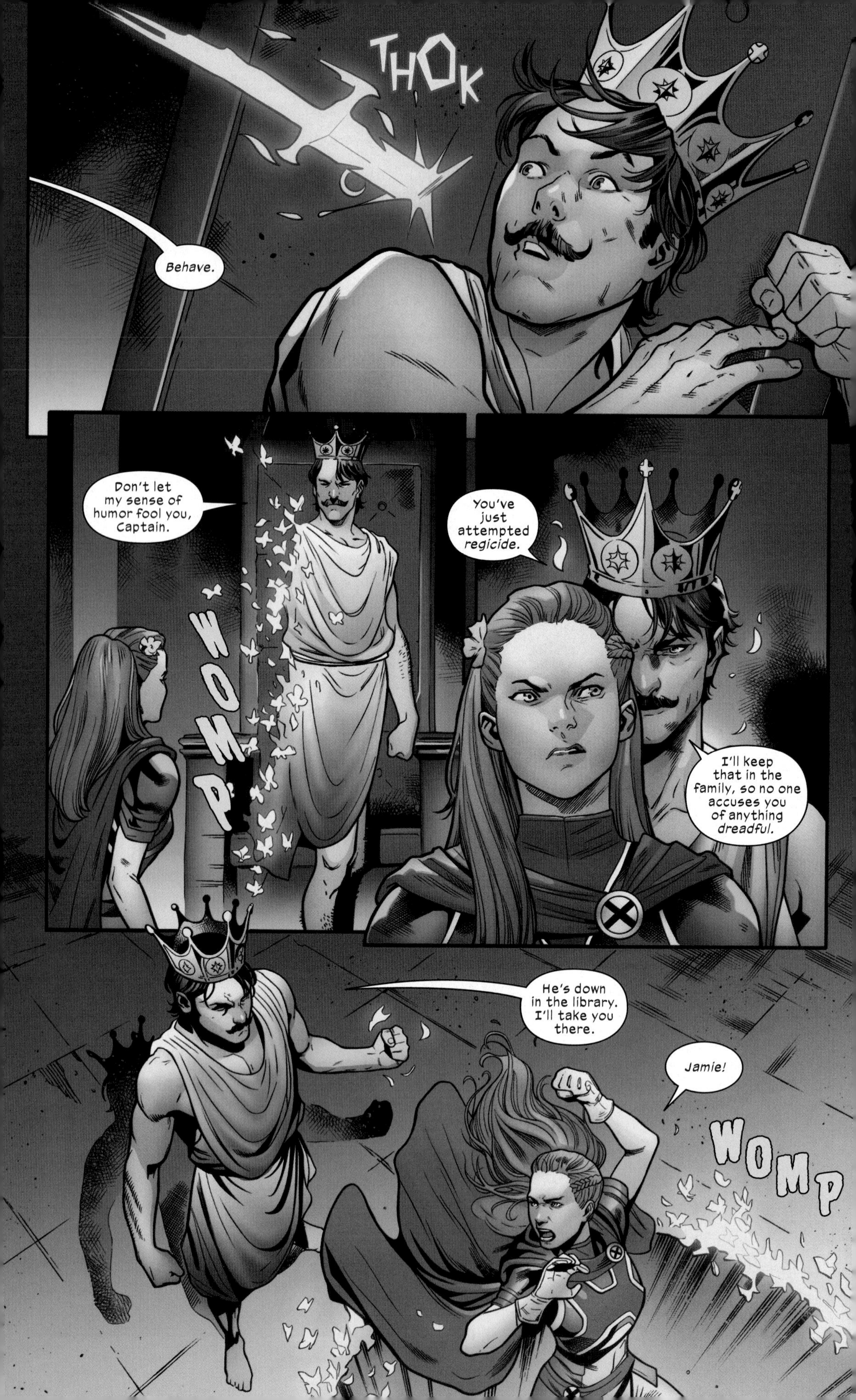
THOK
Behave.
Don't let my sense of humor fool you, Captain.
WOMP
You've just attempted *regicide*.
I'll keep that in the family, so no one accuses you of anything *dreadful*.
He's down in the library. I'll take you there.
Jamie!
WOMP

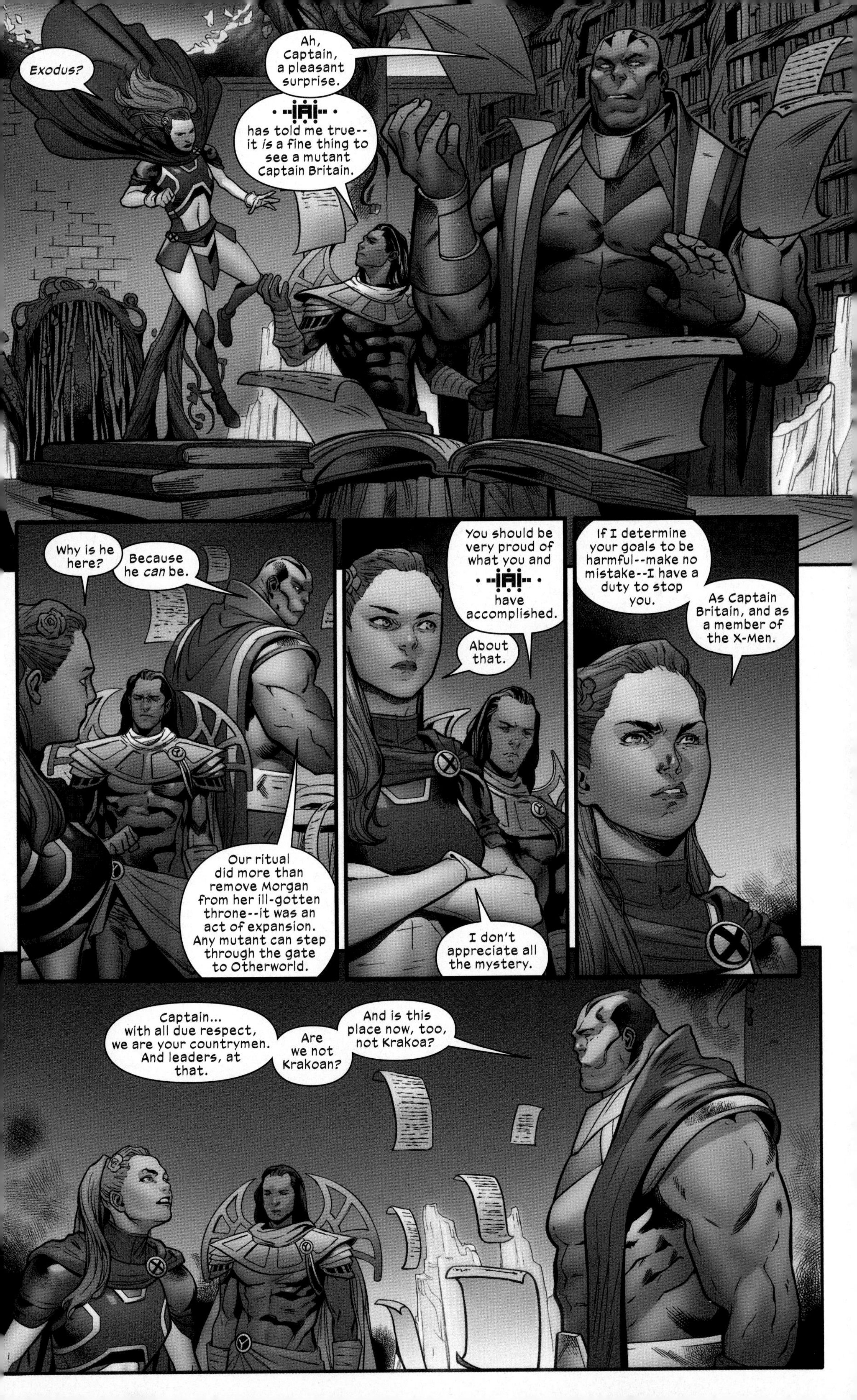
Exodus?
Ah, Captain, a pleasant surprise.
has told me true--it *is* a fine thing to see a mutant Captain Britain.
Why is he here?
Because he *can* be.
Our ritual did more than remove Morgan from her ill-gotten throne--it was an act of expansion. Any mutant can step through the gate to Otherworld.
You should be very proud of what you and
have accomplished.
About that.
I don't appreciate all the mystery.
If I determine your goals to be harmful--make no mistake--I have a duty to stop you.
As Captain Britain, and as a member of the X-Men.
Captain... with all due respect, we are your countrymen. And leaders, at that.
Are we not Krakoan?
And is this place now, too, not Krakoa?

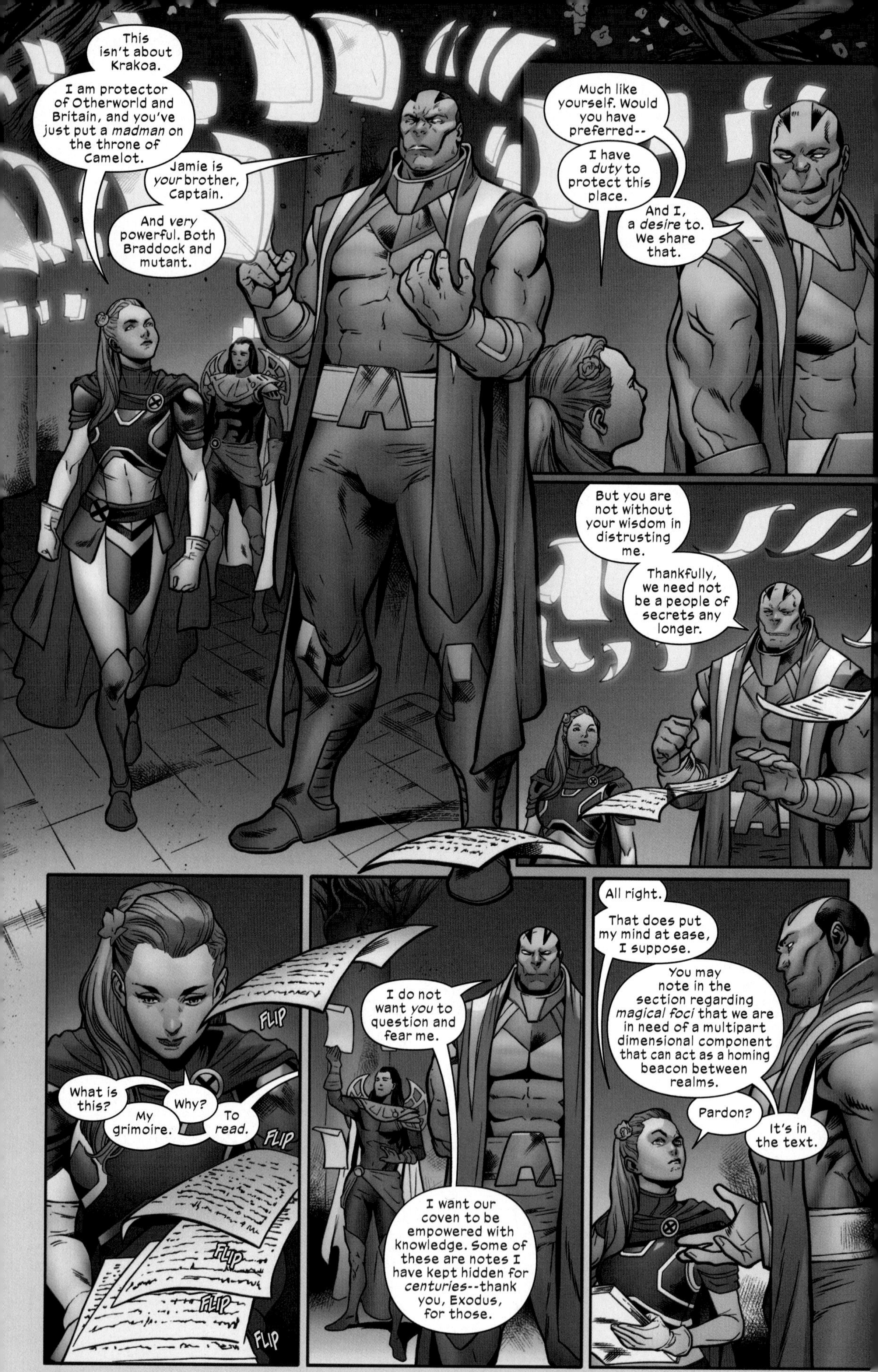
This isn't about Krakoa.
I am protector of Otherworld and Britain, and you've just put a madman on the throne of Camelot.
Jamie is your brother, Captain.
And very powerful. Both Braddock and mutant.
Much like yourself. Would you have preferred--
I have a duty to protect this place.
And I, a desire to. We share that.
But you are not without your wisdom in distrusting me.
Thankfully, we need not be a people of secrets any longer.
FLIP
What is this?
Why?
My grimoire.
To read.
FLIP
FLIP
FLIP
FLIP
I do not want you to question and fear me.
I want our coven to be empowered with knowledge. Some of these are notes I have kept hidden for centuries--thank you, Exodus, for those.
All right.
That does put my mind at ease, I suppose.
You may note in the section regarding magical foci that we are in need of a multipart dimensional component that can act as a homing beacon between realms.
Pardon?
It's in the text.

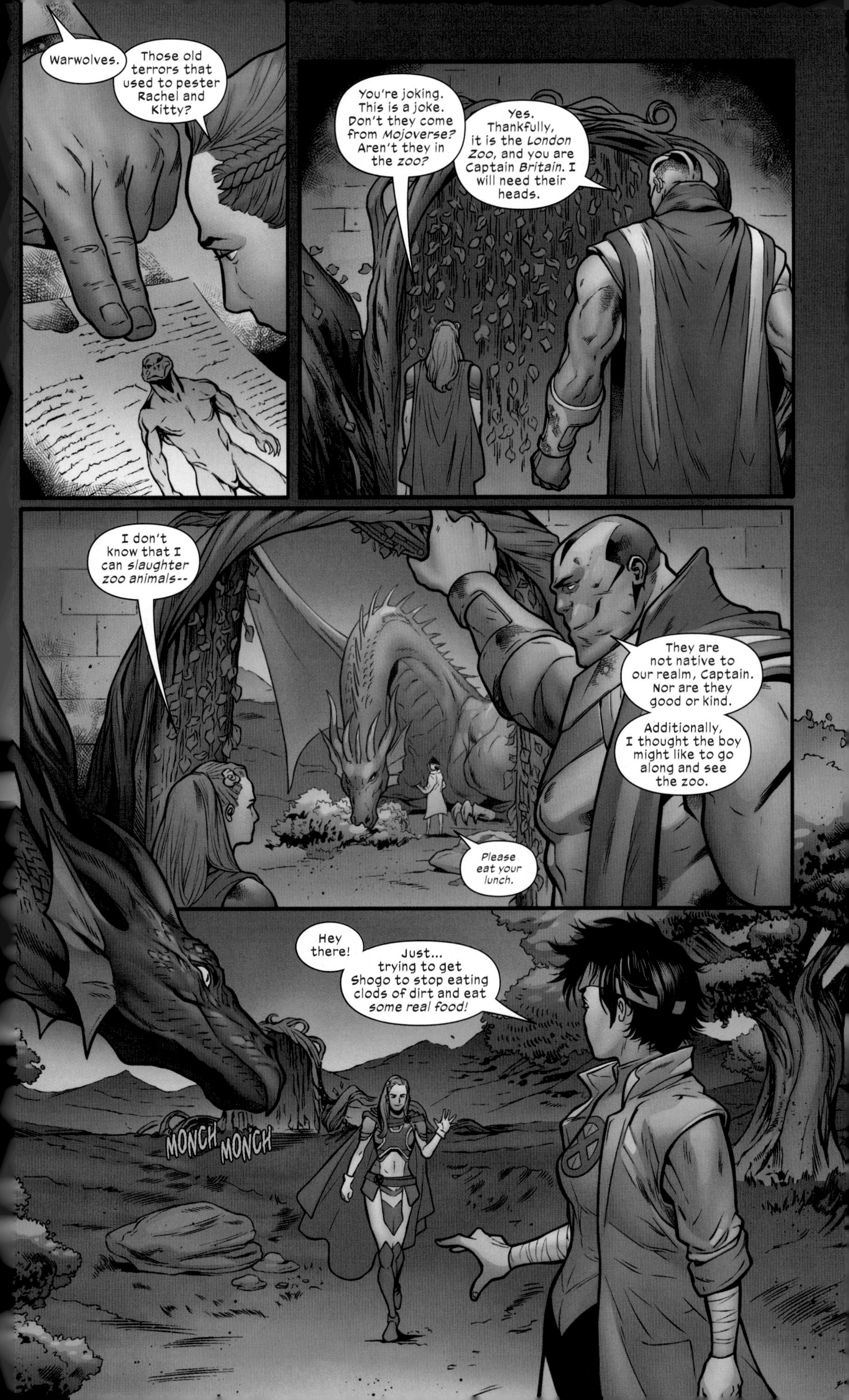

Warwolves.
Those old terrors that used to pester Rachel and Kitty?
You're joking. This is a joke. Don't they come from Mojoverse? Aren't they in the zoo?
Yes. Thankfully, it is the London Zoo, and you are Captain Britain. I will need their heads.
I don't know that I can slaughter zoo animals--
They are not native to our realm, Captain. Nor are they good or kind.
Additionally, I thought the boy might like to go along and see the zoo.
Please eat your lunch.
Hey there!
Just... trying to get Shogo to stop eating clods of dirt and eat some real food!
MONCH MONCH

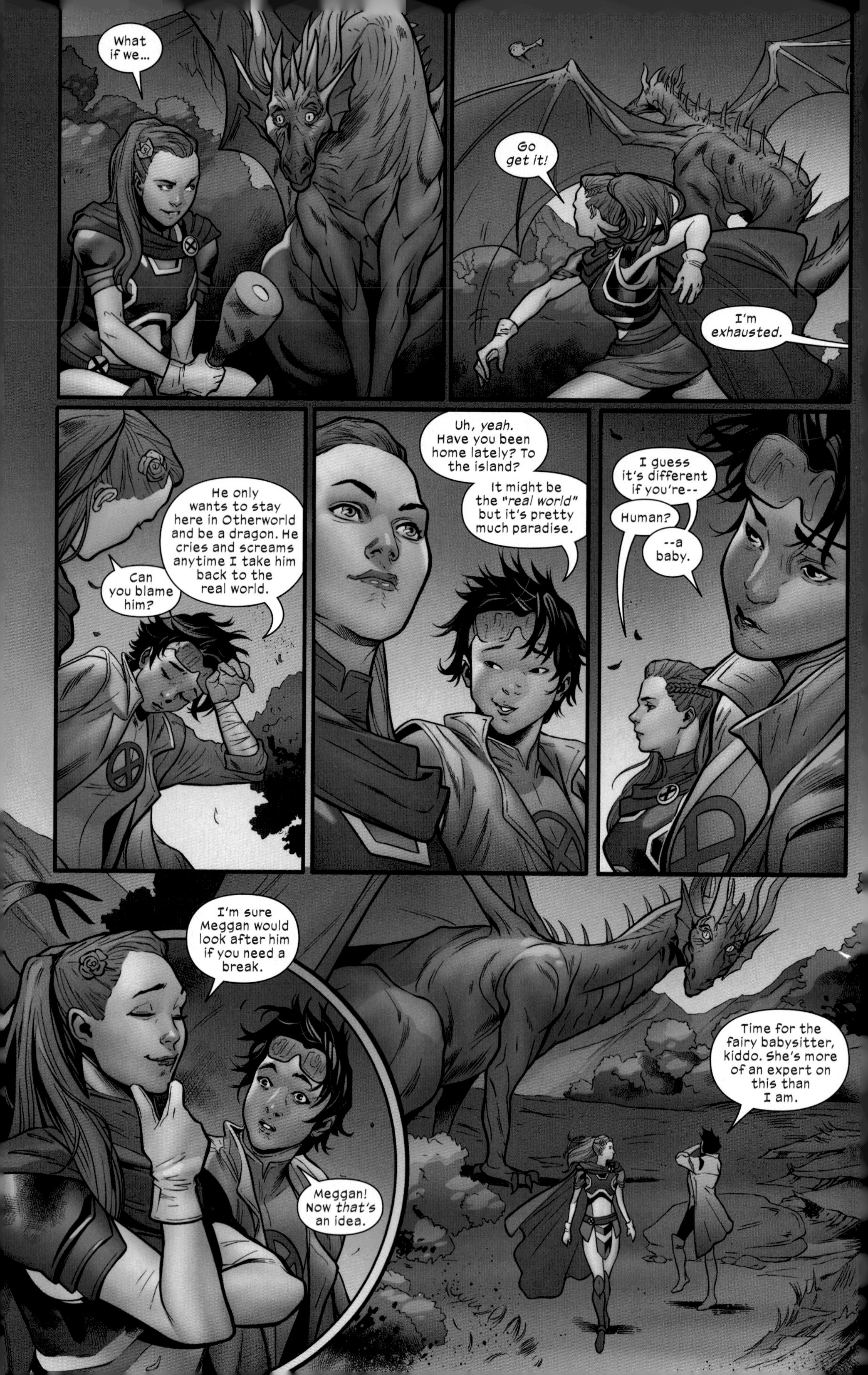
What if we...
Go get it!
I'm exhausted.
He only wants to stay here in Otherworld and be a dragon. He cries and screams anytime I take him back to the real world.
Can you blame him?
Uh, yeah. Have you been home lately? To the island?
It might be the "real world" but it's pretty much paradise.
I guess it's different if you're--
Human?
--a baby.
I'm sure Meggan would look after him if you need a break.
Meggan! Now that's an idea.
Time for the fairy babysitter, kiddo. She's more of an expert on this than I am.

FROM THE GRIMOIRE OF

EX MAGICA: BESTIARY (Fig. 23)

WARWOLF -

Otherdimensional predator species - Genus unknown.

Once an elevated species hailing from , recent research suggests a decline in the supernatural faculties of these hybrids. A cross between humanoid and lupine, attempts were made by *Homo sapiens* to socialize and appeal to their more humanoid nature during the beasts' tenure in the London Zoo.

These amateur and somewhat mocking socialization attempts succeeded in a marked regression among the warwolves, appearing to diminish their faculties for shapeshifting, speech, and other signs of higher intelligence to incidental and reactionary at best.

Like most species, they become more violent, animalistic, and harmful under the guidance of *Homo sapiens*, losing the abilities that once made them unique.

The otherdimensional nature of their flesh is a potentially powerful conduit. [see: *EX MAGICA: ALMANAC* fig 1.]

Numbers: 5 (in captivity)

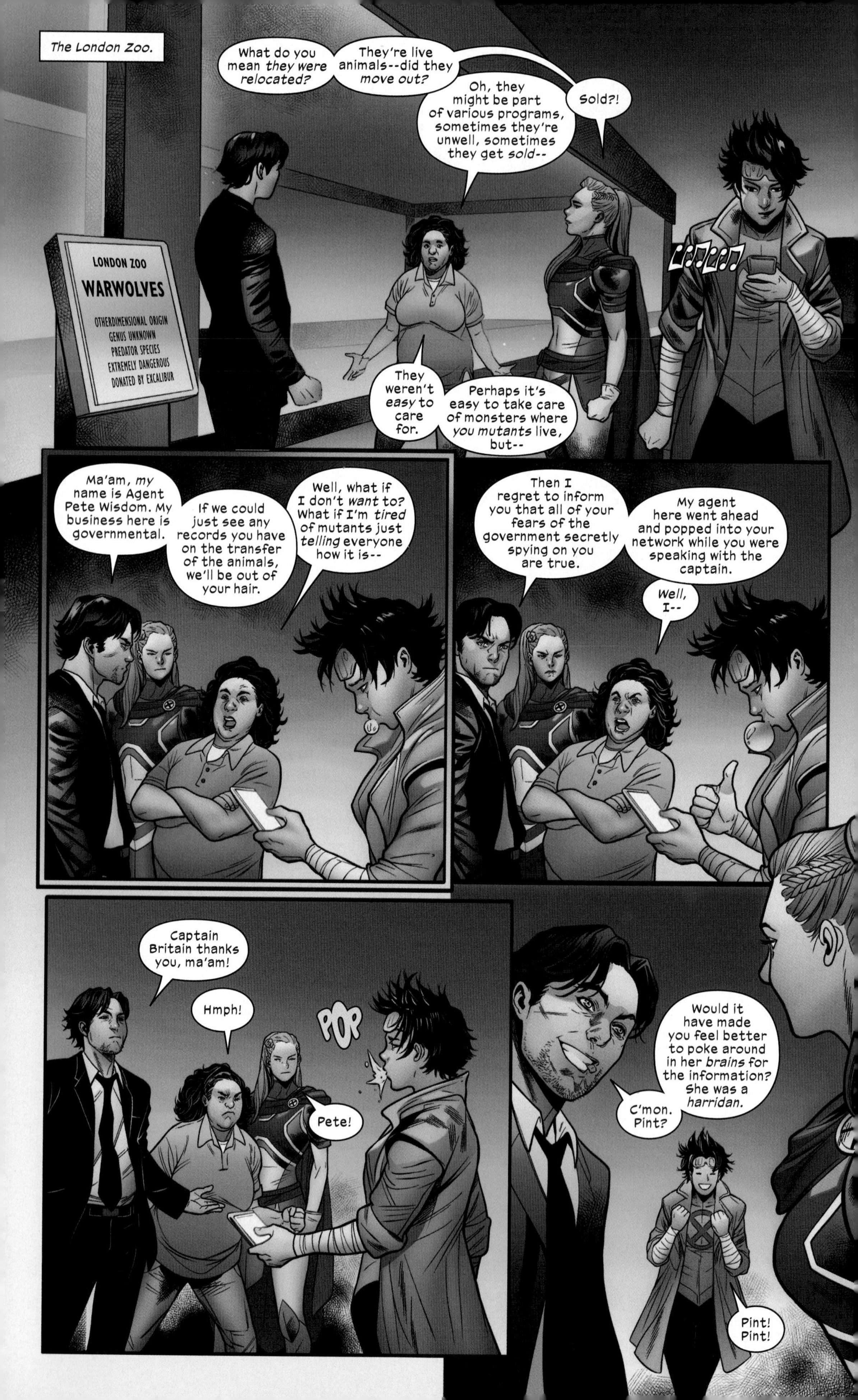
The London Zoo.
What do you mean they were relocated?
They're live animals--did they move out?
Oh, they might be part of various programs, sometimes they're unwell, sometimes they get sold--
Sold?!
LONDON ZOO
WARWOLVES
OTHERDIMENSIONAL ORIGIN
GENUS UNKNOWN
PREDATOR SPECIES
EXTREMELY DANGEROUS
DONATED BY EXCALIBUR
They weren't easy to care for.
Perhaps it's easy to take care of monsters where you mutants live, but--
Ma'am, my name is Agent Pete Wisdom. My business here is governmental.
If we could just see any records you have on the transfer of the animals, we'll be out of your hair.
Well, what if I don't want to? What if I'm tired of mutants just telling everyone how it is--
Then I regret to inform you that all of your fears of the government secretly spying on you are true.
My agent here went ahead and popped into your network while you were speaking with the captain.
Well, I--
Captain Britain thanks you, ma'am!
Hmph!
POP
Pete!
Would it have made you feel better to poke around in her brains for the information? She was a harridan.
C'mon. Pint?
Pint! Pint!

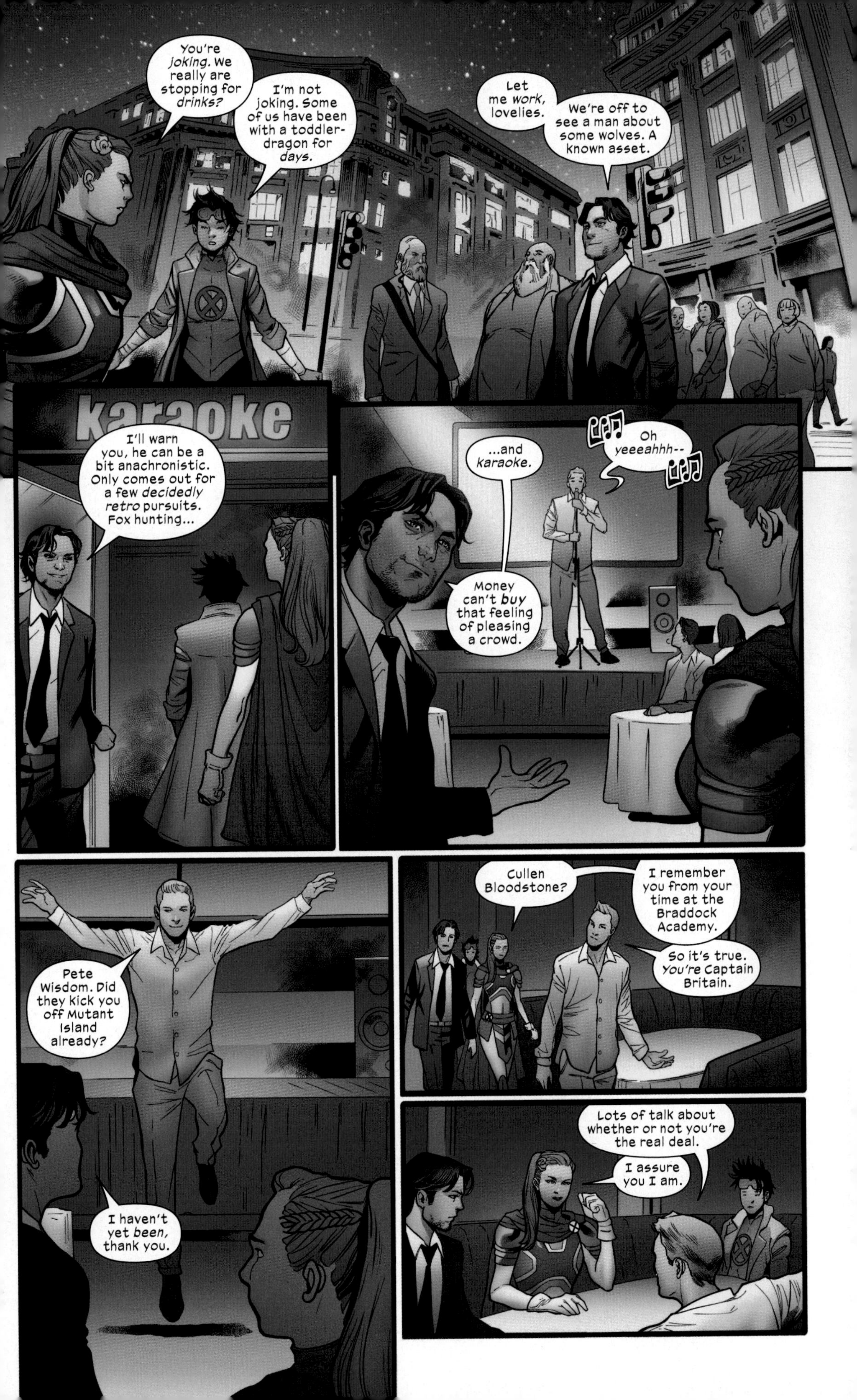
You're joking. We really are stopping for drinks?
I'm not joking. Some of us have been with a toddler-dragon for days.
Let me work, lovelies.
We're off to see a man about some wolves. A known asset.
karaoke
I'll warn you, he can be a bit anachronistic. Only comes out for a few decidedly retro pursuits. Fox hunting...
...and karaoke.
Oh yeeeahhh--
Money can't buy that feeling of pleasing a crowd.
Pete Wisdom. Did they kick you off Mutant Island already?
I haven't yet been, thank you.
Cullen Bloodstone?
I remember you from your time at the Braddock Academy.
So it's true. You're Captain Britain.
Lots of talk about whether or not you're the real deal.
I assure you I am.

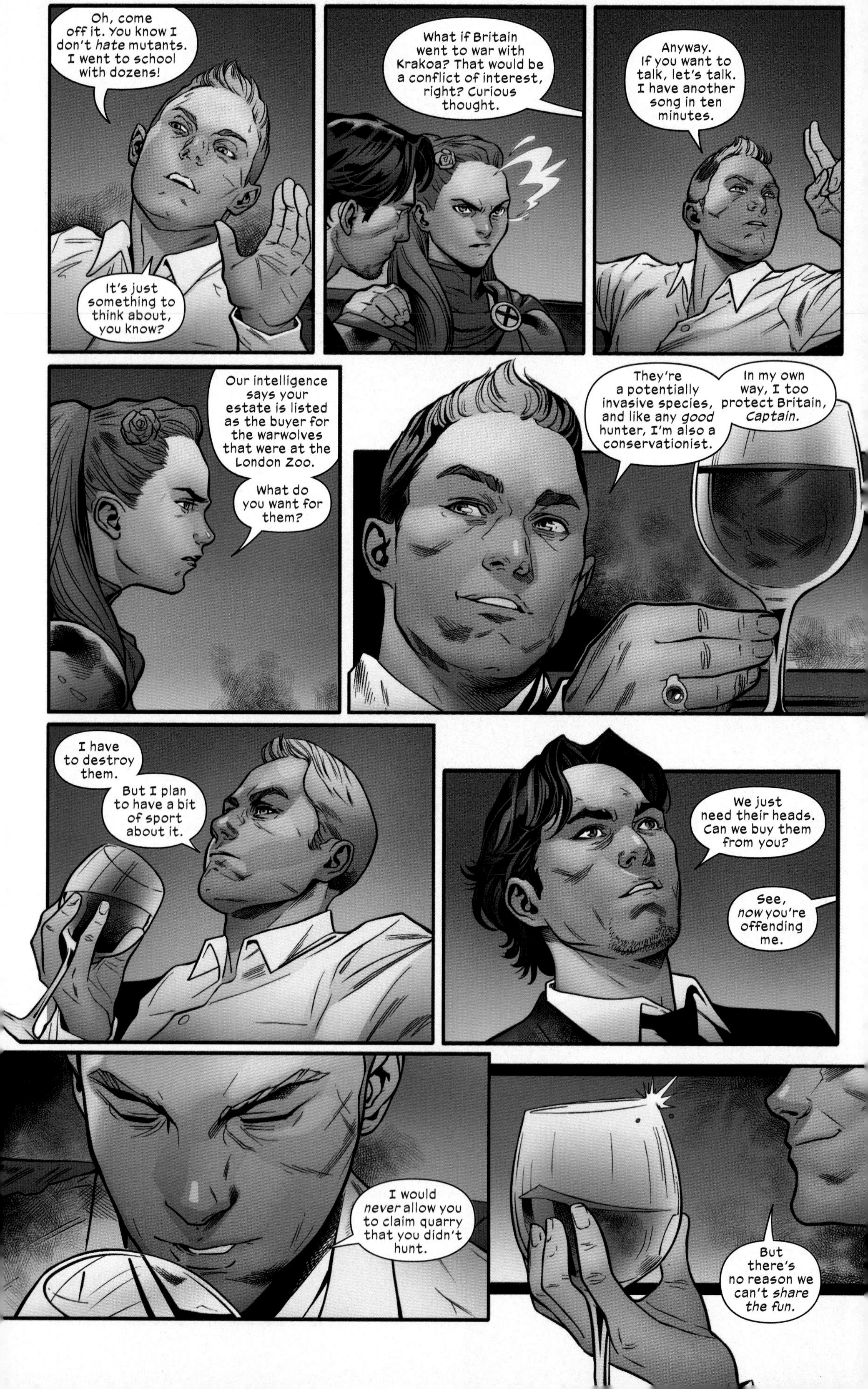

Oh, come off it. You know I don't *hate* mutants. I went to school with dozens!
It's just something to think about, you know?
What if Britain went to war with Krakoa? That would be a conflict of interest, right? Curious thought.
Anyway. If you want to talk, let's talk. I have another song in ten minutes.
Our intelligence says your estate is listed as the buyer for the warwolves that were at the London Zoo.
What do you want for them?
They're a potentially invasive species, and like any *good* hunter, I'm also a conservationist.
In my own way, I too protect Britain, *Captain.*
I have to destroy them.
But I plan to have a bit of sport about it.
We just need their heads. Can we buy them from you?
See, *now* you're offending me.
I would *never* allow you to claim quarry that you didn't hunt.
But there's no reason we can't *share* the fun.

The **Bloodstone Summer Lodge and Preserve**
cordially requests the pleasure of your company at

A Warwolf Hunt

Rules of Engagement:

· NO GATES OR KRAKOAN FLORA OF ANY
KIND ARE PERMITTED ON THE
BLOODSTONE PRESERVE

· SPORTSMANSHIP IS REQUIRED

· YOUR HOST DOES NOT TAKE KINDLY
TO UNFAIR GAMES

Champagne reception at sundown following
the first evening's activities.

Attire: Cape Casual

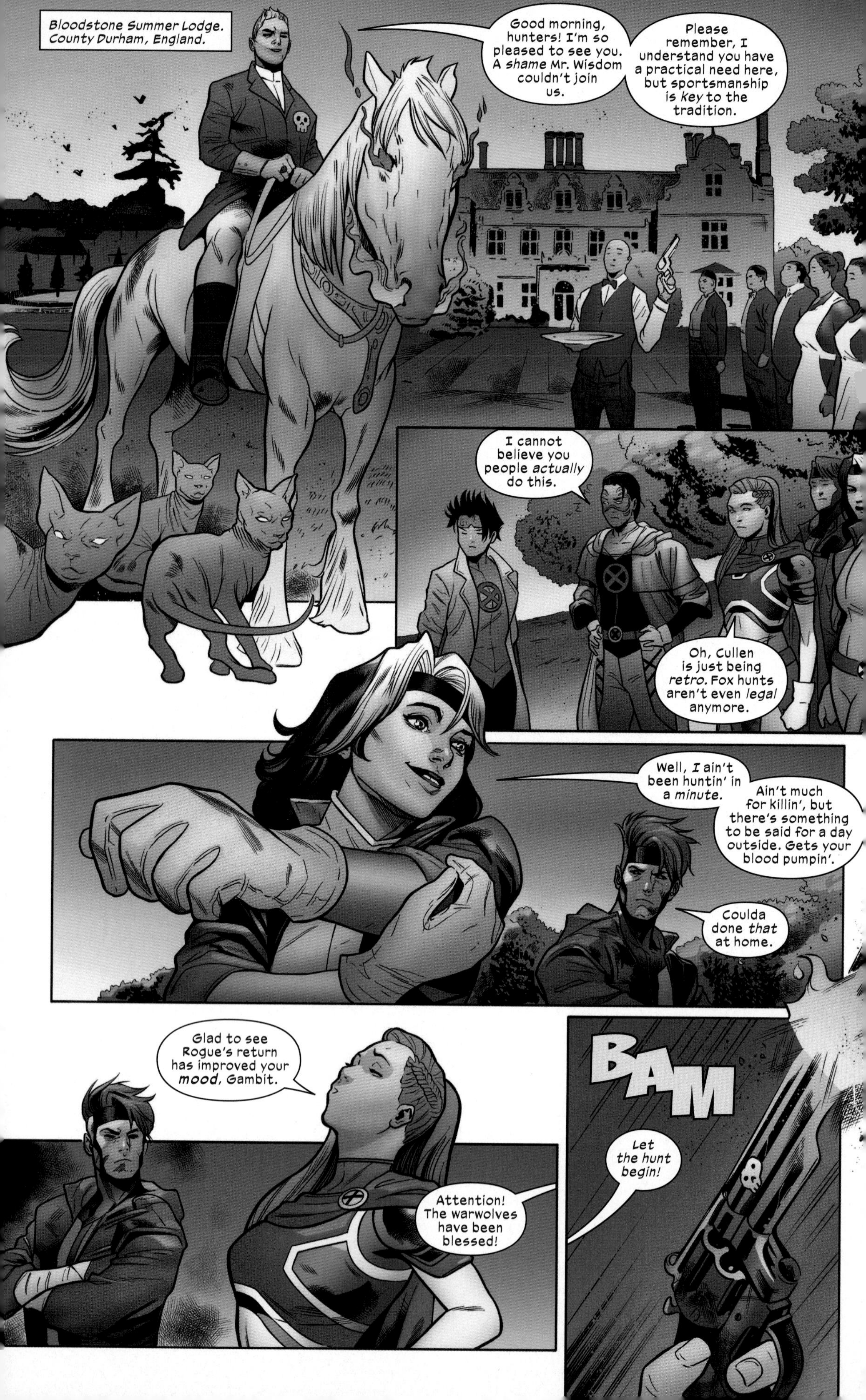
Bloodstone Summer Lodge. County Durham, England.
Good morning, hunters! I'm so pleased to see you. A *shame* Mr. Wisdom couldn't join us.
Please remember, I understand you have a practical need here, but sportsmanship is *key* to the tradition.
I cannot believe you people *actually* do this.
Oh, Cullen is just being *retro*. Fox hunts aren't even *legal* anymore.
Well, *I* ain't been huntin' in a *minute*.
Ain't much for killin', but there's something to be said for a day outside. Gets your blood pumpin'.
Coulda done *that* at home.
Glad to see Rogue's return has improved your *mood*, Gambit.
Attention! The warwolves have been blessed!
BAM
Let the hunt begin!

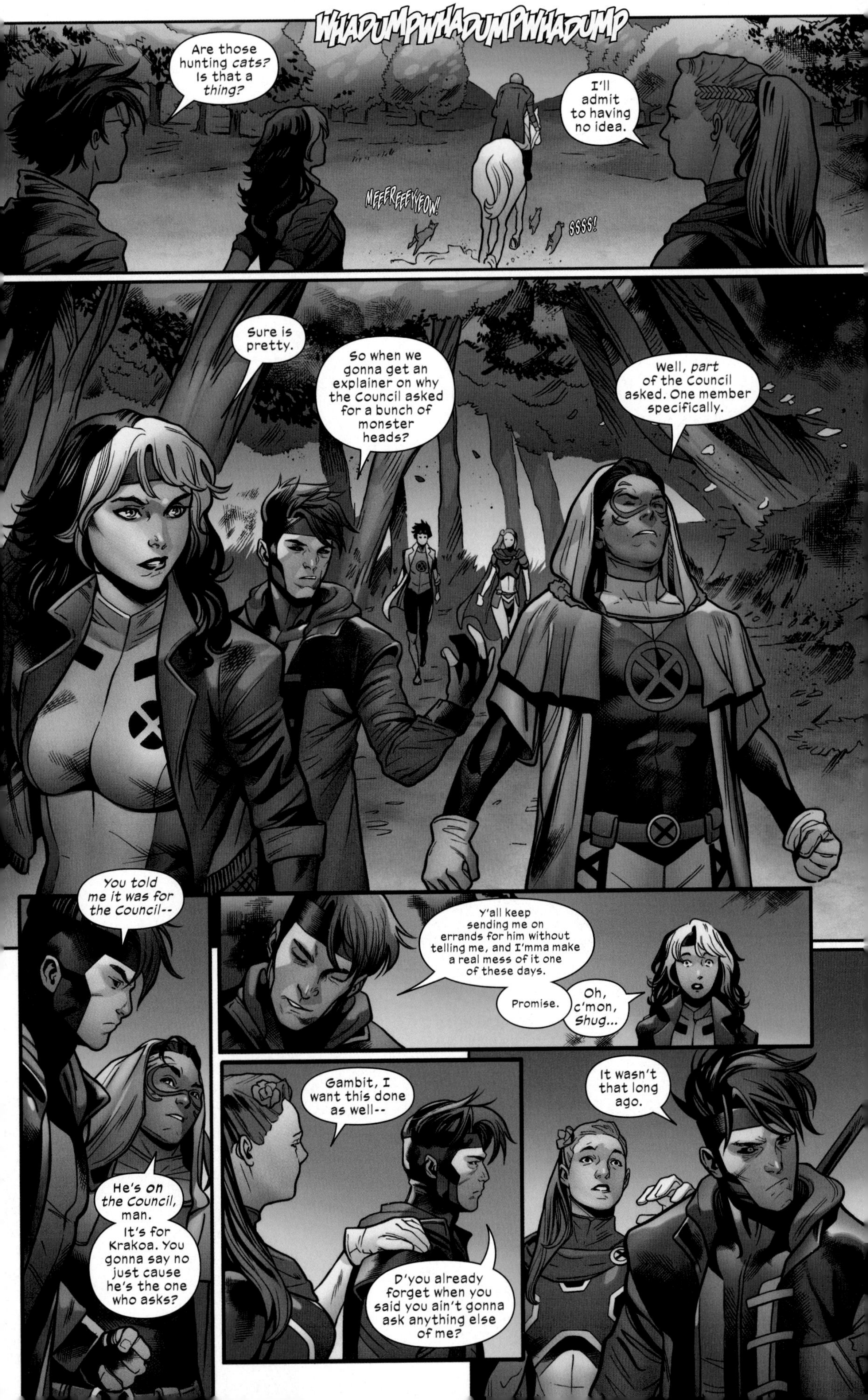
WHADUMPWHADUMPWHADUMP
Are those hunting cats? Is that a thing?
I'll admit to having no idea.
MEEERREEEYYEOW!
SSSS!
Sure is pretty.
So when we gonna get an explainer on why the Council asked for a bunch of monster heads?
Well, part of the Council asked. One member specifically.
You told me it was for the Council--
He's on the Council, man.
It's for Krakoa. You gonna say no just cause he's the one who asks?
Y'all keep sending me on errands for him without telling me, and I'mma make a real mess of it one of these days.
Promise.
Oh, c'mon, Shug...
Gambit, I want this done as well--
D'you already forget when you said you ain't gonna ask anything else of me?
It wasn't that long ago.

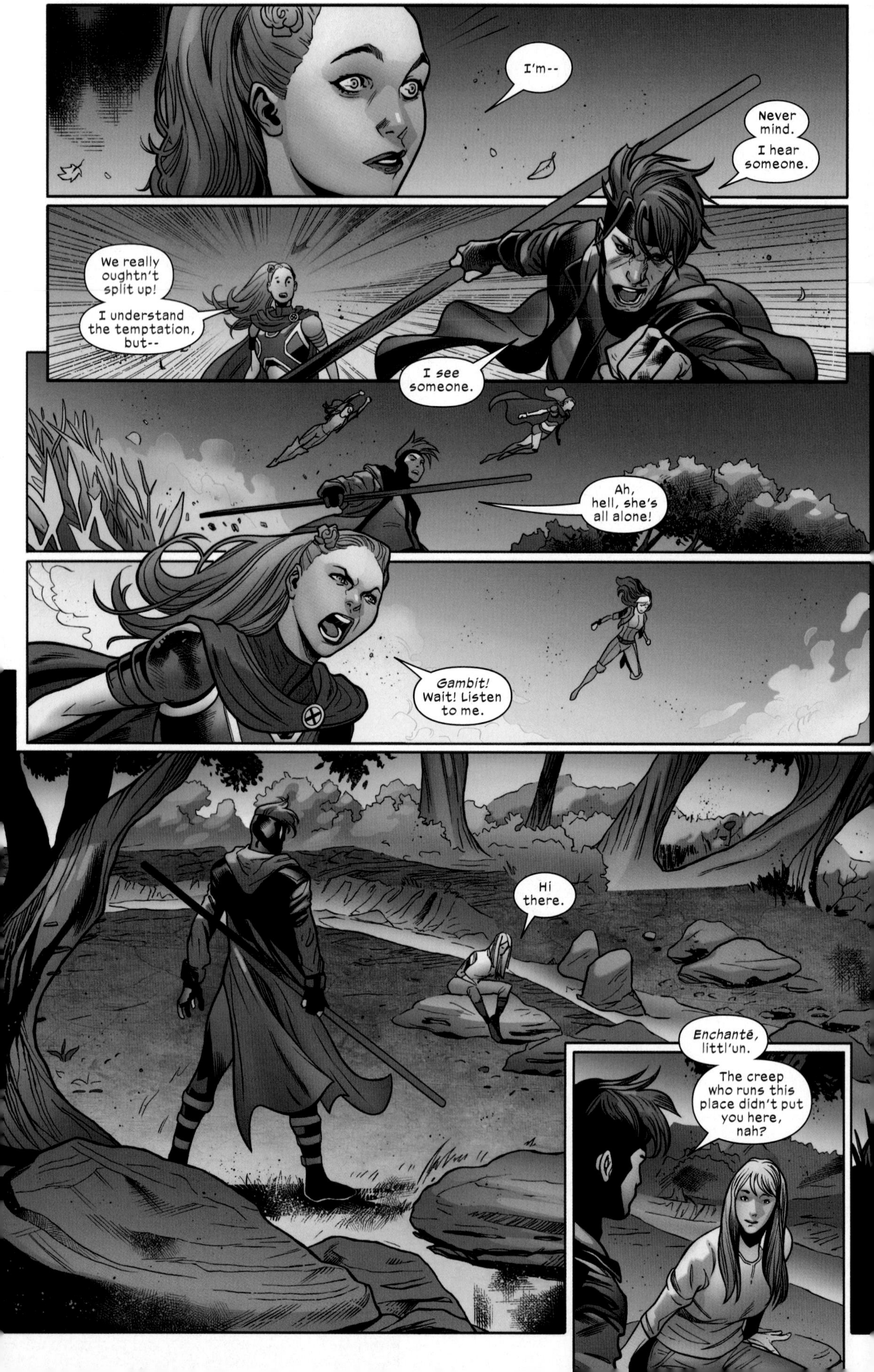
I'm--
Never mind.
I hear someone.
We really oughtn't split up!
I understand the temptation, but--
I see someone.
Ah, hell, she's all alone!
Gambit! Wait! Listen to me.
Hi there.
Enchanté, littl'un.
The creep who runs this place didn't put you here, nah?

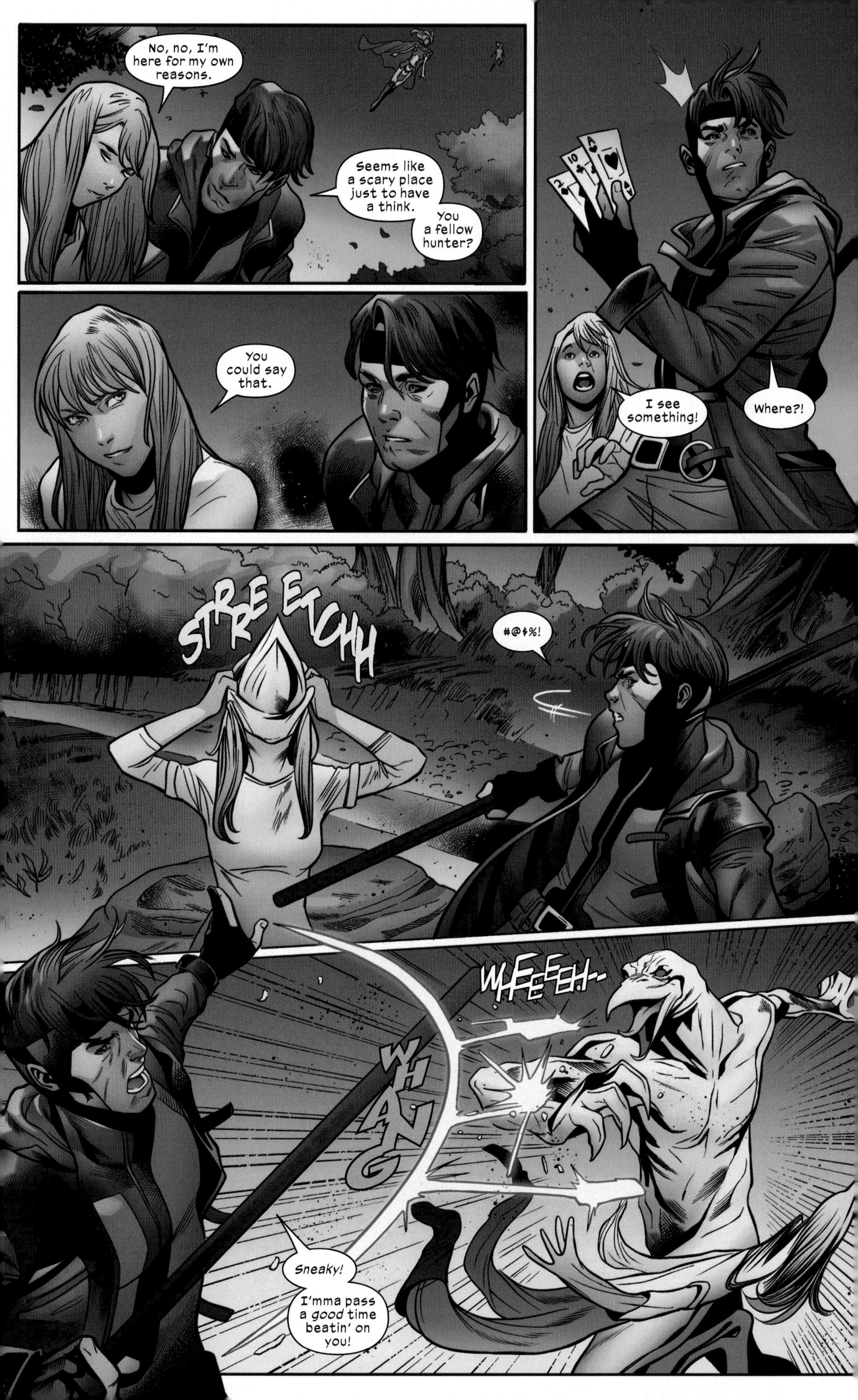

No, no, I'm here for my own reasons.
Seems like a scary place just to have a think.
You a fellow hunter?
You could say that.
I see something!
Where?!
STRREETCHH
#@$%!
WHEEEH--
WHANG
Sneaky!
I'mma pass a *good* time beatin' on you!

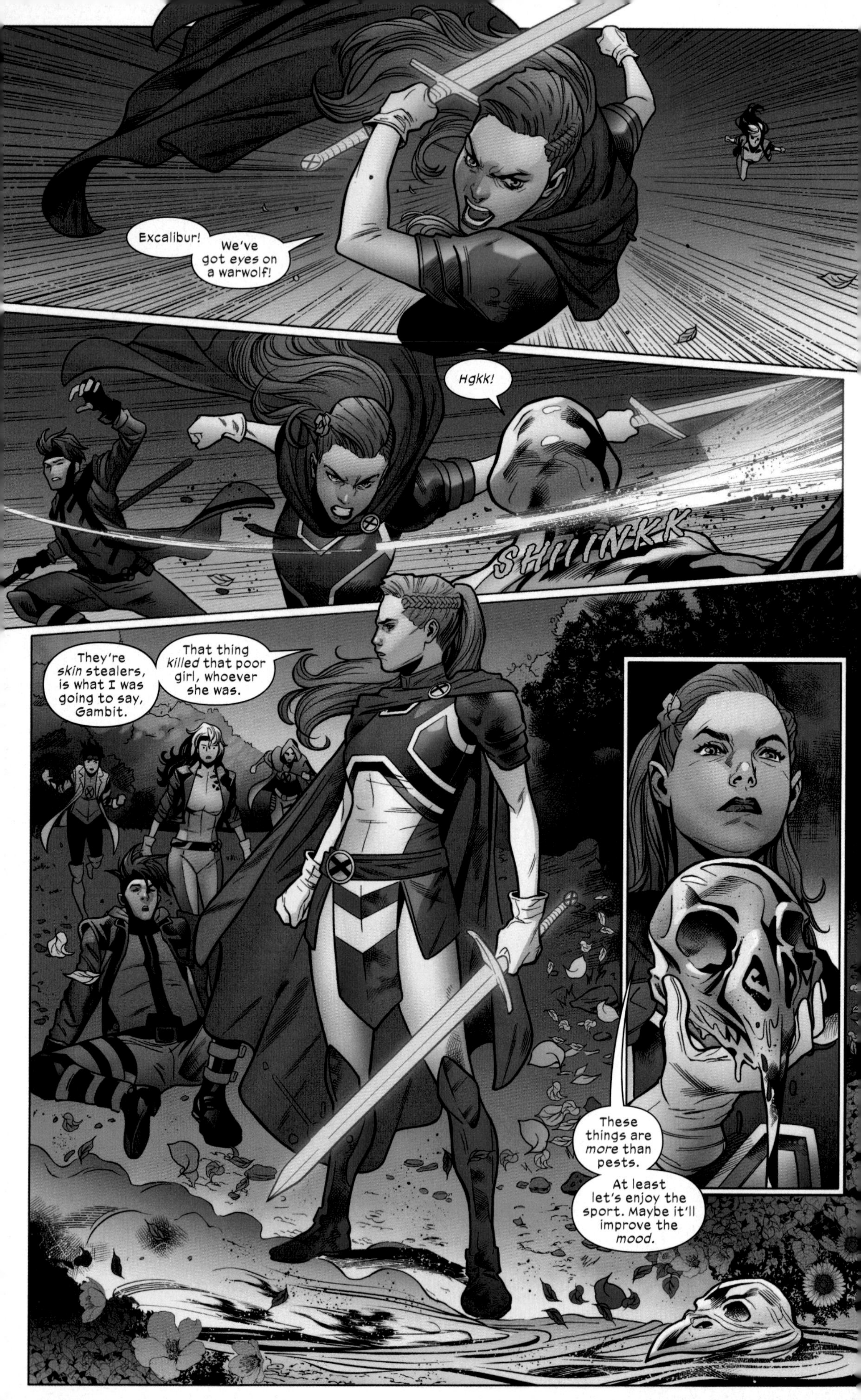

Excalibur!
We've got eyes on a warwolf!
Hgkk!
SHIIINKK
They're skin stealers, is what I was going to say, Gambit.
That thing killed that poor girl, whoever she was.
These things are more than pests.
At least let's enjoy the sport. Maybe it'll improve the mood.

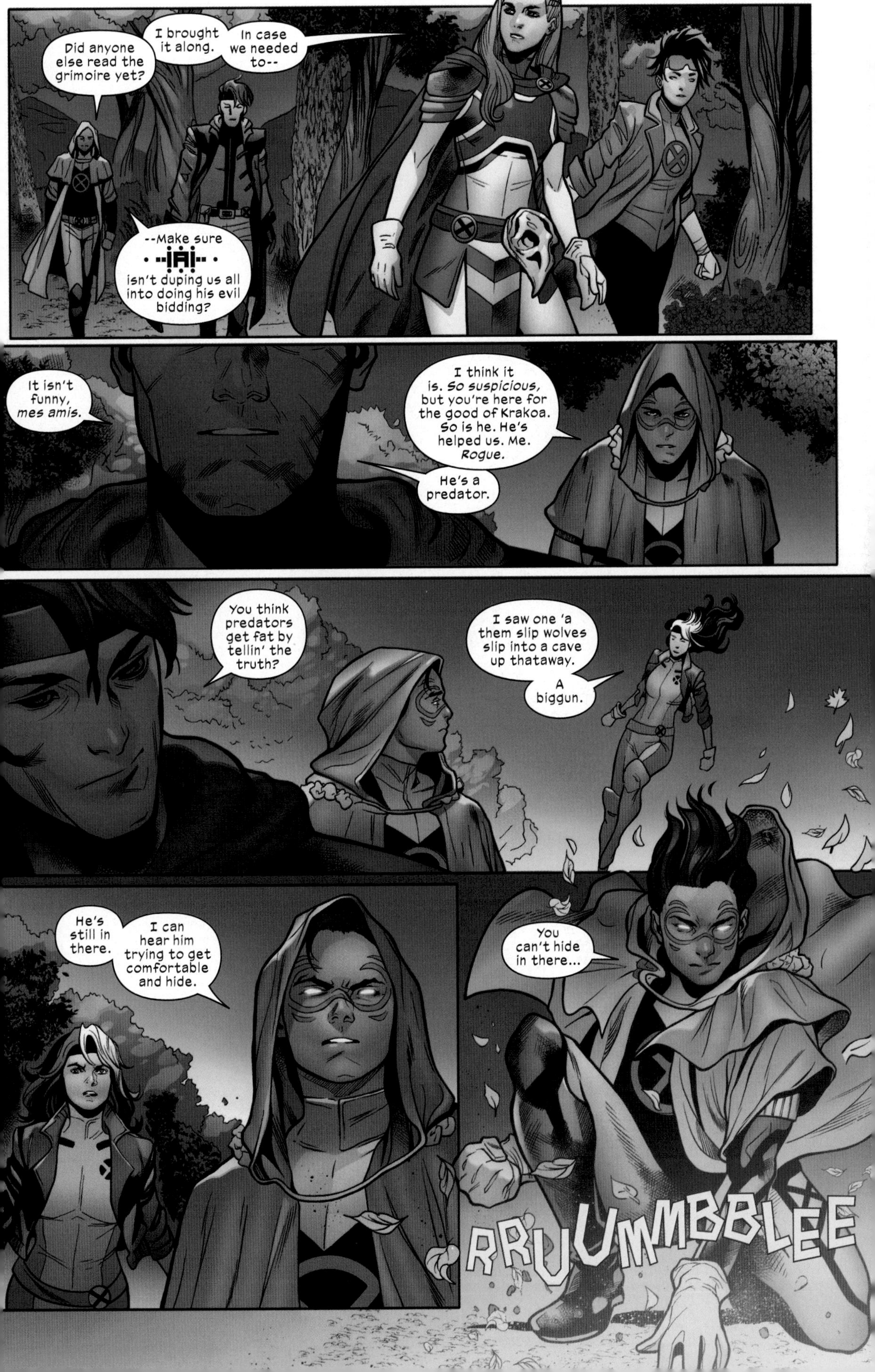
Did anyone else read the grimoire yet?
I brought it along.
In case we needed to--
--Make sure
isn't duping us all into doing his evil bidding?
It isn't funny, *mes amis.*
I think it is. *So suspicious,* but you're here for the good of Krakoa. So is he. He's helped us. Me. *Rogue.*
He's a predator.
You think predators get fat by tellin' the truth?
I saw one 'a them slip wolves slip into a cave up thataway.
A biggun.
He's still in there.
I can hear him trying to get comfortable and hide.
You can't hide in there...
RRUUMMBBLEE

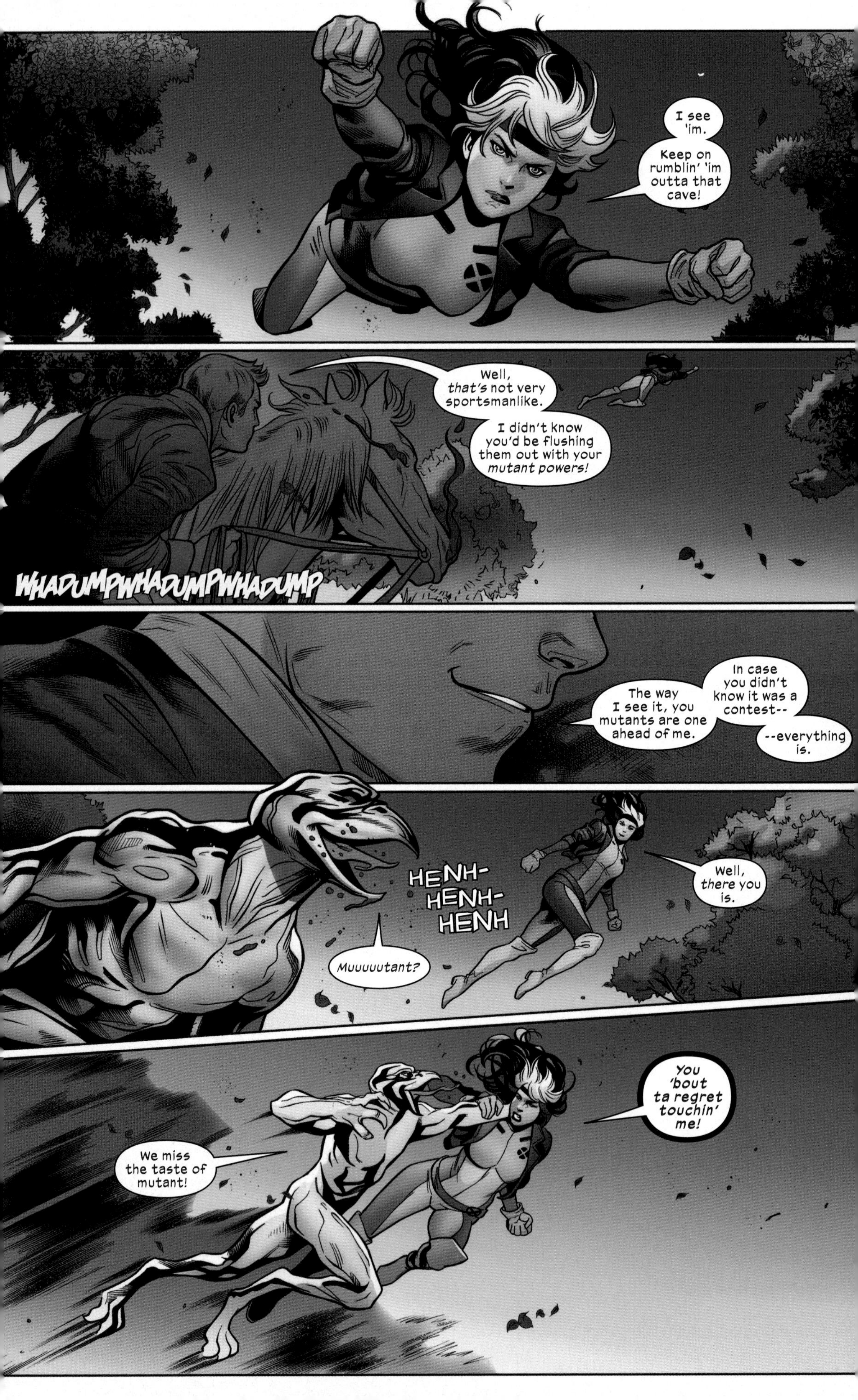
I see 'im.
Keep on rumblin' 'im outta that cave!
Well, *that's* not very sportsmanlike.
I didn't know you'd be flushing them out with your *mutant powers!*
WHADUMPWHADUMPWHADUMP
The way I see it, you mutants are one ahead of me.
In case you didn't know it was a contest--
--everything is.
HENH-HENH-HENH
Muuuuutant?
Well, *there* you is.
You 'bout ta regret touchin' me!
We miss the taste of mutant!

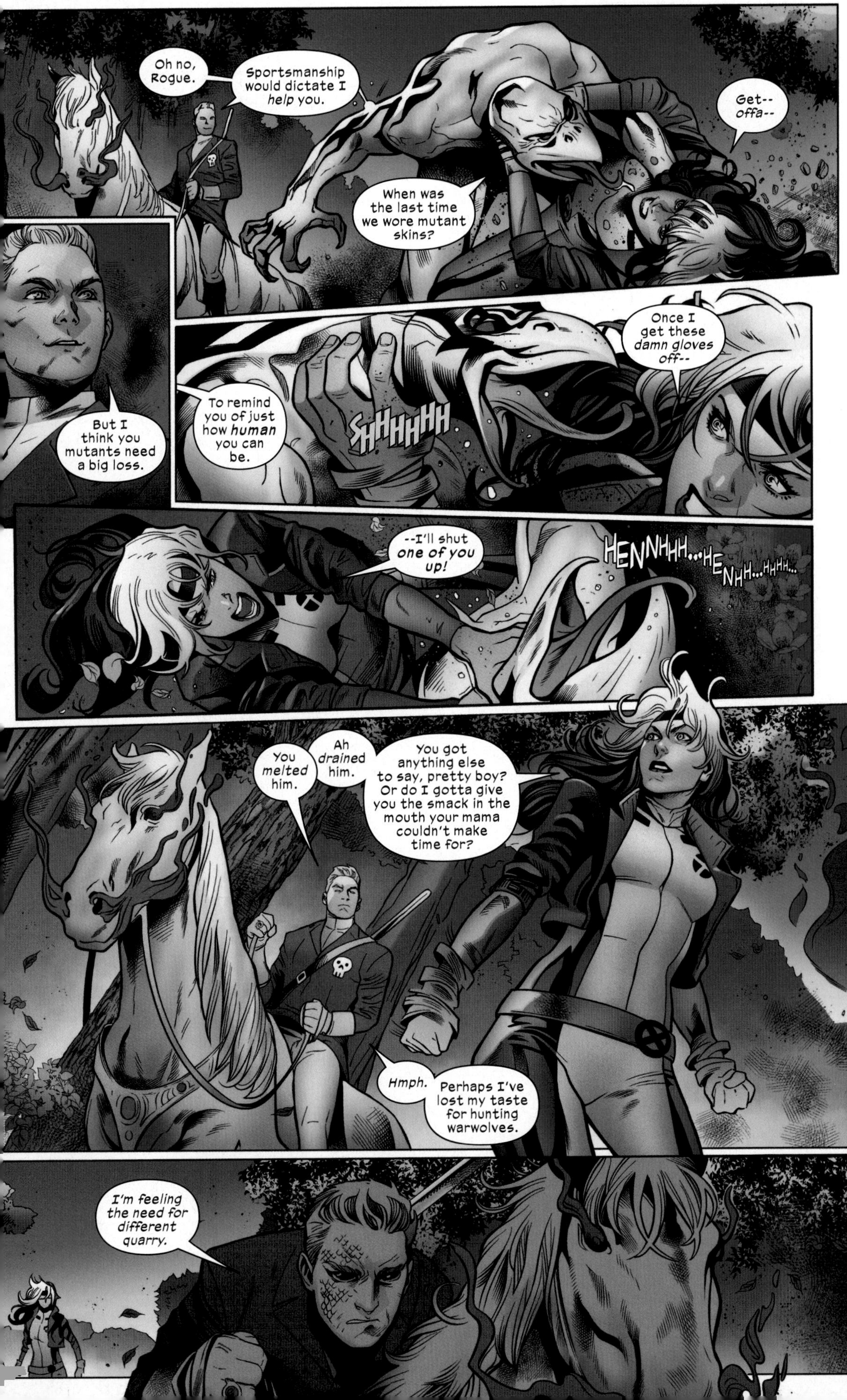
Oh no, Rogue.
Sportsmanship would dictate I *help* you.
Get-- offa--
When was the last time we wore mutant skins?
But I think you mutants need a big loss.
To remind you of just how *human* you can be.
Once I get these *damn gloves off--*
SHHHHHH
--I'll shut *one of you up!*
HENNHHH...HENHH...HHHH...
You *melted* him.
Ah *drained* him.
You got anything else to say, pretty boy? Or do I gotta give you the smack in the mouth your mama couldn't make time for?
Hmph.
Perhaps I've lost my taste for hunting warwolves.
I'm feeling the need for different quarry.

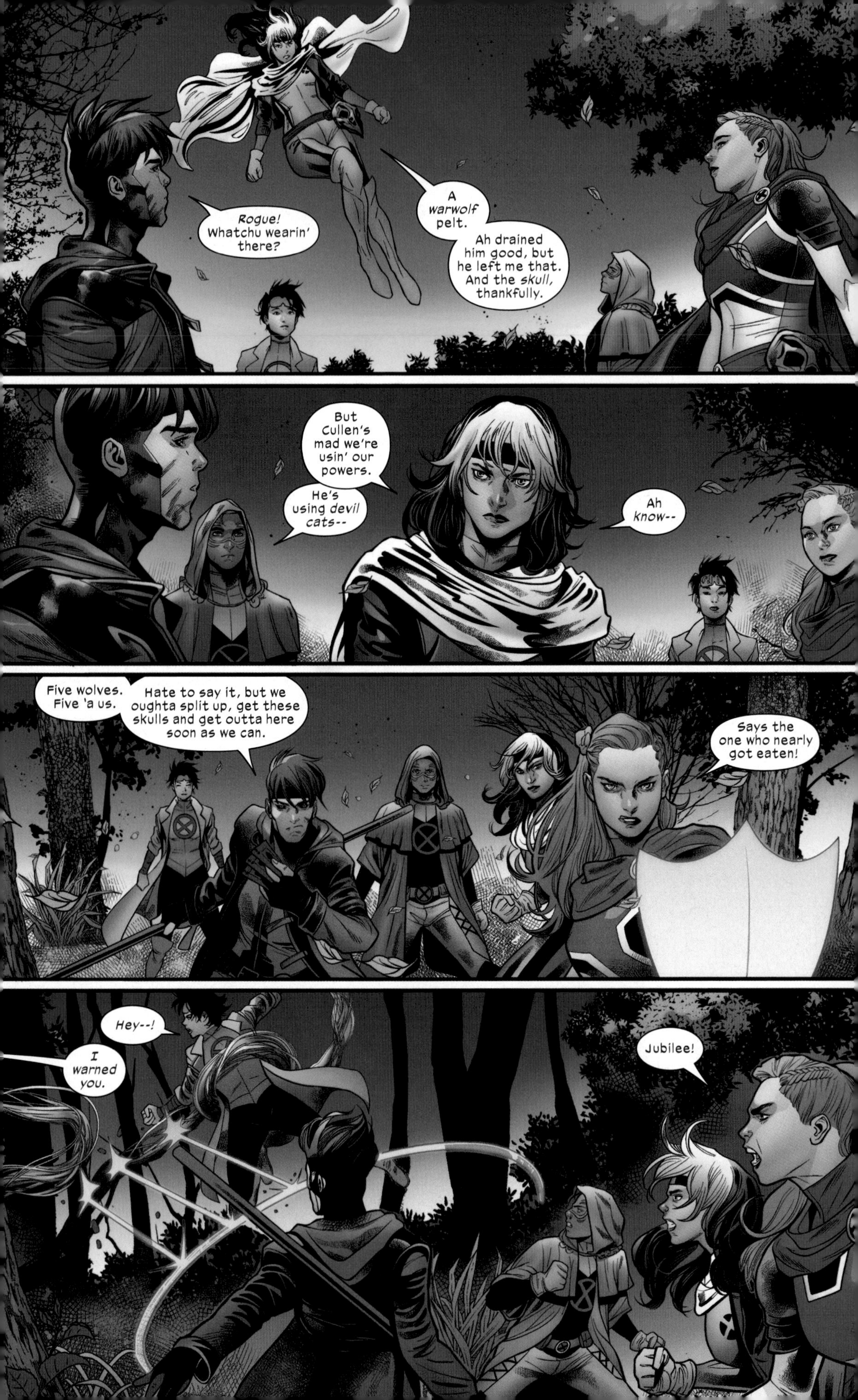
Rogue! Whatchu wearin' there?
A warwolf pelt.
Ah drained him good, but he left me that. And the skull, thankfully.
But Cullen's mad we're usin' our powers.
He's using devil cats--
Ah know--
Five wolves. Five 'a us.
Hate to say it, but we oughta split up, get these skulls and get outta here soon as we can.
Says the one who nearly got eaten!
Hey--!
I warned you.
Jubilee!

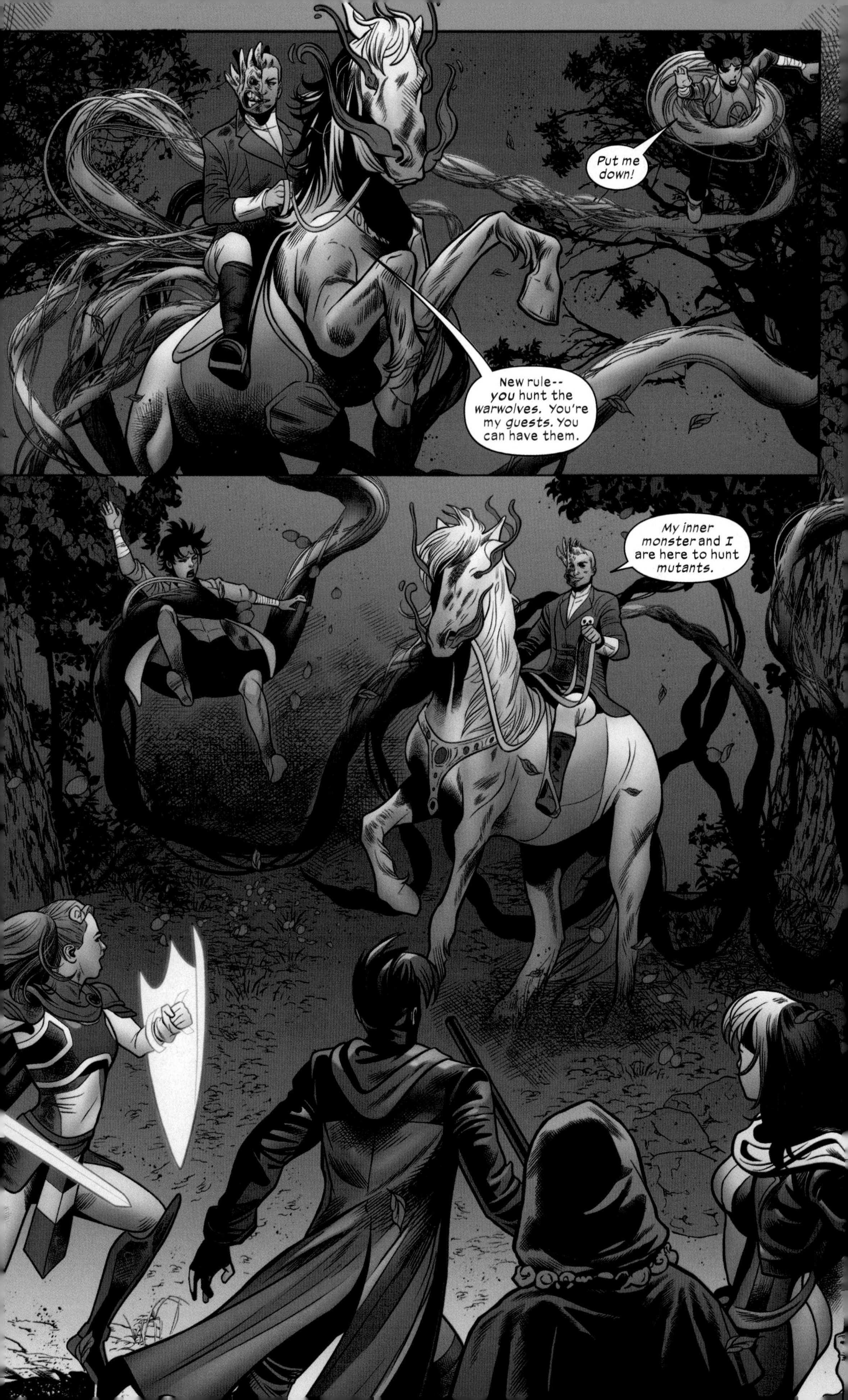
Put me down!
New rule-- you hunt the warwolves. You're my guests. You can have them.
My inner monster and I are here to hunt mutants.

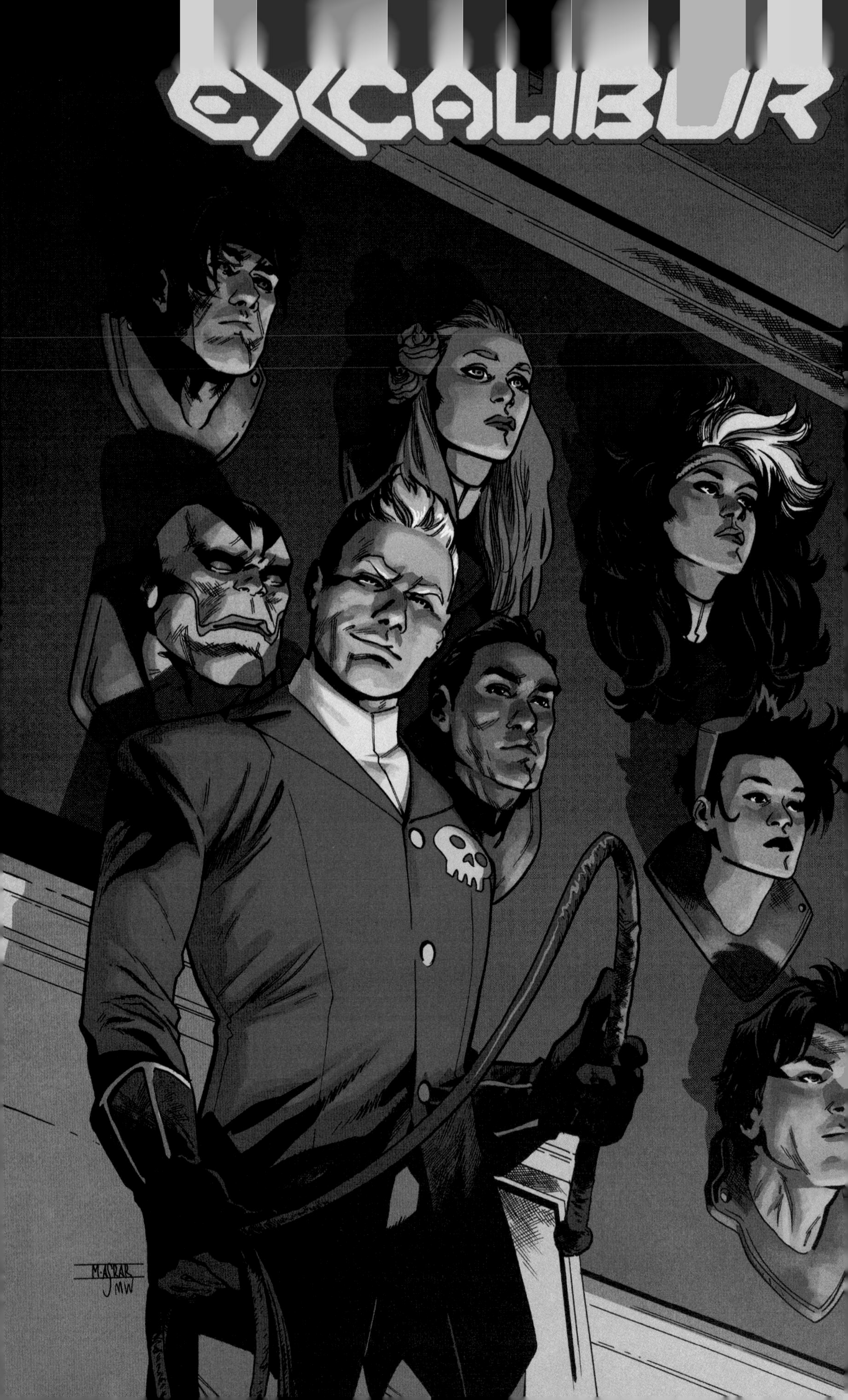
EXCALIBUR
M. ASRAR
MW

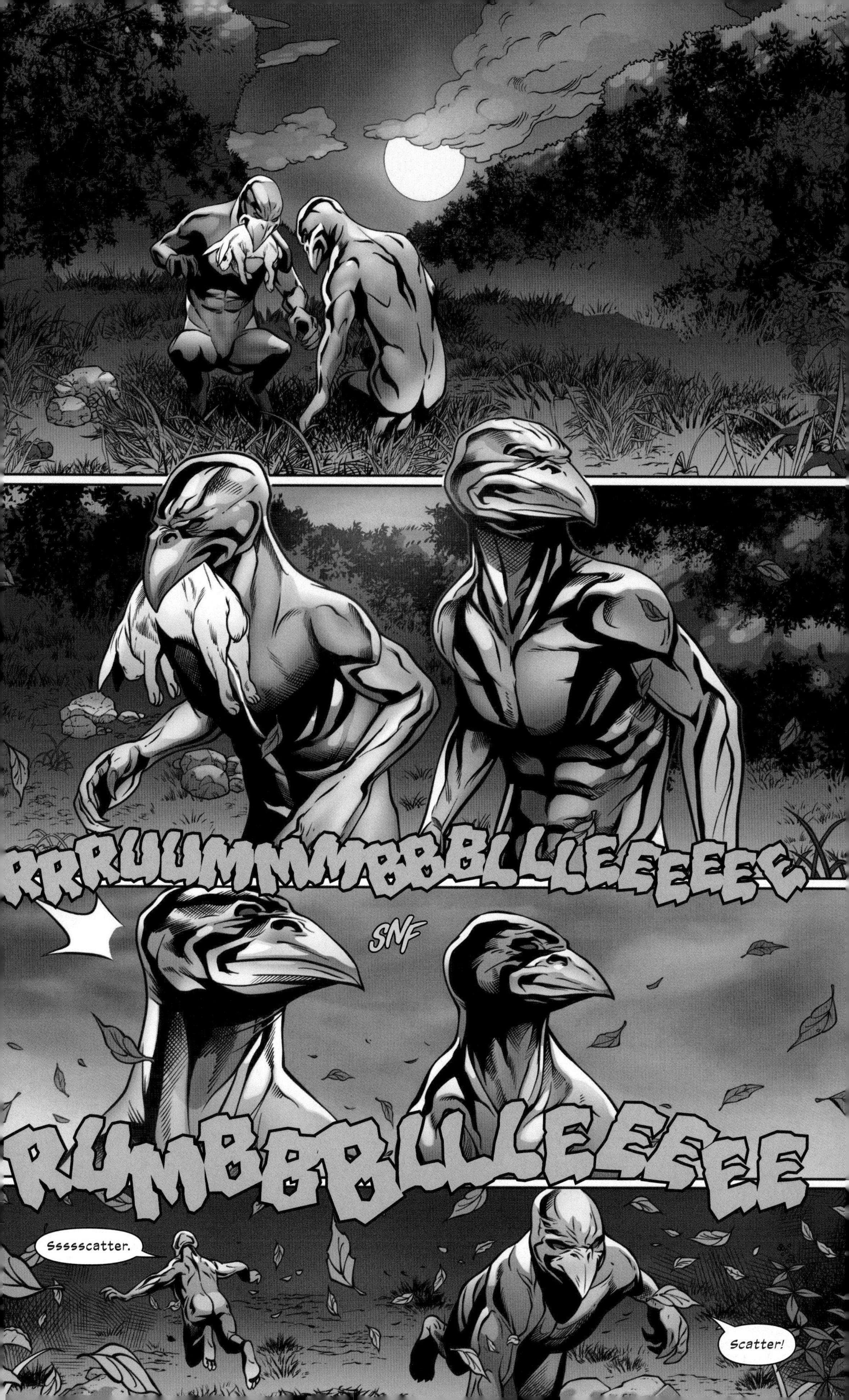
RRRUUMMMMBBBLLLEEEEEE
SNF
RUMBBBLLLEEEEE
Ssssscatter.
Scatter!

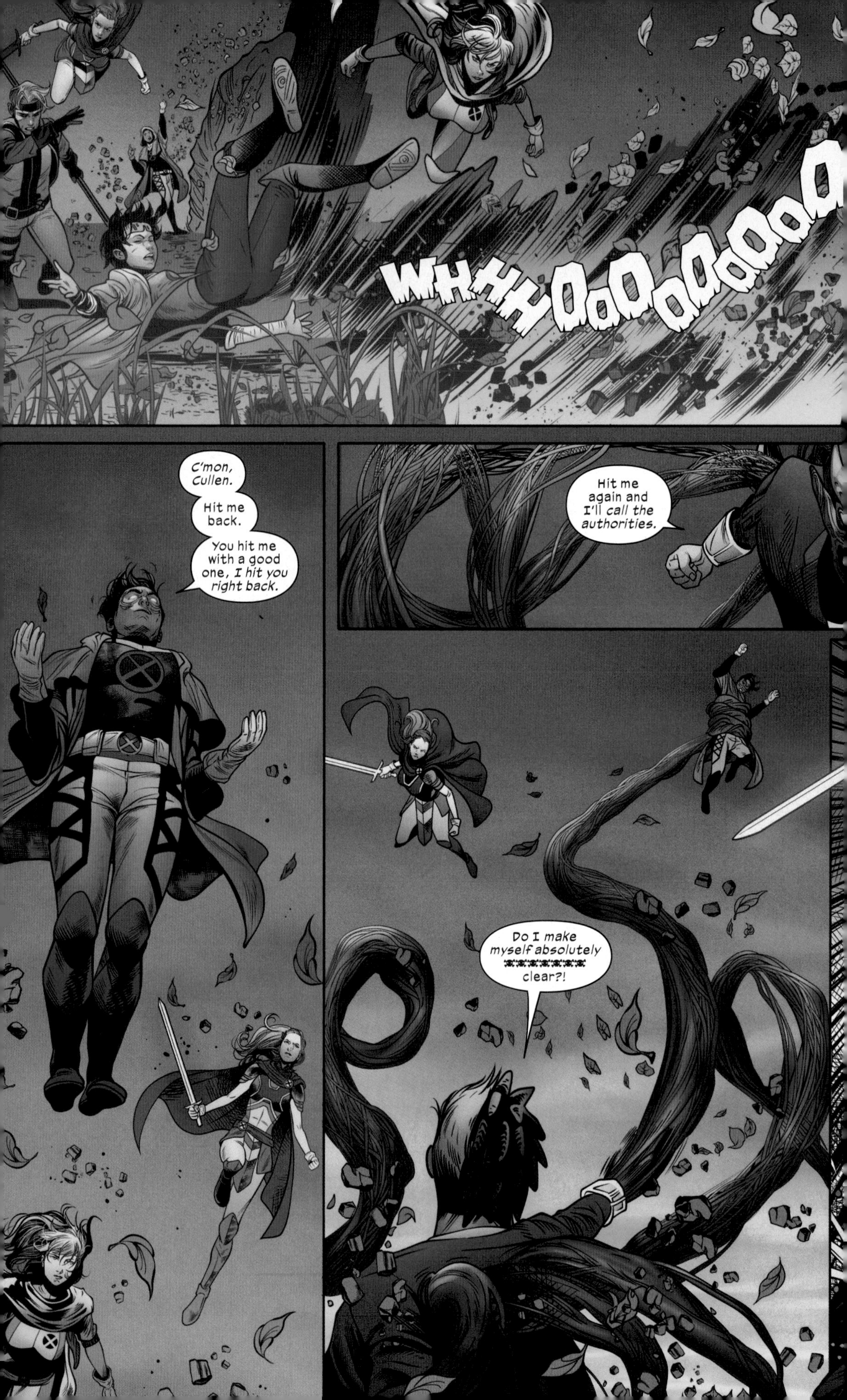
WHHHOOOOOOOOO
C'mon, Cullen.
Hit me back.
You hit me with a good one, *I hit you right back.*
Hit me again and I'll *call the authorities.*
Do I make *myself* absolutely
clear?!

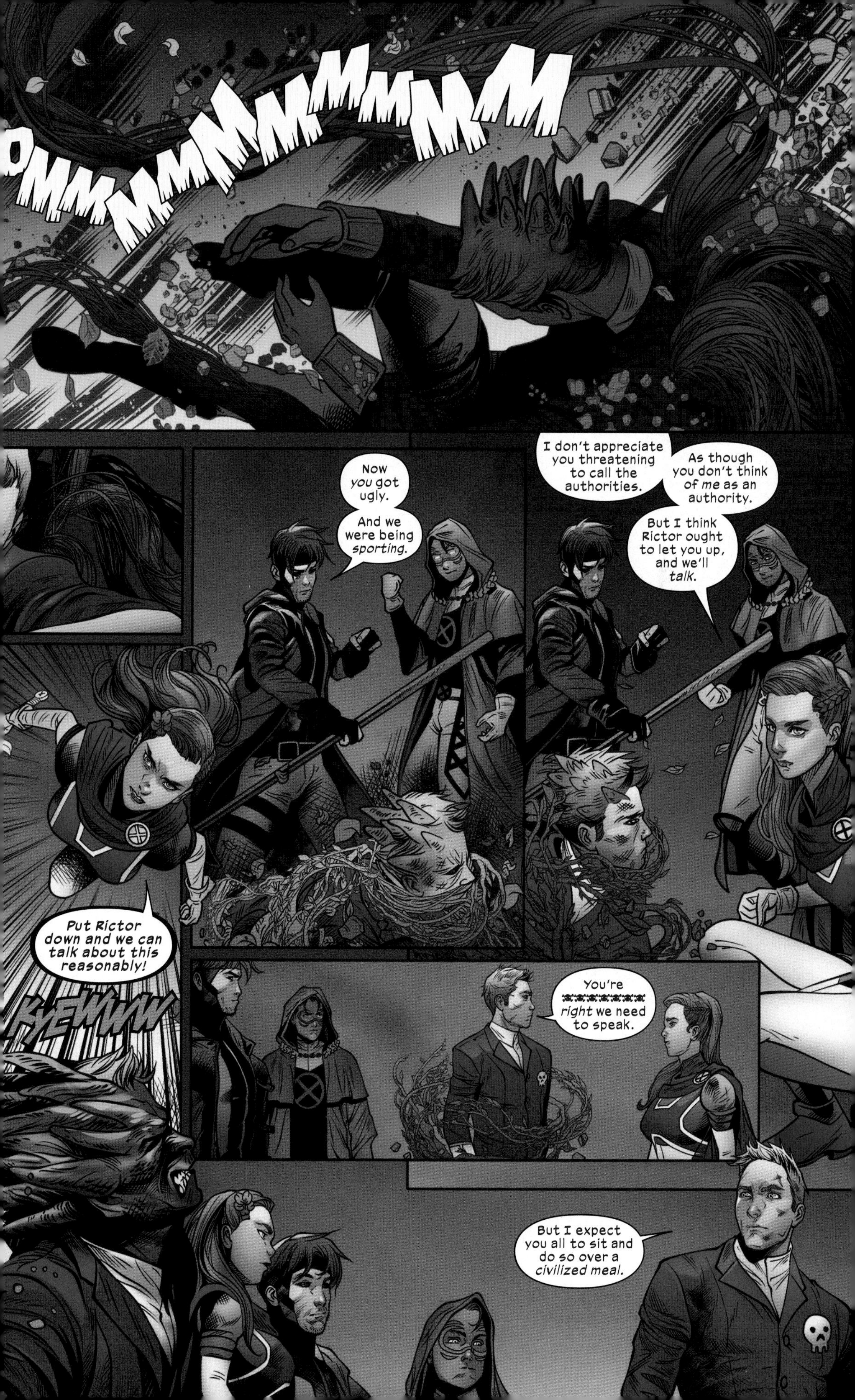
OMMMMMMMMMMMM
Now you got ugly.
And we were being sporting.
Put Rictor down and we can talk about this reasonably!
KYEWWW
I don't appreciate you threatening to call the authorities.
As though you don't think of me as an authority.
But I think Rictor ought to let you up, and we'll talk.
You're right we need to speak.
But I expect you all to sit and do so over a civilized meal.

[00_so_below_X]
[00_as_above_X]

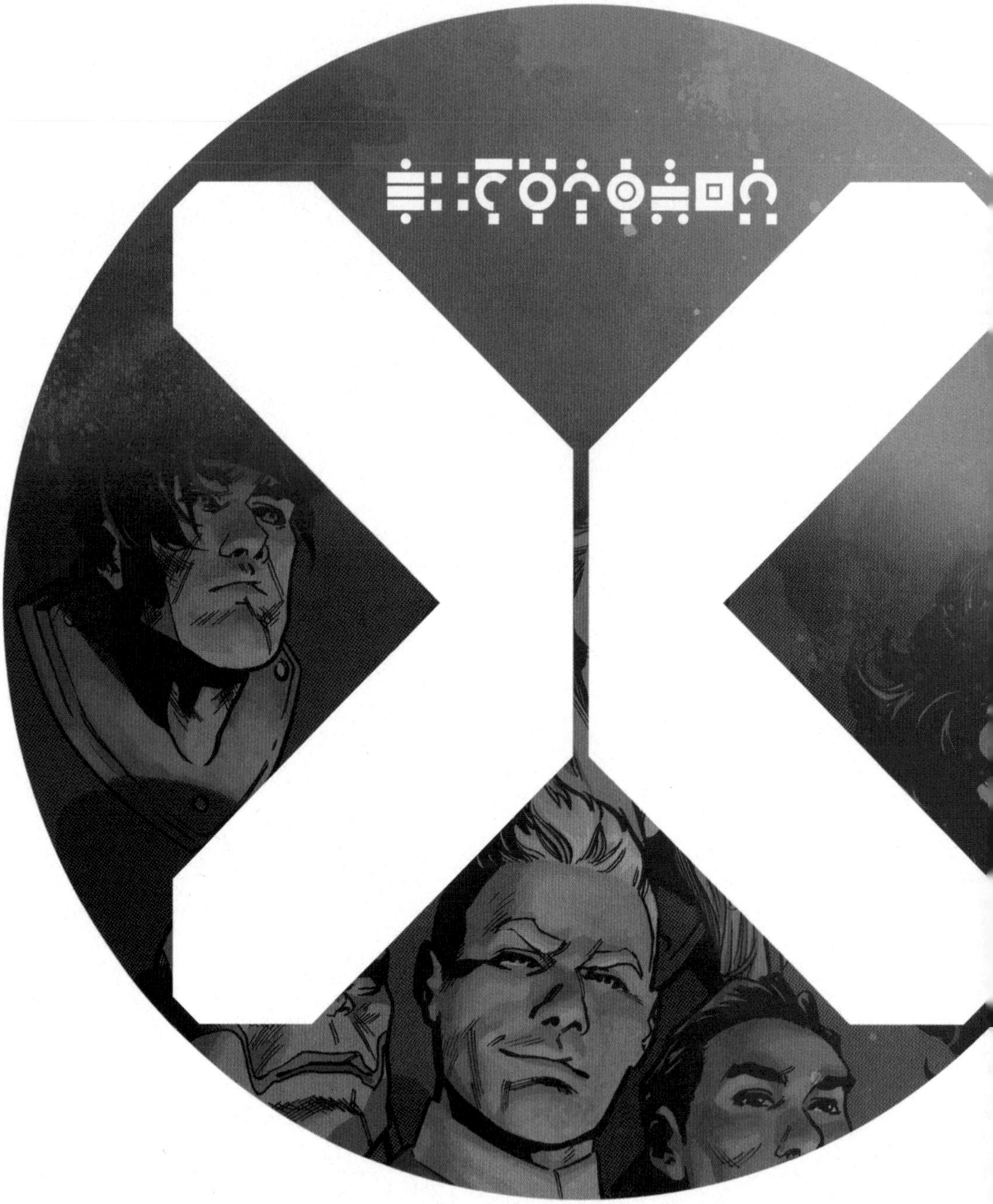

```
TINI HOWARD.....................................[WRITER]
WILTON SANTOS & MARCUS TO...................[PENCILERS]
SEAN PARSONS, MARCUS TO, ROBERTO POGGI & VICTOR NAVA
...............................................[INKERS]
ERICK ARCINIEGA.........................[COLOR ARTIST]
VC's JOE SABINO............................[LETTERER]
TOM MULLER...................................[DESIGN]

MAHMUD ASRAR & MATTHEW WILSON...........[COVER ARTISTS]

NICK RUSSELL.............................[PRODUCTION]

JONATHAN HICKMAN...........................[HEAD OF X]
ANNALISE BISSA......................[ASSISTANT EDITOR]
JORDAN D. WHITE..............................[EDITOR]
C.B. CEBULSKI........................[EDITOR IN CHIEF]
```

[08] EXCALIBUR

[ISSUE EIGHT]...............VERSE VIII:
...THE UNSPEAKABLE AND THE UNEATABLE II

[00_so_below_X]
[X‾ənoqɐ‾sɐ‾00]

[00_00.....0]
[00_00.....8]

[00__fine___]
[00_day_____]

[00_for_a___]

[00___hunt__]

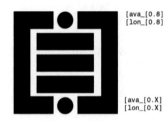

[ava_[0.8]
[lon_[0.8]

[ava_[0.X]
[lon_[0.X]

CIVILITY

Charged by Apocalypse to retrieve strange components
for a necessary ritual, EXCALIBUR went on the hunt!
Chasing down the last remaining warwolves at Cullen
Bloodstone's family hunting lodge was going well
enough -- until the team's unsporting conduct
brought out Cullen's...less gracious side.

Gambit

Rogue

Rictor

Jubilee

Shogo

Captain
Britain

Cullen
Bloodstone

Apocalypse

[ava_[0.8]...]
[lon_[0.8]...]

[Tally....HO.]

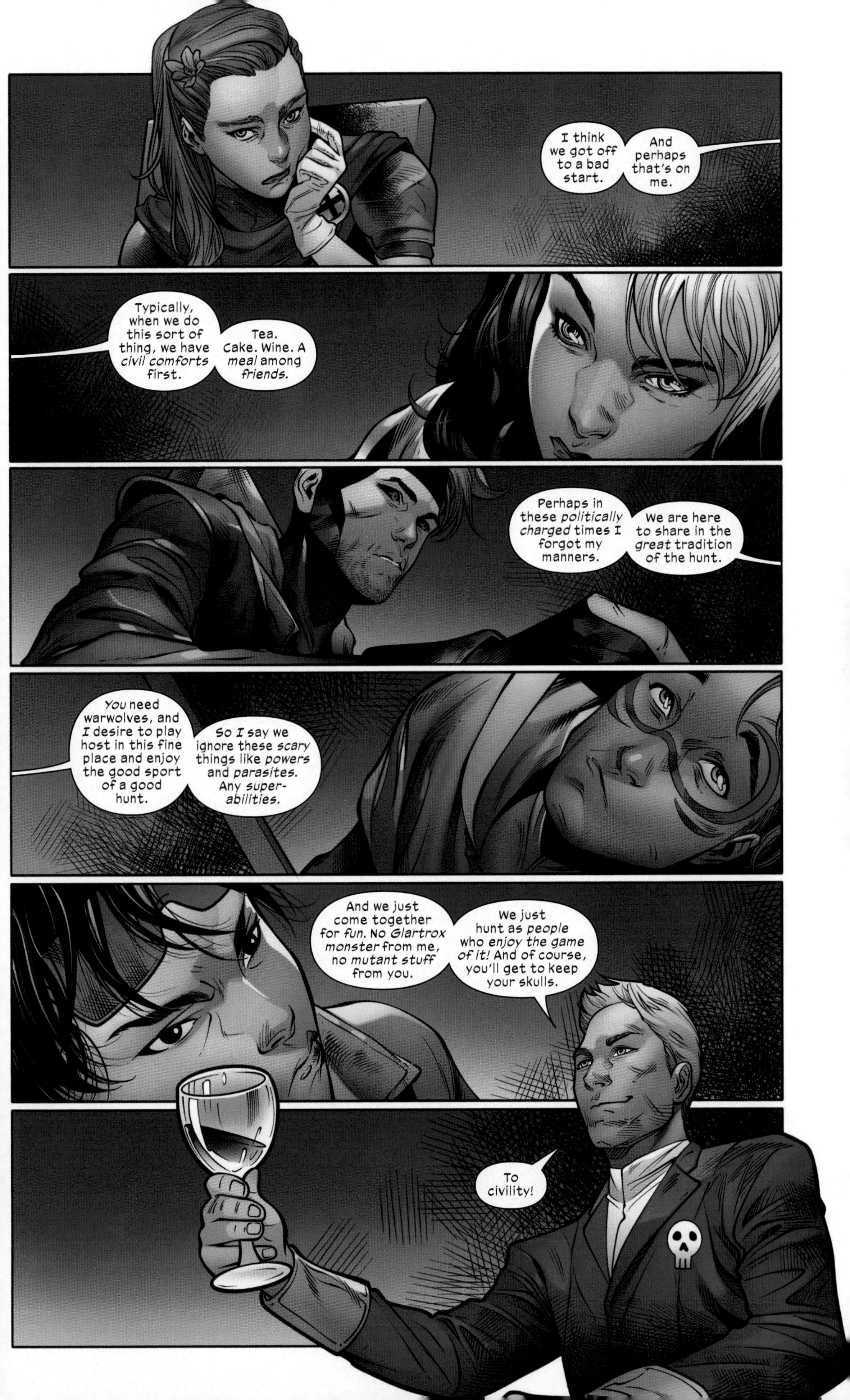

I think we got off to a bad start.
And perhaps that's on me.
Typically, when we do this sort of thing, we have *civil comforts* first.
Tea. Cake. Wine. A *meal* among *friends*.
Perhaps in these *politically charged* times I forgot my manners.
We are here to share in the *great* tradition of the hunt.
You need warwolves, and *I* desire to play host in this fine place and enjoy the good sport of a good hunt.
So *I* say we ignore these *scary* things like *powers* and *parasites*. Any *super-abilities*.
And we just come together for *fun*. No *Glartrox monster* from me, no *mutant stuff* from you.
We just hunt as *people* who *enjoy the game of it!* And of course, you'll get to keep your skulls.
To civility!

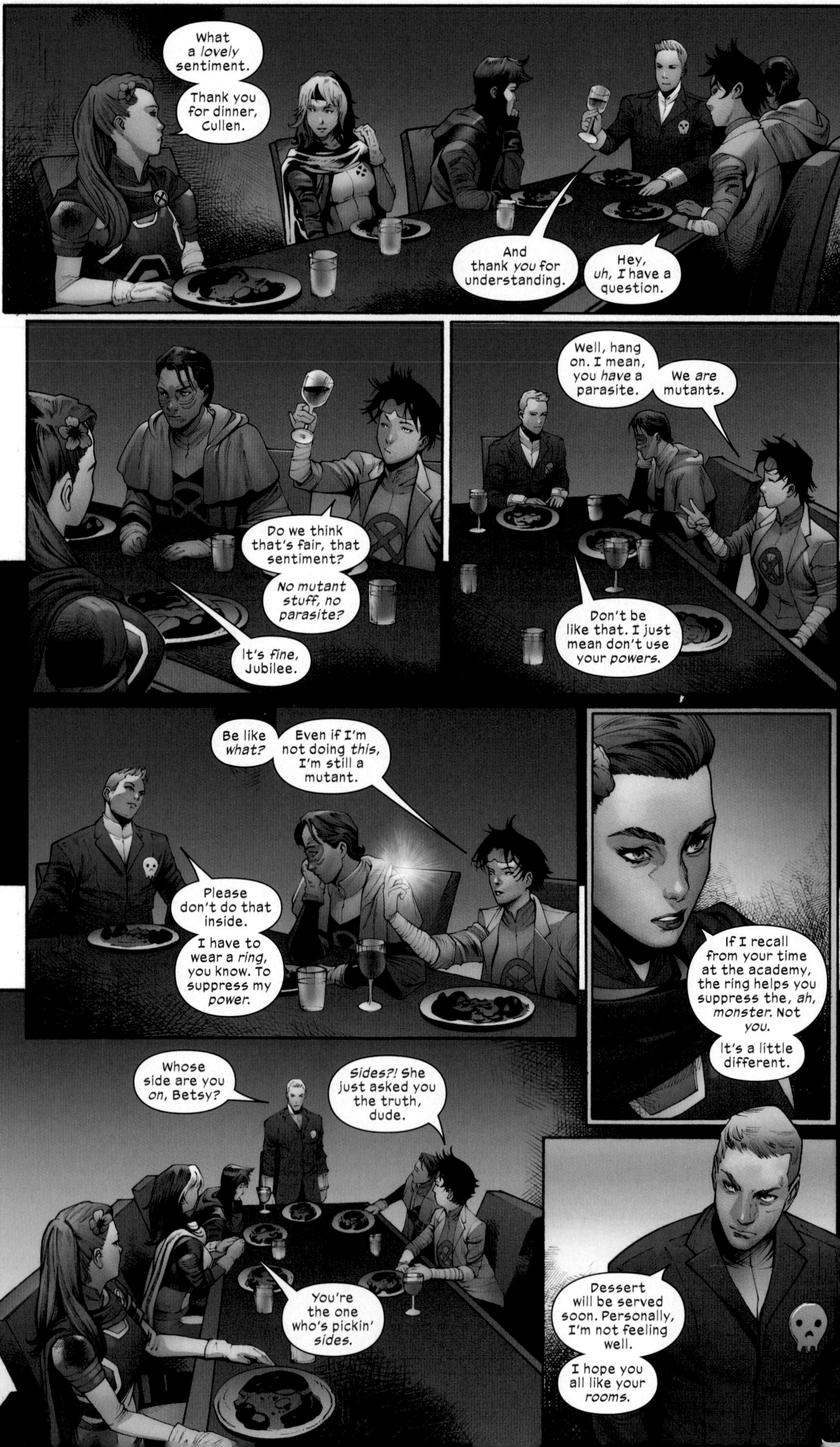
What a *lovely* sentiment.
Thank you for dinner, Cullen.
And thank *you* for understanding.
Hey, *uh,* I have a question.
Do we think that's fair, that sentiment?
No mutant stuff, no parasite?
It's *fine,* Jubilee.
Well, hang on. I mean, you *have* a parasite.
We *are* mutants.
Don't be like that. I just mean don't use your *powers.*
Be like *what?*
Even if I'm not doing *this,* I'm still a mutant.
Please don't do that inside.
I have to wear a *ring,* you know. To suppress my *power.*
If I recall from your time at the academy, the ring helps you suppress the, *ah, monster.* Not *you.*
It's a little different.
Whose side are you *on,* Betsy?
Sides?! She just asked you the truth, dude.
You're the one who's pickin' *sides.*
Dessert will be served soon. Personally, I'm not feeling well.
I hope you all like your *rooms.*

A LETTER TO THE NOBLE *HOMO SAPIENS* OF BRITAIN
THE BLOODSTONE ESTATE OR EXECUTOR THEREOF;

Attn: Master of the House

Dear fellow protector of the Commonwealth:

Greetings. I wish I could come to you with better tidings.

As you well know, the recent establishment of the nation of Krakoa has been seen by some as an act of terrorist isolation. Those who call themselves "superior" dangle lifesaving drugs over the heads of our brave nation, patronizing the powerful abilities of our own countrymen.

Protection from and mastery of the supernatural has long been part of our national fabric. The power inherent in our connection to the land is vital to our culture and our defense.

These Krakoans have put us on the defensive.

We reach out to you today not only to ask for your support as one of Britain's most vital supernatural families, but also to offer our own. Should the presence of Krakoans in Britain make you uncomfortable or threatened, we encourage you to reach out to us immediately. As an alternative to MI-13, we are not burdened by many of the same concerns of diversity.

Merry part,

R. Brousseau

Reuben Brousseau
Coven Akkaba
London

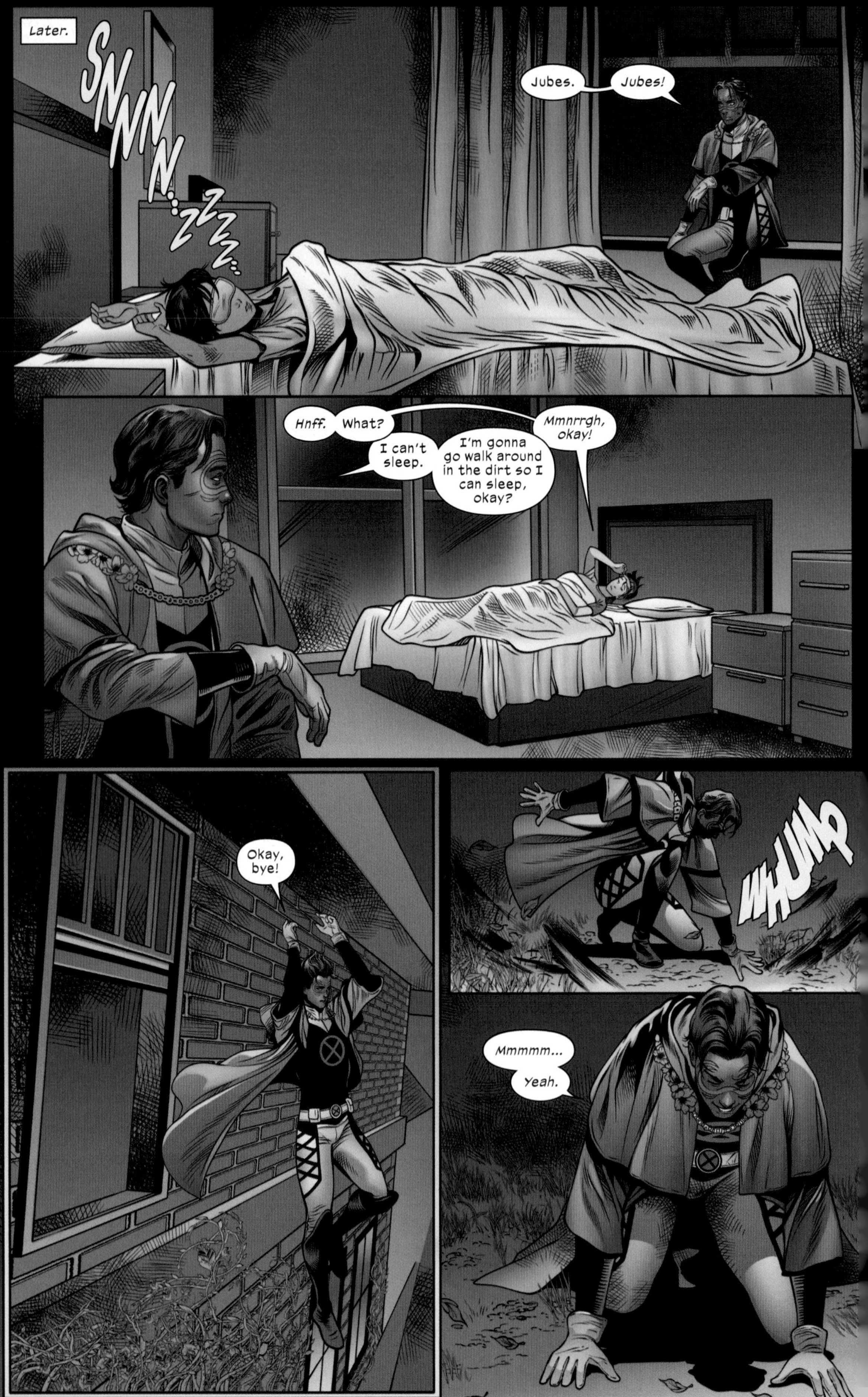

Later.
SNNNN...
ZZZZ...
Jubes.
Jubes!
Hnff.
What?
I can't sleep.
I'm gonna go walk around in the dirt so I can sleep, okay?
Mmnrrgh, okay!
Okay, bye!
WHUMP
Mmmmm...
Yeah.

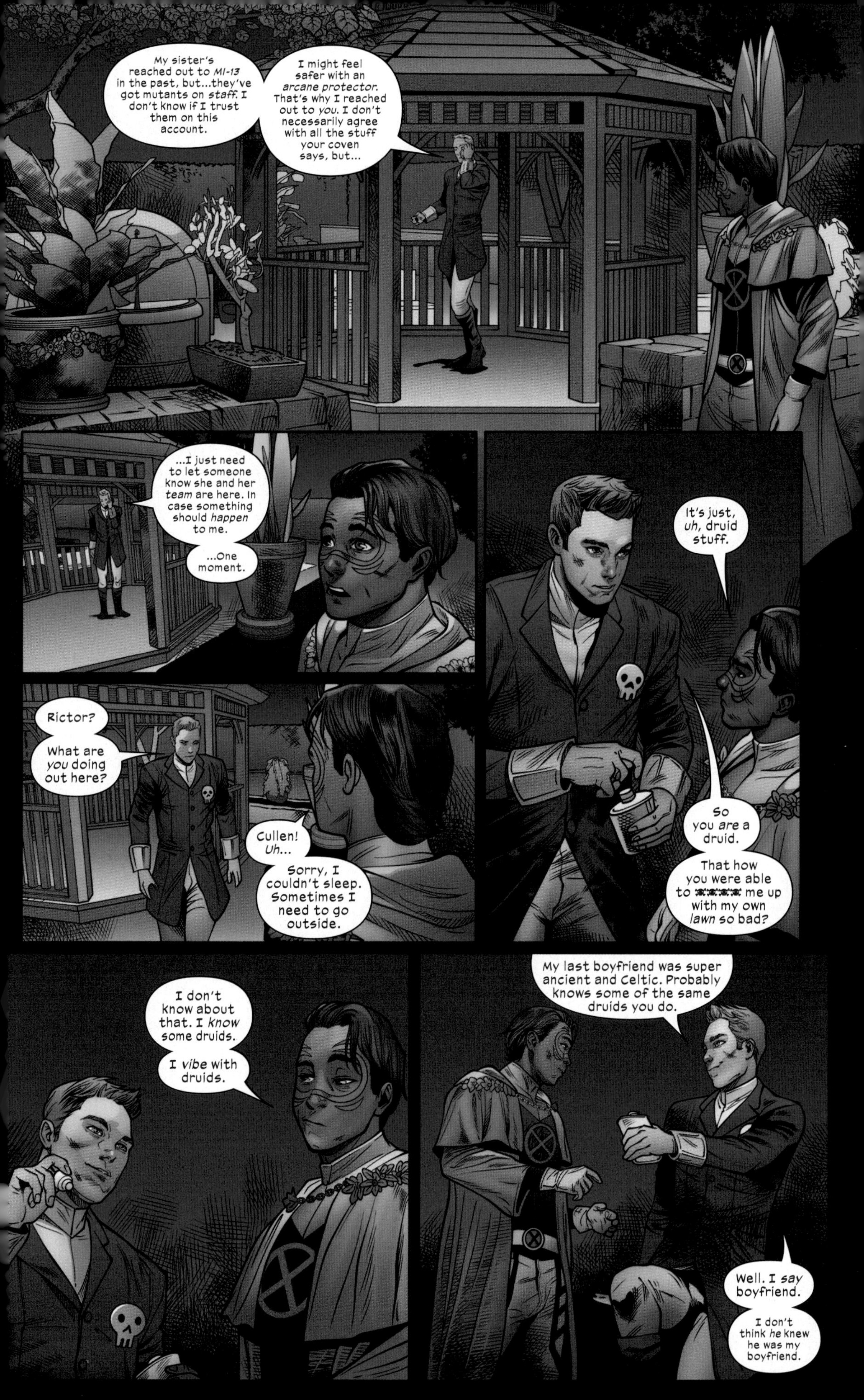

My sister's reached out to *MI-13* in the past, but...they've got mutants on *staff*. I don't know if I trust them on this account.
I might feel safer with an *arcane protector*. That's why I reached out to *you*. I don't necessarily agree with all the stuff your coven says, but...
...I just need to let someone know she and her *team* are here. In case something should *happen* to me.
...One moment.
Rictor?
What are *you* doing out here?
Cullen! *Uh...*
Sorry, I couldn't sleep. Sometimes I need to go outside.
It's just, *uh*, druid stuff.
So you *are* a druid.
That how you were able to ☠☠☠☠ me up with my own *lawn* so bad?
I don't know about that. I *know* some druids.
I *vibe* with druids.
My last boyfriend was super ancient and Celtic. Probably knows some of the same druids you do.
Well. I *say* boyfriend.
I don't think *he* knew he was my boyfriend.

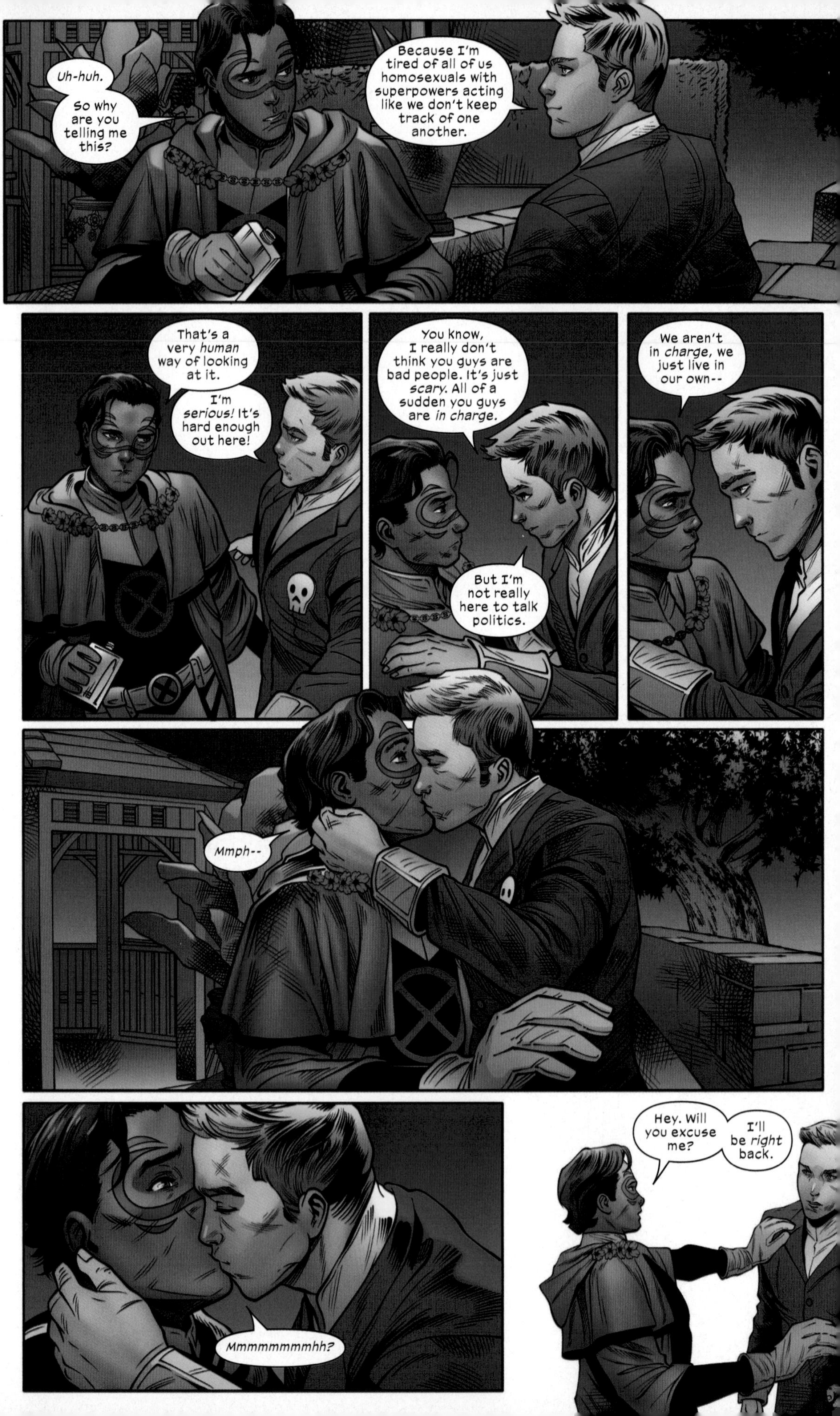
Uh-huh.
So why are you telling me this?
Because I'm tired of all of us homosexuals with superpowers acting like we don't keep track of one another.
That's a very *human* way of looking at it.
I'm *serious!* It's hard enough out here!
You know, I really don't think you guys are bad people. It's just *scary*. All of a sudden you guys are *in charge*.
But I'm not really here to talk politics.
We aren't in *charge*, we just live in our own--
Mmph--
Mmmmmmmmhh?
Hey. Will you excuse me?
I'll be *right* back.

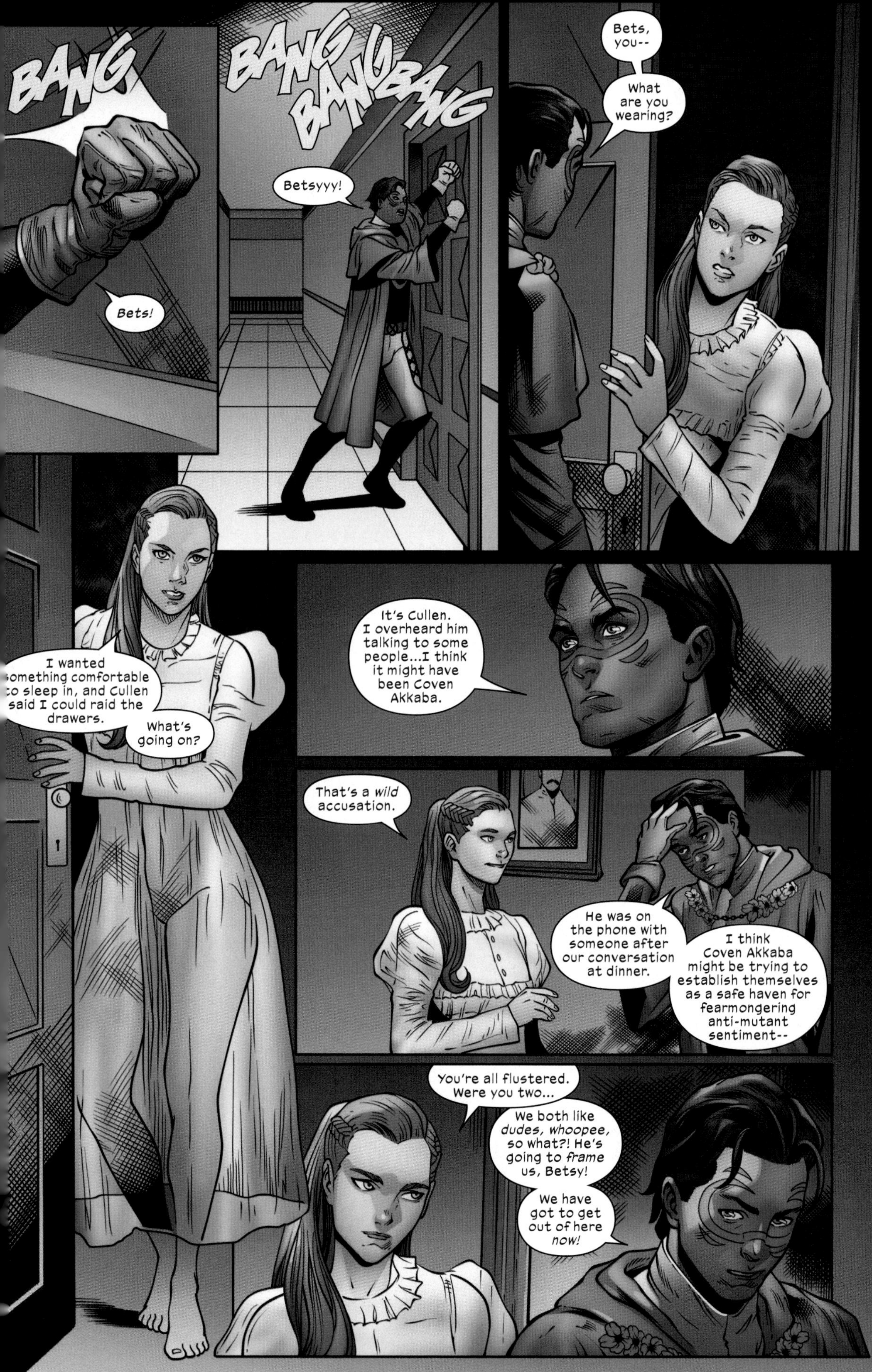
BANG
Bets!
BANG BANG BANG
Betsyyy!
Bets, you--
What are you wearing?
I wanted something comfortable to sleep in, and Cullen said I could raid the drawers.
What's going on?
It's Cullen. I overheard him talking to some people...I think it might have been Coven Akkaba.
That's a *wild* accusation.
He was on the phone with someone after our conversation at dinner.
I think Coven Akkaba might be trying to establish themselves as a safe haven for fearmongering anti-mutant sentiment--
You're all flustered. Were you two...
We both like *dudes, whoopee,* so what?! He's going to *frame* us, Betsy!
We have got to get out of here *now!*

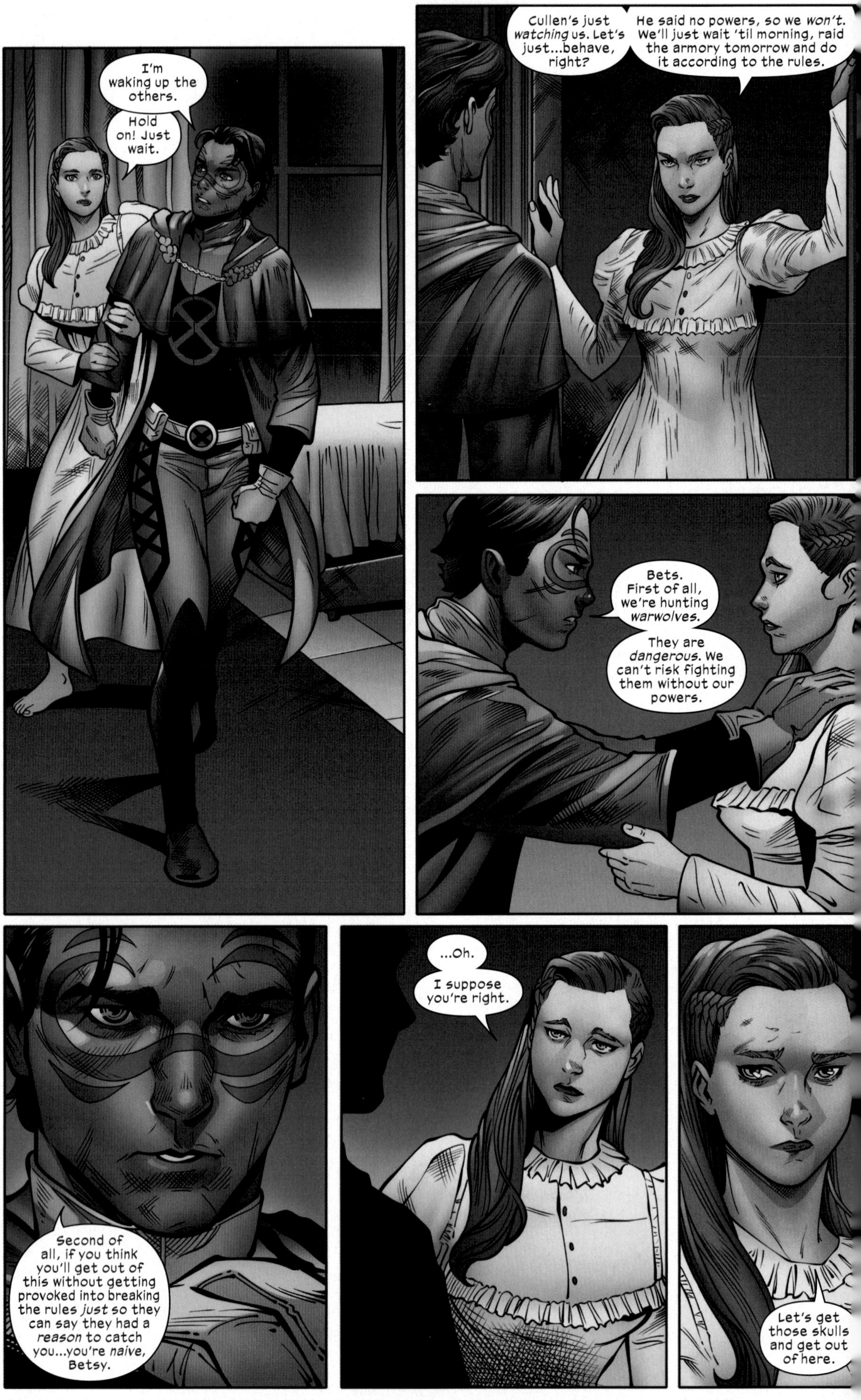
I'm waking up the others.
Hold on! Just wait.
Cullen's just *watching* us. Let's just...behave, right?
He said no powers, so we *won't*. We'll just wait 'til morning, raid the armory tomorrow and do it according to the rules.
Bets. First of all, we're hunting *warwolves*.
They are *dangerous*. We can't risk fighting them without our powers.
Second of all, if you think you'll get out of this without getting provoked into breaking the rules *just* so they can say they had a *reason* to catch you...you're *naive*, Betsy.
...Oh.
I suppose you're right.
Let's get those skulls and get out of here.

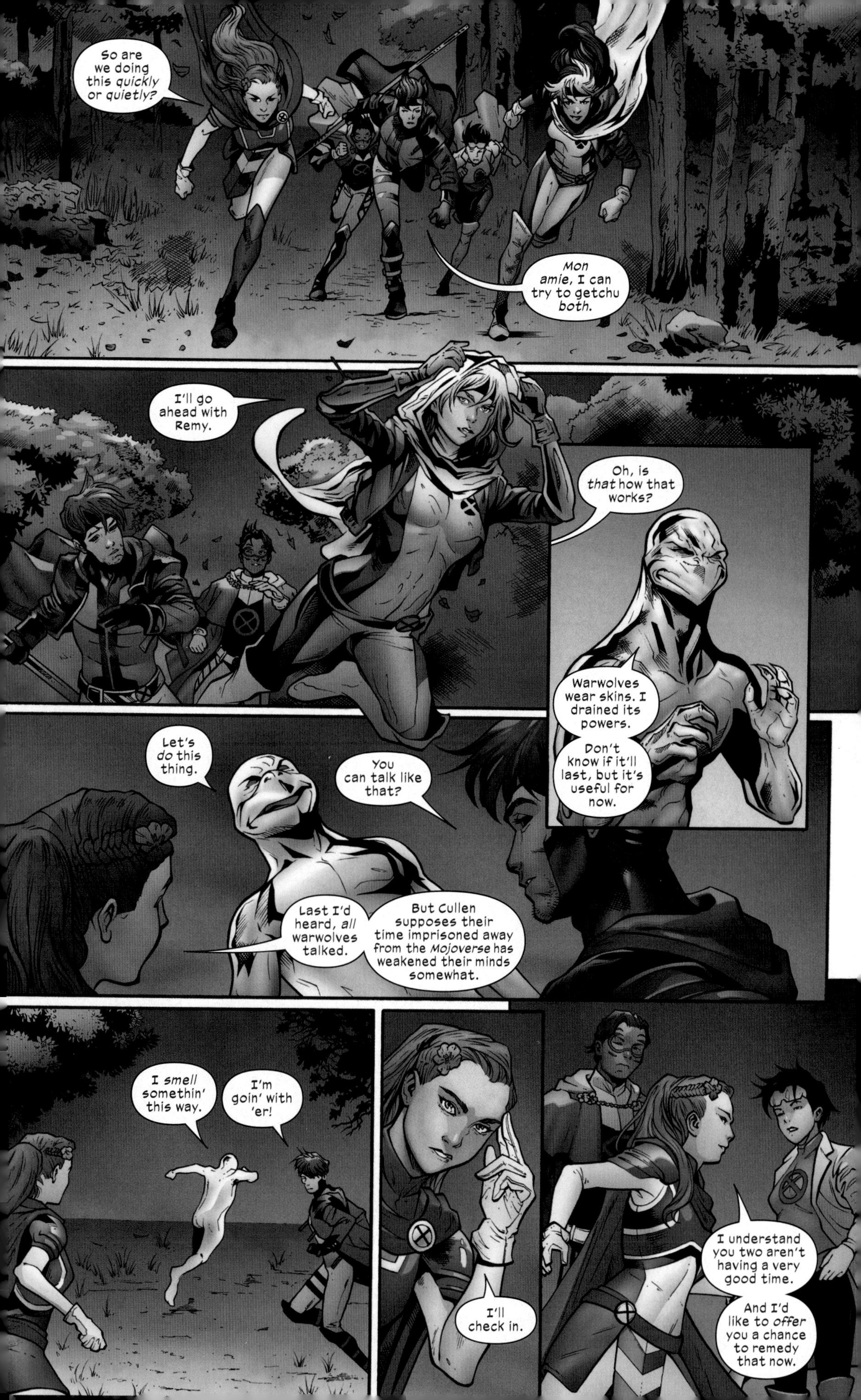
So are we doing this *quickly* or *quietly?*
Mon amie, I can try to getchu *both*.
I'll go ahead with Remy.
Oh, is *that* how that works?
Warwolves wear skins. I drained its powers.
Don't know if it'll last, but it's useful for now.
Let's *do* this thing.
You can talk like that?
Last I'd heard, *all* warwolves talked.
But Cullen supposes their time imprisoned away from the *Mojoverse* has weakened their minds somewhat.
I *smell* somethin' this way.
I'm goin' with 'er!
I'll check in.
I understand you two aren't having a very good time.
And I'd like to *offer* you a chance to remedy that now.

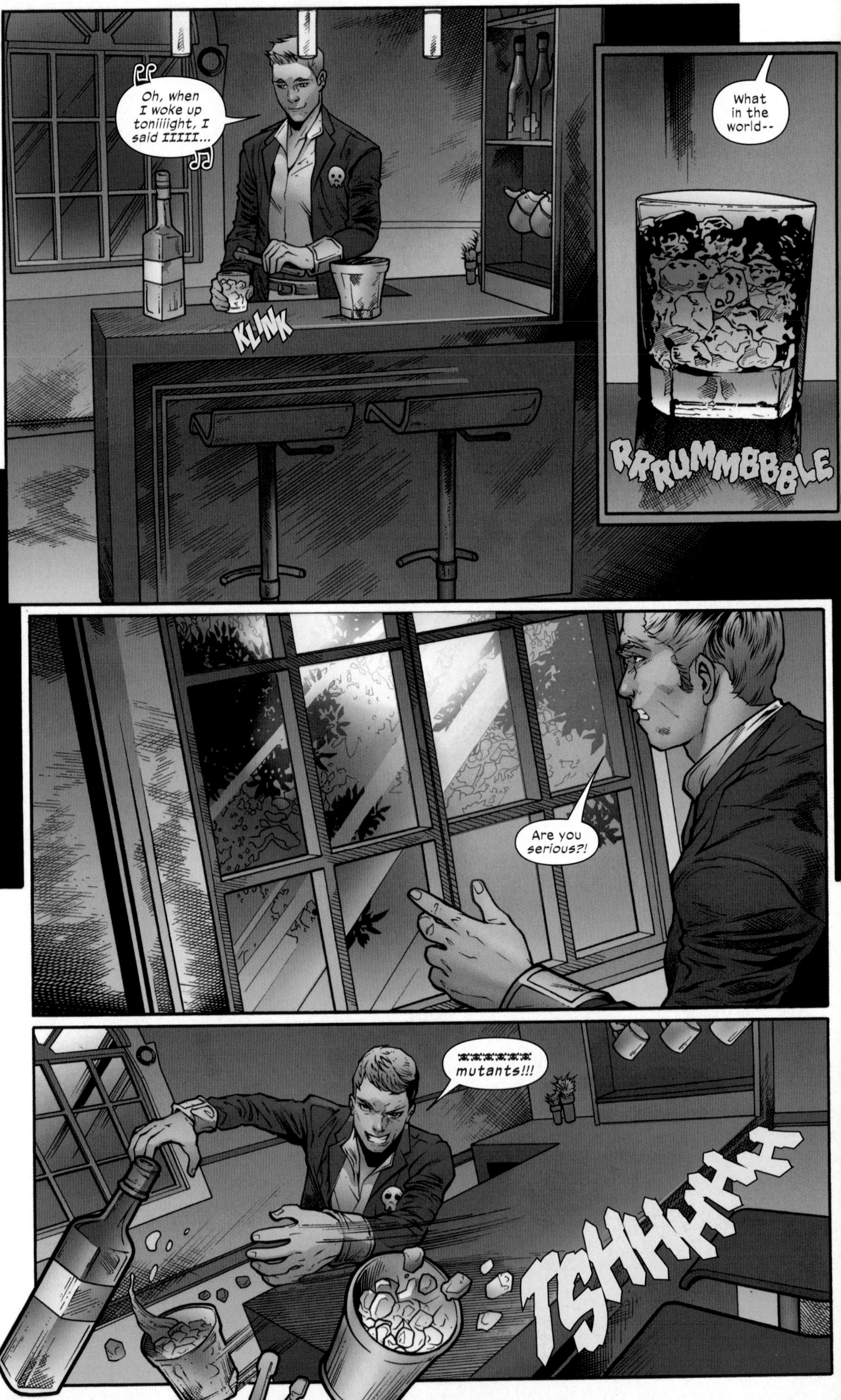
Oh, when I woke up toniiiight, I said IIIII...
KLINK
What in the world--
RRRUMMBBBLE
Are you serious?!
mutants!!!
TSHHHH

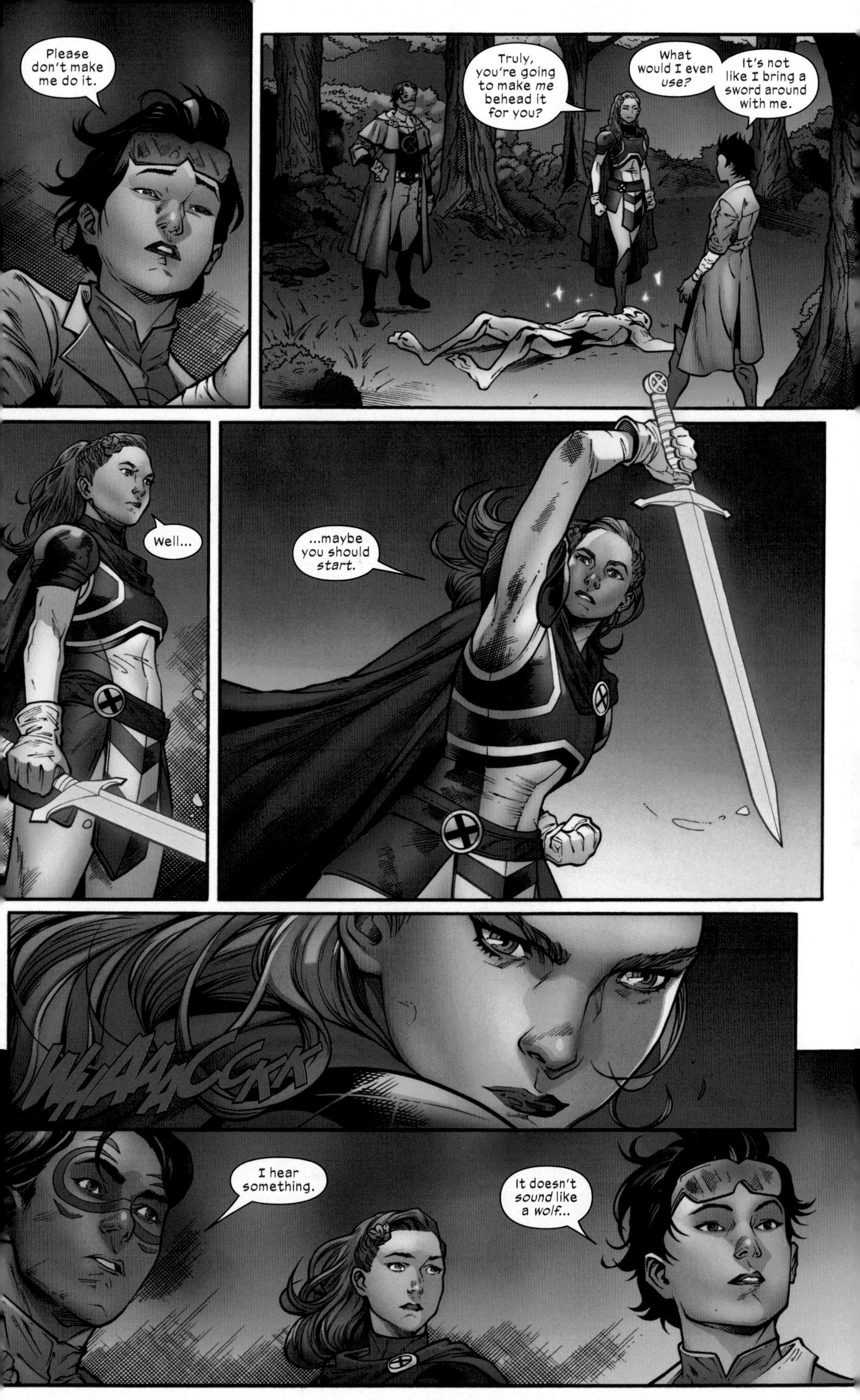

Please don't make me do it.
Truly, you're going to make *me* behead it for you?
What would I even *use?*
It's not like I bring a sword around with me.
Well...
...maybe you should *start.*
WHAACCKK
I hear something.
It doesn't *sound* like a *wolf*...

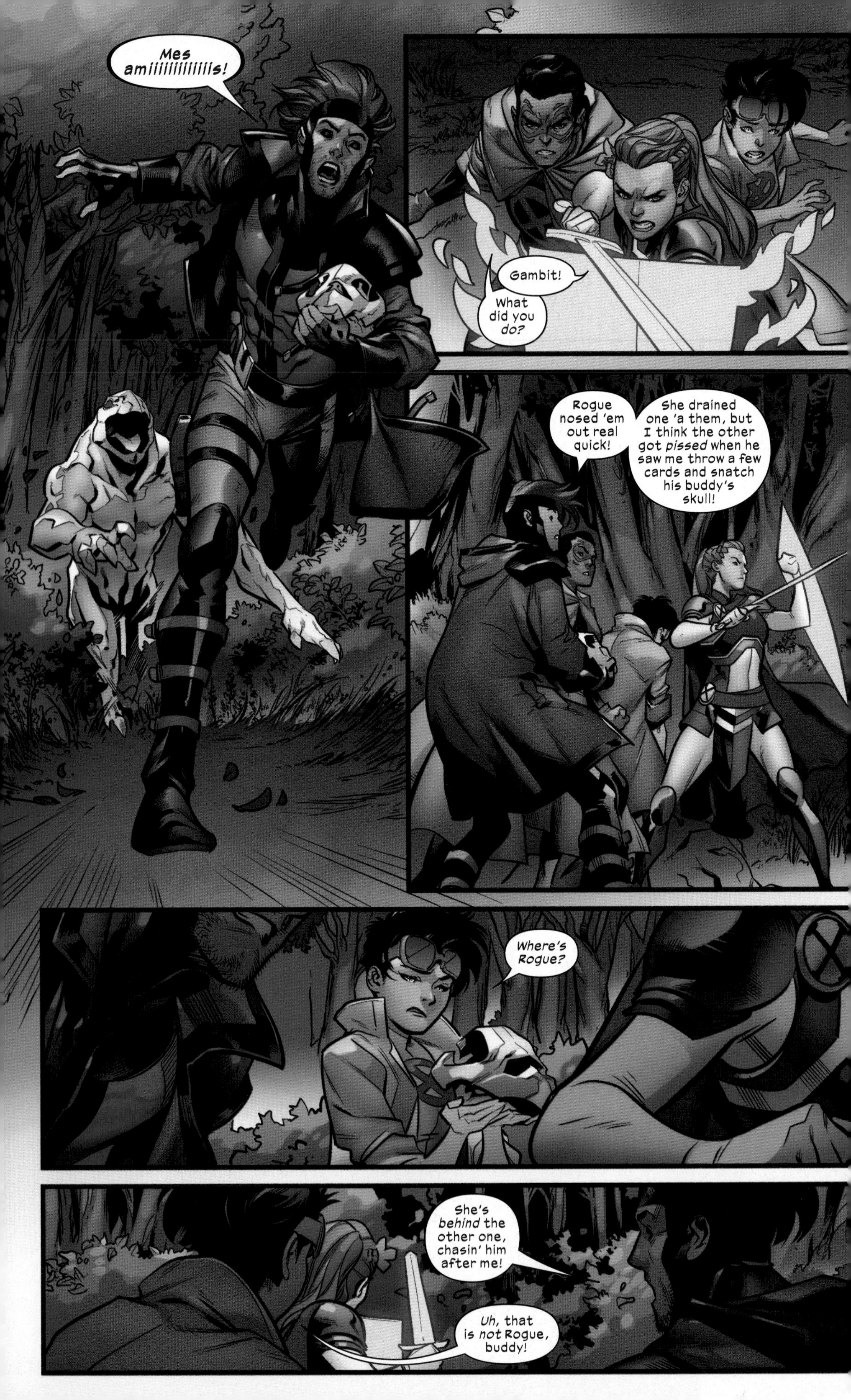
Mes amiiiiiiiiiiiiis!
Gambit!
What did you *do?*
Rogue nosed 'em out real quick!
She drained one 'a them, but I think the other got *pissed* when he saw me throw a few cards and snatch his buddy's skull!
Where's Rogue?
She's *behind* the other one, chasin' him after me!
Uh, that is *not* Rogue, buddy!

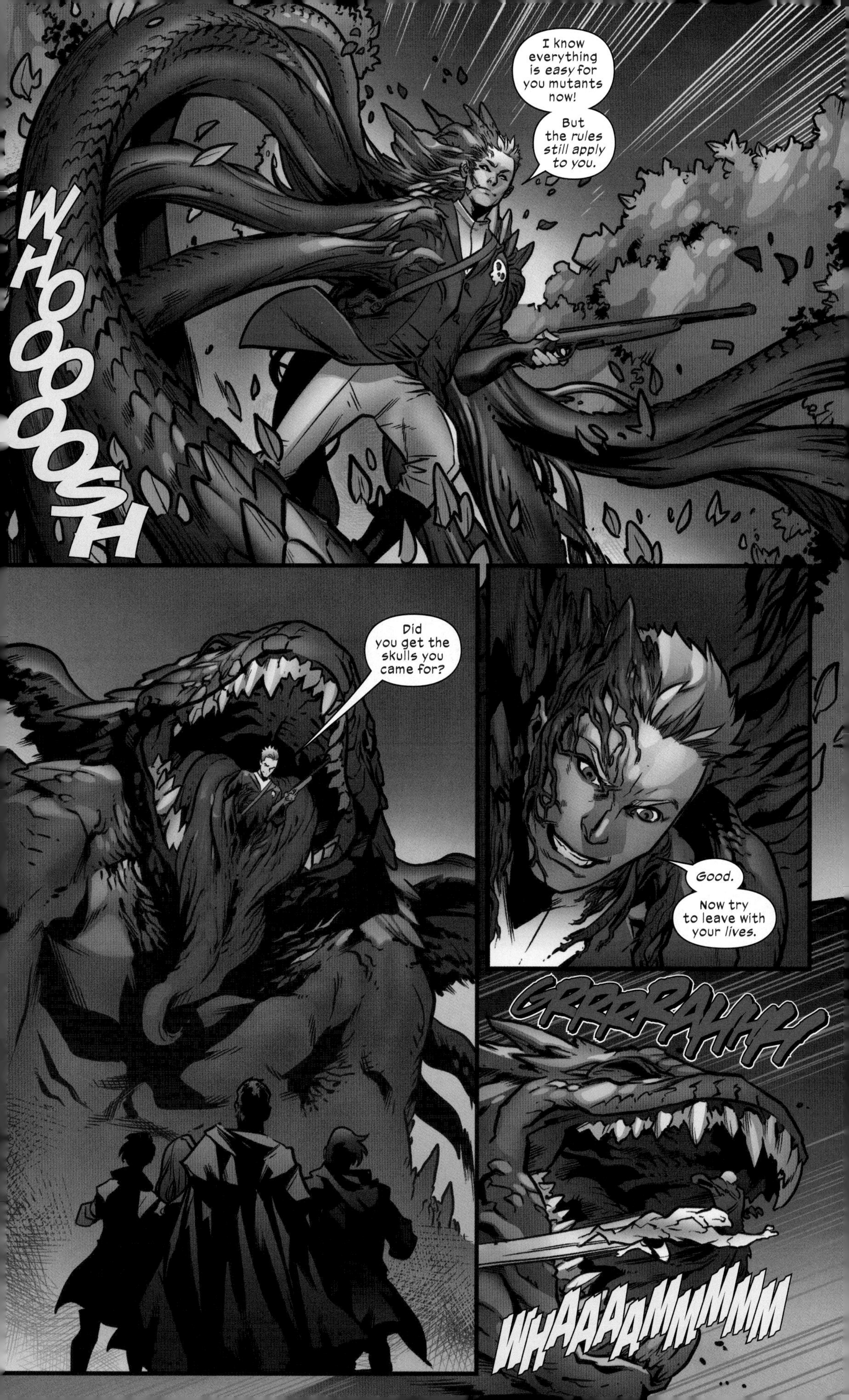

WHOOOOOOSH
I know everything is *easy* for you mutants now!
But the *rules still apply* to you.
Did you get the skulls you came for?
Good.
Now try to leave with your *lives.*
GRRRRAHHH
WHAAAAMMMMMM

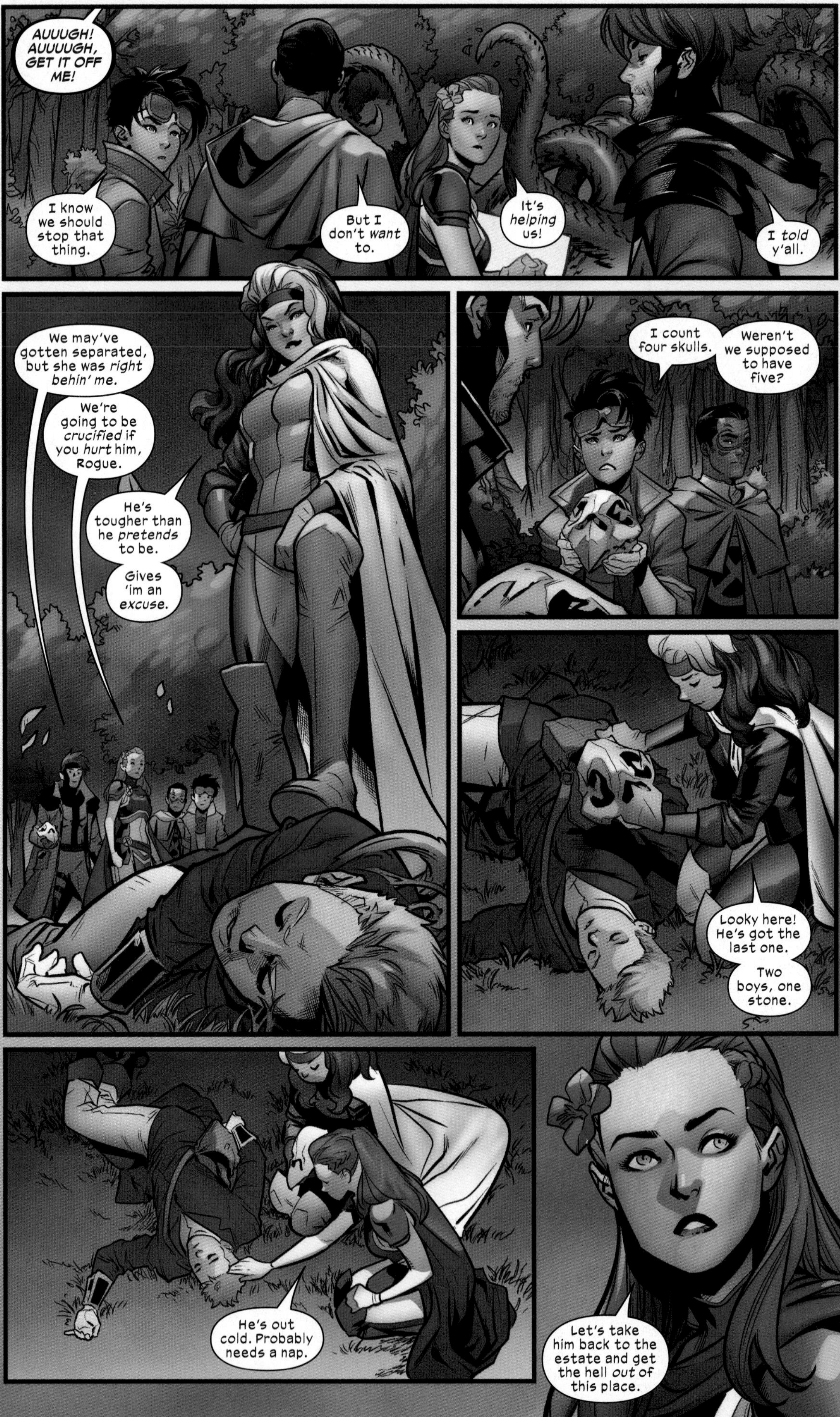
AUUUGH! AUUUUGH, GET IT OFF ME!
I know we should stop that thing.
But I don't want to.
It's helping us!
I told y'all.
We may've gotten separated, but she was right behin' me.
We're going to be crucified if you hurt him, Rogue.
He's tougher than he pretends to be.
Gives 'im an excuse.
I count four skulls.
Weren't we supposed to have five?
Looky here! He's got the last one.
Two boys, one stone.
He's out cold. Probably needs a nap.
Let's take him back to the estate and get the hell out of this place.

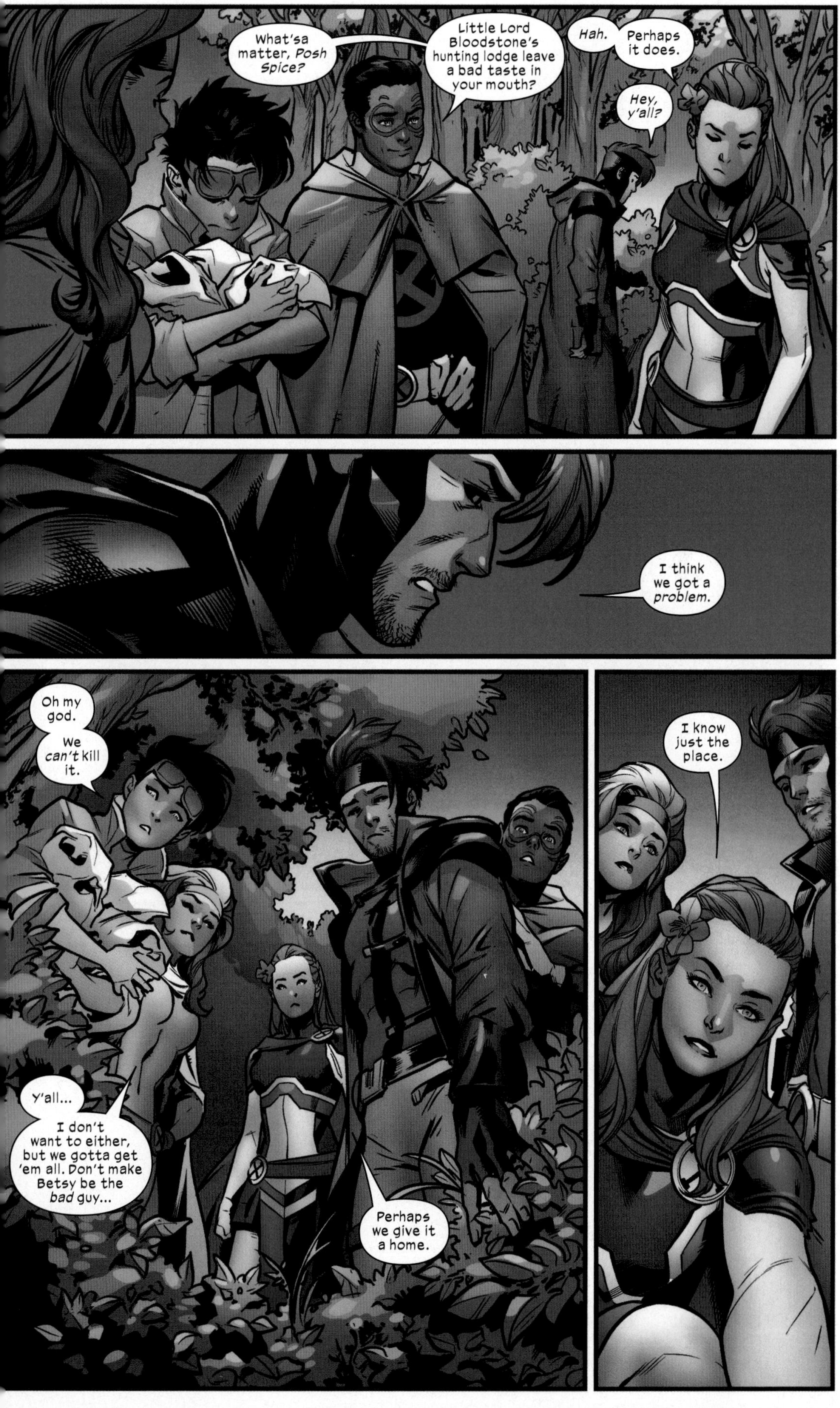
What'sa matter, *Posh Spice?*
Little Lord Bloodstone's hunting lodge leave a bad taste in your mouth?
Hah.
Perhaps it does.
Hey, y'all?
I think we got a *problem.*
Oh my god.
We *can't* kill it.
Y'all...
I don't want to either, but we gotta get 'em all. Don't make Betsy be the *bad* guy...
Perhaps we give it a home.
I know just the place.

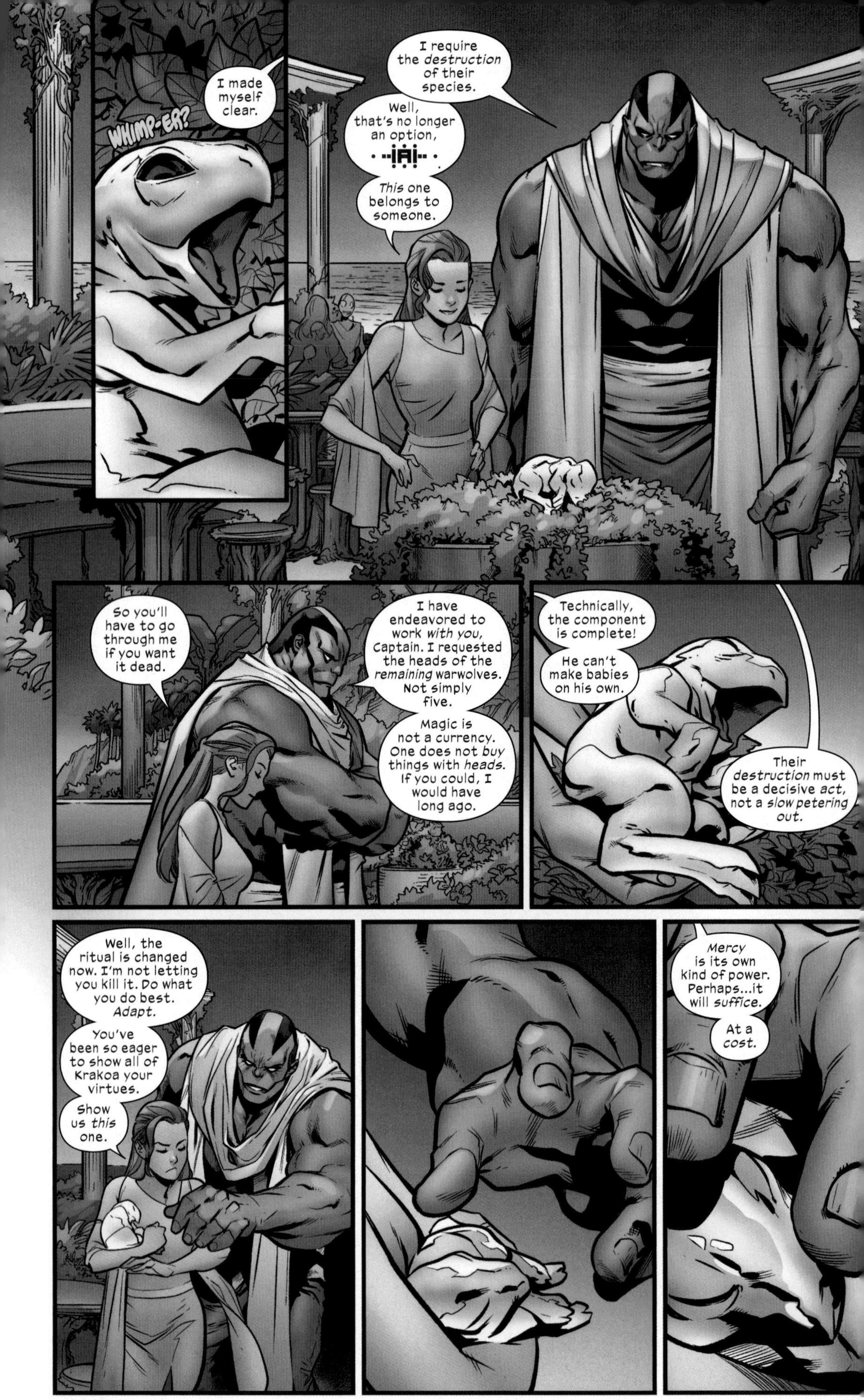

I made myself clear.
WHIMP-ER?
I require the destruction of their species.
Well, that's no longer an option,
This one belongs to someone.
So you'll have to go through me if you want it dead.
I have endeavored to work with you, Captain. I requested the heads of the remaining warwolves. Not simply five.
Magic is not a currency. One does not buy things with heads. If you could, I would have long ago.
Technically, the component is complete!
He can't make babies on his own.
Their destruction must be a decisive act, not a slow petering out.
Well, the ritual is changed now. I'm not letting you kill it. Do what you do best. Adapt.
You've been so eager to show all of Krakoa your virtues.
Show us this one.
Mercy is its own kind of power. Perhaps...it will suffice.
At a cost.

★TO THE STARS, FROM THE STARS★

Out here, the sky is silent. Harmonious pulses of binary stars in time with Krakoa's heart are heard in the quiet refuge of the flowers.

These messages come from the stars outside to the stars within us.

We share them, interpreted from startongue, with our brothers and sisters below.

- 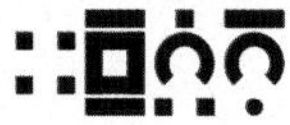

"A sword with two edges is not the same as two swords with a single edge each."

- the pulsar known as RX J0806.4-4123

It is a very bad week to procrastinate. If you sleep facing westward to put your back to the dawn, you will stay up late digging your own grave.

Have you a song that is haunting you? Turn it off. It is drowning out your truth.

A message for those who were born at sunrise -- trust your instinct. Remember that sometimes your instinct is louder than your ego. Dim the lights if you must in order to confront the self.

"If you hunt a beast you do not wish to eat, you become the hand of the cook."

- the Methuselah star, HD 140283

Though it pains us to say, it is an inauspicious era for twins.

We invite you to join us to pray for luck.

★★

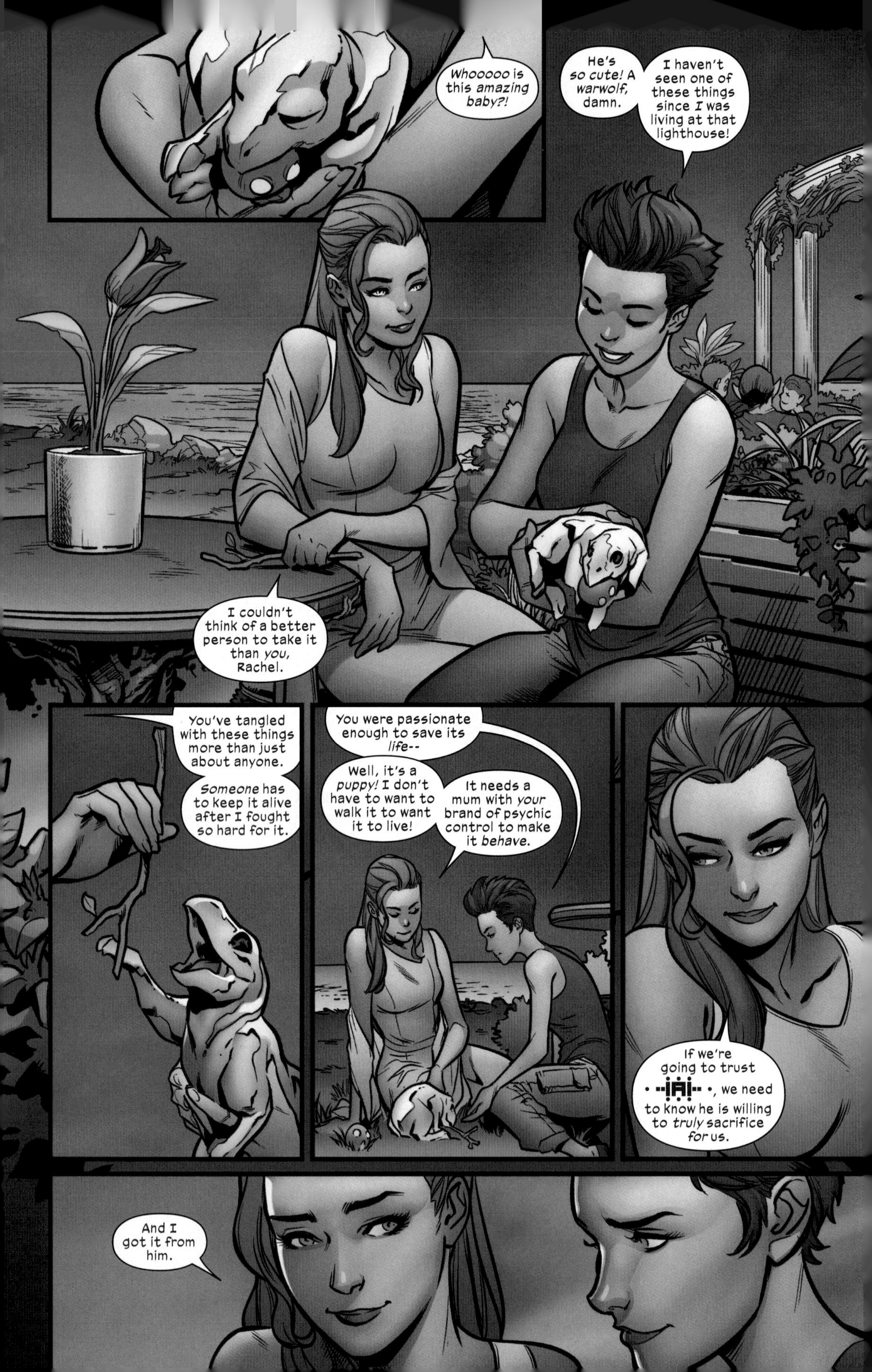
Whoooooo is this amazing baby?!
He's so cute! A warwolf, damn.
I haven't seen one of these things since I was living at that lighthouse!
I couldn't think of a better person to take it than you, Rachel.
You've tangled with these things more than just about anyone.
Someone has to keep it alive after I fought so hard for it.
You were passionate enough to save its life--
Well, it's a puppy! I don't have to want to walk it to want it to live!
It needs a mum with your brand of psychic control to make it behave.
If we're going to trust , we need to know he is willing to truly sacrifice for us.
And I got it from him.

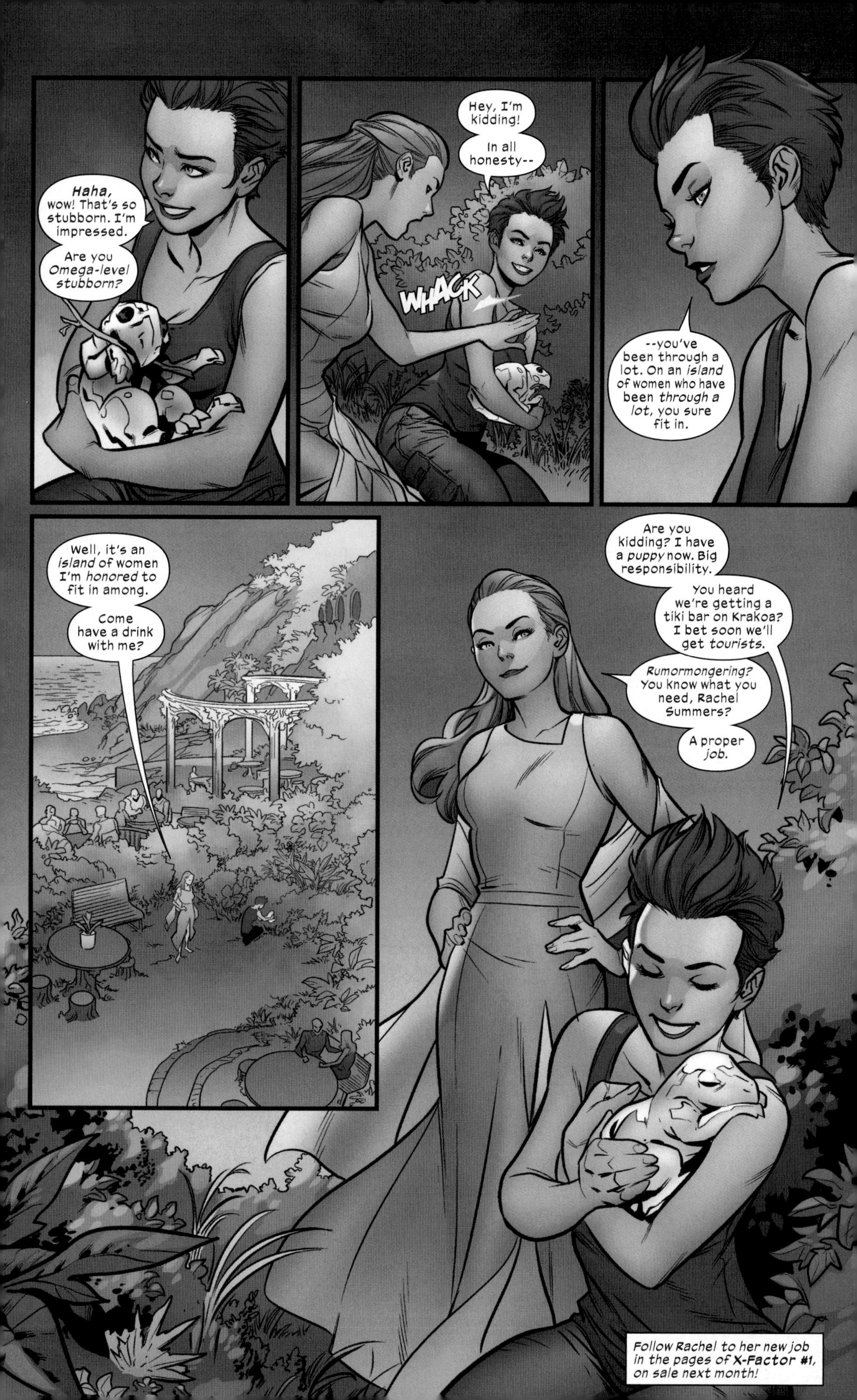

Haha, wow! That's so stubborn. I'm impressed.
Are you *Omega-level stubborn?*
Hey, I'm kidding!
In all honesty--
WHACK
--you've been through a lot. On an *island* of women who have been *through a lot,* you sure fit in.
Well, it's an *island* of women I'm *honored* to fit in among.
Come have a drink with me?
Are you kidding? I have a *puppy* now. Big responsibility.
You heard we're getting a tiki bar on Krakoa? I bet soon we'll get *tourists.*
Rumormongering? You know what you need, Rachel Summers?
A proper *job.*
Follow Rachel to her new job in the pages of **X-Factor #1,** *on sale next month!*

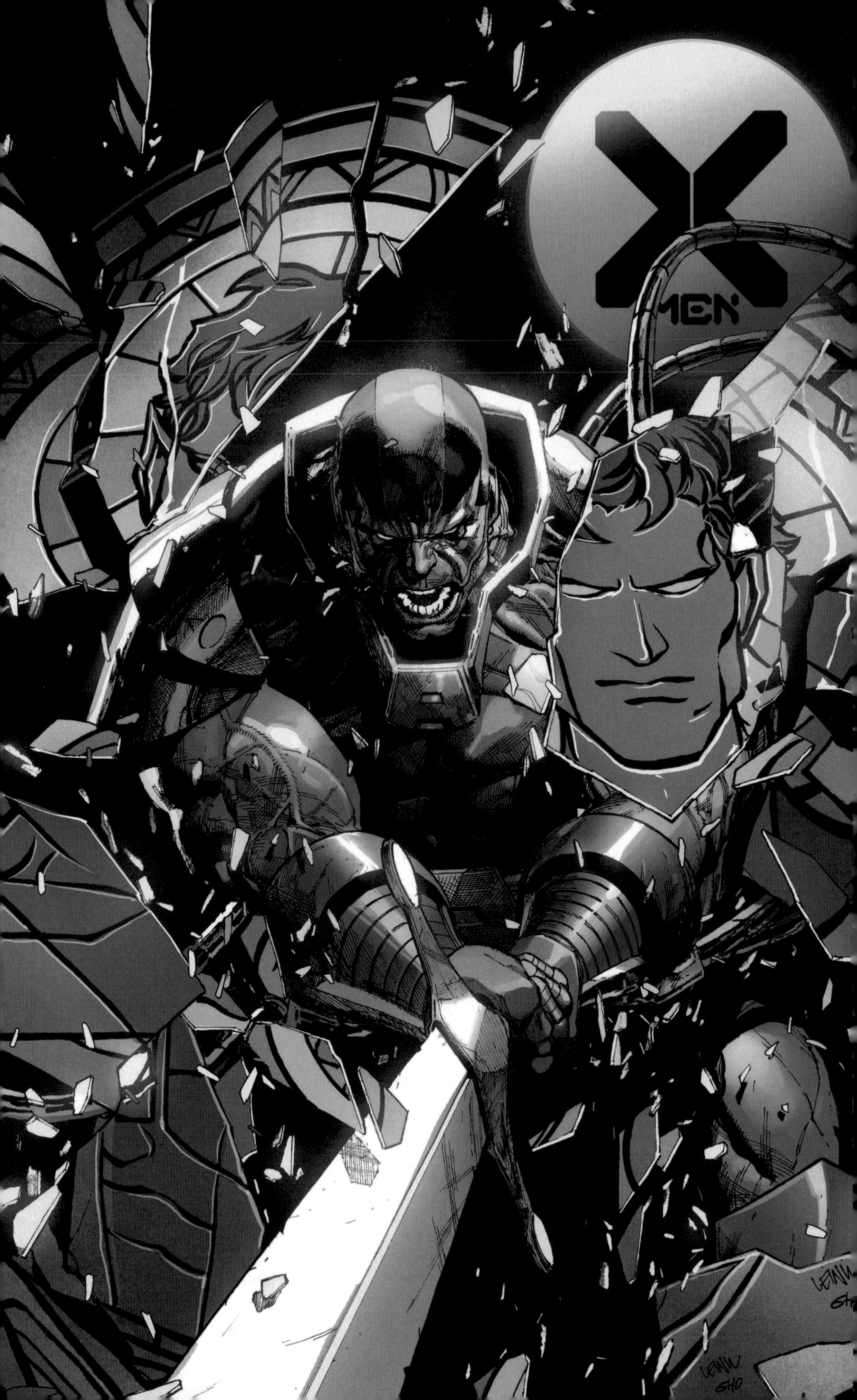
X
MEN

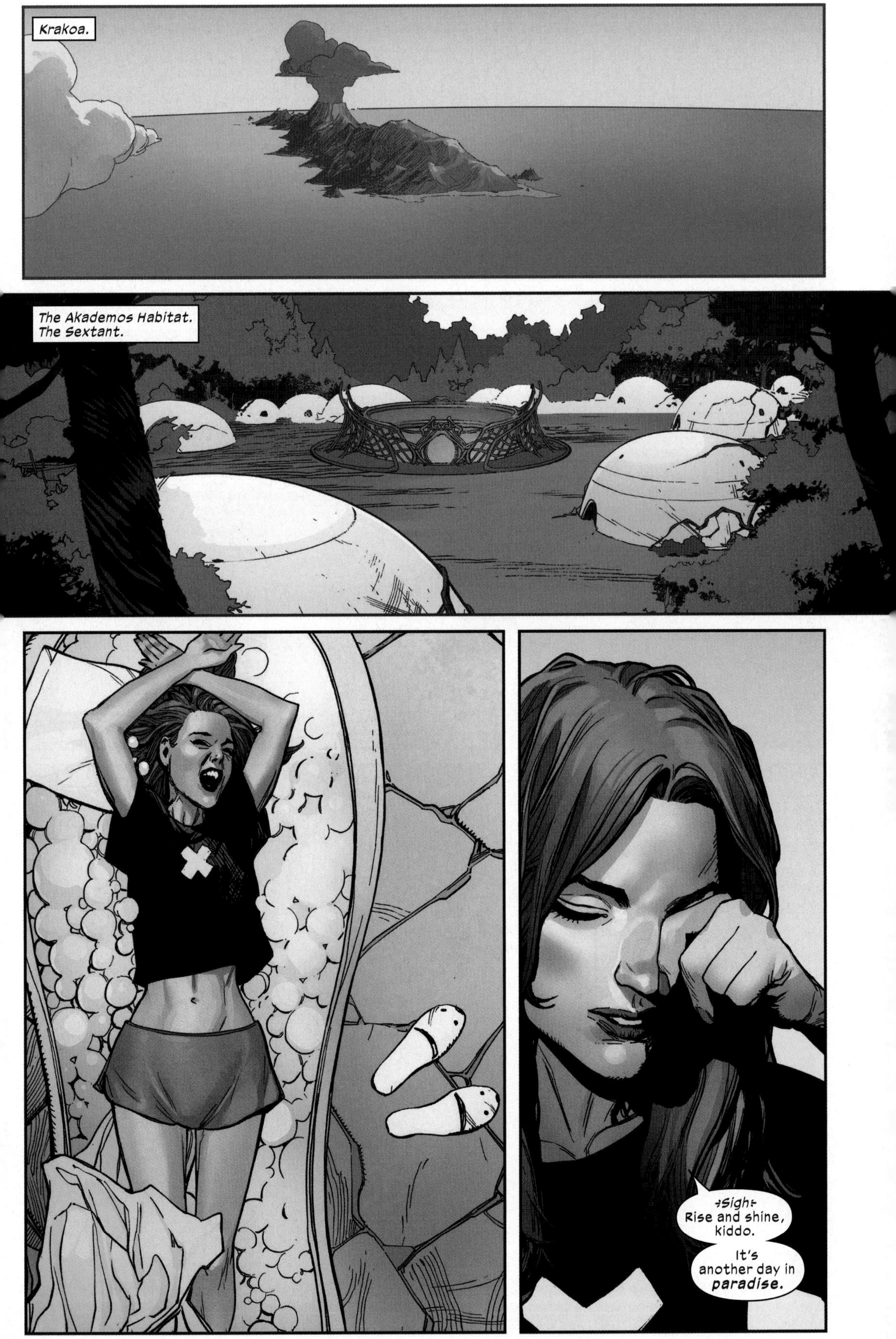

Krakoa.
The Akademos Habitat.
The Sextant.
-Sigh-
Rise and shine, kiddo.
It's another day in paradise.

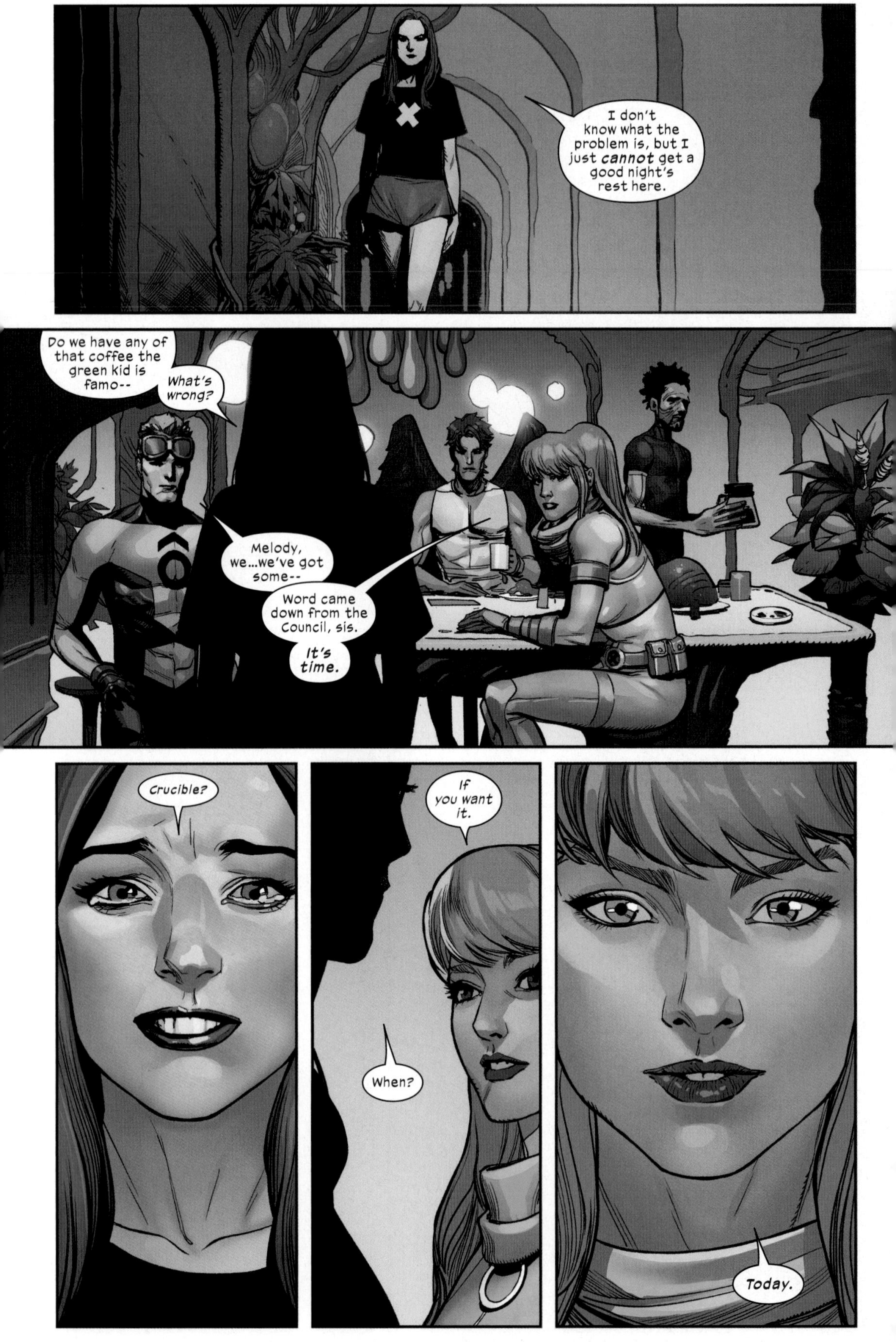

I don't know what the problem is, but I just *cannot* get a good night's rest here.
Do we have any of that coffee the green kid is famo--
What's wrong?
Melody, we...we've got some--
Word came down from the Council, sis.
It's time.
Crucible?
If you want it.
When?
Today.

[kra_[0.7]
[koa_[0.7]

[kra_[0.X]
[koa_[0.X]

FAITH

By combining their mutant powers, the Five have given the X-MEN -- and the Krakoan people -- the miraculous opportunity to be reborn after death. But nothing so incredible comes without a cost...

| Melody Guthrie | Paige Guthrie | Sam Guthrie | Joshua Guthrie |

| Cyclops | Wolverine | Cypher |

| Nightcrawler | Exodus | Apocalypse |

[00_mutants_of_X]
[00_the_world__X]

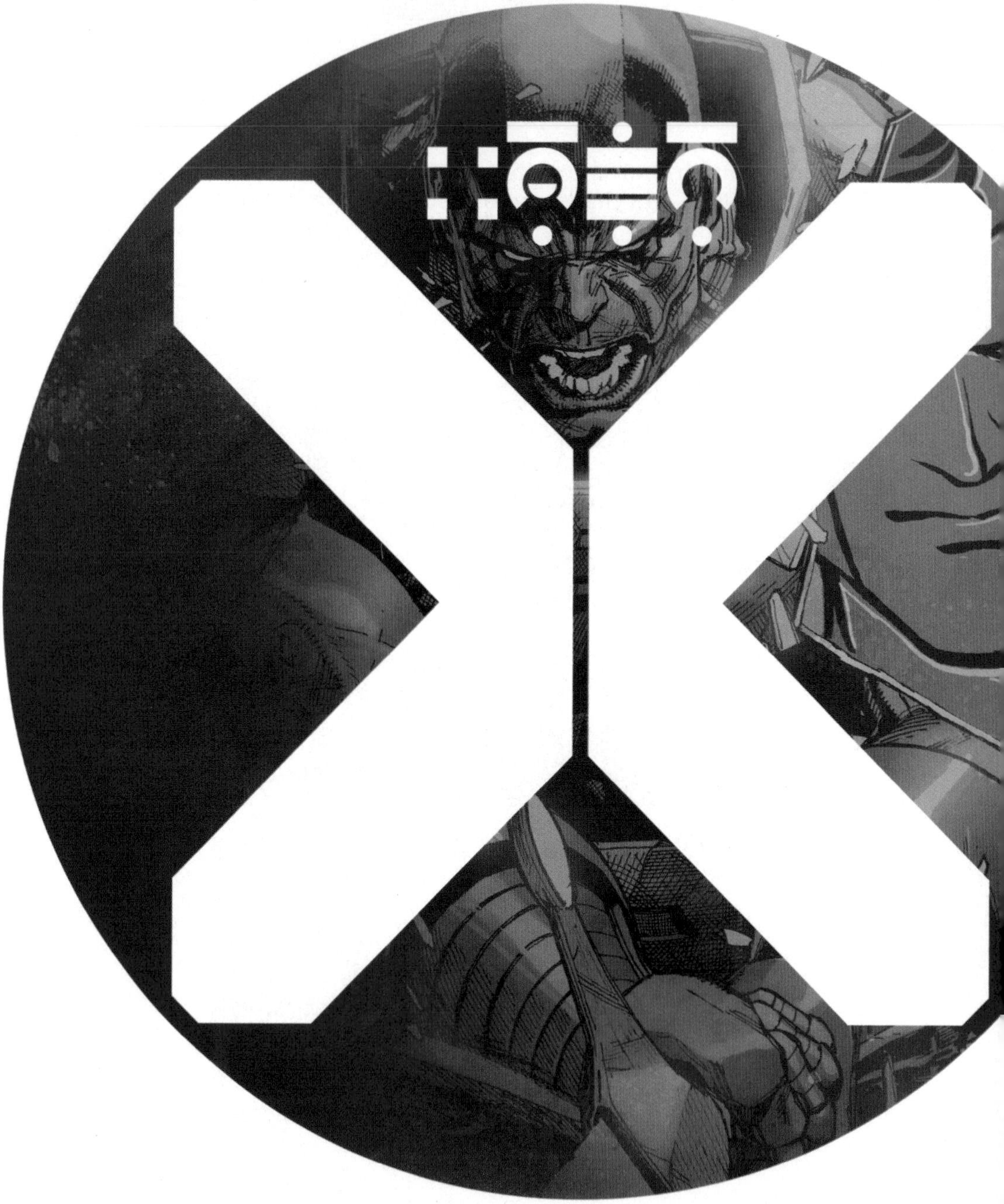

[00_mutants_of_X]
[00_the_world__X]

JONATHAN HICKMAN..................................[WRITER]
LEINIL FRANCIS YU.................................[ARTIST]
SUNNY GHO...............................[COLOR ARTIST]
VC's CLAYTON COWLES.........................[LETTERER]
TOM MULLER..[DESIGN]

LEINIL FRANCIS YU & SUNNY GHO...........[COVER ARTISTS]

MIKE DEL MUNDO...................[VARIANT COVER ARTIST]

NICK RUSSELL...............................[PRODUCTION]

ANNALISE BISSA......................[ASSISTANT EDITOR]
JORDAN D. WHITE..................................[EDITOR]
C.B. CEBULSKI........................[EDITOR IN CHIEF]

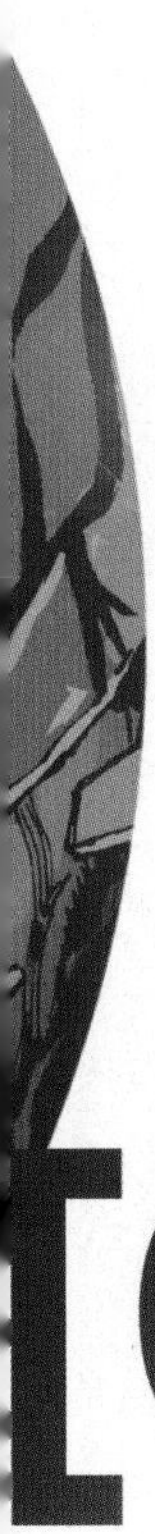

[07] X-MEN

[ISSUE SEVEN]...................LIFEDEATH

X-MEN CREATED BY.................STAN LEE & JACK KIRBY

[00_mutants_of_X]
[00_the_world__X]

[00_00...0]
[00_00...7]

[00_unite_]
[00______]

[00______]

[00______X]

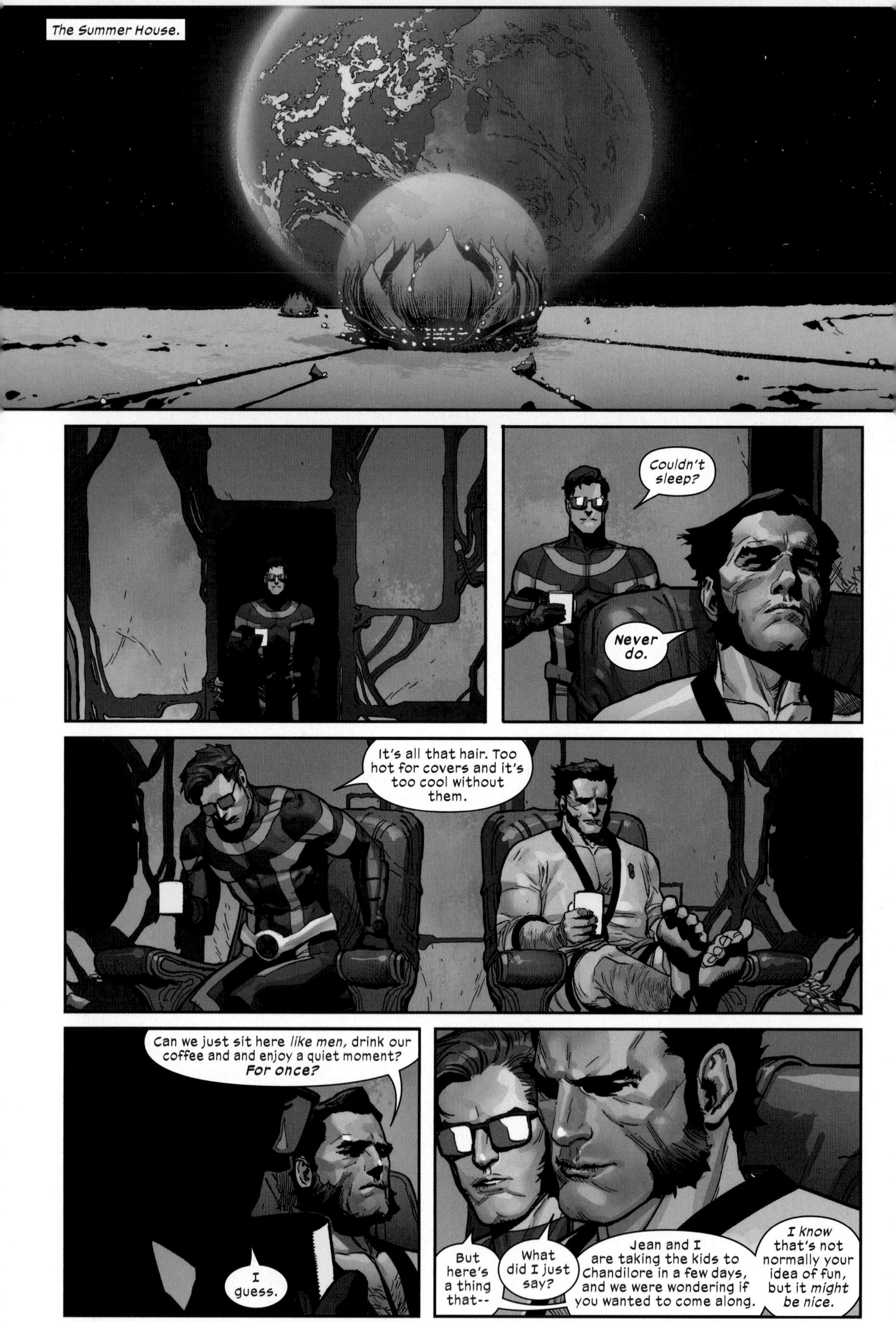
The Summer House.
Couldn't sleep?
Never do.
It's all that hair. Too hot for covers and it's too cool without them.
Can we just sit here *like men*, drink our coffee and and enjoy a quiet moment? *For once?*
I guess.
But here's a thing that--
What did I just say?
Jean and I are taking the kids to Chandilore in a few days, and we were wondering if you wanted to come along.
I know that's not normally your idea of fun, but it *might* be nice.

The scenery at that place is something else.

It sure is.

Jeannie in a bikini. Scott in a Speedo.

Heh.

Well, who could say no to that?

Great.

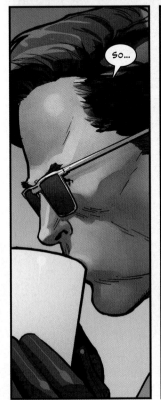

So...

Crucible is today.

Yes, it is.

Are you going?

No.

No, I am not.

You think it's wrong?

Didn't say that. Even if I felt that way...it ain't our choice to make, is it?

Logan, that feels like a cop out.

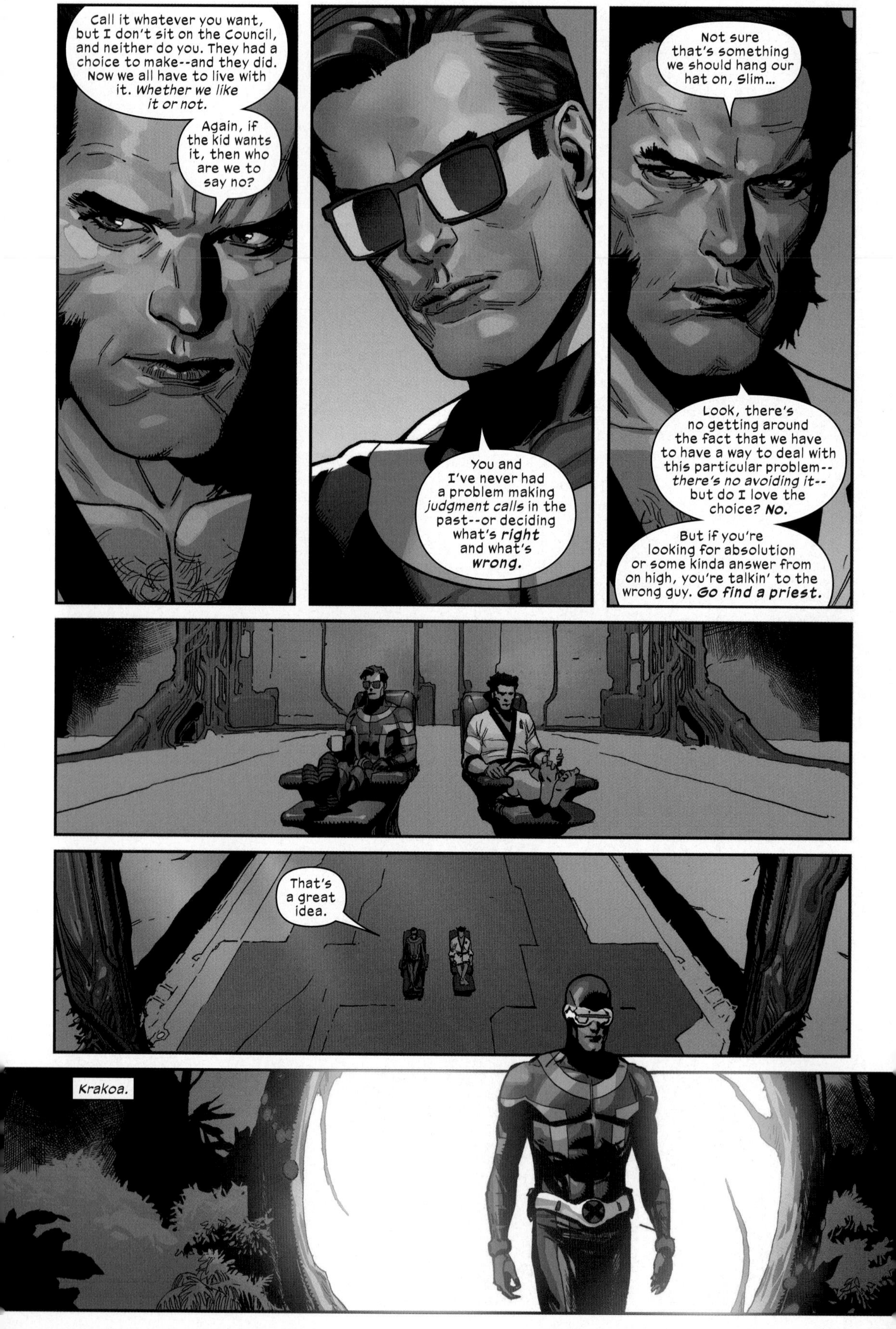

Call it whatever you want, but I don't sit on the Council, and neither do you. They had a choice to make--and they did. Now we all have to live with it. *Whether we like it or not.*
Again, if the kid wants it, then who are we to say no?
You and I've never had a problem making *judgment calls* in the past--or deciding what's ***right*** and what's ***wrong.***
Not sure that's something we should hang our hat on, Slim...
Look, there's no getting around the fact that we have to have a way to deal with this particular problem-- *there's no avoiding it--* but do I love the choice? ***No.***
But if you're looking for absolution or some kinda answer from on high, you're talkin' to the wrong guy. ***Go find a priest.***
That's a great idea.
Krakoa.

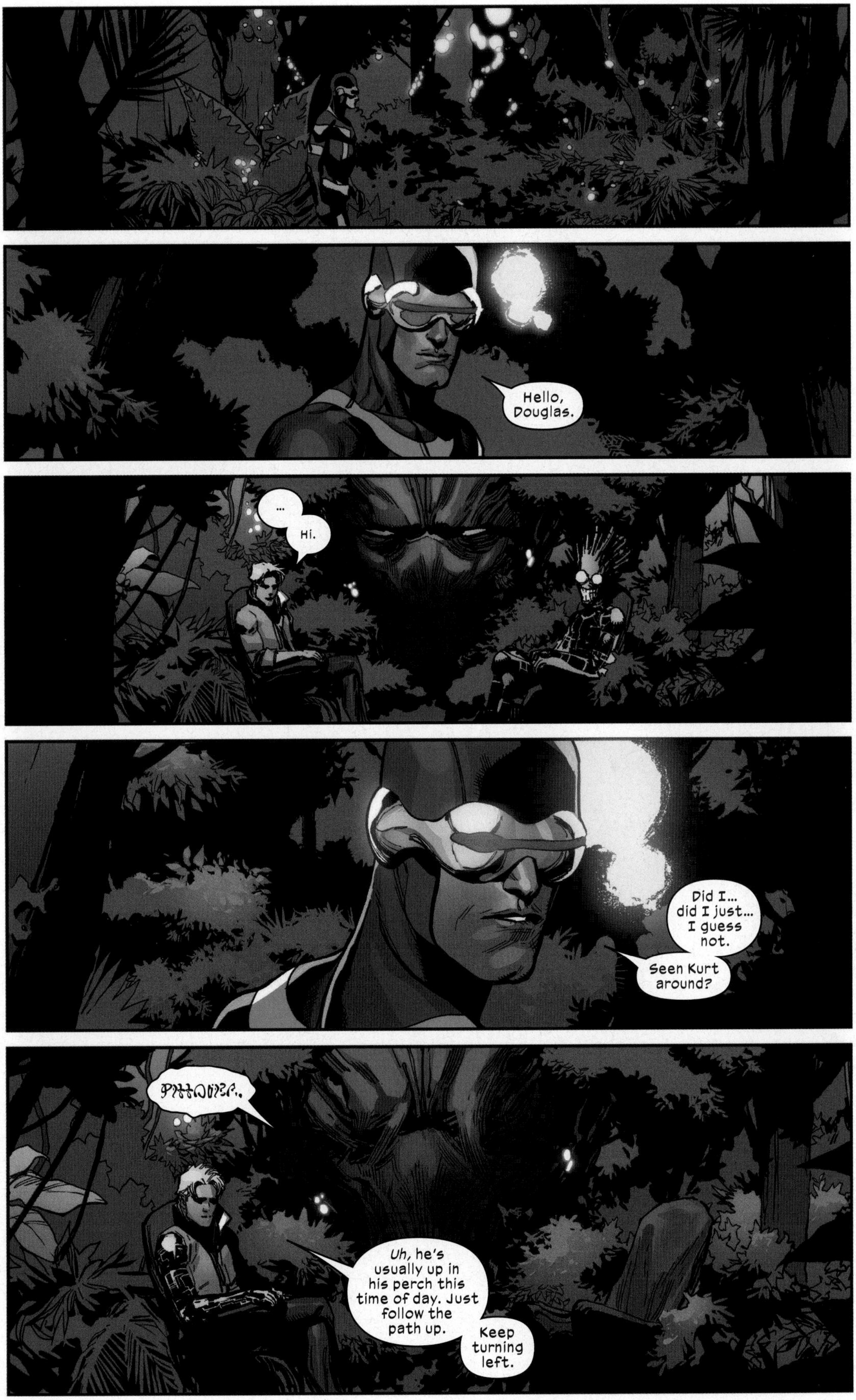
Hello, Douglas.
...
Hi.
Did I... did I just... I guess not.
Seen Kurt around?
Uh, he's usually up in his perch this time of day. Just follow the path up.
Keep turning left.

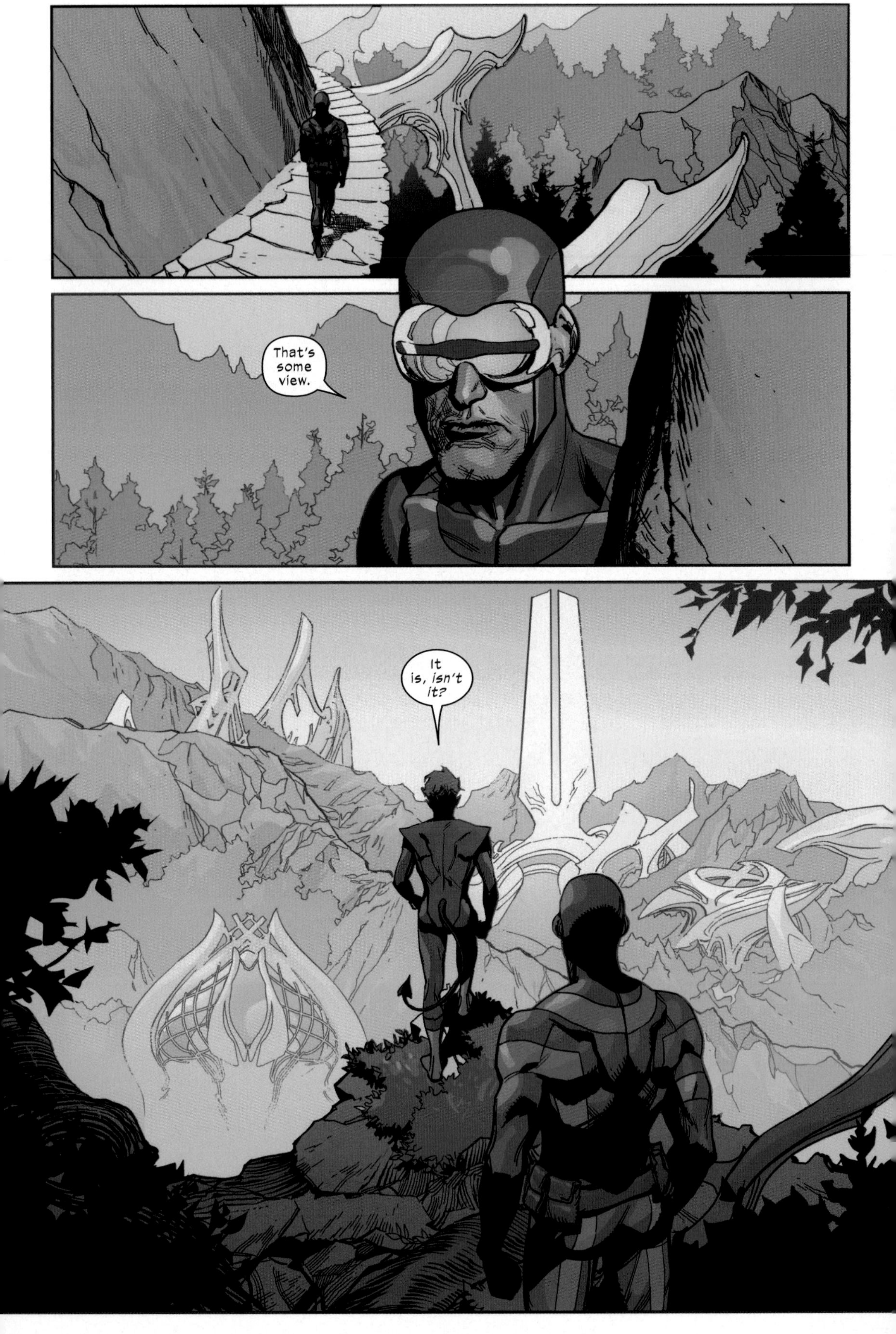
That's some view.
It is, isn't it?

You see that building in the distance? The tall one-- the forked towers?

Hard to miss.

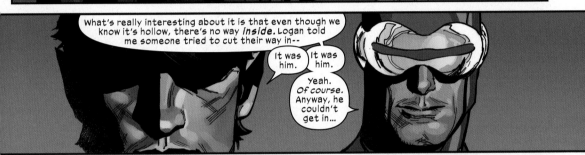

What's really interesting about it is that even though we know it's hollow, there's no way *inside*. Logan told me someone tried to cut their way in--

It was him.

It was him.

Yeah. Of course. Anyway, he couldn't get in...

"It just immediately sealed back up.

"So *no one's* been in there."

I have.

Is that so?

Yes. Curiosity got the best of me. So in I went. Leap of faith and all that.

Well? What did you find?

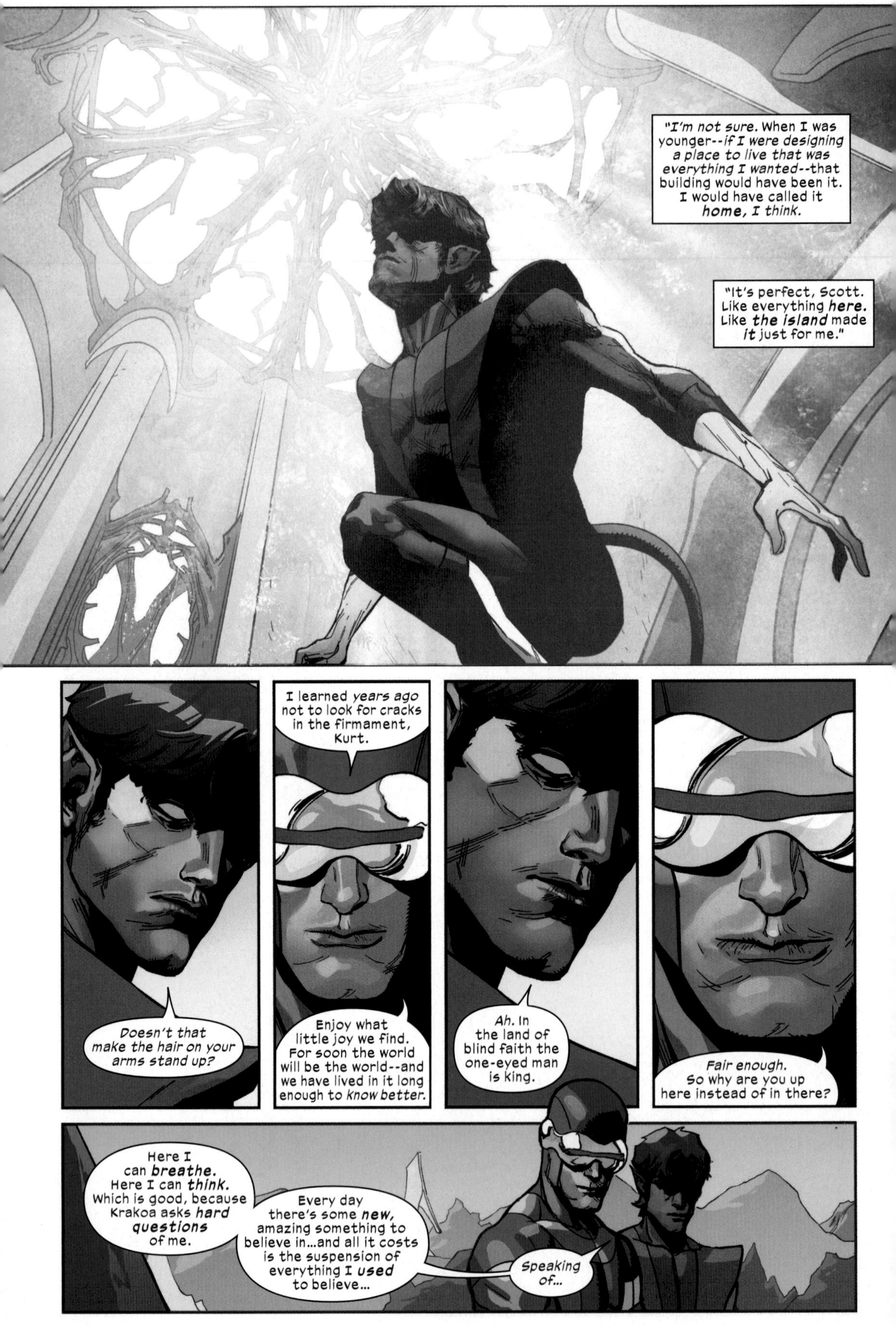
"*I'm not sure.* When I was younger--*if I were designing a place to live that was everything I wanted*--that building would have been it. I would have called it ***home, I think.***
"It's perfect, Scott. Like everything ***here.*** Like ***the island*** made ***it*** just for me."
I learned *years ago* not to look for cracks in the firmament, Kurt.
Doesn't that make the hair on your arms stand up?
Enjoy what little joy we find. For soon the world will be the world--and we have lived in it long enough to *know better.*
Ah. In the land of blind faith the one-eyed man is king.
Fair enough. So why are you up here instead of in there?
Here I can ***breathe.*** Here I can ***think.*** Which is good, because Krakoa asks ***hard questions*** of me.
Every day there's some ***new,*** amazing something to believe in...and all it costs is the suspension of everything I ***used*** to believe...
Speaking of...

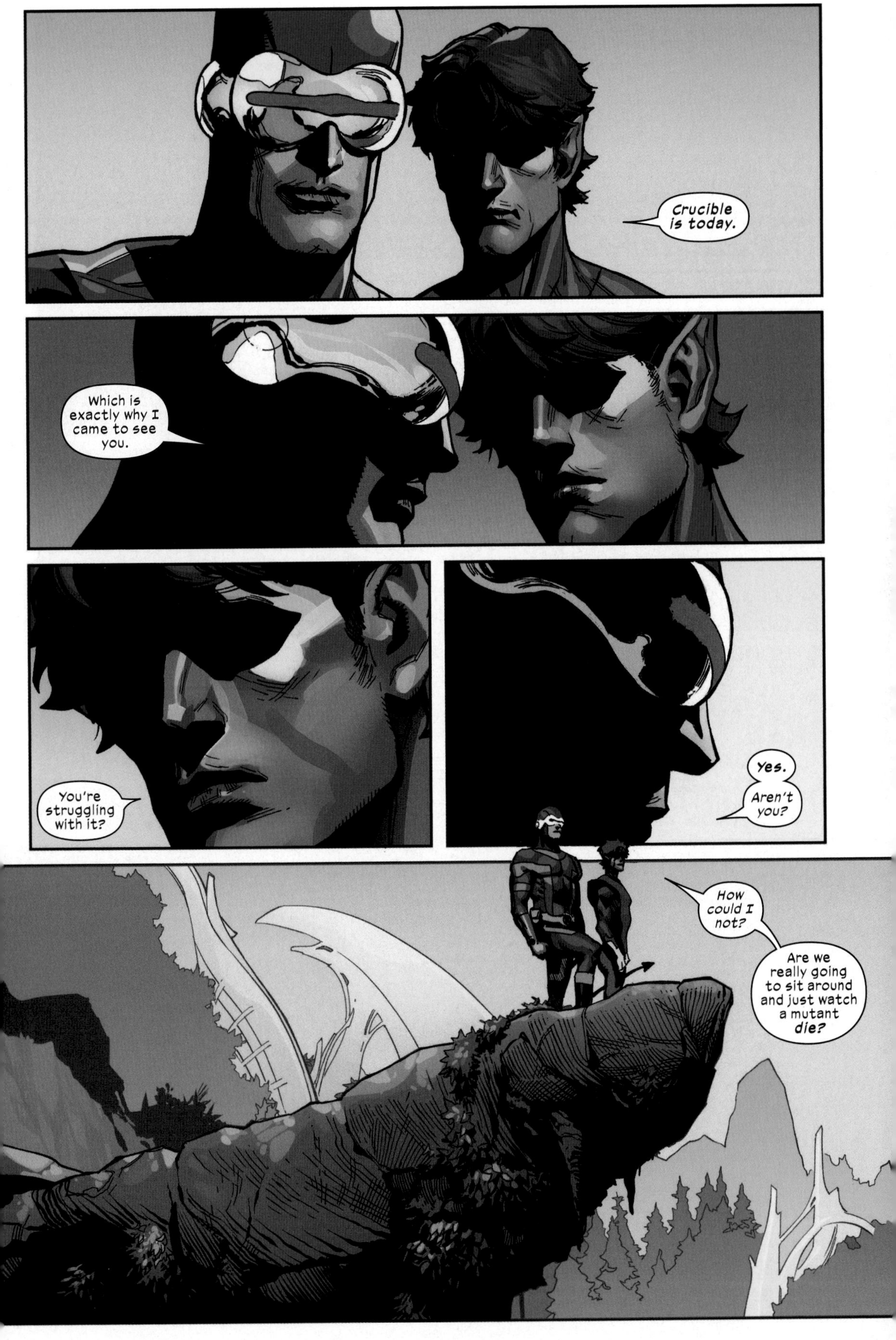
Crucible is today.
Which is exactly why I came to see you.
You're struggling with it?
Yes.
Aren't you?
How could I not?
Are we really going to sit around and just watch a mutant die?

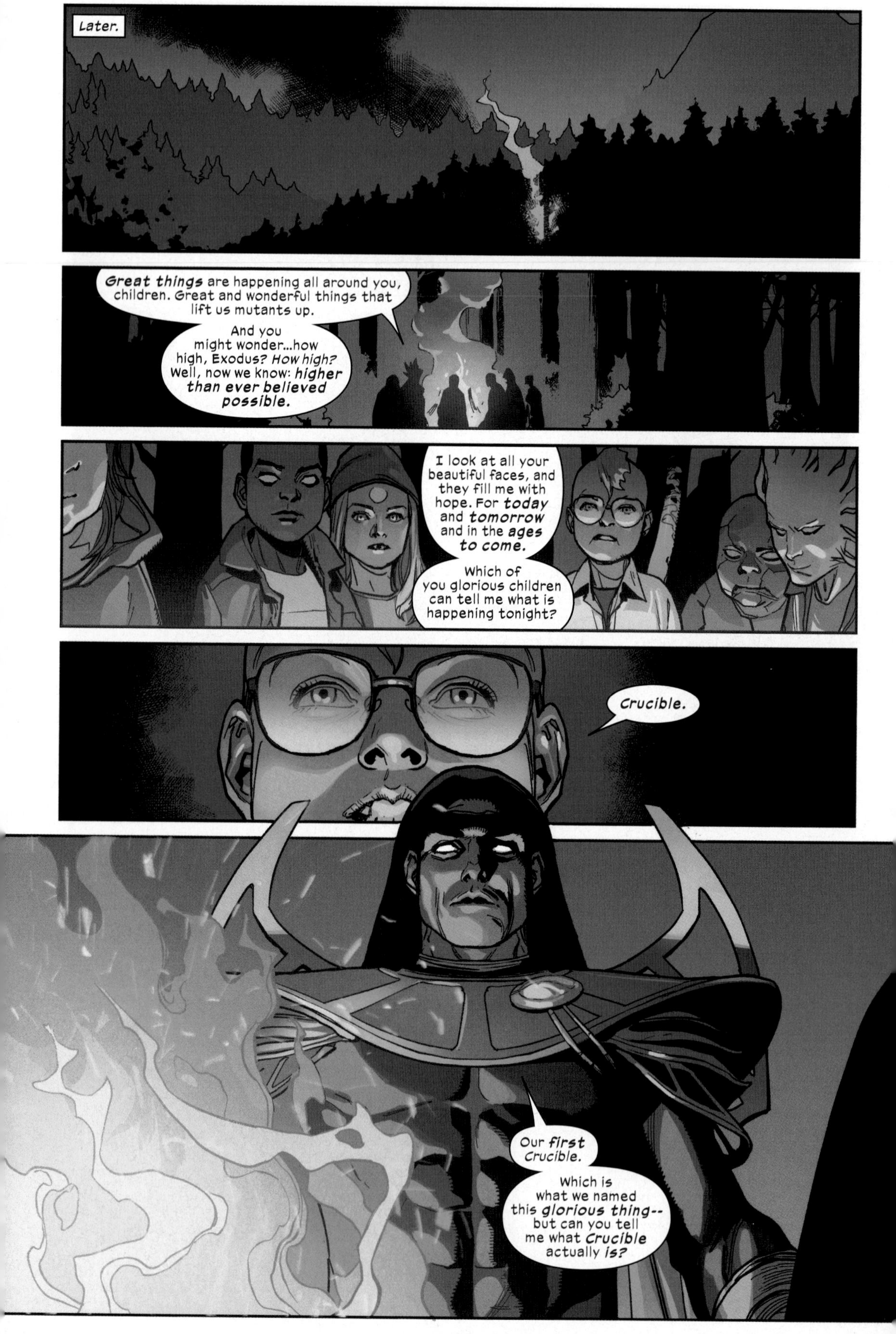
Later.
Great things are happening all around you, children. Great and wonderful things that lift us mutants up.
And you might wonder...how high, Exodus? How high? Well, now we know: higher than ever believed possible.
I look at all your beautiful faces, and they fill me with hope. For today and tomorrow and in the ages to come.
Which of you glorious children can tell me what is happening tonight?
Crucible.
Our first Crucible.
Which is what we named this glorious thing--but can you tell me what Crucible actually is?

I think it's where a *broken mutant* has to *die* so they can be an *unbroken mutant*.

Is that right?

Your answer has the ring of truth...but not *the whole truth.*

Would you like to hear the whole truth?

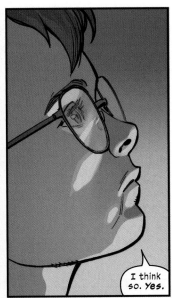

I think so. *Yes.*

Then listen closely, children, for this is *truth.*

It is the story of a woman. Her name was *Scarlet Witch.*

Pretender! Pretender!

Stop! Stop! We don't say her name!

Pretender! Pretender!

Of course you know her--*we all know her*--her and her great sin.

She erased the powers of one million mutants. She made *mutant* into *man*...

"She made so many of us less. She spoke the words..."

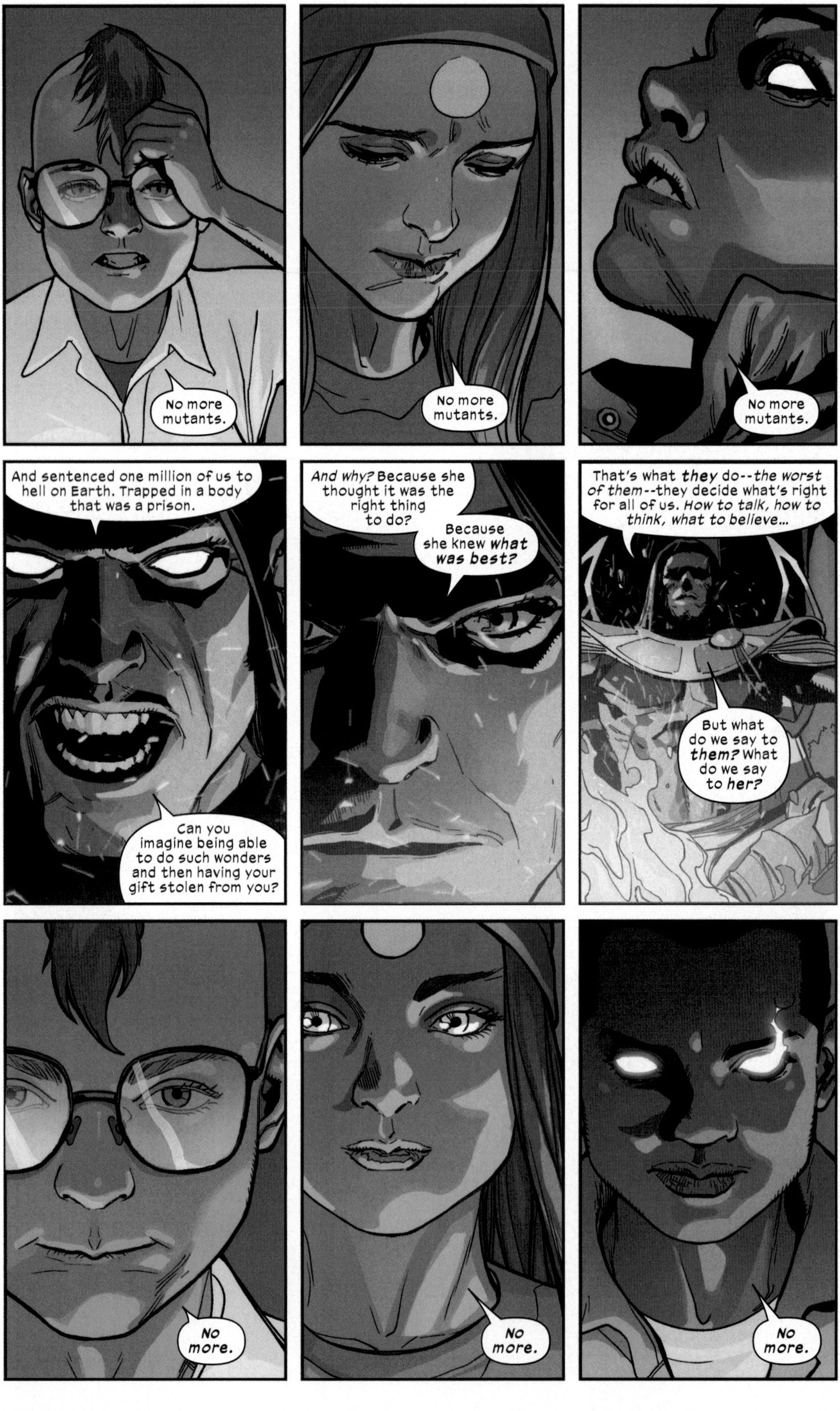
No more mutants.
No more mutants.
No more mutants.
And sentenced one million of us to hell on Earth. Trapped in a body that was a prison.
Can you imagine being able to do such wonders and then having your gift stolen from you?
And why? Because she thought it was the right thing to do?
Because she knew *what was best?*
That's what *they* do--*the worst of them*--they decide what's right for all of us. *How to talk, how to think, what to believe...*
But what do we say to *them?* What do we say to *her?*
No more.
No more.
No more.

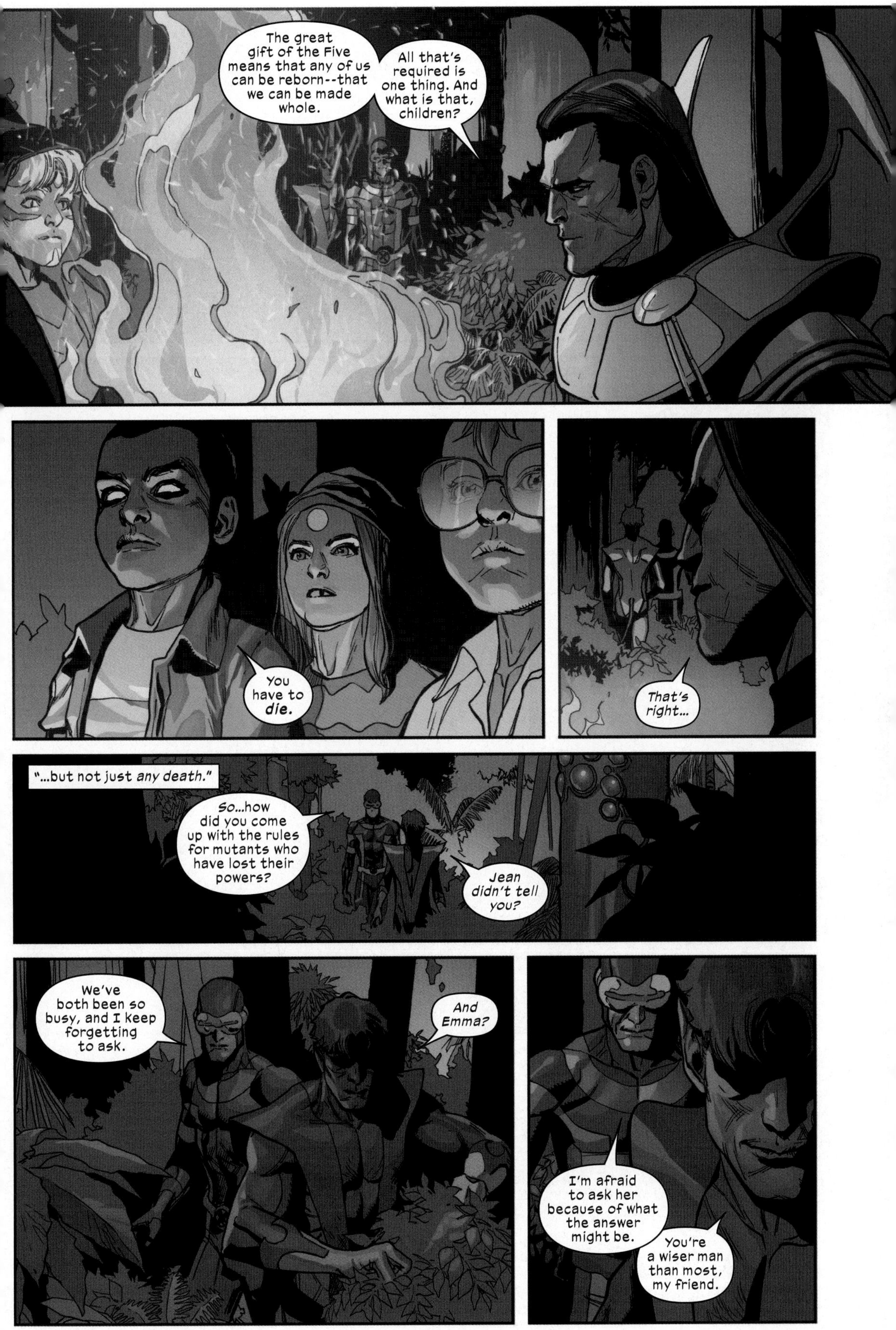
The great gift of the Five means that any of us can be reborn--that we can be made whole.
All that's required is one thing. And what is that, children?
You have to *die*.
That's right...
"...but not just *any death*."
So...how did you come up with the rules for mutants who have lost their powers?
Jean didn't tell you?
We've both been so busy, and I keep forgetting to ask.
And Emma?
I'm afraid to ask her because of what the answer might be.
You're a wiser man than most, my friend.

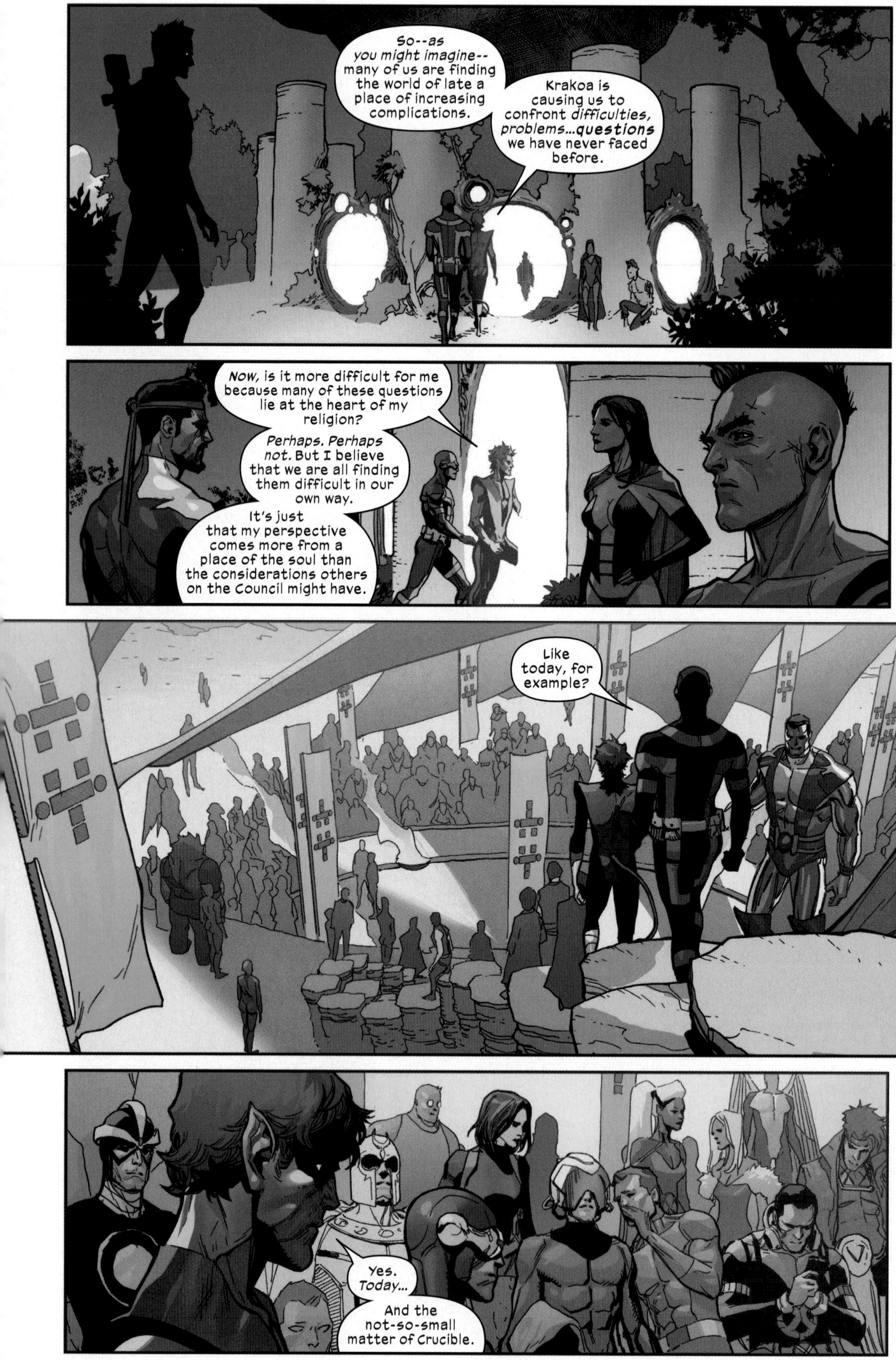
So--as you might imagine--many of us are finding the world of late a place of increasing complications.
Krakoa is causing us to confront difficulties, problems...questions we have never faced before.
Now, is it more difficult for me because many of these questions lie at the heart of my religion?
Perhaps. Perhaps not. But I believe that we are all finding them difficult in our own way.
It's just that my perspective comes more from a place of the soul than the considerations others on the Council might have.
Like today, for example?
Yes. Today...
And the not-so-small matter of Crucible.

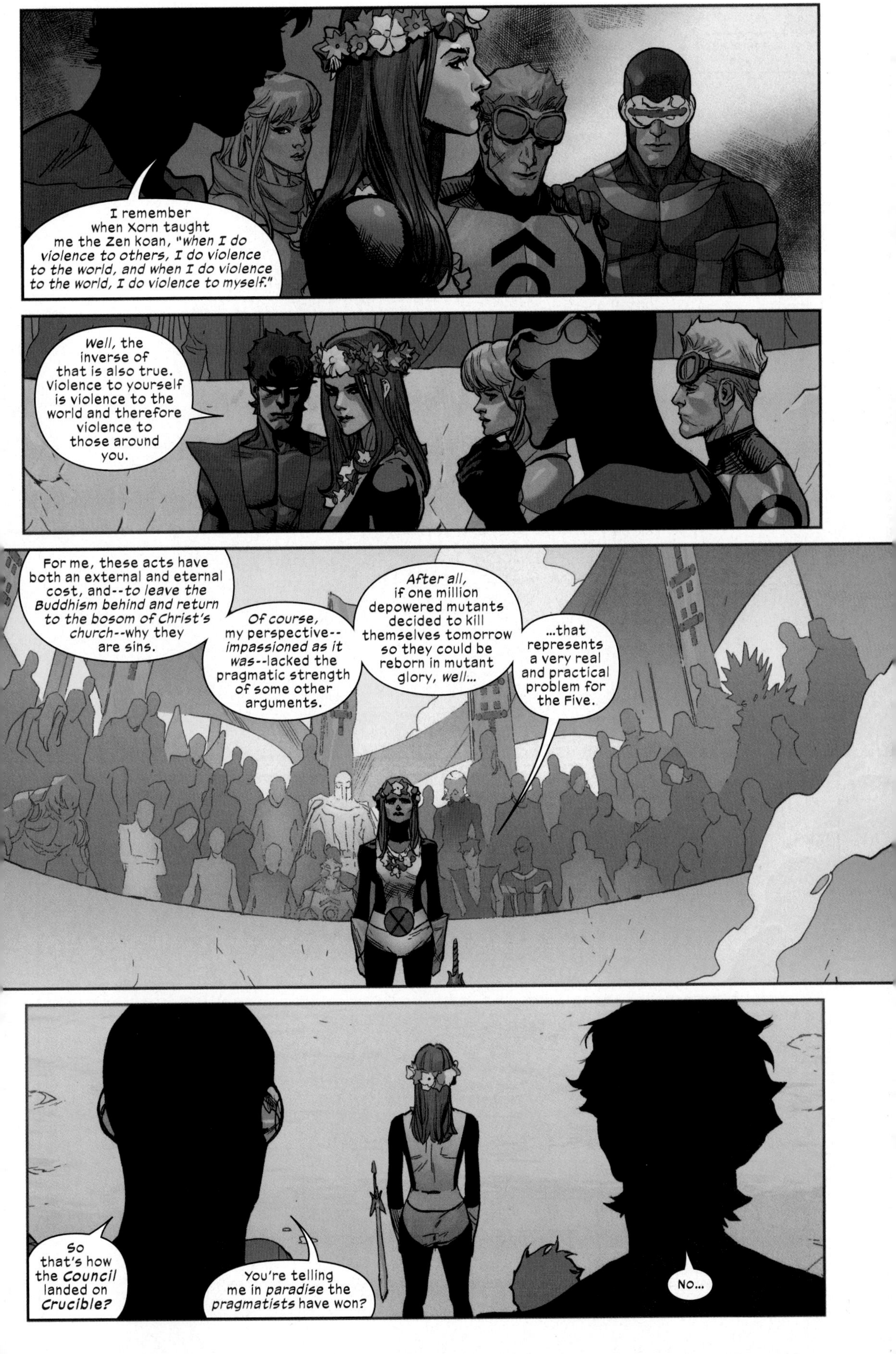
I remember when Xorn taught me the Zen koan, "when I do violence to others, I do violence to the world, and when I do violence to the world, I do violence to myself."
Well, the inverse of that is also true. Violence to yourself is violence to the world and therefore violence to those around you.
For me, these acts have both an external and eternal cost, and--to leave the Buddhism behind and return to the bosom of Christ's church--why they are sins.
Of course, my perspective--impassioned as it was--lacked the pragmatic strength of some other arguments.
After all, if one million depowered mutants decided to kill themselves tomorrow so they could be reborn in mutant glory, well...
...that represents a very real and practical problem for the Five.
So that's how the Council landed on Crucible?
You're telling me in paradise the pragmatists have won?
No...

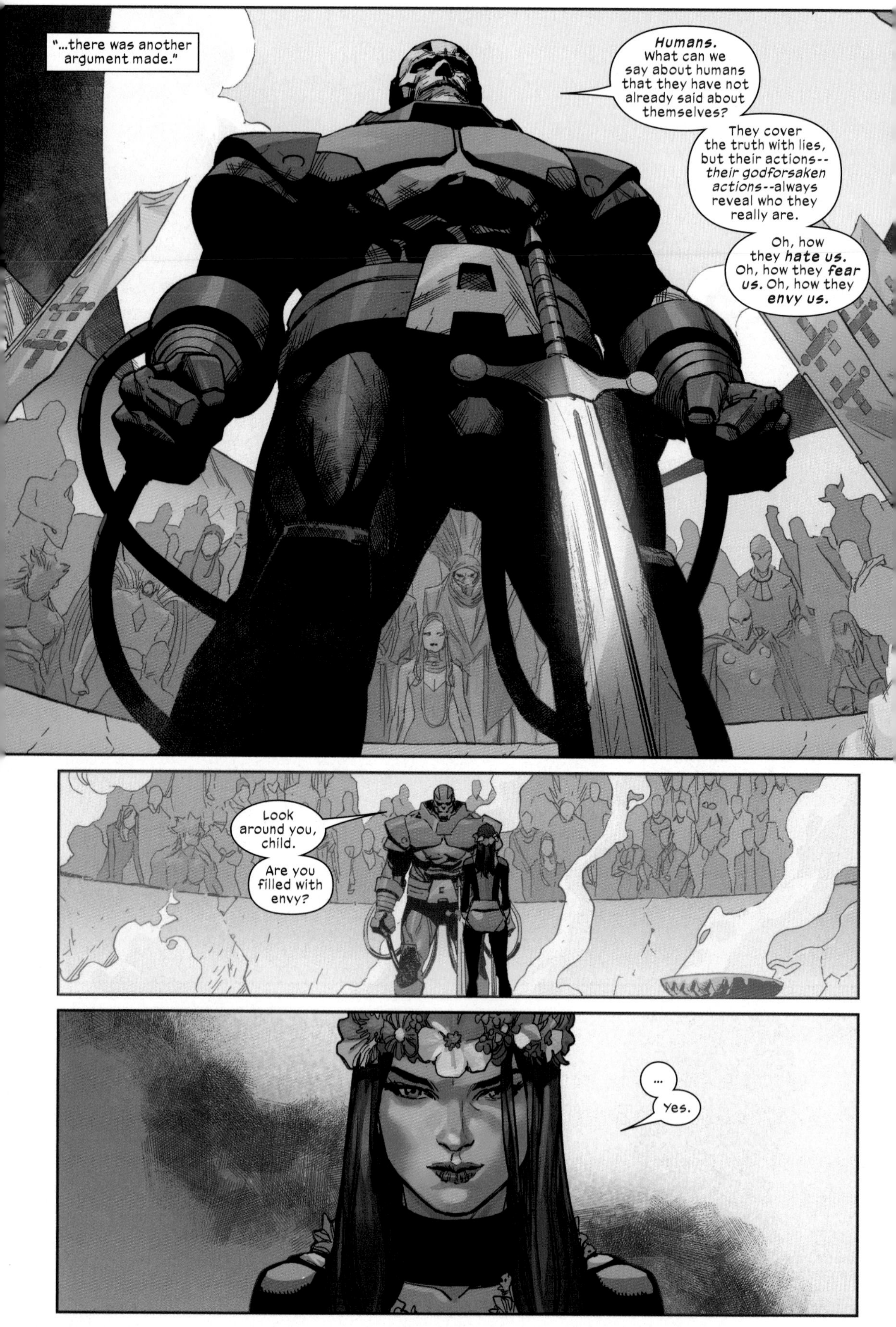
"...there was another argument made."
Humans. What can we say about humans that they have not already said about themselves?
They cover the truth with lies, but their actions--their godforsaken actions--always reveal who they really are.
Oh, how they hate us. Oh, how they fear us. Oh, how they envy us.
Look around you, child.
Are you filled with envy?
...
Yes.

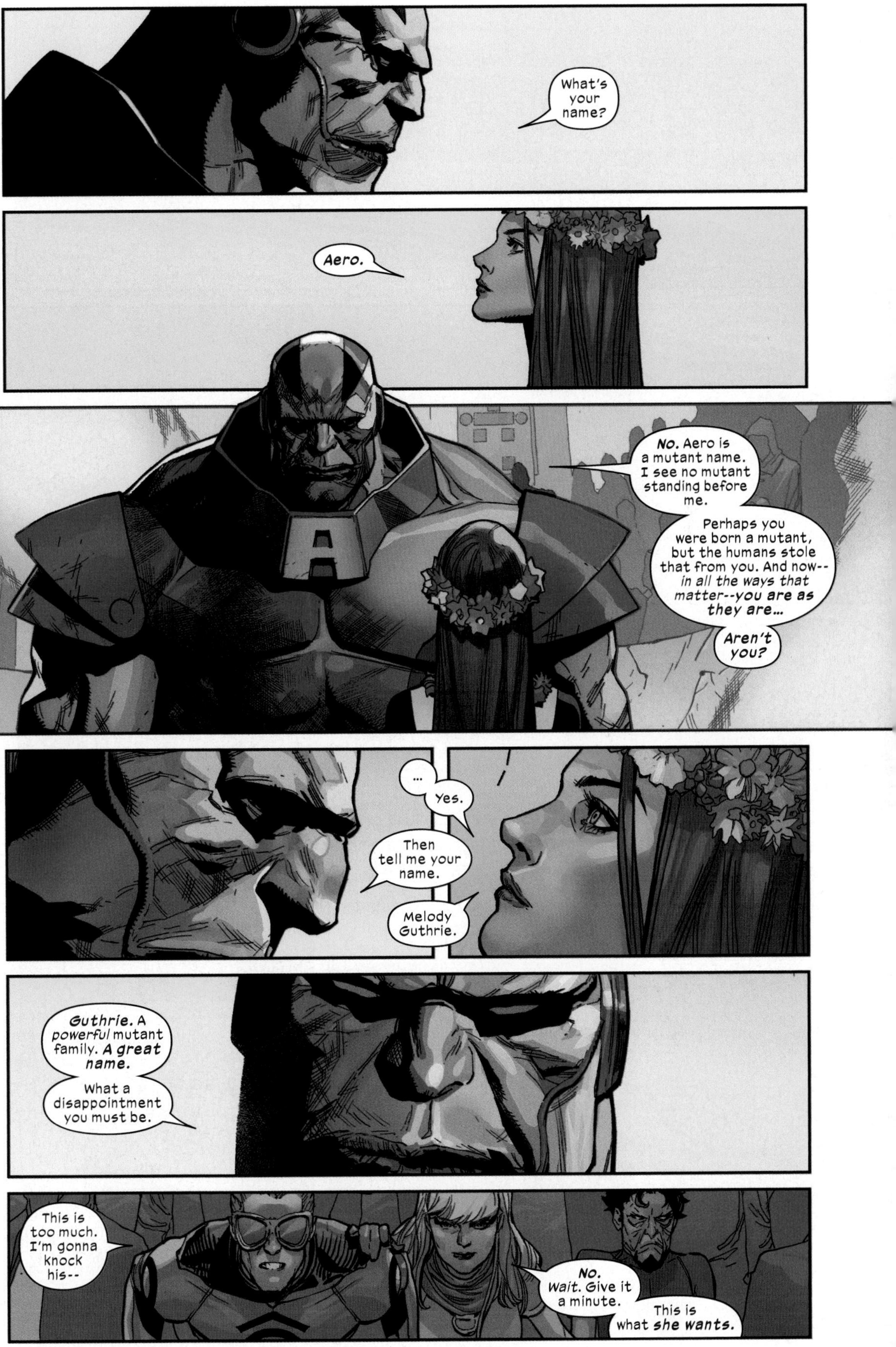
What's your name?
Aero.
No. Aero is a mutant name. I see no mutant standing before me.
Perhaps you were born a mutant, but the humans stole that from you. And now-- in all the ways that matter--you are as they are...
Aren't you?
... Yes.
Then tell me your name.
Melody Guthrie.
Guthrie. A powerful mutant family. A great name.
What a disappointment you must be.
This is too much. I'm gonna knock his--
No. Wait. Give it a minute.
This is what she wants.

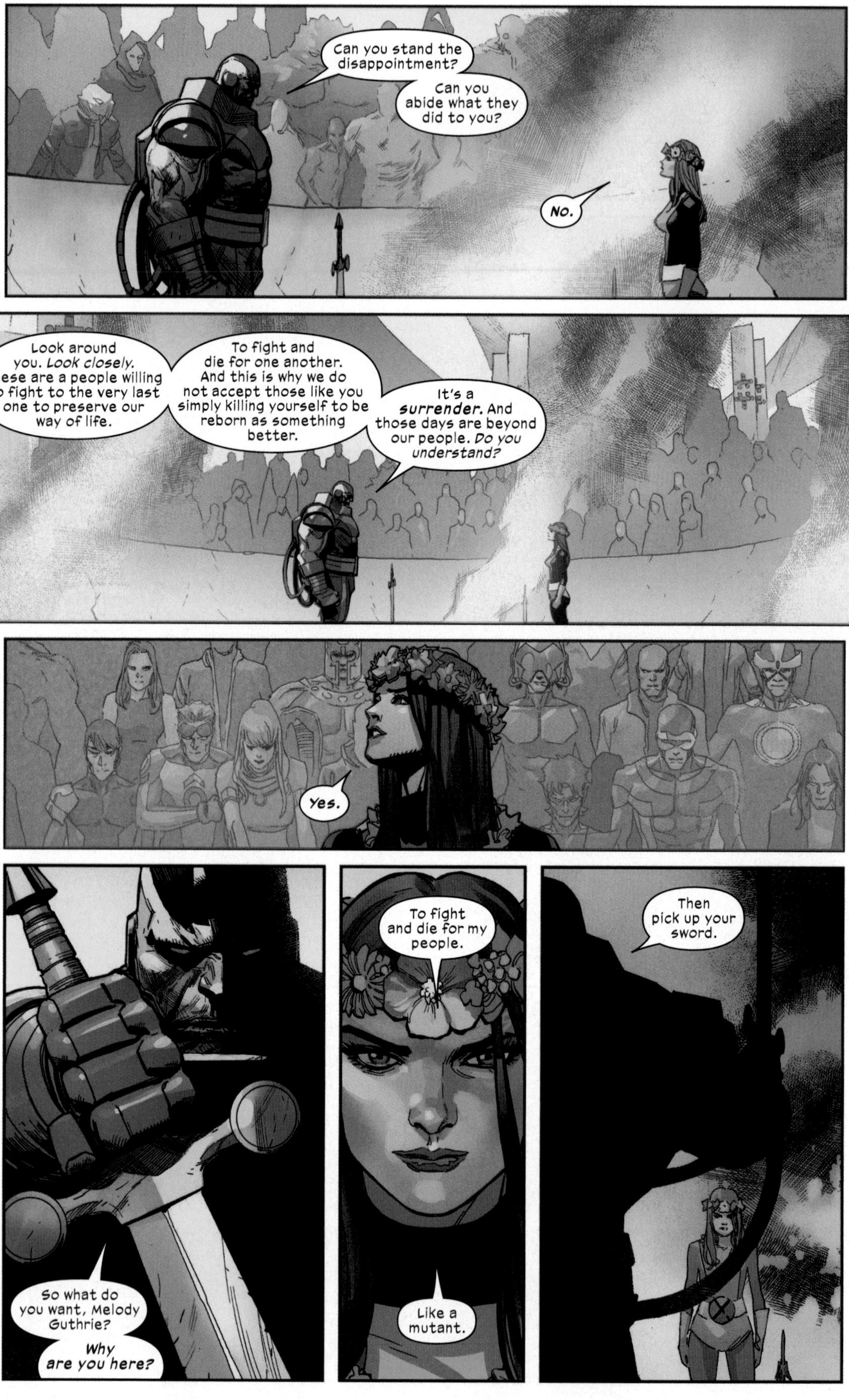

Can you stand the disappointment?
Can you abide what they did to you?
No.
Look around you. *Look closely.* These are a people willing to fight to the very last one to preserve our way of life.
To fight and die for one another. And this is why we do not accept those like you simply killing yourself to be reborn as something better.
It's a **surrender.** And those days are beyond our people. *Do you understand?*
Yes.
So what do you want, Melody Guthrie?
Why are you here?
To fight and die for my people.
Like a mutant.
Then pick up your sword.

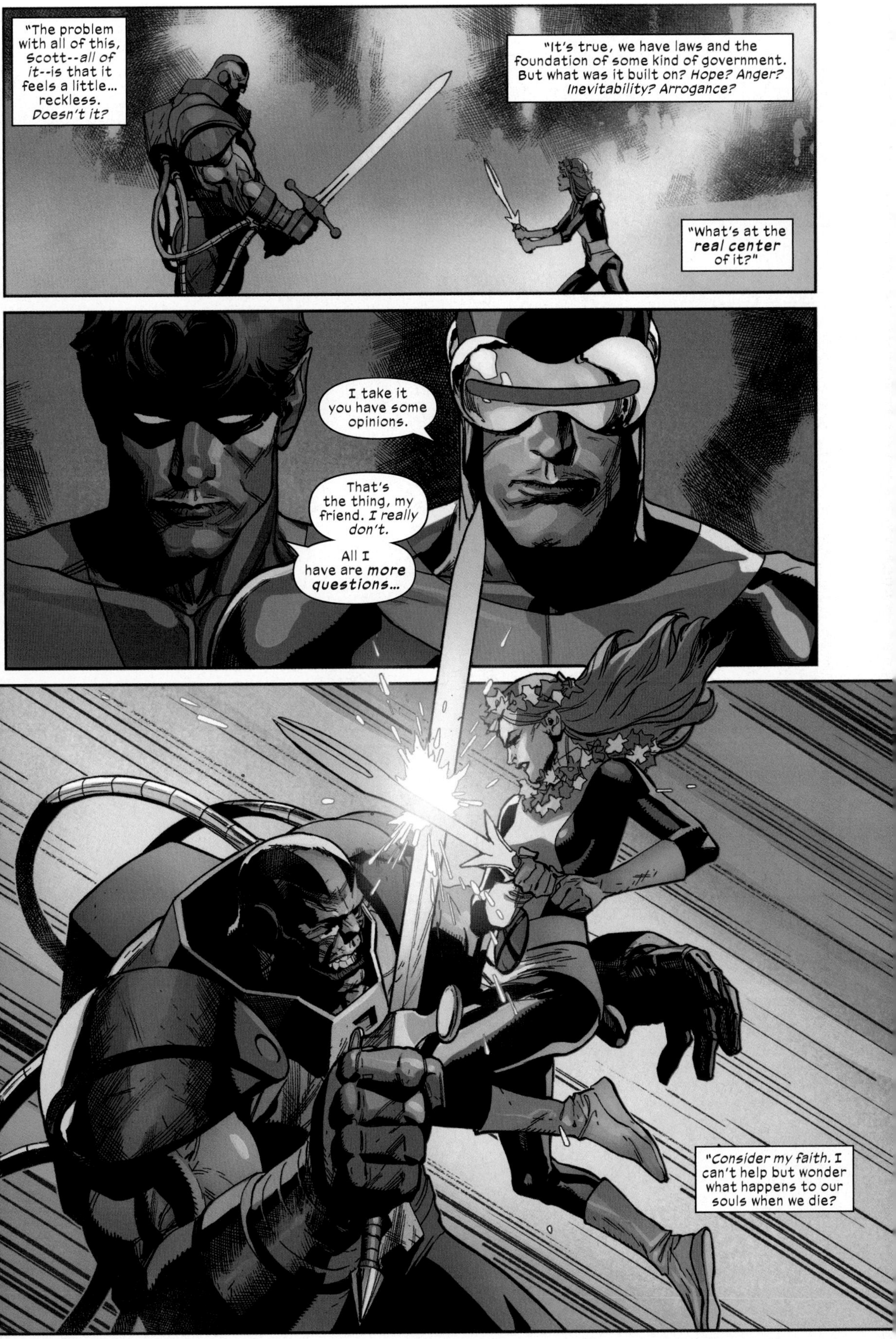
"The problem with all of this, Scott--*all of it*--is that it feels a little... reckless. *Doesn't it?*
"It's true, we have laws and the foundation of some kind of government. But what was it built on? *Hope? Anger? Inevitability? Arrogance?*
"What's at the ***real center*** of it?"
I take it you have some opinions.
That's the thing, my friend. *I really don't.*
All I have are ***more questions...***
"*Consider my faith.* I can't help but wonder what happens to our souls when we die?

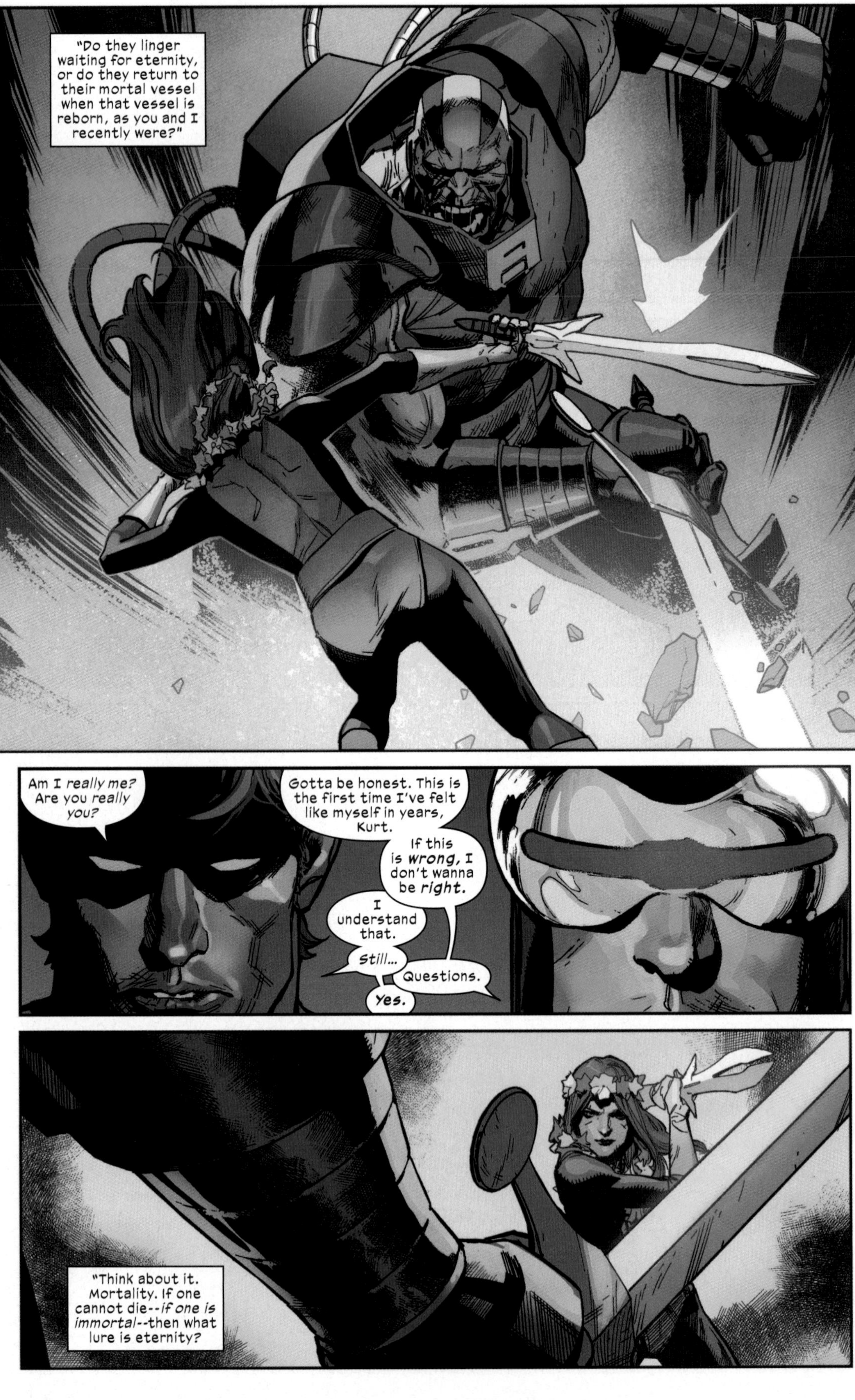
"Do they linger waiting for eternity, or do they return to their mortal vessel when that vessel is reborn, as you and I recently were?"
Am I *really me?* Are you *really you?*
Gotta be honest. This is the first time I've felt like myself in years, Kurt.
If this is *wrong,* I don't wanna be *right.*
I understand that.
Still...
Questions.
Yes.
"Think about it. Mortality. If one cannot die--*if one is immortal*--then what lure is eternity?

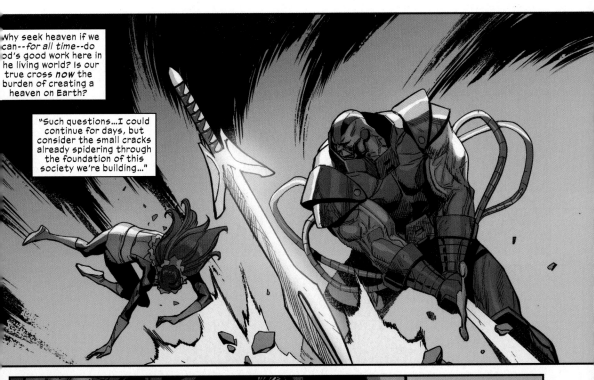

Why seek heaven if we can--*for all time*--do God's good work here in the living world? Is our true cross *now* the burden of creating a heaven on Earth?

"Such questions...I could continue for days, but consider the small cracks already spidering through the foundation of this society we're building..."

You've heard about *the wills?*

Yes.

And?

It's going to be a problem.

"I agree, but some might say it isn't. Especially after witnessing Crucible."

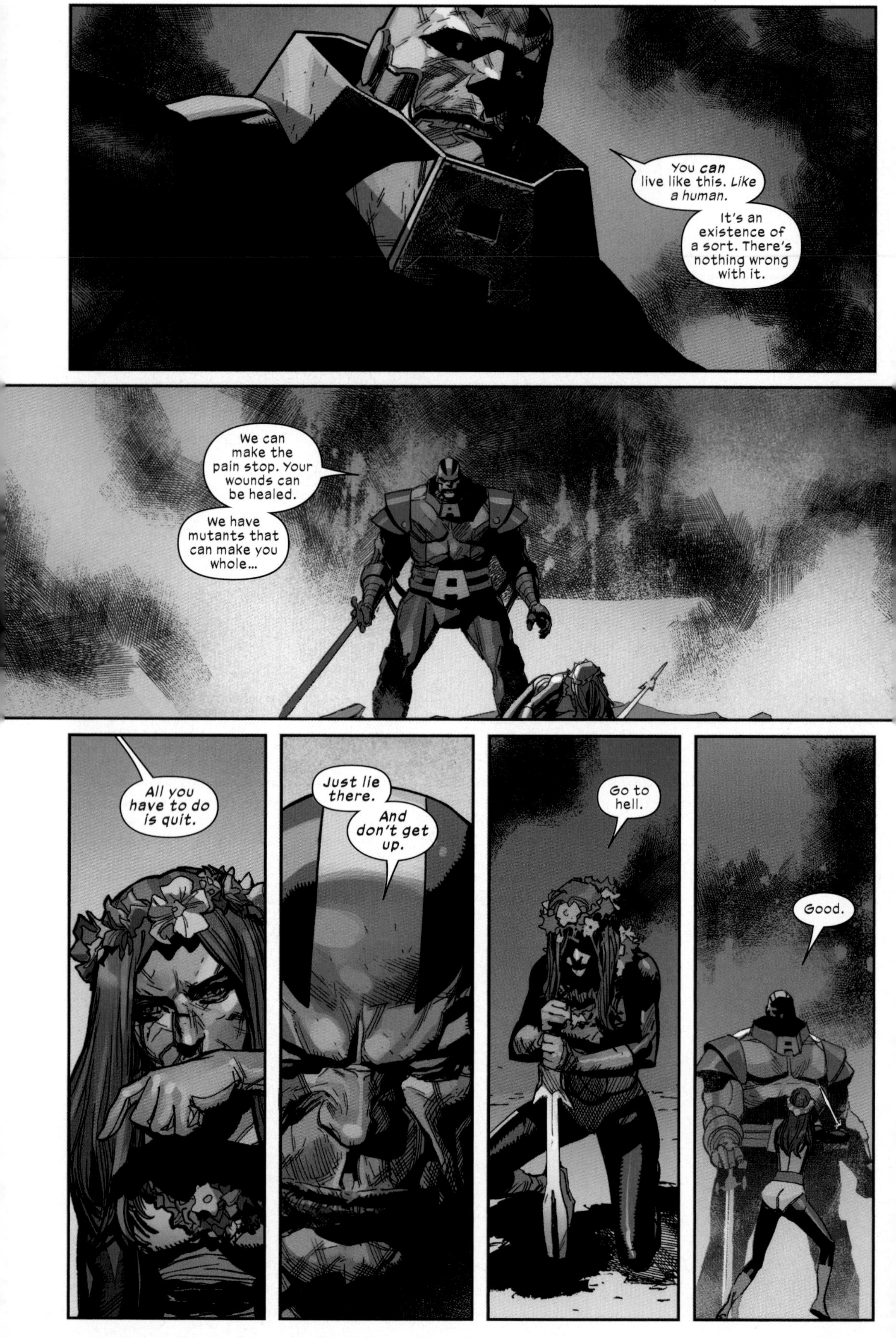
You *can* live like this. *Like a human.*
It's an existence of a sort. There's nothing wrong with it.
We can make the pain stop. Your wounds can be healed.
We have mutants that can make you whole...
All you have to do is quit.
Just lie there.
And don't get up.
Go to hell.
Good.

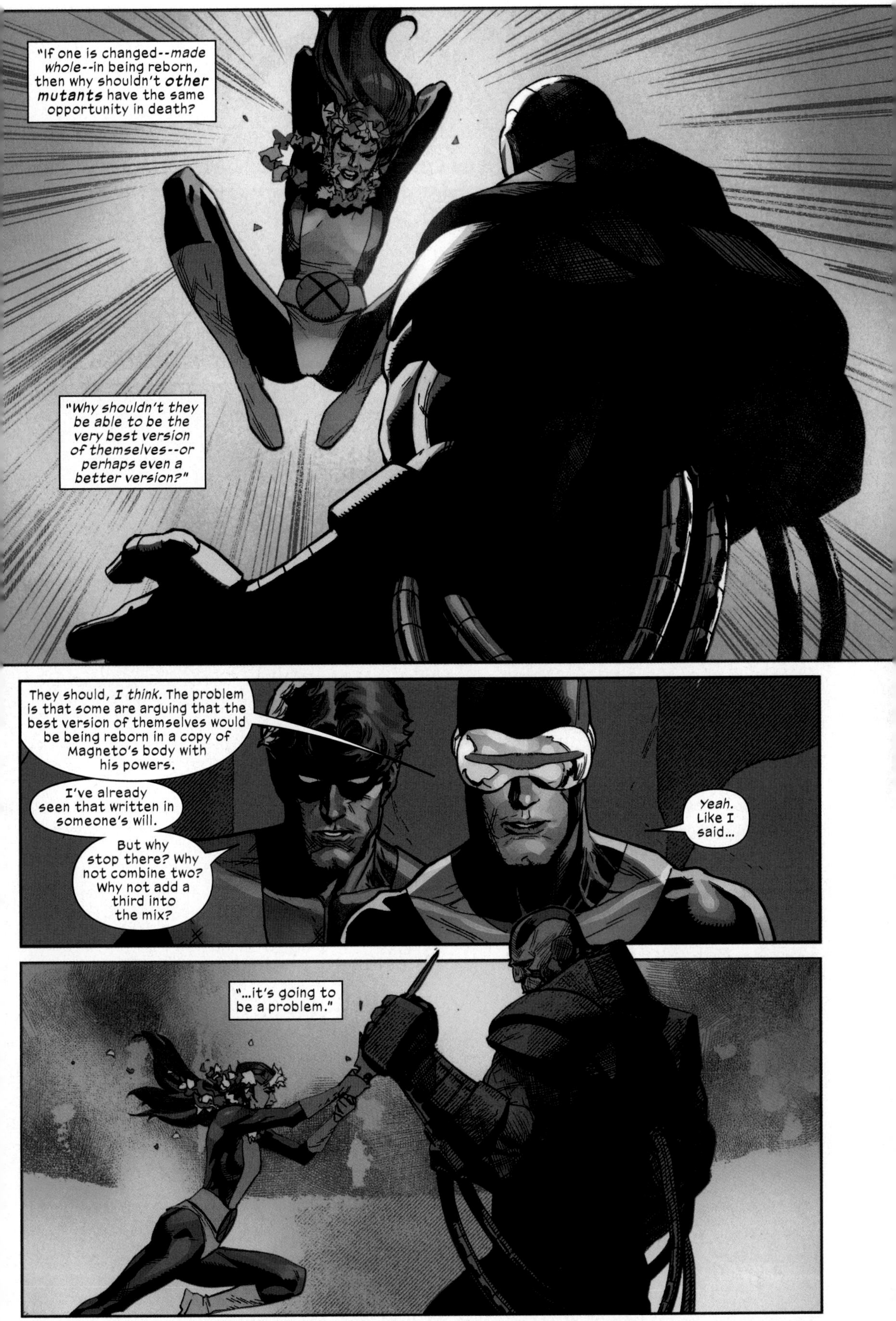
"If one is changed--made whole--in being reborn, then why shouldn't other mutants have the same opportunity in death?
"Why shouldn't they be able to be the very best version of themselves--or perhaps even a better version?"
They should, I think. The problem is that some are arguing that the best version of themselves would be being reborn in a copy of Magneto's body with his powers.
I've already seen that written in someone's will.
But why stop there? Why not combine two? Why not add a third into the mix?
Yeah. Like I said...
"...it's going to be a problem."

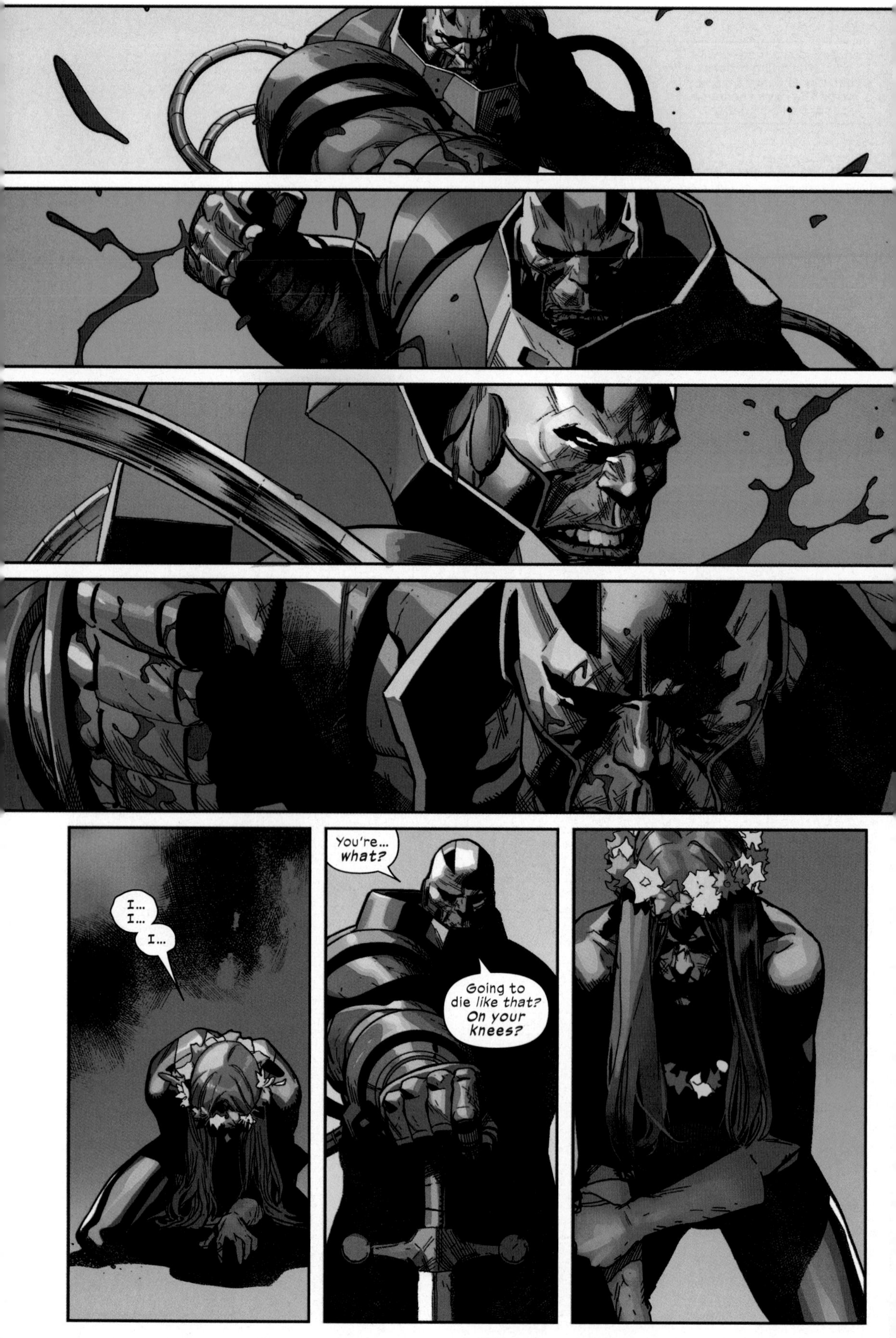

I... I... I...
You're... what?
Going to die like that? On your knees?

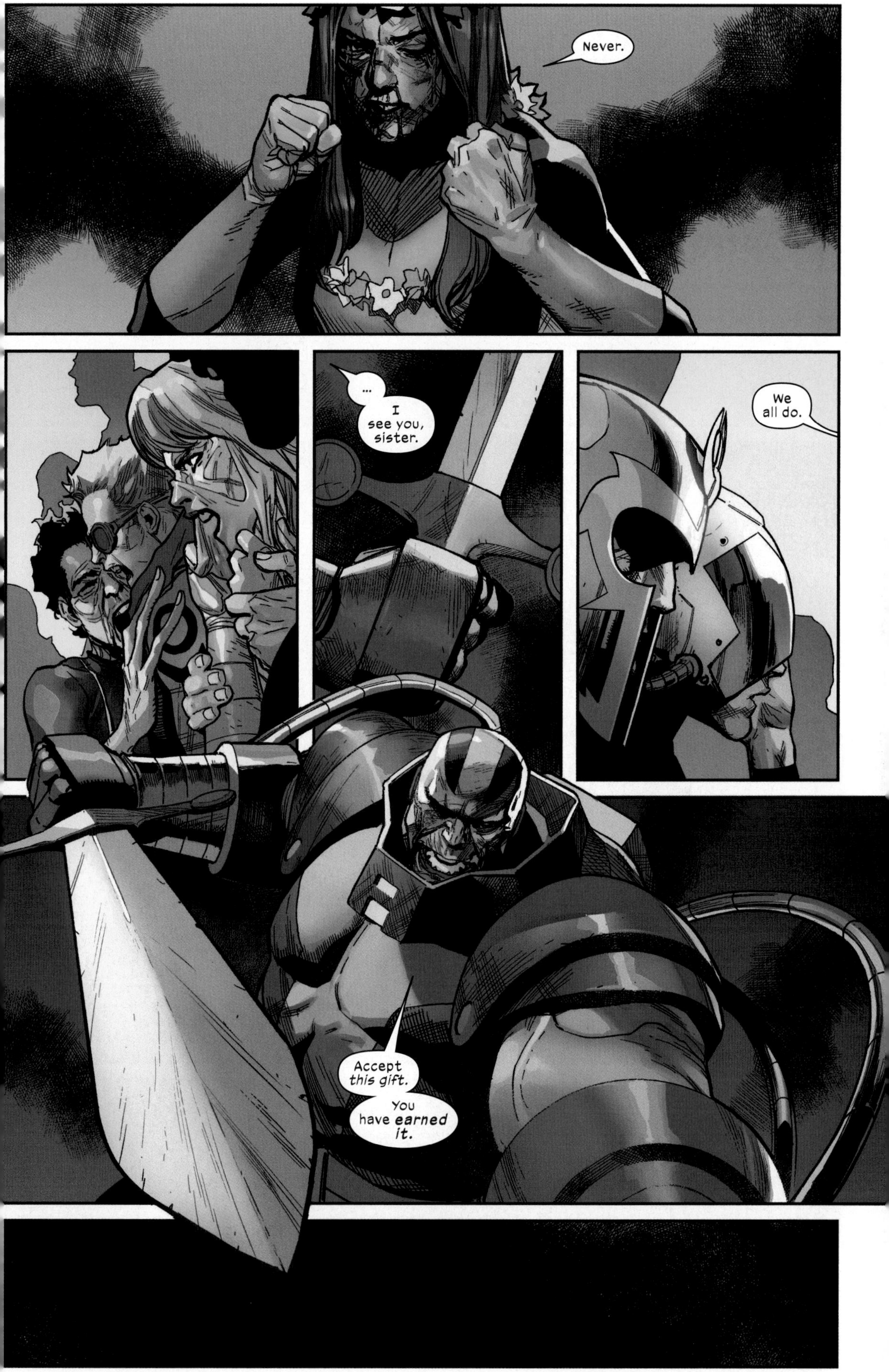
Never.
...
I see you, sister.
We all do.
Accept this gift.
You have earned it.

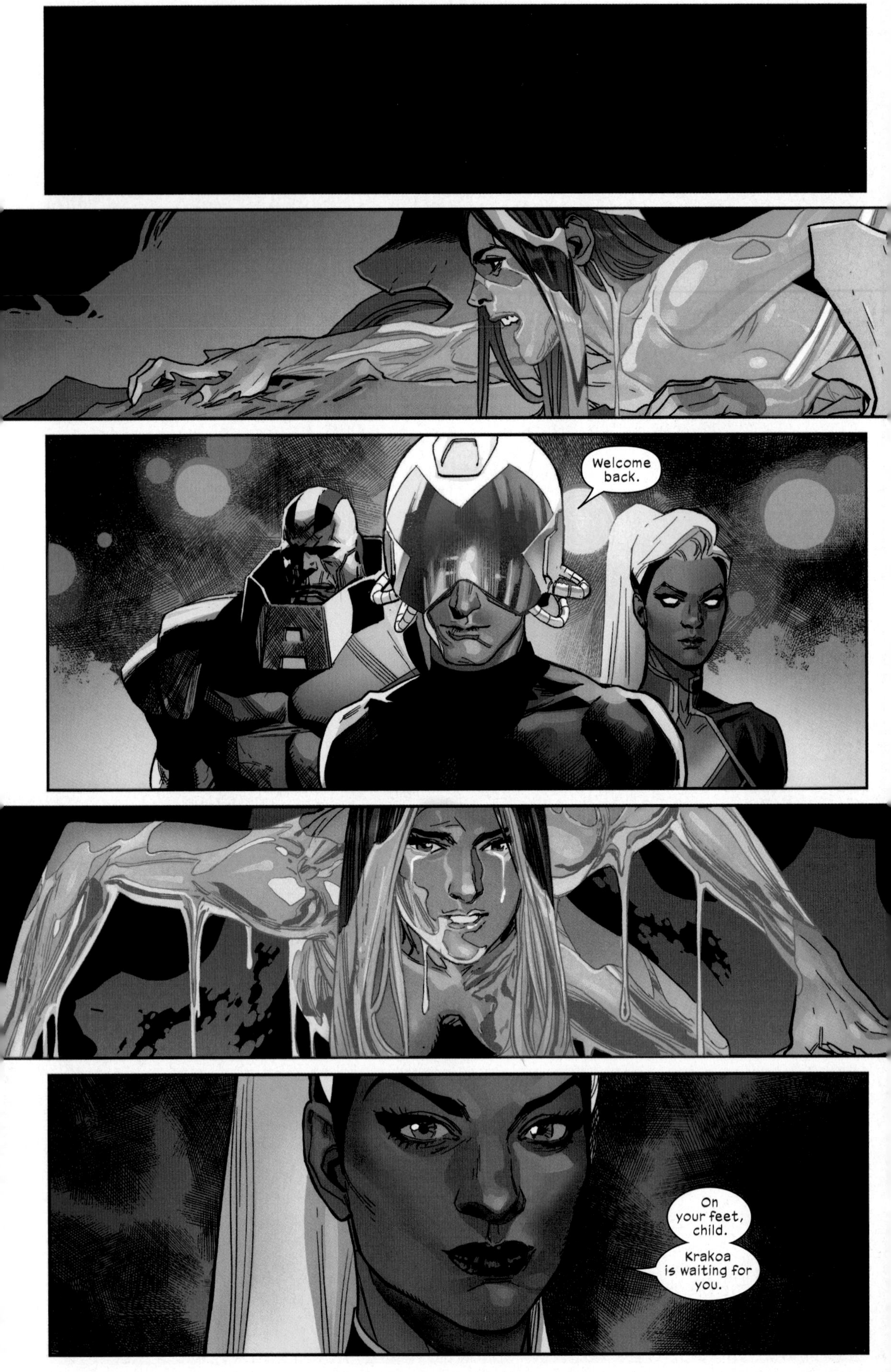
Welcome back.
On your feet, child.
Krakoa is waiting for you.

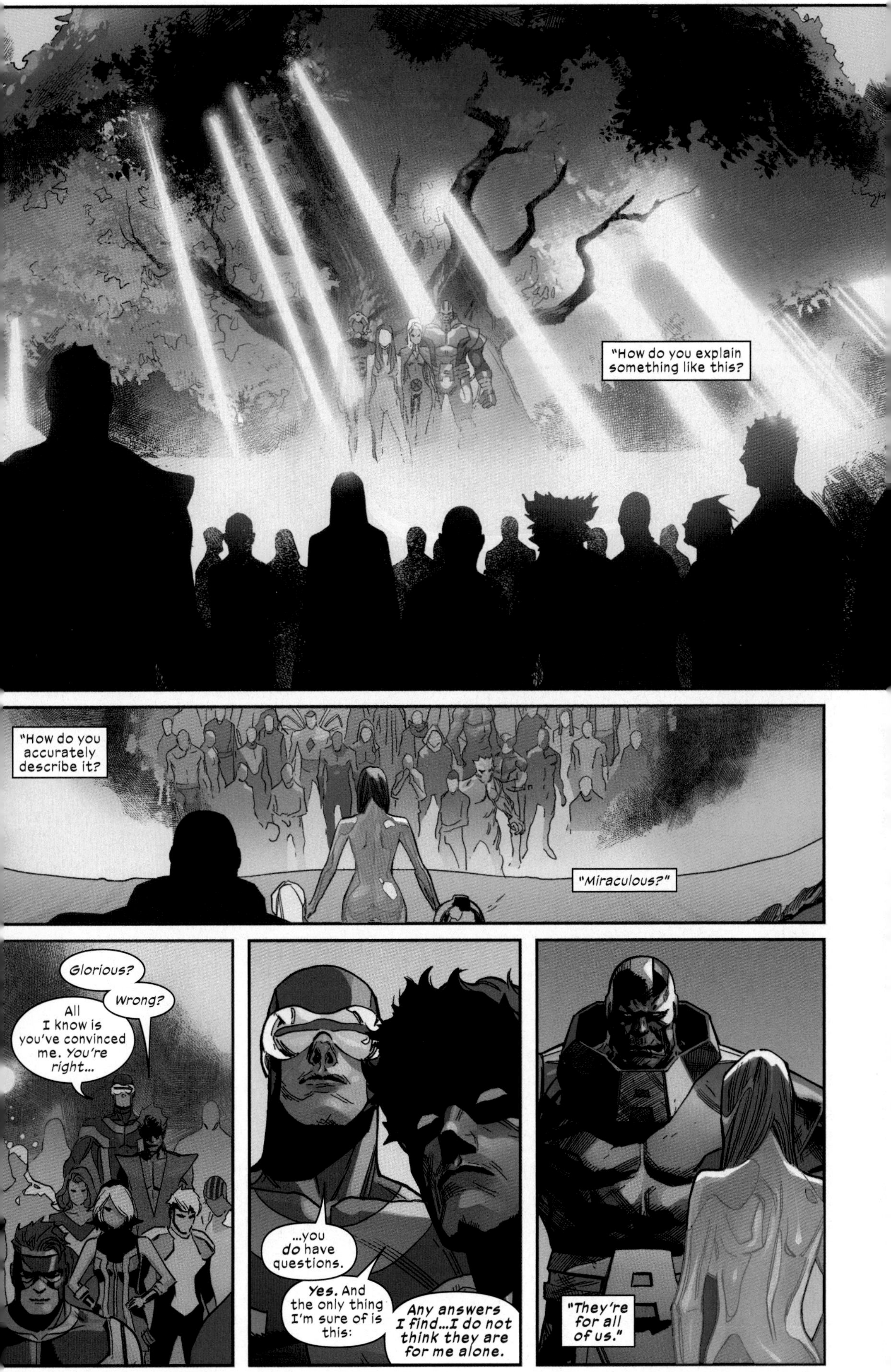
"How do you explain something like this?
"How do you accurately describe it?
"Miraculous?"
Glorious?
Wrong?
All I know is you've convinced me. You're right...
...you do have questions.
Yes. And the only thing I'm sure of is this:
Any answers I find...I do not think they are for me alone.
"They're for all of us."

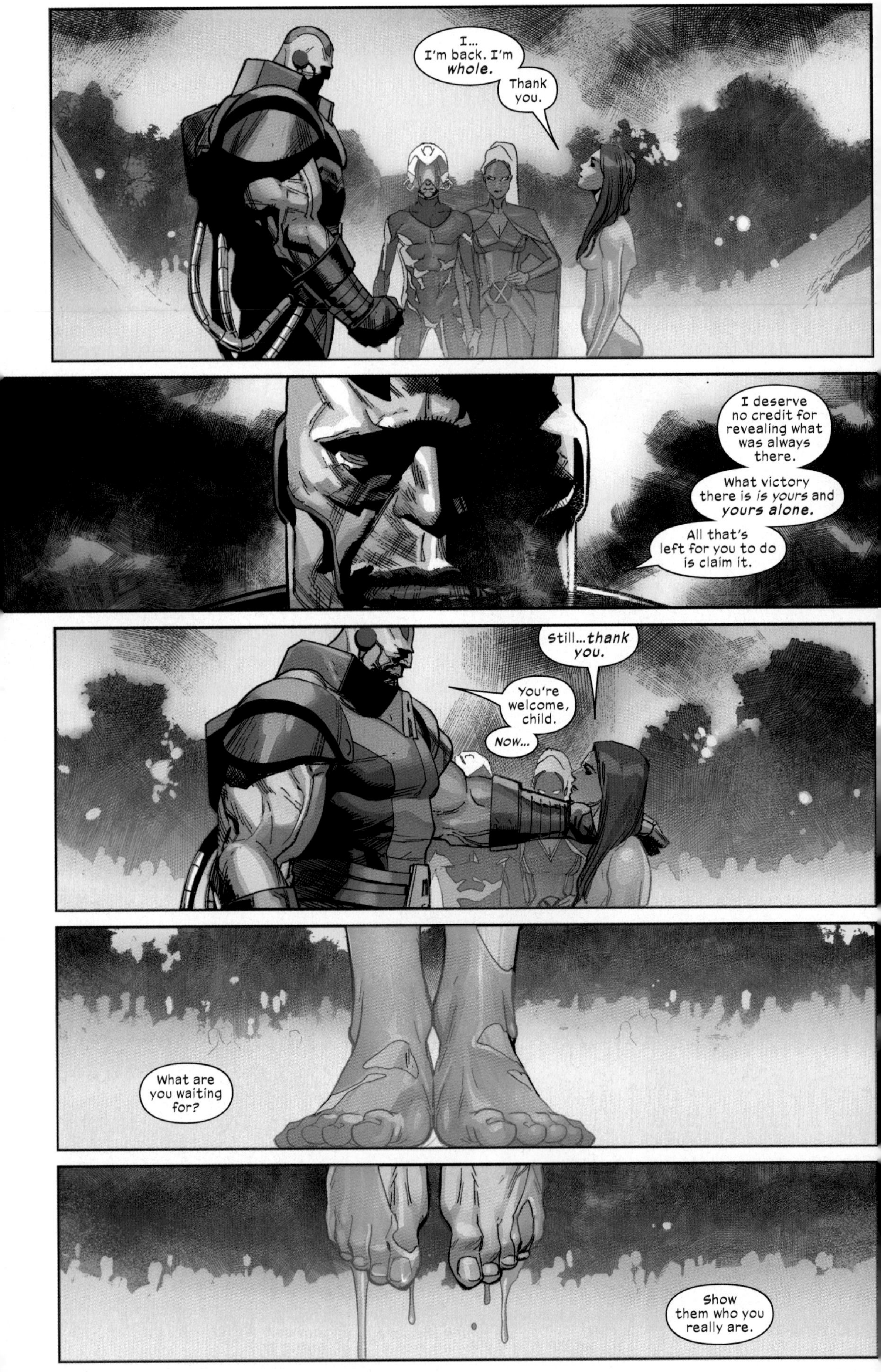
I... I'm back. I'm *whole.*
Thank you.
I deserve no credit for revealing what was always there.
What victory there is *is yours* and ***yours alone.***
All that's left for you to do is claim it.
Still...*thank you.*
You're welcome, child.
Now...
What are you waiting for?
Show them who you really are.

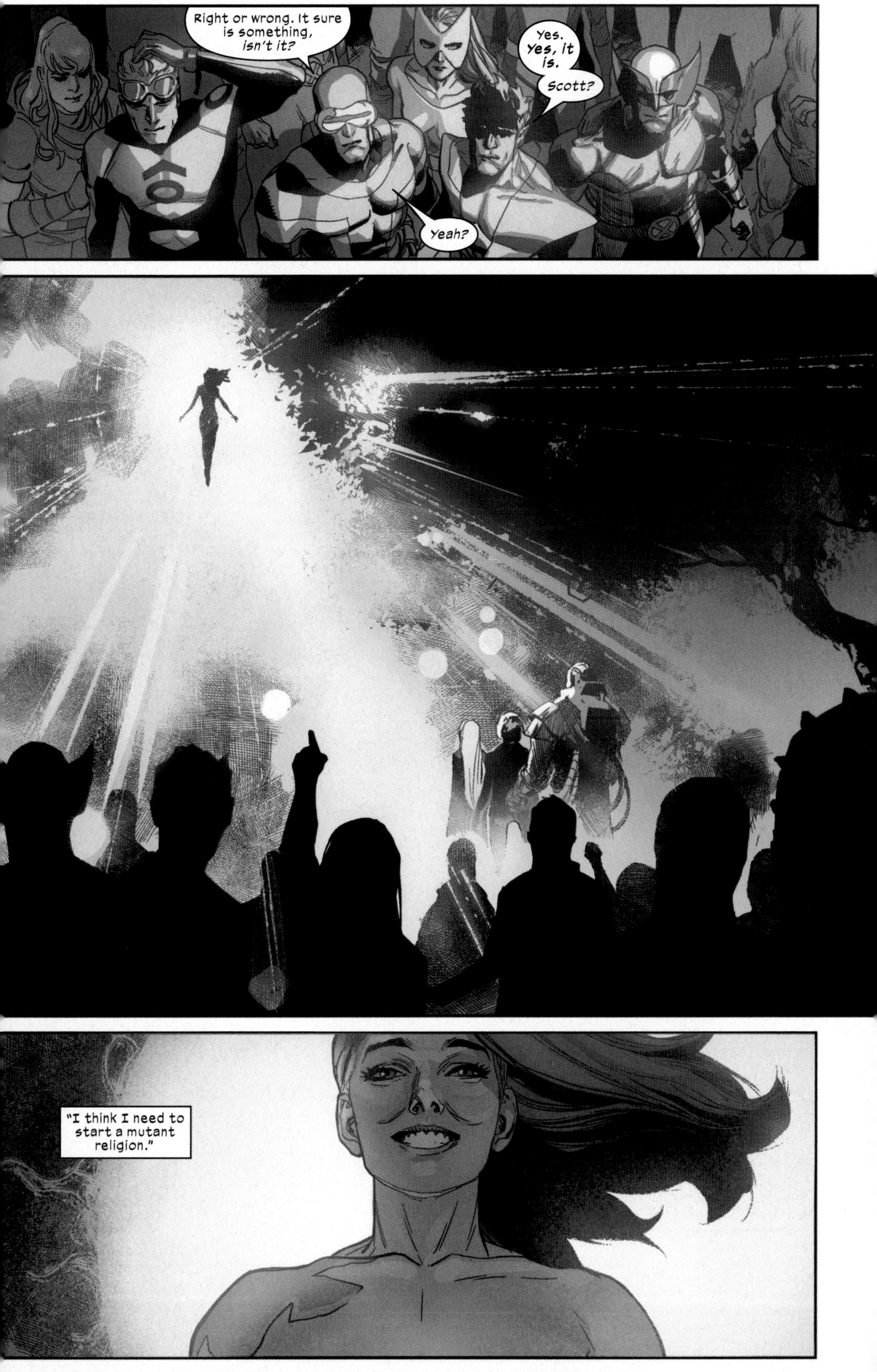
Right or wrong. It sure is something, isn't it?
Yes. Yes, it is.
Scott?
Yeah?
"I think I need to start a mutant religion."

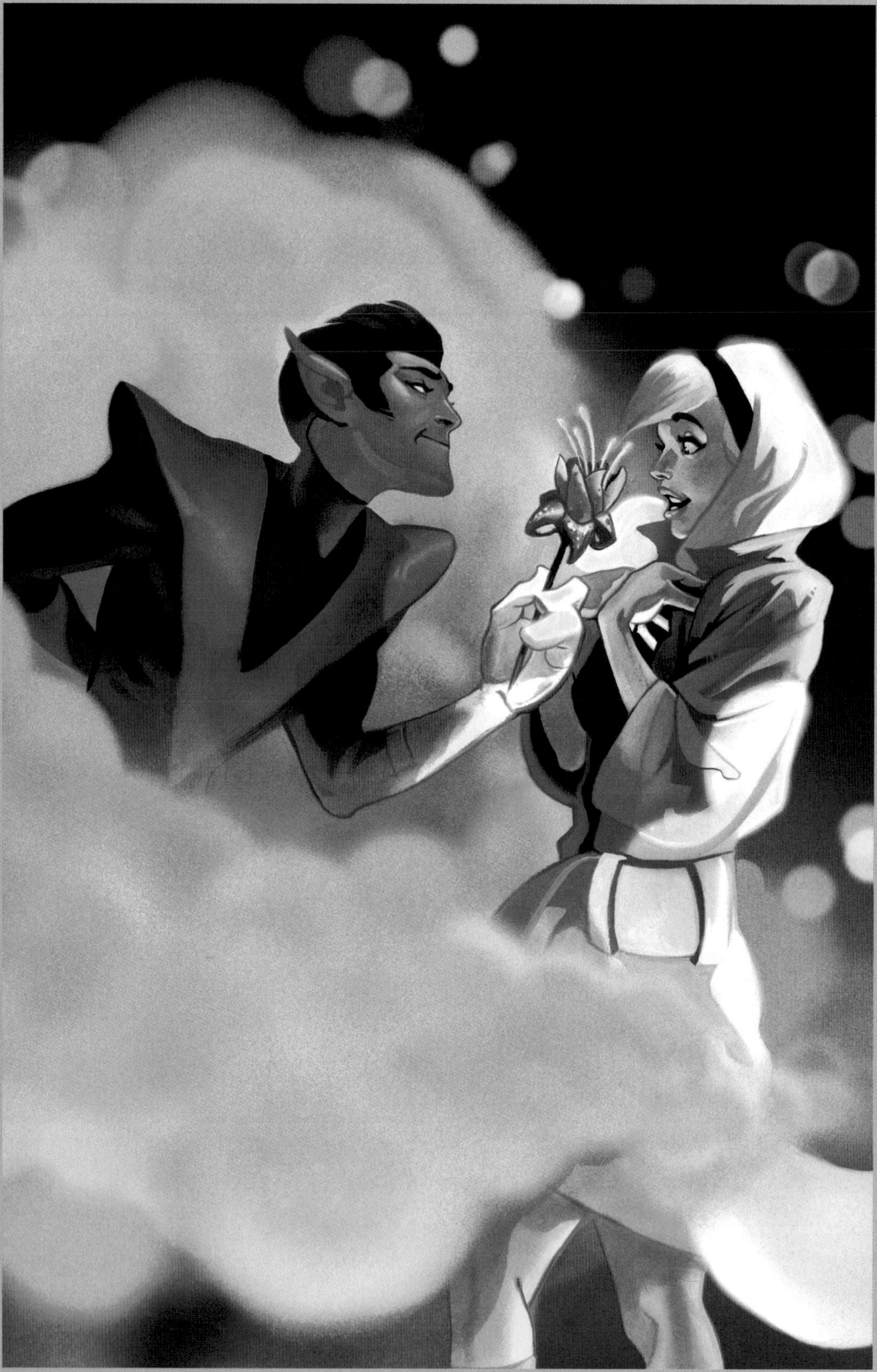

X-Men #7 Gwen Stacy Variant by Mike Del Mundo

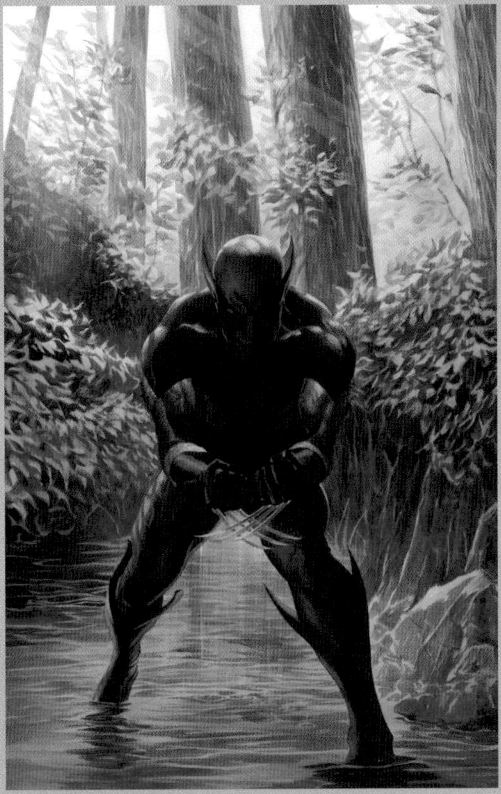

Wolverine #1 Variant
by Alex Ross

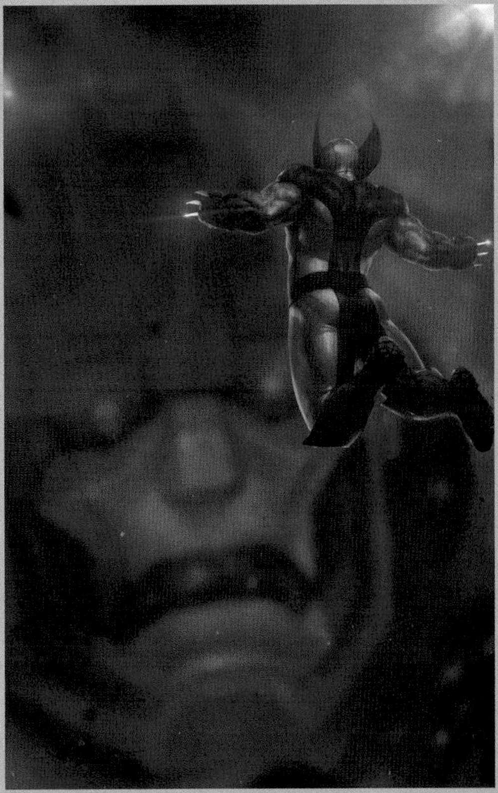

Wolverine #1 Variant
by Jeehyung Lee

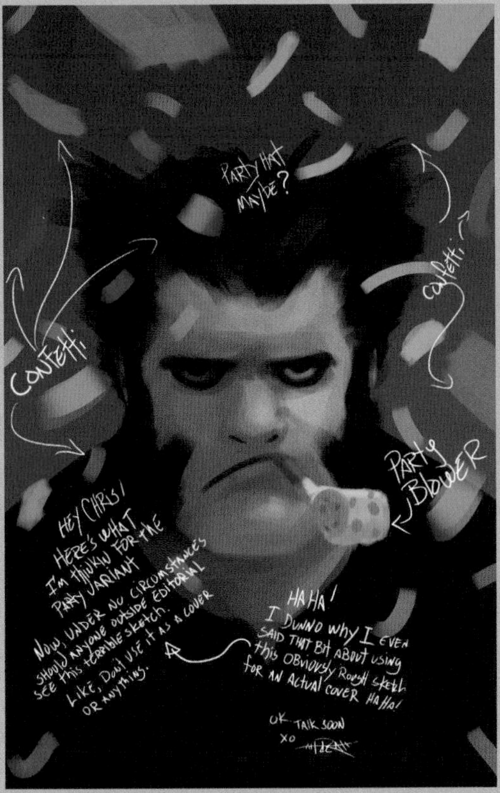
Party Hat maybe?
Confetti!
Confetti!
Party Blower
HEY CHRIS! HERE'S WHAT I'm thinkin FOR the Party Variant
Now, UNDER NO CIRCUMSTANCES should ANYONE OUTSIDE EDITORIAL SEE this terrible sketch.
Like, Don't USE it AS A COVER OR ANYTHING.
HA HA! I DUNNO why I EVEN SAID THAT BIT ABOUT USING this OBVIOUSLY Rough sketch FOR AN ACTUAL COVER HA HA!
OK TALK SOON
XO

Wolverine #1 Party Sketch Variant
by Rahzzah

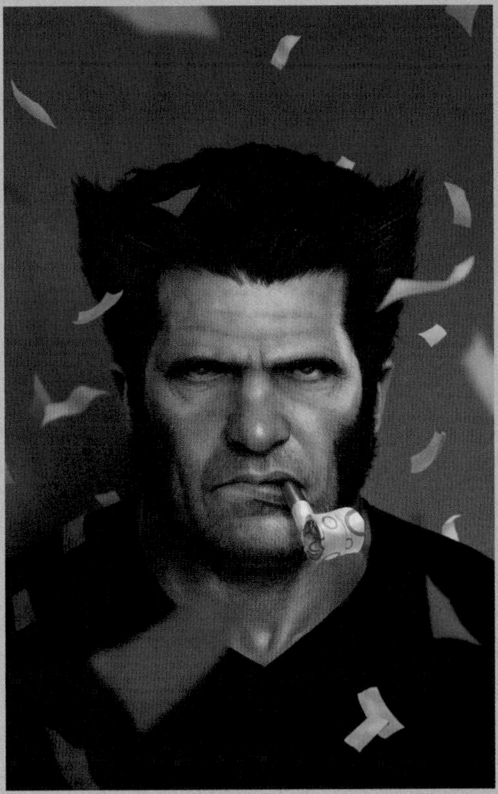

Wolverine #1 Party Variant
by Rahzzah

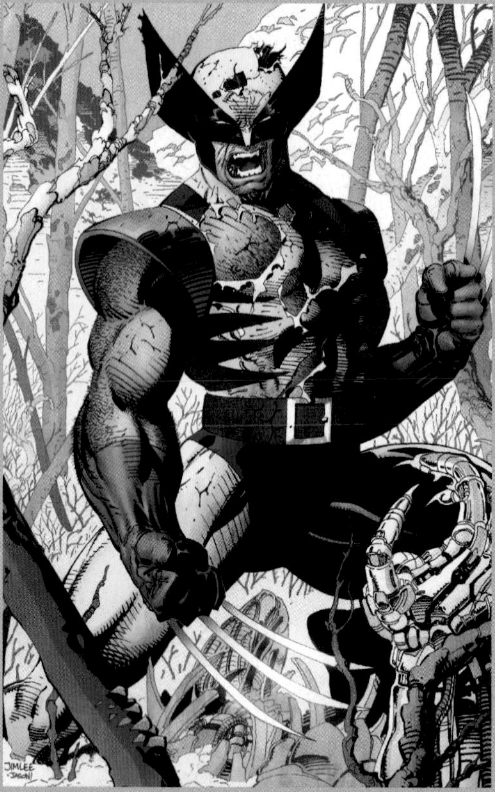

Wolverine #1 Hidden Gem Variant
by Jim Lee & Jason Keith

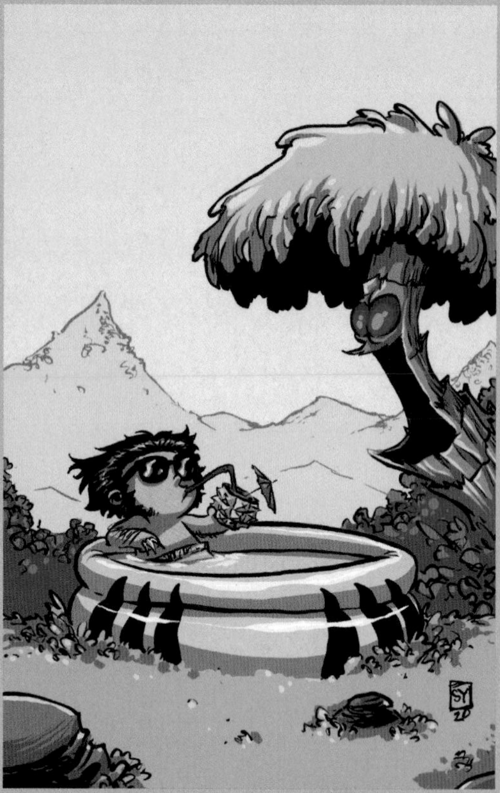

Wolverine #1 Variant
by Skottie Young

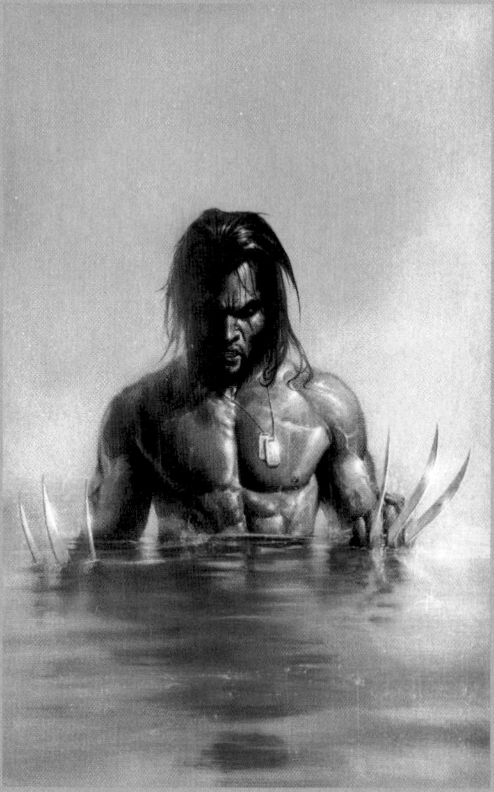

Wolverine #1 Variant
by Gabriele Dell'Otto

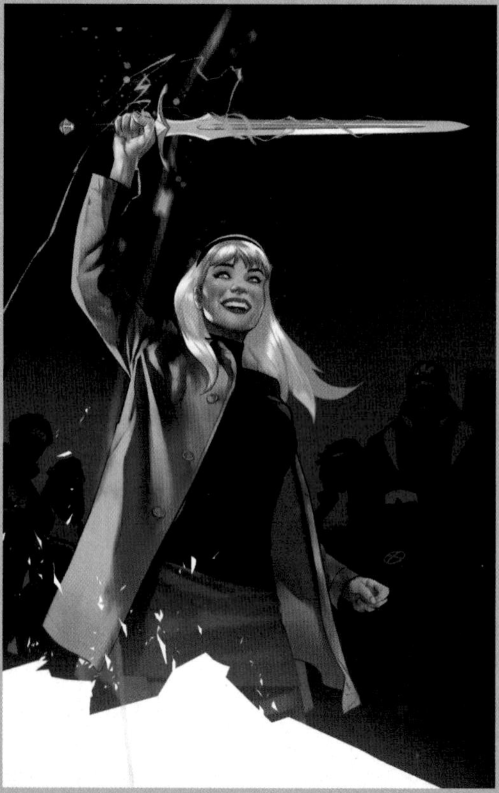

Excalibur #7 Gwen Stacy Variant
by Ben Oliver